CLARK'S

FOREIGN

THEOLOGICAL LIBRARY.

FOURTH SERIES.

VOL. XII.

Dr H. M. Martensen's Christian Dogmatics.

EDINBURGH:

T. & T. CLARK, 38 GEORGE STREET.

MDCCCLXXIV.

CHRISTIAN DOGMATICS.

A

COMPENDIUM OF THE DOCTRINES OF CHRISTIANITY.

BY

DR. H. MARTENSEN,

BISHOP OF SEELAND, DENMARK.

TRANSLATED FROM THE GERMAN

BY THE

REV. WILLIAM URWICK, M.A.

EDINBURGH:

T. & T. CLARK, 38 GEORGE STREET.

LONDON: HAMILTON, ADAMS & CO.   DUBLIN: J. ROBERTSON & CO

MDCCCLXXIV.

1874

TRANSLATOR'S PREFACE.

THE work of the learned and pious Dr Martensen, Bishop of Seeland, in Denmark, which is now presented in an English dress, was originally written in Danish, and has gone through several editions. A German translation of it soon appeared, but the Author not being satisfied with that rendering of his work, re-wrote it himself in German, and the present English version is a translation of this later German edition prepared by Dr Martensen himself.

The work is what we call a *text-book*, or manual of Christian Dogma; and while here and there the English reader may perceive a degree of abstruseness in the method of treating certain doctrines,—the Doctrine of the Trinity, for example,—which is only a reflection of the profoundness of the Author's thought, he will find throughout, a clearness and conciseness, not always to be met with in German theological works.

The Author's plan is simple; his mode of treatment is marked by brevity; yet he seldom fails, with the accuracy of a master mind, to deal with and throw light upon the cardinal points and bearings of each dogma of the Christian system. His interpretations and applications of various texts of Scripture are fresh and suggestive, so that the work, with the help of the Index now appended, will be found valuable as a book of reference, by all ministers and expounders of God's Holy Word.

Being a Lutheran, we find that the Autnor gives prominence to the efficacy of our Saviour's redemption upon
man's body and the kingdom of nature. We English Protestants differ with him here, specially in the application of
his theory to the sacraments, but the recollection of this bias
is necessary, in order to the right understanding of some expressions in the work.

The Translator, whose name appears on the title-page, begs
to state, that for the first 180 pages of this English version
the Rev. Dr Simon of Berlin, the translator of Dorner in this
series, is responsible. The work then came into the present
writer's hands, and the remainder, as well as the revision of
the whole, and the conduct of it through the press, has de-
volved upon him.

HATHERLOW, CHESHIRE, 5th Nov. 1866.

CONTENTS.

I.

INTRODUCTION.

II.

THE CHRISTIAN IDEA OF GOD.

III.

THE DOCTRINE OF THE FATHER.

INTRODUCTION.

DOGMATIC THEOLOGY.

§ 1.

Dogmatic theology treats of the doctrines of the Christian faith held by the community of believers, in other words, by the Church. A confessing and witnessing church cannot be conceived to exist without a definite sum of doctrines or *dogmas*. A dogma is not a δόξα, not a subjective, human opinion, not an indefinite, vague notion ; nor is it a mere truth of reason, whose universal validity can be made clear with mathematical or logical certainty : it is a truth of *faith*, derived from the authority of the word and revelation of God ;—a positive truth, therefore, positive not merely by virtue of the positiveness with which it is laid down, but also by virtue of the authority with which it is sealed. Dogmatics is the science which presents and proves the Christian doctrines, regarded as forming a connected system.*

§ 2.

Dogmatics is not only a science *of* faith, but also a knowledge grounded *in*, and drawn *from* faith. It is not a mere historical exhibition of what has been, or now is, true for others, without being true for the author ; nor is it a philosophical knowledge of Christian truth, obtained from a stand-point outside of faith and the church. For even supposing—what yet we by no means concede—that a scientific insight into Christian truth is possible, without Christian faith, yet such philosophizing about Christianity, even though its conclusions were ever so favourable to the church, could

---

* Cf. Mynster: "Ueber den Begriff der Dogmatik "—in the "Studien and Kritiken."

A

not be called dogmatics. Theology stands within the pale of Christianity; and only that dogmatic theologian can be esteemed the organ of his science, who is also the organ of his *church;*—which is not the case with the mere philosopher, whose only aim is to promote the cause of pure science. This desire to attain an intelligent faith, of which dogmatics is the product; this intellectual love of Christian truth, which should be found especially in the *teachers* of the church, is inseparable from a personal experience of Christian truth. And, as this intellectual apprehension of what faith is grows out of personal faith, modified by a recognition of the experience of other believers, so its ultimate aim is to benefit the community of believers, and bring fruit to the church. We may say, therefore, that dogmatic theology nears its goal just in proportion as it satisfies equally the demands of science and of the church. We hear it, indeed, often said at the present day,—*e.g.*, by Strauss, who, viewing dogmatic speculation from the stand-point of modern science, has sought to represent it as antiquated,—that the notions "scientific" and "ecclesiastical" are absolutely incompatible with one another; that only the so-called pure science, which starts without presuppositions, deserves the name of science, etc.: but such objections need occasion the church no surprise, since in the very first centuries of its existence many such were made by heathen philosophers. In spite of all these objections, there has been from the first a constant effort in the church to produce a science of the church that shall accord with the distinctive nature of Christian truth, and with the conditions imposed in this temporal form of existence upon the apprehension of truth in general; and this effort will continue to be made till the end of time—made by those, and for those, who cannot, and will not, take a position outside of Christianity; who, on the contrary, feel it indispensable that their life and modes of thought should be shaped by Christianity.

Observations.—The limits within which dogmatic theology is confined, may be given, in a general way, as the Catechism on the one hand, and on the other, philosophy, in so far as it proposes to make Christianity its object, yet takes a position outside of the Christian faith. In the popular catechetical exhibition of truth is contained the

germ of all dogmatical theology. But the scientific
element is found here only in a potential form, the main
object being practical and ecclesiastical. Not until the
scientific element, as such, appears, can we speak of dogmatic knowledge. This, as is well known, has, in its
development, assumed various forms, among which are
speculations, which involve a certain relation between
dogmatics and philosophy. Now, although the question,
how far dogmatic theology has a speculative character,
is much disputed, it is at all events clear that that
speculation which treats the truthfulness of Christianity
as something problematical, which looks for certainty respecting it in the results of its own investigations, cannot
be called dogmatical speculation. For dogmatics assumes
at the outset the absolute truth of Christianity, independently of all speculation. The δὸς ποῦ στῶ, so often expressed
by an inquiring philosophy, is for dogmatic theology
answered at once ; the theologian does not make the truth
depend on his investigation, but only seeks to gain by his
thought a firmer grasp of the truth which he already
accepts as absolutely certain, and at which he first arrived
in quite another way than that of speculation. The
scientific interest felt by the theologian is therefore
radically different from that purely logical enthusiasm
which Fichte lauds—that logical enthusiasm which urges
one to think merely for the sake of thinking, unconcerned
and indifferent as to the results to which one may be
brought. The theologian confesses himself to be in so far
a Realist, that he thinks, not for the sake of thinking, but
for the sake of *truth;* he confesses, to use Lessing's
pertinent simile, that the divine revelation holds the same
relation to his investigations as does the answer of an
arithmetical problem, given at the outset, to the problem
itself. Dogmatics, therefore, does not make *doubt* its
starting-point, as philosophy is often required to do ; it is
not developed out of the void of scepticism, but out of
the fulness of faith ; it does not make its appearance in
order by its arguments to prop up a tottering faith, to
serve as a crutch for it, as if, in its old age, it had become
frail and staggering. It springs out of the perennial,

juvenile vigour of faith, out of the capacity of faith to unfold from its own depths a wealth of treasures of wisdom
and of knowledge, to build up a kingdom of acknowledged
truths, by which it illumines itself as well as the
surrounding world. Dogmatics serves, therefore, not to
rescue faith in the time of its exigency, but to glorify it,
—*in gloriam fidei, in gloriam dei.* A mind starved by
doubt has never been able to produce a dogmatic system.
If we look at the great theologians who rank in this
department as masters and models—at Athanasius,
Anselm of Canterbury, Thomas Aquinas, or at the Reformers and their successors,—we always find that it was
faith which moved and impelled them to their work; that
in their meditations and studies they were not wandering
about in the uncertainty of doubt, but stood firm in the
certainty of faith. Indeed, it may be said in general that
it is faith which has furnished the impulse to all genuine
ecclesiastical structures. And if we consider the *few*
dogmatic productions of our time which bear the stamp of
independent thought, we find again that what distinguishes
them from the great mass of philosophical productions, is
just this effort to evolve the cognitions that are involved
in faith. In this respect, *Schleiermacher's* Dogmatics
marks a turning-point of modern times. For, whatever
may be thought as to the depth of the views, and the
purity of the faith there expressed, still at all events one
of the great results accomplished by that work is that
many have been aroused by it to see that dogmatic
theology has an independent principle quite its own, and
is not obliged to hold its domain in fee from a philosophy
foreign to itself.—In saying that the sphere of dogmatics
is bounded on the one side by the catechism, on the other
by that philosophy which merely makes faith an object
of its examination, we aimed to give a preliminary,
temporary definition. For within these limits there is room
for a great variety of more or less perfect forms of presenting dogmas; and it is, therefore, the object of this
Introduction to describe the kind of knowledge, the
genus cognoscendi, which constitutes the peculiarity of
the science of dogmatics.

§ 3.

What dogmatic theology is, can be explained only in connection with a definition of Christianity and the Christian Church, of the Church Catholic and Evangelical; and this in turn takes us back to the more general notions of Religion and Revelation. Although these points can be fully discussed only in the dogmatic system itself, yet they must be here treated in a preliminary and general way, in order to fix the true meaning of dogmatics.

RELIGION AND REVELATION.

§ 4.

All religion is a sense of God's existence, and of man's relation to God; including the difference and opposition between God and the universe, God and man; but at the same time, the solution, the removal of this opposition in a higher unity. Religion may therefore be more accurately described as man's consciousness of his communion with God, of his union with God. Religion differs from art and from philosophy. For, although philosophy, too, consists in a recognition of God, *inasmuch as its subject is God, His relation to the universe,* and to man; and, although art *may* likewise have the same character, since it may make God's revelations the subject of its representations;—yet there is between these spheres and that of religion the essential difference, that the speculative and aesthetic relation to God is only one of a secondary order, a relation mediated by ideas, thoughts, and images; whereas the religious relation to God is a relation of existence—a relation of personal life and being to God. We may, therefore, say that religion, in the true sense of the word, is a *life* in God. While thus the heroes of art and science have God only in the reflected image of thought and fancy, the pious man has God in his very being, —a difference whose reality forces itself upon us when we set prophets and apostles over against poets and philosophers. There is, therefore, the same difference between philosophy and art on the one hand, and religion on the other, as between the ideal conception or pictorial representation of one who prays and labours for the kingdom of God, and personal life, prayer and labour for the kingdom of God.

§ 5.

The religious relation to God must therefore be still more particularly defined as a *holy,* a personal relation to God, finding its universal expression in the conscience. For conscience has not merely a side directed towards the world, it is not merely the consciousness of the moral law which should control human life ; it has also a side directed towards God, although in most men this side is obscured. Conscience is man's original *knowing together* with God *(con-scientia)* the relation of his personal being to God ; an immediate, perceptible, co-knowledge with God. For, as I know myself to be in my conscience, so I live, and so I am. The relations between God and men acquire religious significance only as they spring from, or are received into, this fundamental relation ; and certainty respecting divine and human things is a *religious* certainty only when it is the certainty of conscience. But this holy relation to God can be sustained only by Theists, not by Pantheists ; it pre-supposes necessarily a free Creator, who knows and wills, and who makes known His eternal power and Godhead in the creation. Only when the creature and the human person, have in reference to God a relative independence ; only in case the created will meets the eternal will of God, can we speak of holiness in man, as distinct from God, or as united with Him. Holiness and conscientiousness, as the history of heathenism shows, are not characteristics of pantheistic religions : at best they are only feebly developed therein. Hence these are imperfect and untrue forms of religion ;—or as we may otherwise express it, the heathen's sense of divine things is polluted by mixture with his sense of earthly things ; his religious sentiments, as all myths show, are polluted by mixture with his aesthetic and speculative sentiments.

§ 6.

As man is designed in general to be at once *himself,* and a *member* of a greater whole, this is pre-eminently true of religion, for which he is pre-eminently designed. Accordingly, a man's religious sense, though it is of the most individual and personal nature, involves the consciousness of his belonging to a community. For only in a *kingdom* of God, only in a kingdom of individuals animated by God, standing to one another in the reciprocal relation of productivity and receptivity, of giving and taking, can religion develop its real wealth. History abounds in illustrations of the power of religion to form communities. This is shown not only by the temple and the synagogue under the Old Covenant ; not only by the Christian Church and the Christian Conventicle, but also by the religions of heathen nations. Where religion becomes a merely private thing, *only* a concern of individuals, then we may discern a sign of a state of dissolution, of a break between the individual and society.

Observations.—The assertion sometimes made of late, that religion is a *talent,* and that we can no more demand that every man be religious than we can require every man to possess artistic or philosophic talent, is false. For though there may be men who have more religious capacity than others ; though we may speak of a talent and of a genius for religion, yet, since religion is the *central* vocation of man, the obligation rests on every one to be religious, just as every one is required to be moral ; though this obligation does not imply that there may be no such thing as a genius for morality. It is, however, an oft-repeated assertion that there are many men who are moral without being religious ; and we do not deny its truth : we only maintain that such a morality is neither radical nor deep. Without some sort of religion, without a certain belief in Providence, be it only a vague belief in an all-controlling power, no self-conscious morality is conceivable.

§ 7.

In seeking to gain a more definite view of the psychological forms in which religion manifests itself, we may assume it to be now universally admitted that psychologically religion presents itself exclusively neither as feeling alone, nor as perception alone, and volition ; that we are to treat the question no longer as one of an *either—or,* but as one of a *both—and.* Schleiermacher, in his Dogmatics, makes the feelings the exclusive seat of religion ; and, inasmuch as feeling is a term designating the most immediate contact of consciousness with its object, it may be said, indeed, that the foundation of a religious character is denoted by it—its foundation, but not its completion. In designating religious feeling as a feeling of absolute de-

pendence, he follows the mystics in describing piety as a
theopathic state, as a state in which man feels his inmost soul
touched by the power in which we live and move and have
our being,—a holy πάϑος, in which man feels himself to be a
vessel and an abode of the Deity. This description not only
reminds one of mysticism ; it is itself mystical ; for it leaves
us in dusky uncertainty as to *what* the absolute power is on
which we feel ourselves dependent ; whether it be an impersonal Absolute, a Fate, or an ethical, holy, good Power. Only
in the latter case can the theopathic state, the feeling of absolute dependence, be a feeling that elevates and makes free.
For it is only by relation to a good, a holy Power that the
feeling of one's own personality is confirmed ; not by relation
to an impersonal Absolute. In order, therefore, to avoid this
ambiguity, we would define * the religious feeling in its fundamental form as a feeling of *unbounded reverence.* In this is
involved the deepest feeling of dependence, of finiteness, of
creatureship, of humility ; at the same time, it implies that
the Power on which I feel myself to be dependent is the good,
the holy Power to which I feel myself in my conscience bound ;
not a Fate, which can be an object of fear only, not of reverence. This reverential dependence is the germ of the trust,
devotion and love, which we see in the religion of the patriarchs. In Abraham's reverence we find expressed the dependence of the creature on the Almighty Creator of heaven and
earth ; but we also find in it a faint anticipation of the
glorious freedom of the sons of God.

§ 8.

Man, in so far as his religion is one of mere feeling,
is in a state of passive subjection to God ; in so far as his
religion, on the contrary, consists in knowledge, he is,—to
use again a term borrowed from the mystics,—*free* in relation
to God. It is the light of knowledge through which the
religious feeling of dependence, instead of being an oppressive
one, becomes an elevating feeling of freedom ; only by means
of this light can the obscure, mystical feeling of dependence
be transfigured into a feeling of reverence, devotion, and love.
For it is only in the light of knowledge that God becomes a
distinct *object* of consciousness ; only when this light is
enjoyed can the afore-mentioned relation of distinction and

* With Mynster.

of unity between God and man be a *free* relation. The knowledge of which we speak is, however, not a knowledge *of* religion, but, as Daub designates it, a knowledge *in* religion, as indeed is implied in the very idea of conscience, which is not only a feeling, but also a perception. Hegel's definition of religious knowledge as an immediate knowledge we are very willing to adopt, only we mean by the immediate, not the lower, imperfect knowledge, which is to be superseded by philosophy as the perfect knowledge, but the original, primitive knowledge which lies at the basis of speculation.

Religious cognizance of God is not knowledge in the form of abstract thought; but the idea of God assumes shape in a comprehensive *view* of the world, and of human life in its relation to God, a view of heaven and earth, nature and history, heaven and hell. Piety cognizes not merely by thoughts growing out of the relations of conscience and confined to these relations, but also by means of the mental *picture* which springs from these same relations. When we now denominate not only the reason, but also the *imagination* as the organ of religious perception ; when we say that without fancy no one can get a lively conception of God, the assertion may to many sound strange. But experience shows that no religion has ever assumed an important historical character without developing a comprehensive ideal view of the universe, an imaginative view by which the invisible is blended with the visible ; whether this blending or marriage has the significance of a mere myth and symbol, or connects itself with a truly divine revelation. We will not here appeal to the Grecian religion of beauty, nor to the grand, fanciful conceptions embodied in the myths of the North ; for it might justly be said that in these the religious element is corrupted by its mixture with the poetical. We appeal to Judaism and to Christianity itself, both of which most distinctly teach that God's essence is invisible, like thought and spirit; both of which, however, by their sacred history, their symbolic and figurative language (incomprehensible without a corresponding religious fancy) most emphatically confirm our assertion that fancy appertains not merely to superstition, but also to true religion. But it must be constantly kept in mind that the religious conceptions generated by fancy are in their origin

religious conceptions, that they are the views of those who
stand in a religious relation to God, not the product of culture
or of art.   It is true even of myths, that they are no product
of culture, but, on the contrary, are implied in culture.

Observations.—One's religious views may be held at second
hand, *i.e.*, in a philosophical or aesthetic way.   And
just because religious perception deals with an objective element, that of thought and fancy, it may be
sundered from its vital source in the affections, and be
exercised in a merely aesthetic or philosophic way, independent of personal faith.   Thus there are philosophers,
poets, painters, and sculptors, who have represented
Christian ideas with great plastic power, yet without
themselves having a religious possession of those ideas;
being brought into relation to them only through the
medium of thought and fancy.   Thus too, a large proportion of the men of the present time hold religious views
only in an aesthetic way, or merely make them the subject
of refined reflection; hold them only at second hand,
because they know nothing of the personal feelings and
the determinations of conscience which correspond to
them; because, in other words, their religious knowledge
does not spring from their standing in right religious
relations.   The adoption of religious notions, nay, even
of a comprehensive religious view of life, is therefore by
no means an infallible proof that a man is himself religious.
The latter is the case only when the religious views are
rooted in a corresponding inward state of the mind and
heart; when the man feels himself in conscience bound
to these views; in short, when he believes in them.   And
even though a man, with the help of Christian views,
could achieve wonders in art and science, could prophesy,
and cast out devils, yet Christ will not acknowledge him
unless he himself stands in right personal relations to
these views.   It is specially necessary at the present time
to call attention to this double manner in which religious
notions may be entertained.

§ 9.

Personal religion is not complete till it assumes the
form of religious volition.   Through feeling and knowledge

God seeks to draw man into his kingdom ; but only through the WILL does religion become, on the part of man, an actual worship of God. No man can absolutely avoid being moved by religious feelings ; no one can avoid being in some sense put into a theopathic state, though it be only for passing moments ; no one can absolutely escape from the light of the religious knowledge which forces itself upon us through the conscience. But it rests with man whether he shall encourage these feelings, whether he shall resolve to let these feelings *prevail*, whether he shall *surrender* himself, and freely assume the relation of a worshipper of the God who has revealed Himself. The will forms, therefore, the key-stone, the determining power, in the religious consciousness.

§ 10.

These several factors, which together make up religion, limit and sustain one another ; for, as the feelings, *e.g.*, are indebted to the will for true profundity, so, on the other hand, energy of will depends on depth of emotion. But these all unite together, and the central point of union we call *faith*. Faith is a life of feeling, a life of the soul, in God (if we understand by *soul** the basis of personal life, wherein, through very fulness, all emotion is still vague) ; and no one is a believer, who has not felt himself to be in God and God in him. Faith *knows what* it believes, and in the light of its intuition it views the sacred truths in the midst of the agitations and turmoil of this world's life ; and though its knowledge is not a comprehensive knowledge, although its intuition is not a seeing face to face, although in clearness it is inferior to these forms of apprehension, yet in certitude it yields to neither ; for the very essence of faith is, that it is firm, confident *certitude* respecting what is not seen. Faith, finally, is the profoundest act of the will, the profoundest act of obedience and devotion. *Nemo credit nisi volens;* therefore, faith necessarily passes over into action ; partly into definite acts of worship (sacrifice, prayer, sacrament), partly into actions belonging to the sphere of morality, which thus receives a religious impress.

Observations.—Whenever either of the above developed

---

* *Gemüth*, *ι. e.*, the seat of the affections, sentiments, and emotions ; the emotional nature. English has for it no specific term.

elements of faith is made prominent to the exclusion of
the others, a false phase of it is presented, and there
results a one-sided, morbid kind of religion. One-sided
preference given to feeling, leads to mysticism. One-
sided stress laid on religious knowledge and sentiments,
leads either to abstract orthodoxy or to an aesthetic play
of the fancy with religious notions. One-sided prominence given to the will, leads, as in the case of Kant and
Fichte, to " moralism."

§ 11.

Faith in God is faith in God's REVELATION, or in God's
communication of Himself to His creatures; a self-communication in which the communications of divine truth,
light and *life* condition each other. Being belief in the
supernatural *transcendental* God, who reveals His nature and
His will in the world, faith distinguishes life in God from life
in the world; the believer knows that his conception of God
is not derived from the world, nor from his own heart, but
from God who reveals Himself to man. This consciousness
of a difference between holiness and worldliness, is inseparable from conscious faith; and for this reason heathendom is
destitute of faith in the strict sense of the word, since in
heathendom there is no real difference between the holy and
the profane, no real difference between a godly and a worldly
spirit. Heathendom may indeed exhibit a sort of piety, an
εὐσέβεια, but no faith, inasmuch as the light of revelation is
lacking, or shines only by transient flashes into the darkness.
At the best there can be found there only sporadic demonstra-
tions of faith; its calm repose is not known.

§ 12.

Revelation being a communication of Spirit to spirit,
the Spirit and not nature must be its only perfect medium.
For, although it is indeed the creative Spirit who speaks
through nature to the created spirit, yet nature with her inar-
ticulate language speaks only in an indirect and figurative
manner of the eternal power and godhead of the Creator. A
direct, unambiguous revelation can be found only in the world
of spirit, of the word, of conscience, and of freedom, in other
words, of *history*. Revelation and history are, therefore, not
to be separated; yet, if there were no other history than pro-

fane history, God's revelation would still be without an adequate medium.   Profane history reveals to us, it is true, a development of ideas, of divine potencies and forces ; but that this development,—inquiring as it does, agreeably to its objective character, only after the great whole, after the race in general, and seeming to be quite indifferent to individuals ;—that this course of worldly events serves to accomplish the designs of a holy will, and to build up a kingdom of God in which God, through the medium of the whole, puts Himself into a personal relation to each individual soul ; this we may learn from conscience.   In the general course of events we look in vain for such a *revelation* of this mystery that we can find repose in it.   We hear, indeed, the sacred voice of God speaking through the voices of profane history ; and in the deeds of men, in secular events, we discern also the deeds of God ; but in the tumult of the world's history our ear confounds God's voice with the voices of men, and the holy, providential design now and then disclosed in the fate of men, is concealed again from our sight amidst the restless stream of events.   If we may, in truth, speak of a sacred, divine revelation, then there must be a history within history, there must be within profane history a *sacred history*, in which God reveals Himself as God; a history in which is revealed the sacred design of the world as such, in which the word of God so encases itself in the word of man that the latter becomes the pure organ for the former, and in which the acts of God are so involved in the acts of men that the latter become a perfectly transparent medium through which the former may be seen.   Sacred history must, therefore, have the form of a history of a *covenant*, in which God, by means of sacred events, enters into a special personal relation to man ; it must be the history of an *election*, a selection from profane history.   And so it appears in the history of Israel, in which everything revolves around the holy purposes, the word, and the acts of God ; and this finds its completion and its fulness in the *sacred history of Christ ;* so that thus the history of the Christian church, as a new history within history, flows through the history of the universe.   The revelation here indicated, involved in sacred history and propagated by the church, we call the *special* positive revelation, as distinguished from the general revelation given in nature and in the moral world, from the revelation presented in the history of a merely natural development of the human race.

§ 13.

When the three great forms of religion, Heathenism, Judaism, and Christianity, are termed three several stages in the development of the religious consciousness, it must not be forgotten that only Judaism and Christianity, with their sacred history, have a common principle of development; while heathenism, with its myths, points to an essentially different principle. To be sure, some ancient and modern Gnostic systems have tried to show that the three religions are all of a piece, pronouncing heathenism, as the natural starting-point in the religious development of man, to be the fundamental form, and representing the sacred history of Judaism and Christianity as only a modification of the mythical spirit. But this effort involves a rejection of the notion of revelation and a disregard of the radical difference between revelation and myth. Myths, it is true, have this in common with revelation, that they are not arbitrarily invented, but, like revelation, have an objective, mysterious origin. But myths have their mysterious origin in the spirit of the world, in the *cosmical* spirit, while revelation has its origin in the *Holy* Spirit. Myths contain, therefore, most certainly, a rich fund of ideas, but contain no expression of a holy will. Precisely because their contents are nothing but ideas, mythical forms have merely a seeming existence; they are for the imagination and the fancy; they are only personifications of ideas. And precisely because revelation is the revelation of a holy *will*, does it demand, as its medium, history, historical facts, historical personages; for only in history is the will in its element; the holy will, only in sacred history. The mythical dream-world with its personifications must vanish before the light of culture, because it presents in the fermentations of fancy only what philosophy and art present in the form of clear consciousness; for in myths the distinctly religious element is found only in a vague, sporadic, and mystical form. Revelation, on the contrary, cannot be supplanted by any science, just because it is not a lower form of knowledge, but is sacred fact and holy life. By this statement we by no means deny that within the sphere of revelation there may, and even must, be constructed a system of symbols in which sacred ideas are symbolised in a manner resembling mythical representations ; nor again do we deny that on the basis of a sacred history a mythology may be developed, as we see it in Catholicism, where a series of legends has entwined itself like a creeping plant around the trunk of sacred history. We only mean to affirm that revelation, being based upon the *principle of personality*, is inseparable from a sacred *history*, and is radically different from the mythical world of dreams and shadows.

§ 14

The designation of the three great forms of religion as different stages of *consciousness*, is not exhaustive. They are rather three stages of *being* :—a truth expressed by Christianity when it describes itself at once as a new *creation* of the human race, and as a *redemption* of it from the untrue, abnormal being exhibited in heathenism ; Judaism exhibiting the incipient and preparatory economy of redemption. Whilst the heathen are estranged from God and stand in relation only to the divine ideas which manifest themselves in the world, without being brought by these into relation to the will of the divine Creator himself, the Jews, as a chosen people, are raised to a higher stage of being, where the way is prepared even for the new creation,—the new creation which first began to be fully accomplished in the Incarnation of God in Christ.

CHRISTIANITY AND THE CHRISTIAN CHURCH.

§ 15.

The widest conceivable contrast of existence between God and the world is presented in the relation of Creator to creature, of the holy God to sinful man. If now we consider the different religions in their relation to this fundamental problem of religion, we may say : Heathenism is unacquainted with the problem ; Judaism lives in it and looks for its solution ; but only Christianity gives the actual solution.

Heathenism is unacquainted with the problem of creation, or the religious problem presented by dependence on a holy creative God. The antithetic relation between God and the universe is viewed only superficially ; as in all forms of pantheism, the antithesis between God and the universe is

only ideal ; and hence the solution is found in figures, myths,
and symbols.   Judaism, on the contrary, feels its relation
of creatureship, and consequently of conscientious obligation ;
but this relation involves a *dualism* between heaven and earth ;
God and the universe are two different beings, not merely two
sides of the same being ; over against God stands a created
world as not-God ; a created spirit stands in the relation of
obligation, of dependence, of obedience ; here the opposition
is *real.*   But the creature strives to return to, yearns to become united with, the Uncreated one.   " Thou hast created
us for thyself, and our heart is restless, and will not rest till
it rests in thee, O Lord ! "   And yet there is an infinite distance between the eternal, the Almighty Creator of heaven and
earth, and the finite, limited human creature who is dust
and ashes,—a chasm which seems incapable of being filled.
Christianity solves this problem by its gospel of the *Incarnation of God* in Christ.   The antithesis is not removed by
figures or myths, for it is an antithesis of being, and must
be removed by a change in the sphere of being.   The Word
became *flesh* and dwelt among us, the Word which was in
the beginning with God and himself was God, the Word by
whom all things were made ; men beheld His glory as of the
only begotten of the Father, full of grace and truth.   As the
incarnate Word, as He in whom the fulness of the Godhead
dwells bodily, Christ is the Mediator between God and the
creature, the Mediator whose office it is to transmute man's
relation of created dependence into one of unlimited freedom,
to transform men from creatures into children of God.   The
idea of an incarnation runs, it is true, also through the myths
of heathendom ; but the union there implied between God and
man is a merely natural union, which does not recognise the
actual separation in point of holiness.   It was, therefore, the
design of Judaism to maintain this truth, until the fulness of
time should come, when heaven and earth could become truly
united in Christ.   The heathen's notion of the union of God
and man is not the notion that God has become man, but that
man becomes God,—not the notion of an incarnation of God,
but of an *apotheosis* of man.   The idea of incarnation dawns
on the Jew in his Messianic hope, but is checked by the constant fear of making God and man one in essence ; for which

reason the perfect conception of the incarnation is not here found. Yet the hope of Israel shows itself to be a *holy* hope in that it conceives the Messiah as coming *from above* through God's *condescending* love, to which human nature stands in a merely passive, receptive, submissive relation.

But the fundamental problem of religion is still more profound than that of creation. The separation between heaven and earth is not only that between Creator and creature, but between the holy God and a sinful world. Heathenism knows nothing of this problem. For to the heathen evil is only limitation, ignorance, a natural defect, a fate which cleaves to finiteness, but not SIN, not the disturbance of a holy relation towards God, originating in the will of the creature. Judaism lives and moves in this problem. Its sacred tradition begins with the account of the *fall* of man ; and this breach between the holy God and sinful man runs through the whole history of Israel, incessantly attested by the law and the prophets. But the *restoration* of the broken relation, the *atonement* for sin, is in Judaism only foreshadowed by types and prophecies. Not until God becomes incarnate in Christ, does the true Mediator enter into the world. " God was in Christ, reconciling the world unto himself."* In this gospel of the crucified One is contained the solution of the hard problem of sinfulness. The atonement was not accomplished by images and myths— " for our sin is not a mock or painted thing, and therefore our Redeemer is also not a painted Redeemer : " the God-man really suffered ; He was really crucified as an atonement for the sin of the world. With Him, the new Adam, the whole race is organically united, and " He died for all, that they which live should not henceforth live unto themselves, but unto Him who died for them and rose again."†

The essence of Christianity is, therefore, nothing else than Christ Himself. The founder of the religion is Himself, its sum and substance. He is not merely the historical founder of a religion ; His person cannot be separated from the doctrine which he proclaims, but has an eternal, ever-present significance for the human race. As he is the Mediator and Propitiator, the sacred point of unity between God and the sinful world, so He is also continually the *Redeemer* of the human race.

* 2 Cor. v. 17. † 2 Cor. v. 15.

B

All regenerating, all purifying, all sanctifying influences by which man is freed from his state of bondage to sin, and made to partake of the mystery of the incarnation and atonement, proceed from the person of Christ, through the Spirit going out from Him into His Church.

§ 16.

The conception of sacred history is inseparable from that of MIRACLES. The full discussion of this subject must be reserved for the dogmatic system itself; but we may here in general terms designate the miracle of the *Incarnation*, of God becoming man in Christ, as the fundamental miracle of Christianity. Christ Himself is the prime miracle of Christianity, since His coming is the absolutely *new beginning* of a spiritual creation in the human race ; a beginning, whose significance is not only ethical, but cosmical. The person of Christ is not only a *historical* miracle, not merely a new starting-point in the world's moral development; as such it would be only relatively a miracle, a wonder, in the same sense, as the appearance of every great genius may be so termed, not being analogous to anything preceding. But Christ is something NEW in the race. He is not a mere moral and religious genius, but the new man, the new *Adam*, whose appearance in the midst of our race has a profound bearing not only on the moral, but on the *natural* world. He is not a mere prophet, endowed with the Spirit and power of God, but God's only begotten Son, the brightness of His glory, and the express image of His person, for whose redemptive appearance, not only man, but nature, waits. The person of Christ is, therefore, not only a historical, but a *cosmical* miracle ; not to be explained by the laws and forces of this world, this world's history and natural phenomena. But in order to be able to appropriate to itself the new revelation in Christ, the human race must receive a new sense, a new spirit ; the spirit of Christ must enter into a permanent union with man, as the principle of a new development—a development conceivable only as proceeding from an absolutely new beginning in the conscious life of the race.

The miracle of the Incarnation is hence inseparable from that of INSPIRATION ; or the outpouring of the Spirit on the day of Pentecost ; through which the principle of the new development is implanted in the human race, and from which the new life of fellowship, and the new sense of fellowship take their rise. The miracle of inspiration is the same in the subjective, as the miracle of the revelation of Christ in the objective, sphere. To these two new commencements, which form two sides of one and the same fundamental miracle, the miracle of the new creation, the Christian Church traces its origin. All the individual miracles of the New Testament are simply evolutions of this one; and all the Old Testament miracles are only foretokens, anticipatory indications of the new creating activity which in the fulness of time is concentrated in the miracle of the Incarnation, and of the founding of the church.

§ 17.

Here we come to the opposing principles of Supernaturalism on the one side, and Naturalism and Rationalism on the other. If a distinction is to be made between naturalism and rationalism—they being in fact only two sides of one and the same thing, each necessarily leading to the other—the former is referable primarily to the objective, the latter to the subjective, side of existence. Both reject miracles; but naturalism directs its opposition chiefly against the miracle of *incarnation*, because it recognises no higher laws than those of *nature ;* rationalism directs its main attacks against the miracle of *inspiration*, because it denies that there is any other and higher source of knowledge than *reason*. But, although there will always be men who affirm that the notions of nature and revelation, of reason and revelation (the latter taken in the positive, Christian sense of the word), are notions that exclude each other, yet within the Christian Church itself this can never be conceded.

We take first into consideration the issue between Supernaturalism and *Naturalism*. Here the decision of the question depends upon how the system of law and forces which we call nature, is conceived—whether it be conceived as a system in itself, finally and eternally fixed, or as a system that is passing through a *teleological* development, a continued creation. In the latter case new potencies, new laws and forces must be conceivable as entering into operation ; the preceding stages in the creation preparing the way for them, and prefiguring them, though not the source from which they can be derived. This is the Christian view of nature. In terming itself the new, the second creation, Christianity by no means calls itself a disturbance of nature, but rather the completion of the work of creation ; the revelation of Christ and the kingdom of Christ it pronounces the last potency of the work of creation ; which power, whether regarded as completing or as redeeming the world, must be conceivable as teleological ; operating so as to change and limit the lower forces, in so far as these are in their essential nature not eternal and organically complete, but only temporal and temporary. Hence the point of unity between the natural and the supernatural lies in the teleological design of nature to subserve the kingdom of God, and its consequent *susceptibility* to, its *capacity of being moulded* by, the supernatural, creative activity. Nature does not contradict the notion of a creation ; and it is in miracles that the dependence of nature on a free Creator becomes perfectly evident. But, while nature does not contradict the notion of a creation, the assumption of a creation is quite as little inconsistent with the notion of nature. For, although the new creation in Christ does do away with the laws of *this* nature, yet it by no means destroys the notion of nature itself. For the very notion of nature implies, not that it is a hindering restraint to freedom, but rather that it is the organ of freedom. And as the miraculous element in the life of Christ reveals the unity of spirit and of nature, so the revelation of Christ at once anticipates and predicts a new nature, a new heaven, and a new earth, in which a new system of laws will appear ; a system which will exhibit the harmony of the laws of nature and of freedom,—a state for which the whole structure of the present creation, with its unappeased strife between spirit and nature, is only a teleological transition period.

Naturalism, on the contrary, regards nature as a system in itself, eternal and organically complete. In this system there is nothing which cannot be explained as a development of the laws, forces, possibilities, and conditions, that are the same from eternity to eternity. The speculative assumption from which speculative naturalism starts, is that of pantheism, the canon of which Spinoza gives us. He identifies God and nature, defines God as *natura naturans*, the universe as *natura naturata ;* thus he shuts miracles out entirely, since the notion of nature which he lays down is utterly incompatible with that of a creation, of a *transcendental beginning*. For even the *first* creation is denied, since nature (*natura naturata*), though it *exists* through God (*natura naturans*), yet did not *come into existence* through God, through a free creative " Let there be," which of itself would have involved a miracle.   But to Spinoza it is no more a miracle that God and the universe should exist together, than that in a circle there should be both centre and circumference, and that centre and circumference should be conceived as simultaneously existent.   And just as Spinoza finds it impossible to conceive a single law of the circle to be annulled, he cannot conceive that any law of nature can be annulled ; because this would be an annulling of God's own nature, which according to Spinoza, is nothing different from the nature of this world. This we consider the only consistent form of naturalism.   For *Deism,*—although, for the sake of maintaining the immutability of natural laws, it denies miracles, yet assumes that the universe was *created,*—assumes thus after all a transcendental beginning ; concedes at least that the first day of this world was made to dawn by a miracle ; concedes that this origin is not self-evident as the propositions of mathematics and physics are, certain relations of time, space, and nature, being assumed. But Deism stops with this miracle ; it regards nature as being from this point completed ; like a clock which, once made and wound up, pursues its changeless course, to all eternity.   He who, on the contrary, admits a *continued* creation, must also assume that nature continues to be susceptible of free, divine agencies ; he must assume the continuance of a transcendental activity in nature and the course of the world.   Wherever men believe in a living Providence ; wherever men believe in the power of *prayer* ; wherever the words, " Blessings come from above," are not an empty sound, there men believe also that miracles are constantly taking place in secret, that we are everywhere surrounded by invisible, supernatural, and sacred influences, which are able to act on nature as something distinct from God.   But this belief must be at once recognised as imperfect, unless men will go further and recognise the great and manifest miracle, the miracle of the revelation of Christ.*

Observations.—In our time we find the denial of miracles fully carried out by Strauss, in the critical life of Jesus, and in his Christian Dogmatics. Strauss' criticism has been called thorough-going scepticism. It is rather thorough-going dogmatism, based on the assumptions of naturalism. The demonstrative force of his criticism rests on the constantly recurring repetition of the thought, developed long ago with much greater brevity and force by Spinoza: "Miracles are impossible; there is no transcendental beginning, for God and nature are one, from eternity to eternity!" But this proposition, on which Strauss everywhere either expressly or tacitly rests the arguments, by which he transforms every portion of sacred history into a myth;—this proposition Strauss has subjected to only a very superficial sceptical examination. This is evident especially from the fact, that he considers only the feeblest representations of the Christian view, and that he caricatures and parodies even these. We, for our part, do not at all pretend to be "free from assumptions;" but we can just as little accord to Strauss "scientific" freedom from assumptions. We accord to him this freedom only in a *religious* respect, *i. e.*, we allow that he has a *lack of interest* in the deepest problems of the religious life.

§ 18.

If we now attend to the relation of Supernaturalism to *Rationalism,* we find that the attacks of rationalism are chiefly directed against Inspiration, and the *miracula gratiæ* connected with it, while those of naturalism are directed against the Incarnation, and the *miracula naturæ* connected with it. If we consider reason as the thinking mind which searches the depths of existence, and ask whether reason, as it manifests itself in *us*, is something finished and complete in itself, the rationalist will very readily concede a progressive development of reason ; a development that leads to new discoveries and cognitions ; nay, the more profound rationalism of our day willingly admits that as " there is more reason in history,

* Mynster: Ueber den Begriff der Dogmatik (in the "Studien und Kritiken.")

so there is also more history in reason, than men in general are inclined to assume." But what the rationalist does not concede is, that there should be a new and different source of knowledge than the universal reason (κοινὸς λόγος) from which the human race has always drawn and will continue to draw ; —that there are other truths than those which are evolved out of the inborn reason of the human race. Hence he reduces Inspiration to the enthusiasm of genius ; sees in revealed Truth only truths of reason clothed in an antique form ; and explains the miracle of regeneration as being the fruit of religious education and *culture*. Thus rationalism falls back upon the assumptions of naturalism ; for, denying that a new source of knowledge has been opened in Christ, it must also deny that in Christ a new source of life is opened different from all other sources of life in creation. If, however, it is certain that in Christ a new source of life is opened, then there must have been also a new source of knowledge opened ; a realm of divine counsels hitherto hidden ; a realm of new cognitions which cannot be explained as the product of a development of reason. But these by no means conflict with the universal cognitions of human reason, although they in various ways modify them. For, on the one hand they serve to fill up and *complete* the rational cognitions ; on the other, they serve to *free* the universal human reason from the darkness with which universal sinfulness has infected it. To suppose that this implies an insoluble dualism in the realm of knowledge, is as incorrect as to suppose that in the system of the universe the two creations imply an insoluble duality. For, as there is only one system of creation, though in this there are two grand stages, so there is also but one system of reason, although herein are involved two degrees in the revelation of reason. Objectively considered, the unity lies in the fact, that it is the same Logos that reveals himself in both creations ; but that the revelation of the Logos in Christ is a higher degree of revelation, differing from His universal revelation in that it is a revelation which *completes* and *redeems* the world ; whereas the other merely creates and preserves. Subjectively considered, the unity is found in the fact, that the human reason stands in a *receptive* relation towards the Spirit of Christ, as the Spirit that completes and

redeems the world ;—a receptivity through which reason is to
be raised to a higher stage of productivity.   That revelation
(as is so often asserted) contradicts the laws of reason, (a term,
by the way, whose meaning is as unfixed as is the science of
dialectics itself), can be admitted only in the same sense as it
may be admitted that the revelation in Christ contradicts the
laws of morality.   For, as Christianity does abolish the moral
laws, considered as independent abstractions, in order to ratify
them all in enforcing the duty of love, which is the fulfilling
of the law : so also it abolishes the laws of reason, as abstractions, in order to ratify them in revealing the wisdom of
Christ, which is the fulfilling of the law of reason (σοφία Θεοῦ
in opposition to σοφία τοῦ κόσμου).

Observations. — Regeneration is for the individual what
inspiration is for the whole church at the period of its
foundation.   It is the new beginning which involves a
susceptibility for the revelation of Christ.   No one can
attain faith by the mere prosecution of his education and
by reflection ; although these may doubtless in various
ways prepare the way for regeneration.   But only in case
this new beginning becomes an object of consciousness,
can a truly Christian knowledge begin.   Even if we
should conceive an ideally perfect system of Christian
theology, this would not suffice to convince an unbeliever.   It would at the most only force from the unbelievers the confession that, *if* he were a believer, *i. e.,* if
he had an *experimental conviction* of the truth of the
objects of faith,—if his very being were brought into
relation to them,—he would follow the same method in
developing his faith and making it clear to himself.

§ 19.

The community of Christian believers, or the Christian Church, differs from every other religious community in
that it was founded by Christ, that the personality of the
God-man is implied in the fact of its existence.   The community of believers is brought into relation to God as Father,
only through Christ, and only through Christ is it a fellowship in the Holy Ghost.   Hence that which remains unchangeable amidst all the developments that are taking place
in the Church, is such by virtue of its uninterrupted connec-

tion with Christ as the Head of the ecclesiastical organism—
a connection at once historical and mysterious, because it is a
relation not only to the Saviour mentioned in history, but
also to the Saviour now present in His Church, who rose
from the dead and ascended to heaven. This positive element
in the doctrines and institutions of the Church, must be sought
in its evolution of the notions, " Word of God " and " Sacrament." But in the more particular definition of these, the
Christian Church is divided by two confessions,—the Catholic,
and the Evangelical or Protestant. An Introduction to a
dogmatic system must confine itself to a discussion of the
Church's principle of cognition, as preparatory to a presentation of its own scientific principle. Hence we shall here consider the difference between the two confessions only, in
laying down our view of the divine word, which is the *canon*,
the guide and norm for the doctrine and life of the Church.

CATHOLICISM AND PROTESTANTISM.
§ 20.

Inasmuch as both confessions profess a general belief in
God as Father, Son, and Holy Ghost; inasmuch as both
reject the ancient and the modern forms of Naturalism
and Rationalism, both recognise the truth that the Christian
Church rests upon a Divine Word, derived from the Founder
Himself, and delivered to the Church through the apostles.
For it is only through the apostles that we have received
Christianity, and that Christianity *only* is genuine, which
can show itself to be *apostolic*. The difference between the
confessions does not consist merely in the difference of the
relation which they assign to the oral and the written word
of the apostles (tradition and Scripture), but in their different
views respecting the scope of the apostolate. The Catholic holds
to a living apostolate in the Church, perpetuating itself through
all time—an inspiration constantly kept up in the representatives of the Church. He claims to possess in the decisions
of the councils and of the pope a divine utterance invested
with apostolic authority, as infallible as the word of the first
apostles which was spoken in the world ; and he claims to have
in these decrees the infallible interpretation, an infallible continuation, of that first apostolic word. The Evangelical

church, like the Catholic, confesses that the Spirit of the Lord is with the Church unto the end of the world, leading it into all truth ; but that perfect union of the Spirit of God and man, which is called Inspiration, and which constitutes the essence of the apostolate, it assigns exclusively to the beginning of the Church, to the period of its foundation ; and, although it admits the relative validity of tradition, it yet regards the Holy Scriptures of the New Testament as the only perfect, authentic and absolutely canonical expression of the original fulness of the apostolic spirit.

But the difference here indicated rests on another which lies still deeper—a difference in the conception of the essence of Christianity itself. The Evangelical Church views Christianity as a Gospel; as glad tidings of the new life and the new creation in Christ, offered to men as a free gift of heavenly grace ; whereas the Catholic Church for the most part regards faith as a new law, and Christ as a new lawgiver. Hence, representing the Gospel merely as an external authority to which the believer must yield, and not recognizing the principle that the gospel is to be freely accepted, and to be developed anew in every believer's inner experience, the legal church, for this very reason, cannot be satisfied with a canon of faith which, like the Holy Scriptures, contains what the church needs for the preservation of the true doctrine only in an undeveloped though completed form. It requires a canon in which every particular element is developed ; it requires a hierarchy endowed with power to expound the law with infallible authority in all its single precepts. Catholicism does not inquire after any internal canon found in the Christian experience of believers, but lays all the more stress on the external canon. It inquires little about *how* faith appropriates Christianity (*fides qua creditur*), for it is secretly afraid of the conflicts accompanying the development of faith, and of the possible errors and abuses that are inseparable from it ; but all the more carefully does it inquire *what* the object of the faith is (*fides quae creditur*). The Catholic doctrine of the infallibility of the church, *i.e.*, of the hierarchy, is thus to be traced ultimately to this legal character of the church, and to the efforts, growing out of this, to *guarantee* to itself, in an external manner, the genuineness of its

Christianity—efforts by which it removes itself farther and farther from the very thing that is to be guaranteed.

Observations.—The Catholic train of thought, in which truth and error are so strangely mixed, is, in its main features, the following :—

What are the external marks of genuine Christianity? For from the earliest times Christianity has stood over against Christianity, since doctrines entirely opposed to each other have been preached in the name of Christianity. The fundamental criterion can be none other than "*the apostolical.*" The Christianity which lays claim to genuineness, must be able to prove that it dates from the apostles. It is only through the apostles that we have Christianity at all ; only from them can we learn what should be called by that name. They are organs of revelation and have the spirit of inspiration ; their minds are the pure, colourless medium through which heavenly truth casts its rays into history ; only through this medium can we see Christ as in a true mirror. Therefore the church in its contest with heresy has the task to perform of making sure to itself its union and connection with the mind of the apostles. But by what means does the church preserve its union with the apostles? The Scriptures are used by heretics as well as by the church. In order to understand them the Christian faith is necessary ; for, considered in themselves, they may be interpreted in the most diverse ways, and every heretic reads them through his own spectacles. Besides this, they are not sufficient ; for many questions may arise that are not answered in the Scriptures, and yet the church in every stage of its progress needs the apostolic spirit for its guidance. The Bible is only an historical monument of this spirit ; but the spirit itself must reveal itself through the church as a living, present reality. Hence, it is concluded, there must be in the church a *living* continuation of the apostolic mind.

The first form in which this living continuation, this actual presence, of the apostolic mind is conceived, is Tradition. As distinguished from the apostolic *writings,* Tradition signifies the apostolic *word,* which propagates itself from generation to generation as a living power, orally delivered by the apostles to their disciples, and handed down by them to their successions. Says Irenaeus, " We can count up the bishops who were installed in the churches by the apostles, and their successors down to the present time. Even if the apostles had left us no writings, we should still have to observe the order of the tradition which they gave to those to whom they intrusted the churches. Many barbarians believe in the gospel of Christ, having written that gospel in their hearts, without paper and ink, by carefully preserving the old tradition." (Irenaeus adv. haer. III.)

If, however, tradition is to be the actual presence of the apostolic mind, its propagation must not be a matter of accident. In the course of time tradition itself needs interpretation, and in this, human caprice and error must be excluded. Therefore there must be in the church an order of teachers appointed by God and endowed by special grace with the power to hand tradition down pure and unadulterated. *The apostolate is continued in the episcopate.* Together with their office the apostles communicated also their spirit ; and, as they themselves were inspired, and only by virtue of that inspiration were strictly organs of revelation, the same is true of their successors. The apostolic spirit continues its deathless existence through the mystical body of the episcopate, which body becomes visible in the *councils.* The Spirit of inspiration hovers over the councils, explains and interprets the words which He himself spoke in past ages, and which He himself wrote in the sacred books. What the sacred authors meant ; what they often made known only in enigmatical hints because the church could not yet bear it ; that is now revealed in the course of time by the same Spirit who came upon them on the day of Pentecost, and under whose inspiration they composed their writings.

The sacred stream of inspiration, therefore, flows through all history. The Spirit accompanies his church in the form of the episcopate, and through it establishes the *unity* of the church, raising it above all the changes of time, and making it indestructible. This unity comes

into view in the councils, the spiritual body of the episcopate. The single bishop, as such, is not inspired : he is
inspired only in so far as he is one with the body. The
diversity of the individual minds that are present at the
council are made harmoniously to blend in the unity of
Spirit, the Spirit moving each one to give up his one-
sidedness for the sake of promoting the unity of the
body. But now the unity of the body must become
visible in one supreme head. The episcopate must be
centralized in the *primacy*. The immediate presence o
the apostolic spirit would not be perfectly realised if it
were not concentrated in one real person. The council is
a person only as having a moral character ; it only represents, signifies the unity of the church, but *is* not
that unity itself, for all bishops cannot be present at
the council ; moreover, controversies may arise among
the representatives, and then the inspiration is only with
the *majority*. But in the Pope, as the supreme head of
the church, the unity of the church is embodied, not
in a mere so-called moral person, not in a mere majority,
but in a real, individual person ; in him is collected the
whole fulness of the divine power and intelligence of the
episcopate ; in him the Spirit of inspiration has found
its personal focus. He is the pure, personal mirror for
the Spirit of truth, whose rays are scattered throughout
all Christendom. As Peter held the primacy in the
circle of apostles, so the Pope holds it in the circle of
bishops. In the doctrine of the primacy the system of
Catholicism reaches its climax. From the Roman chair
the apostle is still speaking on whom, according to
the will of the Lord, His church was to be built ; here
the church has an infallible testimony of the truth, elevated above all doubt ; for, as the central organ of inspiration, the Pope has unlimited authority and power to
ward off all heresy. In so far as he speaks, *ex cathedra*,
his consciousness is a divine-human consciousness ; and
he is so far *vicarius Christi*. As Peter once said to the
Redeemer, " Lord, to whom shall we go ? Thou hast the
words of eternal life," so all Christendom turns in the
same way—not to Christ, but to the successor of Peter

The system of Catholicism grows, therefore, out of an effort to grasp revelation as a purely objective thing;—which involves the task of assuring itself of a living and infallibly apostolic organ for the continued apprehension and communication of the revelation. But in the midst of these efforts the original object of knowledge has been gradually forgotten. Catholicism has developed itself into a great system of *guarantees* of Christianity; but Christianity, the thing itself, which was thus to be guaranteed, has been thrown into the shade. The opposition between genuine and spurious Christianity has been gradually reduced to the affirmation and the negation of these guarantees. To attack the infallibility of the Pope and of the Church is the prime heresy. The spirit of reformation awakes in the Church, and bitterly complains that Judaism and heathenism have crept in under the mask of the hierarchy, that the Word of God has been perverted by the commandments of men (*traditiones humanæ*), that Christ is virtually no more preached, that faith has become to most men an unknown thing, because nothing is preached but faith in the Pope and the Church, instead of the one, the saving faith in the Redeemer, as the true Mediator between God and man. The critical investigations provoked by the spirit of reformation demonstrate that the external criteria of truth, employed by the Catholic Church, are invalid; for tradition stands opposed to tradition, council to council, pope to pope. The Catholic assertion that the Church has a visible unity is unhistorical; it is an idea that is refuted by facts. The Reformation leaves the guarantees of Christianity, and goes back to Christianity itself; and, committing itself to the guidance of the Spirit who is not confined to Rome, but raises up and endows free Christian men wherever and whenever He wills; it undertakes the work of purifying the temple, of cleansing the Church, by means of the Holy Spirit and the Holy Scriptures.

§ 21.

It has often been said that the principle of Protestantism is that of *subjectivity*—a proposition which, expressed in this indefinite, general form, is liable to misconception. The aim

of the Reformation was as much to regain objective Christianity, to separate the true tradition from the false or at least
transient traditions (*traditiones humanæ*), as to revive subjective, personal Christianity. What the Reformation desired
was neither exclusively the objective nor the subjective; it
was the free union of the objective and the subjective, of the
thing believed and the person believing, of divine revelation
and the religious self-consciousness. This free union of the
objective and the subjective the Evangelical Church claims to
have secured through its so-called formal and material principle, which expresses the two sides, the objective and the
subjective side, of the same truth. By the term formal
principle, is meant the Holy Scriptures ; by the term material
principle, is meant justification by faith. On a correct apprehension of these principles, often misunderstood and often
insipidly treated, depends a correct understanding of Protestantism.*

§ 22.

It is obvious that, unless our Christianity is to be a
merely subjective, private Christianity, there must be a canon
of Christianity, independent of our subjective moods and
circumstances. Now, the objective canon for all Christianity
is, it is true, nothing else than *Christ himself,* as a holy,
personal Redeemer ; and, if it is asked *where* we find Christ,
our first answer is the same as the Catholic gives—in the
Church, which is the body of Christ, the organism of which
He is the living, omnipresent Head. In the Church, in its
confessions and its proclamations, in its sacraments and its
sacred services, the exalted and glorified Redeemer is present,
and bears living testimony to Himself in behalf of all who
believe through the power of the Holy Ghost. It is, however,
on the other hand, obvious that a correct relation to the
exalted, glorified Christ is conditional upon a correct relation
to the *historical* Christ, to the historical facts of His revelation, without which one's conception of the exalted and
glorified Christ loses itself in the vagueness of mysticism.
Hence, when we say that we must look for Christ in the
Church, we are led back to the Apostolic Church. The
Apostolic Church exhibits to us not only the original form of

* Cf. Dorner: Das Princip. unserer Kirche.

Christian life, and the relation which it presents, as sustained by Christian believers to the invisible Redeemer after His ascent to heaven ; but it is, at the same time, the possessor of the original image of Christ, the image of the Word, which became flesh and dwelt among us ; the image of Christ as He was historically revealed. Now, it being certain that the Apostolic Church, as opening the progressive development of the Church, contained Christianity in its genuine form, it is quite as certain that there must have been delivered to us a trustworthy exhibition of Christianity as it originally was. For this is certain: *either* no one can now make out what Christianity is ; in which case Christianity is not a divine revelation, but only a myth, or a philosophical dogma; *or* there must have been given a reliable tradition of the manner in which the apostles conceived and received Christ, whereby every succeeding age is enabled to preserve its connection with the Apostolic Church, and with genuine Christianity. So far we agree with the Catholics. Our views, however, differ from theirs, in that we, with the Reformers, find the perfect, trustworthy form of apostolic tradition only in the Holy Scriptures of the New Testament. As to tradition— in the sense of something handed down by the Church, side by side with the New Testament—we hold, with the Reformers, that there is nothing in it which can, with such certainty as can the Scriptures, demonstrate that it had an immediate or even mediate apostolic origin, and that it has preserved through long ages its pure, apostolic form. We hold, therefore, that the Scriptures are the ultimate touchstone of criticism (*lapis lydius*), which must decide on the Christianity of tradition. Even though we must say that the *essentials* of Christianity are found in tradition, that the Spirit of Christ controls its development, still experience teaches that inspiration was not continued in the post-apostolic times, and that very soon, in the formation of traditions, there arose a mixture of canonical and apocryphal elements. Facts likewise show that, in those periods of the post-apostolic church, in which the growth of tradition was not controlled by the Holy Scriptures, a purely apocryphal tradition has been developed. The oral tradition of the apostles had to be exposed very early to disfigurement. But in contrast with the fleeting and mutable character of tradition, the Scriptures remain a firm, immovable witness. *Littera scripta manet.* This faith in the Scriptures which we share with the Reformers ; this faith in their sufficiency as a canon of Christianity, in the completeness of the apostolic testimony therein recorded ; this faith is a part of our Christian faith in Providence, in the guidance of the Church by the Lord ;—a faith which, like every form of faith in Providence, cannot be demonstratively proved, and can be confirmed only by the lapse of time. Within the sphere of our own experience, however, we are able to see, in view of the evident uncertainty of tradition, that without the Scriptures we should have no firm hold, and should not be able to distinguish what is canonical from what is apocryphal. Without the Scriptures a reformation of the Church in that long period of corruption, of darkness, would have been impossible ; and a new founding of the Church, or at least a new mission of apostles, would have been necessary.[*]

§ 23.

The principle maintained by the Reformers respecting the Scriptures assumes primarily a negative attitude towards tradition ; but its relation to tradition is by no means merely negative, although often so conceived. There are indeed those who hold the principle in such a form that they admit nothing to be valid in the Church whose Biblical origin cannot be in the strictest manner authenticated. But this view is entirely foreign to the Lutheran Reformation, although traces of it

---

[*] Cf. Thiersch : Vorlesungen uber Katholicismus und Protestantismus, vol. i., p. 320. " This is an act of the confidence which we put in Divine Providence and in the guidance of the Church by Christ and His Spirit. For it was not unknown to the Most High that a time would come when whatever was derived from the apostles in the form of unwritten tradition would, through the long-continued fault of men, become unstable and unreliable, and that His Church would need a sacred, uncorrupted record accessible to all, such as His people under the Old Covenant had had in the writings of Moses and the prophets. For, if the Holy Scriptures are not the refuge to which the Church is directed to fly, since that which is called tradition has become the object of just offence and insoluble doubt, then the Church has no refuge at all, no secure position, and there would be left for her nothing but to wait to be a second time miraculously founded, or to look for a new mission of apostles." As is well known, the gifted and highly-respected author has himself drawn the latter inference—in which we cannot follow him.

may be found in the Swiss. The Lutheran Reformation, in its original form, took a positive attitude towards both dogmatic and ritual tradition, in so far as it was *œcumenical* tradition ; *i.e.*, so far as it bore the mark of no particular church, being neither Greek Catholic nor Roman Catholic, but simply Catholic. Accordingly, the Evangelical Church adopts the œcumenical symbols, the Apostolic, the Nicaean, and the Athanasian, as the purest expression of dogmatic tradition. Thus Luther's Catechism retains, in the Ten Commandments, the three Creeds, the Lord's Prayer, and the doctrine of the sacrament, of baptism, and of the altar, the same fundamental elements in which primitive Christianity was propagated among the common people through the darkness of the middle ages. Thus, too, the Reformers pointed to a series of testimonies out from early Church, a *consensus patrum*, in proof of the primitive character and age of their doctrine. And Luther and Melanchthon recognized not only the importance of dogmatic tradition, but manifested also the greatest reverence and caution in reference to ritual tradition. The importance which they attached to this is shown especially in their retaining and defending, in opposition to the Anabaptists, infant baptism, a custom which is certainly derived not chiefly from the Scriptures, but from tradition. The same thing is shown by their continuing to observe the principal Christian festivals ; for these, too, were the product of a continued tradition. In like manner they retained many portions of the liturgy and of the hymns of the Church, which had acquired a value for all Christians. Thus we see that, by their principles, Scripture and tradition were not torn asunder, but only placed in their proper relation to each other. And even if it may be said that the Reformers, finding themselves entangled in a web of traditions, in which true and false, canonical and apocryphal elements were almost indissolubly mixed together, sometimes cut the knot instead of untying it,—this proves nothing against the principle of the primacy of Scripture. For this rule cannot be annulled or altered so long as nothing can be put beside the Scriptures that is able to vindicate for itself the same degree of authority.

Observations.—Some among us have thought that the Reformation could be bettered by making simply the bap-

tismal formula or the Apostles' creed the supreme canon
of Christianity,* instituted for this purpose by the apostles,
or rather by our Lord himself, and suited by its simplicity,
brevity, and positiveness to serve as an unchangeable rule
of faith and of biblical interpretation. They claim that
the Reformers, by taking the Scriptures for their rule, opened
the door to all the vague and capricious notions with which
the Evangelical church has been inundated. But, with
all reverence for the Apostles' creed, we can still see in
this proposal no improvement on the doctrine of the
Reformers. We admit the various abuses superinduced by
an unspiritual treatment of the doctrine respecting the
supreme authority of the Scriptures. We acknowledge the
great importance attaching to the Apostles' creed as the
oldest œcumenical testimony of the Christianity of the first
centuries. We concede that this symbol, as to its contents, may be called apostolic, not only because we find
every part of it adopted in all places where the church has
had an existence, but also because we find it in the New
Testament expressed with the same or with equivalent
terms. We know, too, that this symbol is not a mere
extract from the Scriptures, the canon of which was not
completely fixed until about the same time that this symbol itself seems to have received its final form (in the 4th
century). But in thus conceding that it is the oldest and
purest tradition that has come down to us from the ancient church, and that it will always maintain its position
as the foundation of all creeds on account of its biblical
simplicity, we yet by no means concede that it contains *in
itself* an authority supreme and all-decisive. Rather, we
must maintain that its authority rests upon its scripturalness, *i.e.*, not on its derivation from, but on its agreement
with, the language of Scripture. We cannot concede that
this symbol is designed to be the highest *critical* authority in the church; we must rather maintain that its
whole character is such as to make it quite unfit for such
a use. The Apostles' creed cannot of itself be a supreme
and ultimate authority, because, although in substance
apostolic, yet both in its original and its present form it

* The well-known view of Grundtvig.

is a post-apostolic production. It has, to be sure, been maintained as, even in its present form, a work of the apostles or even of our Lord himself. But in reply to such an unhistorical assertion, we only need to point, in the first place, to the complete silence of the New Testament respecting it; and, in the second place, to the unrefuted and irrefutable disclosures that have often been made concerning the various forms which this symbol is found to have had in the early church; forms which, it is true, agree in substance, but by no means give all the parts of the symbol completely, while those that are given are not in all equally complete. From this it is evident that the creed was not handed down by the apostles from the beginning in a finished form, but is the result of various attempts to present the substance of what the apostles taught; finally assuming the fixed form which now the whole church adopts.

Those, however, who maintain that this creed is of strictly apostolic origin, base their proof not so much on history as upon an *idea* of what must necessarily have belonged to the founding of the church. Inasmuch, they say, as the church promises salvation to believers, the question must necessarily, upon its establishment, have been definitely answered,—What and how much must be believed in order to salvation? In other words: the conditions of salvation must at the very outset have been fixed in a manner that should serve for all time; they must in all periods find a concurrent expression in connection with the rite of baptism. Therefore, the confession now made at baptism must have been heard at the first Christian baptism, not a single article can have been taken from, not a single article added to it; for in that case the church would have changed its creed, would have changed the conditions of salvation, if it had declared at one time a shorter, at another a longer summary of doctrines to be necessary to salvation.

But the idea underlying this argument is as little satisfactory as is the argument from history, and seems more suited to the legal than to the evangelical church. The apostolical traditions which have come down to us, and the general experience of Christendom, teach us that Christianity is not primarily a new *law*, but a new life and a new creation ; hence it follows that, when it is asked what is necessary to salvation, we must pronounce the saving agent to be not chiefly a definite *quantum* of doctrinal propositions, but the communication and reception of the principle of the *new creation*, for which reason our elder theologians describe *fides salvifica* as justifying faith in the PERSON *of Christ*. In other words : The apostolic tradition given us in the Scriptures shows us that no *fides explicita* is absolutely necessary to salvation; but that a *fides implicita*—*i.e.*, a faith which, though undeveloped and unconscious, involves the principle and substance of what the Creed expresses with the definiteness of a prescribed rule,—is also a saving faith. It is true only of lifeless, mechanical things (*e.g.*, a ring or a chain), that the whole cannot be had without having all the parts. In living, organic objects, it is very possible to have the whole without having all the parts. But eternal life, and the things that belong to eternal life must, as all will allow, be considered as subject to the laws of life. Hence we find in the Gospels that our Lord adjudges salvation to men who join themselves by faith to Him as the Redeemer, without this faith being developed throughout in all its parts. " Thy faith hath made thee whole," He said, in many instances, without laying down any other conditions. So He declares Peter to be blessed because he confesses Him to be the only begotten Son of God, although many articles of the apostolic creed are lacking in this confession. (Matt. xvi. 16, 17.) This notion of a definitely limited *quantum* of propositions as being *absolutely* necessary to salvation, calls our attention back to the *articuli fundamentales* which were laid down by the early Protestant theologians ; who, notwithstanding their correct definition of the *fides salvifica*, nevertheless designated the *articuli fundamentales* as those articles the acceptance of which was necessary to salvation. But herein they laid themselves open to the charge of teaching error. For clearly salvation is an individual thing, and the misconception of a truth, while it may *in* one individual be no hindrance to his salvation, may endanger the salvation of another who has reached a higher stage of mental development. Hence, if we hold fast to the truth that salvation is an individual thing, and yet are not satisfied with faith in the Redeemer as the ground of salvation, as a principle of life necessarily either present or not present, then we must either hold that in this matter there is something which in its individual applications is indefinable, or we shall be in danger of reposing in a certain set of propositions, trusting that, if we only hold to them, we may be indifferent to everything else.* We cannot determine what is fundamental, by its relation to the salvation of individuals, but by its relation to the preservation and growth of the *church.* Fundamental articles are those on which are conditioned the preservation and growth of the church in sound doctrine ; mediately, therefore, it is true, the education and growth of the individual ; just as the church, by means of its developed faith, supports and maintains the faith of the individual, which is often in various respects imperfect and undeveloped. Although, however, the notion of the necessity of fundamental articles is thus connected with that of the preservation and growth of the church, yet this latter notion must be always somewhat subject to flux and change, inasmuch as times may come in the course of the progressive developments of the church, in which doctrines may be seen to have a fundamental significance which was not before recognized. True, it must be maintained that whatever is really fundamental must at all times have lived and

---

* On this point we fully agree with the excellent sentiments of *Julius Müller* in his work, "Die Evangelische Union" (p. 20) : "As an inalienable acquisition,—derived by the Protestant Church out of the sad decay of its orthodox theology, especially in the latter part of the 17th century and after, out of the pietistic and Moravian reaction, and out of the revival of living faith in the present century—we must regard the conviction that the faith which saves does not consist in the adoption of a series of *articuli fidei fundamentales primarii,* but in an absolute and truthful surrender of one's self to the personal Saviour; a surrender of which the simplest child is capable. Although this conviction may in the next few years have to sustain violent attacks and be branded as heresy— the attacks have, indeed, already begun—yet it is so deeply rooted in the divine word and in the fundamental religious sentiment of the Reformers, that we cannot but have confidence in its final triumph."

moved in the depths of the consciousness of the church ; but it is by no means necessary that the church should at all times have possessed it in an explicit form, still less in the form of a sharply defined formulary. For the first thing, the absolutely necessary thing, is life, life in its fulness; rules, laws, and formularies are secondary, are only *relatively* necessary. Accordingly, so long as the apostolic spirit in its fulness was alive in the churches, there was, so far as can be seen, no necessity for any other formula of faith than that which was given by our Lord himself, Matt. xxviii. 19 (" in the name of the Father, and of the Son, and of the Holy Ghost ") ; for this formula in-cludes the whole of Christianity, the fulness of which was proclaimed by apostolic lips, and which in actual life made itself everywhere felt as a new creation. But after this period of fulness and inspiration had passed, when the church was no longer led by the apostles, when errone-ous doctrines began to force their way, and bring con-fusion, into the churches, then it necessarily became a matter of the greatest consequence to the leaders of the church to *preserve* the treasures which had been handed down by the apostles ; and now they began to put the main points of the preaching of the apostles into the shape of a formula, for which a basis had already been given by our Lord himself. So too a beginning was made in the collection of the apostolic writings into a canon. The great importance of the Apostles' creed lies in the fact that it was the first work of the post-apostolic church, in which the church repeated, in the form of a creed, what had been orally transmitted from the apostles ; just as a catechumen repeats, and says yea and Amen to, what he has received from his teachers, with the resolution to preserve it and transmit it to the next generation.* According to all his-torical evidences the construction of this creed was a gradual process, undergoing many transitions until it finally received the fixed form which it now has. *Now*, to be sure, the confession of the Apostles' creed must be con-

* Cf. A. G. Rudelbach: Ueber die Bedentung des Apostolischen Symbol-ums, p. 22.

sidered as essential to the completeness of the baptismal
act ; since the church testifies its purpose to train up those
who are baptized in this faith ; and the baptized must desire to be partakers of the faith of the church; though, of
course, retaining the right to examine whether the testimony of the church agrees with that of the apostles.
Nevertheless, it can by no means be affirmed that this
confession is the substance of the baptism itself. For no
one can maintain that a baptism, without a complete confession prescribed by the church, is invalid or must be
repeated, in case it is in other respects administered in
accordance with the Lord's own appointment.

The Apostles' Creed is not only, historically considered, a
post-apostolic production; its whole inner form and contents
are such as to prove its insufficiency to serve as the highest
critical standard in the church.   Every word of it would
be unintelligible, if we had not a richer source to which we
could resort for an explanation.   Hence also we find that
the church fathers of the first three centuries never separated tradition from the Scriptures ; and Irenaeus, so often
appealed to on the point of the rule of faith, himself calls
the Scriptures " *columna et fundamentum ecclesiae.*"   It
is quite clear too that without the Scriptures we should
derive from the Apostles' Creed a poor support.   Though
it is a symbol used at baptism, yet it gives us not the
slightest information concerning the sacramental significance of baptism ; and with a full confession of the
Apostles' Creed might be joined such a conception of
baptism as finds in this sacrament only a symbolic ceremony.   It gives us quite as little light respecting the
Lord's supper.   The same is true of the important doctrine of justification by faith, a doctrine whose fundamental importance, doubtless, few among us will have the
courage to question.   Even the doctrine of the person of
Christ is so indefinitely stated that both Arians and
Socinians have been able to adopt the creed ; and the
latter have always appealed to the harmony of their belief
with the Apostles' Creed in order to prove themselves to
be good Christians.   If it is answered that those who
bring heresies into the creed, misinterpret it, and disregard

the consequences which necessarily flow from the creed we assent to this fully. Only we must then express our surprise at the way in which the Nicene and Athanasian creeds are often depreciated by those who affirm that the Apostles' Creed alone has the right to determine what Christianity is. For, if this creed cannot be understood except as inferences are deduced from it, it would seem to be far safer to adopt that development of it which is presented by the œcumenical councils of the church in those later symbols,—in which, through the aid of the Holy Scriptures, the great and comprehensive truths implied in the earlier symbol are drawn out,—than to fancy that we may be indifferent to the later creeds as being only a work of biblical scholars ; and yet that any person whatever may himself deduce the necessary inferences from the Apostles' Creed, and that too, perhaps, without consulting the Scriptures at all. To leap over the intervening symbols in this way, and go back immediately to the Apostles' Creed, is to imitate the course of the Socinians. But whether it is done from the stand-point of infidelity or of faith, it will always be an unhistorical procedure.

We are, therefore, unable to see in this theory respecting the Apostles' Creed, any improvement upon the Reformation. We can see in it only a reaction against the one-sided view of the authority of the Scriptures, which has displayed itself in so many ways within the Protestant churches ;—a reaction kindred to that of Puseyism in the Anglican church, in which, however, we discern no possibility of a new development.

§ 24.

The formal principle of Protestantism, or its objective canon of Christianity, is therefore the Holy Scriptures in their indissoluble connection with the *confessing* church. But the notion of a canon of Christianity, be it found in the Bible or in the church, points to a conscious mind *for* which it is a canon. The external canon points to an internal canon, by whose aid alone it can be correctly understood ; and that internal canon is the *regenerated* Christian mind, in which the Spirit of God bears witness with the spirit of man (*testimonium spiritus sancti*). To the unregenerated and merely natural mind,

both the Bible and the church, the testimony of the church
in word and in deed, in doctrine and worship, will be nothing
more than the outward, sensible presence of Christ was to the
unbelievers of His age.   Only to that mind in which Christianity, in which the spirit of the Scriptures and of the church,
is present as an inner principle of life, do the Scriptures and
tradition unfold their contents; without this internal canon
they remain unintelligible.   It has been said that the Bible
must be interpreted according to the *analogia fidei;* but how
can such an *analogia fidei,* such a summary of the essential
dogmas of the Scriptures, be obtained without a Christian
mind which has come into possession of Christian truth in a
manner relatively independent of the Scriptures; and which,
by virtue of this conception of Christian truth, is able to
recognize what is essential in the Scriptures *as* essential.   It
has been said that the Scriptures should be interpreted according to the rule of faith (*symbolum apostolicum*); but by what
is the rule of faith in its turn to be interpreted, unless by the
Christian mind, which in this summary of doctrinal propositions can detect the invisible principle which gives them their
organic unity, and at the same time is able to distinguish, in
these different propositions, the leading from the subordinate
ones, the central from the peripheral?   For all parts in an
organism cannot be alike central, alike essential.   Lastly, it has
been said (by Augustine) that the Scriptures must be interpreted Ͽεοπρεπῶς, in a manner worthy of God and divine
things ; but how is this possible, unless the Christian idea of
God is alive in the mind ?   The idea of this internal canon
is the internal and *material* principle of Protestantism.   This
material principle is usually called justification by faith.
But we must here guard against that misconception of it which
makes justification by faith only a doctrinal proposition.   For
then it would be merely a *traditum,* an addition to what is
positively given, but not, in relation to this, a new side, something *a priori*.   Justification by faith must here be taken as
an expression for subjective Christianity, for the regenerated
mind, for the new creature in Christ, in whom the certainty
of justification through Christ, the certainty of the forgiveness
of sins, and of adoption into the family of God,—and, accordingly, the certainty of the glorious freedom of the sons of God,

—is the centre of life. And this new creature, by virtue of its living Christian experience, by virtue of the conception, which it carries within itself, of Christian life and Christian truth, knows itself to be, not a *tabula rasa,* but a relatively independent centre, to have an *a priori* existence, in relation, not only to the church, but even to Holy Scripture itself. It is true, Christianity as a subjective thing is born from the womb of the church, and must always stand in a relation of external dependence to the church and the Scriptures ; but, as we above showed in general that man's relation to God must be changed from one of dependence to one of relative freedom, the same holds true in particular of man's relation to the Christian revelation. Personal Christianity must, in the course of its development, come to a point where it no longer stands in a relation of mere dependence to what is imposed from without, but in a free, reciprocal relation to it. It was this self-dependence of the Christian life that displayed itself in an extraordinary degree at the time of the Reformation. Luther's standing-point was the consciousness of " the freedom of a Christian man," the divinely inspired certainty of union with Christ through faith (" Yet not I, but Christ liveth in me," Gal. ii. 20) ; the sure confidence that faith has, not only outside of itself, but in itself, the Spirit that leads into all truth. Governed by these two principles, that of subjective, and that of objective Christianity, in their vital and reciprocal relation to each other, he accomplished the reformation of the church ; and on this same reciprocal relation of these factors depends at all times the prosperity of the Evangelical Church. Here we meet an objection. Christianity in the individual, entering into this reciprocal relation to external Christianity is not only modified by the individual, but exerts a modifying influence on him, reproducing the Scriptures and tradition in a free form, and thus constructing a new tradition ; as we see in the case of the Reformation, by which new creeds were developed. Now it may be said that this subjective Christianity is by no means infallible, because the individual, although regenerated and led by the Spirit of God, is yet not inspired. This we must concede. We grant that the church, so long as it is undergoing the process of development, will never correspond with its ideal. We admit that the Refor-

mation did not bring the church back to its apostolic or its
ideal condition, but that this condition is yet to be realized.
But we affirm that it is only in this way that it *can* be
attained.   It may be granted that there are many things in
tradition, many truths in the Roman Church, which were not
duly appreciated by the Reformers.   But we maintain that
the principle of the Reformation leaves us the possibility of
securing what may have been neglected ; and we maintain,
further, that no reformation can ever be effected in spirit and
in truth, unless the principle is accepted, that nothing shall
pass for truth which cannot stand the final test of the
word of God and the mind of man, freely investigating, in the
liberty wherewith Christ makes us free.

Observations.—When the formal and the material principle
(the Scriptures and the Church on the one side, and the
testimony of the Spirit in the individual Christian on
the other) are taken out of their organic connection with,
and reciprocal relation to, each other, then false notions
of the Church arise.   Church history shows us cases in
which the Christian Church has only the form of a legal
church ; then again cases in which it has merely the form
of a school or of a sect.   But all these phenomena are to be
explained as the dissolution of the vital union, of the vital,
reciprocal relation between the principles above described.

We will now indicate the chief forms which the Church
assumes when the formal principle is maintained and the
material set aside.

The formal principle, when the material principle is
neglected, may be maintained predominantly in the form
of *tradition ;* this gives us one-sided Catholicism.   In
this case the only question asked is, What and how much
shall be believed, and how can this be most securely guaranteed, so as to guard against the evils of individual
caprice ?   Secure in the possession of genuine Christianity,
and confirmed by its guarantees, the mind subordinates
itself to the church, so that there can be no thought of
an internal conflict growing out of the process of testing
and appropriating what the Church teaches.   When such
a conflict takes place, it is a purely individual matter,
not springing from the principle of the church itself.

The formal principle again may, when the material principle is set aside, be maintained predominantly in the form of the *Scriptures;* this gives us a new form of the legal Church, such as was seen within the sphere of Protestantism in the orthodoxy of the seventeenth century. Here the Scriptures are regarded as a book of laws; and, the individual Christian, not maintaining a relative independence over against the Scriptures, is unable to distinguish in the Scriptures between the essential and the incidental, and practices a genuine relic-worship towards the letter of the Bible. That this is a tendency towards Catholicism, is shown by the fact that those who follow it carry the principle on from Scripture to tradition; inasmuch as the church creeds are accepted as a rule for the interpretation of the Scripture; and no divergence from them is tolerated. Secure in the possession of the inheritance left by the fathers, secure in the possession of "the pure doctrine," of the genuine presentation of the plan of salvation, they forget that in their inner life they have not experienced what the creeds describe; that they are calculating with dogmatic *formulæ* without possessing the vital, religious realities denoted by the *formulæ.* The plan of redemption has become a mere theory, for which, nevertheless, in the heat of dogmatic strife they display the extremest zeal. How far men had gone in depreciating subjective Christianity, —the testimony of the Spirit,—is most distinctly seen in the controversy of the orthodox Christians with the Pietists respecting the *theologia irregenitorum.* The orthodox expressly affirmed that the official acts of unregenerate preachers might be attended with as rich a blessing as those of the regenerate, if only they preached the orthodox doctrines, and that it was possible to penetrate into the truths of the Holy Scriptures without a regenerate heart. This is indeed so far true, that thought and fancy may be to a certain degree inspired by Christianity without its taking root in the heart. But this orthodoxy had become estranged not only from the Christian heart,—the living Christian experience, on which all true penetration into the meaning of Scripture is conditioned,

—but also from the *idea* of Christianity. By Christian knowledge it meant in reality nothing but a logical and intellectual appropriation of "the pure doctrine" in its consequences. Judgment on this carnal orthodoxy could not long be delayed. Rationalism stood before the door with the assertion that even the natural man and the natural reason can understand and expound the Holy Scriptures. And what was Rationalism but a great *theologia irregenitorum* which overflowed Protestant Christendom? Orthodoxy having lost the key of knowledge was no longer able to make a stand against Rationalism, and gradually sank down into that form of supernaturalism in which, faint and ready to surrender, it led a sickly existence.

The principle of the authority of the Scriptures now fell into the hands of the rationalists, who maintained it not only to the exclusion of the testimony of the Spirit, but also to the exclusion of all ecclesiastical tradition. Rationalism broke with all the traditions of the Church, seeing very clearly that they were not bone of its bone nor flesh of its flesh. The Church was thus changed into a school in which the learned exercised their acumen in interpreting the Scripture. In its first stage, nevertheless, Rationalism had a religious character, and sought by means of a rational exposition of the Bible to purify Christianity, regarding it as one with the truths of natural religion. In its further course, however, it turned against the Scriptures, disputed the genuineness of its books, transformed sacred history into myths, etc. Although these attacks of the schools on the Bible seem dangerous to many, yet for him who himself lives within the embrace of Christianity they are of subordinate importance. For the individual Christian will recognize in the Church his objective counterpart, bone of his bone and flesh of his flesh ; herein he will find the womb from which his new life was born, the rock from which he was hewn; together with the witnessing Church, he will recognize in the Scriptures the archetypal work of the same Spirit whose workings he feels in itself and out of himself; he will experience the divine power of the biblical Word in his heart, and leave it to the Christian schools to fight the subject out in its scientific form. And when the subject is brought before the forum of science, the history of science shows that, though rationalistic criticisms have been able to raise many doubts and make many difficulties, yet down to the present day, whenever a positive answer should have been given to the question respecting the origin of the Scriptures, of the Church, and of the new life in the hearts of believers, the answer has been wanting. Neither Rationalism nor Naturalism has thus far been able to give a scientific explanation of this new creation ; they have been unable to furnish an *adequate* explanation.

While a one-sided adherence to the formal principle leads now to a one-sided catholicizing tendency, now to a rationalistic scholasticism, a new series of one-sided forms of the church appears, when the material principle is maintained, and the formal principle sacrificed. When the individual Christian severs himself from all connection with history and tradition, and lightly esteems the written word, relying upon his being born of the Spirit, and accordingly needing no Christ outside of himself, because he has Christ in himself,—then originate *sects*, based on visionariness and fanaticism. Here is displayed the religious *a priori*, without limitation. As there is in science an *a priori*, through which thought transforms all nature, the whole external world, into a shadow and allegory of itself, so there is a religious *a priori* by means of which fanatical piety transforms the church and the Scriptures into a mere reflection of the inner, spiritual Christian life which it lives within itself. Since this disregard of the church and of the Bible is at the same time a disregard of "Christ outside of us," it leads logically to the denial of the miracle of the Incarnation; and then the subjective religion ceases to be subjective Christianity. For what it calls Christ " in us," is nothing but a general idea ; what it calls the inner light, is merely the light of nature wrapped in a mist coloured by Christianity.

To this extreme, however, not many of the sects have proceeded. Most of them bow to the authority of the Scriptures, but break with the church and tradition. This, however, is their mistake, that they fancy that they are able to put themselves into immediate connection with the apostolic church. For, as Christianity in individuals owes its birth to the church, so church history and tradition form the connecting link between us and the apostolic church. Although the thread which binds the present with the apostolic church, is not visible and palpable as the Roman Catholics think, yet it extends through the history of the church, through its doctrines and institutions; it can be traced with the eye of the Spirit *by means* of the Holy Scriptures; whereas every independent attempt to establish a purely biblical church must necessarily fail. And although we do not accept in the Roman sense the proposition : *evangelio non crederem, nisi me suaderet ecclesiæ auctoritas,* yet the principle has a validity which cannot with impunity be overlooked. For, although the church must submit to the authority of the Scriptures, yet it is the church that has to educate the individual and lead him to the sources of the Holy Scriptures, if he is to reach that stage of maturity at which he can himself judge of the relation between what is ecclesiastical and what is Christian.

In order to overcome the various forms of one-sidedness here referred to, there must exist an organic, reciprocal, relation between Scripture tradition and the Christian individual born of the Spirit. On this reciprocal relation depends the health of the church ; and, if we conceive a time when these factors shall have thoroughly permeated one another, then will the church have reached its highest earthly goal ; it will have returned through the strifes of its period of development back to the fulness of life revealed by the apostolic church as a model for all time. But just because in the Evangelical notion of the church, *freedom* is one of the factors, the Evangelical Church cannot be expected to enjoy a perfectly uninterrupted progress, but rather to pass through temporary periods of fermentation and dissolution. For where there is freedom, there are also abuses of freedom. Seemingly the Catholic church knows no such states of disintegration and confusion as does the Protestant. The principle of authority throws a veil over the secret injury, the secret unbelief and doubt, that assert themselves within the church. In the Protestant church, on the contrary, all these defects are manifest. Many members of the Protestant church, however, have become weary of the abuses of freedom, of arbitrary interpretations of Scripture, of the numerous vague appeals to the Spirit, &c., and are seized with a longing for *surer ecclesiastical guarantees,* for a tradition possessing not merely relative, but absolute authority, in order thus to obtain rest. This security they seek, now in the *consensus* of the first three centuries, now in that of the first five or six centuries. "A Catholic current is passing through the world," says Geijer, in one of his last writings; and this "Catholic current" will become more and more noticeable, the nearer the time of the great religious movements and crises approaches. But to lay down a tradition which can claim to be *in itself* infallible; to impose ecclesiastical guarantees which shall make superfluous for the church all internal struggles for freedom, will fortunately be impossible— fortunately for the development of freedom, which needs not only a given truth, but a truth which, being given, must continually be *acquired* anew by an internal process of appropriation. The various manifestations of sympathy with Catholicism exhibited of late, are of use in *awakening* what in many had been slumbering, viz., an appreciation of the importance of the church and of tradition as the natural connecting link between faith and the Bible. But whenever these sympathies have turned into antipathy to the principle and the inmost essence of the Reformation, they lead, as various facts have lately shown, to *Rome,* and to a repose in the guarantees which are there offered.

§ 25.

The Evangelical church appears in two leading forms, the Lutheran and the Reformed. The Swiss Reformation started primarily from the formal principle, that of the authority of the Scriptures; whereas the Lutheran originated more especially in the material principle, in the depths of the Christian consciousness, in an experience of sin and redemption. The first Lutheran written creed, the Augsburg Con-

fession, has no *locus* respecting the Scriptures; in it the
Christian consciousness gives expression to the truths contained within itself, their scripturalness being presupposed.
With this freedom, this delicacy of emotion,* which is a special characteristic of the Lutheran church, is joined a profound reverence for what the church has inherited from history. The Lutheran Reformation manifested the greatest
caution in regard to tradition, and observed the principle of
rejecting nothing that could be reconciled with the Scriptures;
whereas the Swiss Reformation introduced in many respects
a direct opposition between the biblical and the ecclesiastical,
and in several particulars followed the principle that all ecclesiastical institutions should be rejected unless they could be
deduced from the letter of the Bible. In these diverse views
of the principle of the Reformation, and in the carrying out of
them in the formation of church creeds, there is betrayed a
diversity in the tendency of the Christian spirit, which is but
inadequately designated by the antithesis between "emotion"
and "intellect." † The antithesis is better expressed by saying that the Reformed church, although vigorously protest-
ing against the legal church of Rome, is nevertheless infected with the legal spirit, whereas the germ of the fulness
of the gospel is found in Lutheranism. Still the antithesis
can be fully seen only by considering the difference between
the two churches in the main points of their doctrinal system, especially in that point in which the Christian view of
life finds its highest expression, viz., in the *doctrine of the
sacraments.*

PROTESTANT AND EVANGELICAL DOGMATICS.

§ 26.

The Theology of the Evangelical churches must be developed out of their principles. *Qualis ecclesia, talis theologia.* It must have therefore not only a biblical and ecclesiastical, but also a free, scientific character, by virtue of
the idea of Christian truth that is involved in living faith.

* *Gemüthsinnerlichkeit*, an untranslatable expression. Literally, "inwardness
of emotion, or affection."—V. P. *Tr.*
† "Gemüthlichkeit und Verständigkeit."

Under the first two forms the formal principle, under the latter the material principle, find in dogmatics their place.

Observations.—The foregoing statement implies a separation of dogmatics from ethics. What in actual life should not be separated, viz., Christian conceptions and Christian actions, must in science be treated as distinct. In dogmatics the relation between God and man is exhibited as an *existent* relation, whereas in ethics it is regarded as a relation still *future*, to be attained by the free efforts of believers. Hence dogmatics presents the Christian sense of God in its repose ; ethics presents the same in its motion. This difference is, it is true, only relative, but it is yet of importance that these leading aspects of the general theme be kept apart, since otherwise the one may easily be supplanted by the other, especially the ethical by the dogmatical, ethical principles being treated only as supplements to the dogmatic principles, and not as being in themselves independent. The statement that dogmatics is only the scientific expression of the same doctrine which is to be preached, is true only in so far as that the foundation of all Christian preaching—namely, the *confession* and the *testimony* of the revealed truth,—finds in dogmatics its corresponding scientific presentation. In so far, however, as the thing aimed at is to introduce revealed truth into the life, to apply it to ourselves and others,—and in Christian preaching the main point always is this, since it should not only impress on us what we ought to believe, but also what we ought to do,—then preaching receives its corresponding scientific presentation and answer in ethics, which science contains the rules and patterns of Christian conduct.

DOGMATICS AND THE HOLY SCRIPTURES.

§ 27.

The biblical character of dogmatics is seen primarily in the fact that the New Testament holds to it the relation of the supreme *critical* standard, respecting everything that is laid down as dogmatic truth. It is the last touchstone which furnishes a corrective against all *traditiones permanæ* which have been mixed up with the development of dogmas. Nothing therefore can be propounded as Christian doctrine which cannot be traced back to apostolic testimony and the apostolic course of thought—which cannot be traced back to something that foreshadows it in the statement or intimations contained in apostolic doctrine. But the Scriptures form the supreme canon, not only in relation to criticism, but also in relation to the church as an organism. Dogmatic thought is not only to be tested by the Bible, must not only not contradict the Bible, but it must be organically fructified and continually reinvigorated by the fulness of scriptural doctrine. As the archetypal work of the Spirit of inspiration, the Scriptures include within themselves a world of germs for a continuous development. While every dogmatic system grows old, the Bible remains eternally young, because it does not give us a systematic presentation of truth, but truth in its fulness, involving the possibility of a variety of systems. That which is said of the kingdom of heaven, that it is like leaven, which is to leaven the whole lump, is true in like manner of the relation of Scripture to human thinking. Hence it is correctly said : *Theologus in scripturis nascitur.* Theology must always sustain to the Scriptures the relation of a humble receiver, of a constant disciple, and may in this respect be compared to Mary, who sat at the Lord's feet and listened to His words.

But holding to the Bible the relation of disciple does not forbid, but rather requires, that the contents of biblical doctrine should be *reproduced* as the truths of one's own consciousness. Hence, when we say that dogmatic propositions must bear evidence that they are based on the Word of God, we must still on the other hand say that one must be able to exhibit them as inward and present truths of consciousness ; accordingly there is to be considered not only the scripturalness of these propositions, but also the validity and significance which they have in themselves, apart from the fact that they are written. In proportion as these two demands are complied with, dogmatic propositions have value. So long as the theologian can only pronounce a dogma biblical, without at the same time being able to show its inner and permanent significance, and, *vice versa,* so long as the theologian can only express the religious and ideal significance of the dogma, without being able to prove its harmony with the teachings of Scripture,—so long the problem of dogmatics is unsolved. The use of the Scriptures in dogmatics must not, however, consist in a mere appeal to single passages, or in a comparison of single passages; this mode of procedure too often betrays the narrow-minded view that nothing is true which cannot be proved to be literally found in the Bible. We agree rather on this point with Schleiermacher, when he says that in our biblical studies there should be constantly developed a more comprehensive use of the Scriptures, in which stress shall not be laid on single passages taken apart from the context, but in which attention is paid only to the longer and specially fruitful section, in order thus to penetrate the course of thought of the sacred writers, and find there the same combinations as those on which the results of dogmatic study themselves rest.*

Observations.—For Christians the Old Testament is sanctioned only by the New; and no canonical authority can belong to it except what belongs to the preparatory testament after that of the fulfilment has come. On account of its profound organic connection with the New Testament, it is of importance not only as an exegetical auxiliary in the study of the New Testament, but as the delineation of the way in which God led and trained His chosen people, as the testament of the law and of prophecy, as the type or foreshadowing of the eternal treasures, it will always be profitable for doctrine, for correction, for instruction in righteousness.† Hence we reject the Gnostic view of the Old Testament, that it is of no account to the Christian Church; but not less do we reject the Jewish view, which would retain in the Christian Church the Old Testament as an independent canon by the side of the New Testament. For the Old Testament is not *ἰδίας ἐπιλύσεως*,‡ and if it is to serve for Christians as *present* truth, it must first be interpreted *πνευματικῶς, i.e.*, from the standpoint of the New Testament, as we see it done especially by the Apostle Paul. This is true even of the

---

* Schleiermacher: der Christliche Glaube 4 ed. I., 148.
† 2 Tim. iii. 16.   ‡ 2 Peter i. 20.

Psalms and Prophets, the most evangelical portions of the Old Testament. For, rich and exhaustless as are the treasures therein contained for the illumination and edification of the Church, yet the contents cannot be received by the Christian mind as *present* truths, without being regenerated by the *new* Spirit of Christianity and in various respects reconstructed.

Dogmatics and Church Confessions.

§ 28.

A dogmatic treatise claiming to be biblical, but not ecclesiastical, would *eo ipso* not be biblical, since the Bible itself points to a *confessing* church, which is to perpetuate itself through all ages. Dogmatics, in order to be such for the whole Church, must harmonize with the œcumenical symbols of the Christian Church, among which the Apostles' Creed takes the first place. But dogmatic works must not only have a meaning for the Church in general; they must also have a *confessional* character—a demand which in our days is made with renewed energy. What "nationalities" are in the world, "confessions" are in the Church; and although the thought of a *union* of Christian churches cannot be given up, yet every union will be objectionable whose only object is to extinguish individuality and reduce everything to a latitudinarian basis. If, now, we ask in what sense ecclesiastical symbols have a canonical character in relation to dogmatics, the answer is—they have it as being *normæ normatæ*, or QUIA et QUATENUS *cum sacra scriptura consentiunt*. By the first of these specifications (*quia*) we would indicate the essential *oneness* of church doctrines with biblical doctrines; by the second (*quatenus*), that there is nevertheless a relative *difference* between the ecclesiastical and the Christian, between the letter of the symbols and their spirit, between form and idea. Accordingly, in announcing that we intend to adhere not only to the œcumenical symbols, but also to the creed of the Lutheran Church, particularly as this is given in the Augsburg Confession, we mean thereby that we intend to hold to that *type* of sound doctrine which is therein contained, being convinced that we are in this way most sure of preserving our connection with the Apostolic Church. We do not regard the Lutheran Confession as a work of inspiration ; yet no more do we regard it as a mere work of man, inasmuch as the age of the Reformation had a special vocation to bear testimony and put forth confessions, just as had those periods of the Church in which the earlier creeds were formed. We make a distinction between type and formula. By the *type* of Lutheranism we mean its ground form, its inextinguishable, fundamental, and distinctive features. As we recognise in a man or in a people an inward peculiarity, an impress, which belongs to them from eternity, never appearing in perfect clearness in time, and yet recognisable even amidst temporal imperfections : so we can detect in the Christian confessions a church individuality, a fundamental abiding form, which, amidst change and growth, is constantly reproducing itself ; whereas the theological *formulæ* in which this form is expressed are more or less characterized by relativity and transitoriness. To wish to canonize formulæ and letters in the symbols, betrays a defective view of history ; for the symbols originated in the midst of great movements of particular periods, and in various ways exhibit the traces of the peculiar theological culture, the peculiar needs and defects of those times. We know very well how scandalously the distinction between " spirit and letter," " idea and form," may be abused ; but this abuse will not prevent its proper and necessary use. And a candid consideration will always lead to the conviction that the chief importance to be attached is not to the formulæ, but to the fundamental conceptions of the Church.

Therefore, while dogmatic science on the one hand holds to the Church creeds a relation of dependence, it must, on the other hand, in this relation be free to pass critical judgments on the formulæ of the symbols, and also to exhibit the fundamental ideas contained in these symbols in a fresh form, corresponding to the present stage of the development of the Church and of theology.

Observations.—The opposition between orthodoxy and heterodoxy is in the Protestant Church other than in the Catholic. Catholics, assuming the perfect identity of the church and of Christianity, make orthodoxy something

merely historical, that finds a perfect expression in the
doctrinal systems of the church.   Protestants, on the other
hand, maintaining that there is a relative difference between
the church and Christianity, must regard orthodoxy as
something which not merely is, but is yet to be, attained.
During the course of historical development, the difference
between orthodoxy and heterodoxy is relative and variable ;
and propositions which at one time on account of their
novelty are branded as heretical innovations, may at a
later time be justly pronounced orthodox, or purer presen-
tations of the essence of Christianity.   Every new dogmatic presentation of truth must thus necessarily contain
propositions which have the *appearance* of being heterodox,
since otherwise it would leave everything as it was, and
would be only a repetition of the dogmas of the church
without attempting to evolve a purer conception of Christian truth.   It is manifest that *that* only is both seemingly
and really heterodox and heretical, which under the semblance of Christianity denies its essence.   Hence all heresies
are derived from Judaism and heathenism, that is, from
the standpoint of "the old man," and are always forms of
Judaism or heathenism under a Christian mask.   Therefore, heresies are chiefly developed in regard to the
doctrine of the Person of Christ, who is the centre of the
new revelation.   As it is from this starting-point that new
views of God and man are unfolded, so it is from this that
heresies proceed.   Branching out from this point in every
direction taken by Christian thought, they are in their inmost essence nothing but attempts to conceive Christianity
as a renovated Judaism or heathenism.   But just as there
must be in every healthy, social development, a constant
effort to eliminate the foreign elements which seek by
stealth to gain admission, in order to check and undermine
that which is peculiar in the development : so there must
be in the Christian church a constant effort to eliminate
the Jewish and heathen elements (στοιχεῖα τοῦ κόσμου),
which seek to creep into the church under the semblance
of Christianity ; and this effort implies a constant spiritual
return to Christ, and, what is inseparable from a true conception of Christ, the gift of being able to try the spirits.*

* 1 John iv. 1.

DOGMATICS AND THE CHRISTIAN IDEA OF TRUTH.

§ 29.

In saying that a mind, regenerated by Christianity, must be able to reproduce from its own depths the doctrines of the Bible and the church in a *scientific* form, we express only what is involved in the doctrine, rightly understood, of the *testimonium spiritus sancti.* The witness of the Spirit is taken in a sense quite too limited, when it is taken as merely a practical testimony in the conscience, the feelings, the heart, and not at the same time as a testimony borne by the Spirit of God, as the Spirit of truth, through the medium of the thoughts and cognitions of men. We know that the chief witness, on which all else depends, is that which is borne in " demonstration of power;" yet Christian knowledge is one element which belongs to the *completeness* of the testimony which the Spirit bears to the truth of Christianity. In thus attaching to the *testimonium spiritus sancti* not only a practical, but also theoretical importance, and in presupposing in the believing mind a *Christian truth-idea* which meets the truth positively presented to it;—in thus assuming a relatively independent source of Christianity, different from the Scriptures and from the church, we are propounding in respect to speculation, nothing but what, in respect to ethics and art, is conceded by all without hesitation. In respect to morals, we are obliged to assume a (relatively) *a priori* source of Christianity; for, to say nothing of Christian ethics as a science, there has been developed in life, in history, a variety of ethical views and notions, which, it is true, modify, and are modified by, the views and notions originally given, but are by no means a copy of them; they have, therefore, been developed out of the inmost depths of the Christian consciousness, by which new problems have been both presented and solved. In regard to aesthetics, we are obliged to make the same assumption. For Christian art has produced a world of new creations, which have, to be sure, their archetypes in the positive revelation, but yet point to a Christian idea of beauty which must have stirred in the minds of the artists themselves. Now, as we may thus speak of a Christian idea of morality, without which all independent ethical productivity would be impossible ; and, as we may speak of a Christian idea of beauty, without which Christian art would be inconceivable ; so we must also be able to speak of a Christian idea of truth, without which Christian science, all the dogmatic labours, whose monuments are found in the most important works both of ancient and modern times,—nay, even the construction of church creeds, would be impossible and inconceivable.

Observations.—The biblical expression for this idea is Wisdom,* not wisdom as a divine attribute, but as a divine thought which, before the creation of the world, played before the face of God.   Hence, objectively considered, the Christian truth-idea is the holy wisdom-thought which has assumed shape in the Christian revelation, and in the life-giving fulness of this revelation constitutes the regulating, distinguishing, and co-operating principle which amidst variety produces connection, plan, and purpose. But this holy wisdom-thought must also be present as an " inner light," in the human spirit which has believingly received the revelation ; it must give light to the believer's own view of revelation.   By virtue of this sacred wisdom-thought, which in the believer's consciousness is the principle of thought, human thought is able to search the deep things of revelation (1 Cor. ii. 14), to trace out the connection and the foundation of Christian conceptions, and to endeavour to produce a mental counterpart of the eternal, revealed wisdom.

§ 30.

Christian knowledge is a knowledge in *faith ;* for only through faith can the human mind become partaker of divine wisdom.   *Credo ut intelligam.*   A gnosis, which starts from an autonomy that discards all assumptions, which assumes that the human mind is able by its own powers to evolve the truth out of itself, which desires at the outset to occupy the theocentric stand-point, forgets that the human mind is created, and denies the *creatureship* of man.   For faith confesses that human knowledge is that of a creature, that it must rest on experience, that it must begin with an immediate perception of, and contact with, its object, that it must receive the

* Prov. viii., Sirach xxiv., Book of Wisdom vii.

light of truth as a gift which comes down from above, and that it must stand in a relation of humility and trust to the giver.* For human knowledge all independence is conditioned by dependence; all self-activity, all *intellectus activus*, is conditioned on susceptibility, on *intellectus passivus*. The false gnosis which will not believe in order to know, denies not only the creatureship of man, but also his *sinfulness* and *need of redemption*. For it is only through regeneration that the human mind, darkened by sin, can be lifted up to that stage of life and existence, at which it can have a correct view of divine and human things. But regeneration expresses itself in faith. The assertion of Christians, that faith is the mother of knowledge, is substantially confirmed by the analogy of all other spheres of human knowledge; for all human knowledge has its root in an immediate perception of the object. And, as it is useless for one who lacks hearing to talk about music; as it is useless for one who has no sense for colours to develop a theory of colour, the same holds true respecting the cognition of sacred things. "The Strasburg minster," says Steffens, "and the Cologne cathedral, tower up high into the air, and yet, like Herculaneum and Pompeii, they have been to whole generations buried, and men have not seen them, because they lacked the faculty." And so, we may add, there are whole generations who have not seen, and do not see, the Christian Church in history, although it is like a city on a hill. They have no eye for it because they have no faith.

§ 31.

By its "*credo ut intelligam*" Christian dogmatics is distinguished from that form of knowledge which starts with the proposition, "*de omnibus dubitantum est*," so far, namely, as this proposition means that thought must cut itself loose from all presuppositions and start off on a voyage of discovery, in order to find truth, be the truth what it may. In Christian knowledge the motive power is not doubt, but faith. Yet we may allow the existence of a sceptical element in Christian theology, if we use the expression to denote the *critical* and *dialectic* impulse contained in faith. Since faith finds itself

* Cf. the Author's "Dissertation von der Autonomie des Menschlichen Selbstbewusstseins."

in a world of sinfulness, of falsehood, and error ; and since the church has the world not only out of itself, but in itself, faith must have a tendency to criticise, to try the spirits whether they are of God, to test whether the church and Christianity coincide, to test itself in order to assure itself of its own genuineness. And, since faith is also a cognition (§ 8), it must have a dialectical impulse to make clear to itself the antitheses involved in its own trains of thought. Christian faith is very different from artless credulity ; and what has been said in recommendation of childlike and simple faith must be understood *cum grano salis;* for true simplicity of faith requires one to try the spirits and to try one's self. Accordingly, Luther had doubts respecting ecclesiastical traditions and respecting the genuineness of his own monastic Christianity ; and the different periods of the history of the church show that church teachers who were distinguished alike for the simplicity and the heroic strength of their faith, felt an impulse to make their faith clear to themselves by means of the sharpest dialectics. From the earliest ages of the Church this critical tendency has manifested itself in the sharp line of separation drawn between the proper doctrines of Christianity and heretical elements. This procedure necessarily, in every case, gave occasion to a dialectic examination of the particular points in question ; for to draw a distinction between orthodoxy and heresy must surely be impossible, unless we test each individual doctrine by our view of the essence of Christianity ; and test our view of the essence of Christianity by its harmonious conformity with the entire chain of Christian conceptions. In this sense, taking it as critical and dialectic, we may concède the presence of an element of scepticism in dogmatic theology ; to a certain extent we must doubt, not merely in order to *know* aright, but also to *believe* aright. But if we break loose from the foundation of faith, if we become regardless of the vital interest we have in Christianity, if we cast aside its fundamental idea instead of seeking to correct our view of it, and to understand it more completely, and set up our scepticism as an independent source of truth, we shall fall, as the history of Protestantism plainly illustrates, into Rationalism with its all-dissolving criticism and empty dialectics.

Observations. — It frequently occurs that thorough-going

doubt relative to the foundations of Christianity becomes the means of leading the soul to a living conviction of its truth ; important, however, as may be the influence of such doubt, not only in a religious and moral, but even in a scientific respect, it has nothing whatever to do with dogmatic theology as such.   One who entertains doubt as to the very basis of Christianity cannot feel an interest in dogmatic theology ; for his sole enquiry is δός μοι ποῦ στῶ ; a demand which must be substantially satisfied ere strictly dogmatic investigations can begin.

§ 32.

The proposition—*credo ut intelligam*—to which we have just given prominence in opposition to every form of autonomic Rationalism, is not to be taken either in the scholastic sense or in that of the theology now commonly designated the "Theology of Feeling." The scholastic divines fell very soon into a mechanical view thereof ; for they drew the substance of their faith without any sort of critical examination from the creeds prevailing in the church, and started with preliminary principles which totally lacked an inner reality answering to their outward form. The mystics, and more recently Schleiermacher, struck into a path directly opposite to that pursued by the scholastics :—they viewed faith as an inner vital principle, and constituted religious feeling the guide and pioneer of religious knowledge. In consequence, however, of the mystics misapprehending the nature of revelation, and Schleiermacher's defining dogmatic theology as a description of religious states and experiences, both of them fell into a new error, relatively to the "*credo ut intelligam.*" Dogmatic theology became in their hands a mere doctrine concerning the nature of a religious man, or of piety, instead of being a doctrine of the nature of God and His revelation ; it treated rather of man's *need* of Christianity and his experience of its *workings* in his soul, than of Christianity itself, in its eternal truth and its claim to be accepted as such by men. Thus defined, it relates simply to the subjective *ordo salutis;* whilst the facts of revelation, the pillars and foundations of the truth, are left to be accepted and moulded, agreeably to the particular ideas and needs of individual believers. If the full significance of faith as an inner vital principle is to be recognized, it must be considered not merely as the experience of the practical workings of Christianity, but also as the intellectual organ, or the contemplative eye, for the domain of revelation. This latter aspect is recognized by speculative mystics and theosophists (like Joseph Böhme), who teach that faith itself involves a vision. And although they, in their turn, fell into an error, the error of attaching too slight importance to the historical, attention was called in a profound manner to the objective religious relation of faith. Taking for granted therefore the relation to an objective historical revelation, we define dogmatic theology, not *primarily* as the science of " the believer" (the proper and only place for treating fully of the " Christian Believer," his character, life, and the roots thereof, is Christian Ethics) ; but as the science or doctrine of faith (*fides quœ creditur*), not primarily as a system of pious emotions, but as the science of the truths of the Christian Faith ; not primarily as a description of the states of pious souls, but as a development of the believing view of revelation. We are aware, indeed,—and many illustrations of the fact might be adduced from the history of speculation, both in former and modern times,—that the demand for such an objective mode of consideration has frequently led to revelation being treated in a purely theoretical spirit by men totally destitute of religious experience ; has given rise to an intellectualism which paid no regard to the practical aspects of Christianity : but this is by no means necessarily involved in the idea of a knowledge which, besides being the knowledge of religion, is itself *religious*. Whilst we cannot regard feeling as a principle of knowledge :—for the proper and only *principle* of knowledge is the idea, the thought of the divine wisdom ;—we must maintain it to be a condition. The idea, which is the true principle of knowledge in matters of faith, can never arise save in a man that is actually religious ; and our intellectual eye grows dim the moment it ceases to draw nourishment from the heart ; it becomes like the lamp of the foolish virgins which went out for lack of oil. On this ground the profoundest thinkers of the middle ages justly demanded that Scholasticism should be united with mysticism, that the *intellectus* should not be without *affectus*.

Observations.—The view of dogmatic theology as the science of pious states of mind seems to be favoured by certain features of the Reformation ; for example, by the special and new stress it laid on the "*fides qua creditur,*" and consequently on the subjective *ordo salutis,* in opposition to the vain and barren metaphysical discussions indulged in by the scholastic divines. The *Application* was made with new force, *Edification* was aimed at with new zeal, as we remark in particular in the well known and somewhat one-sided passage of the First Edition of Melanchthon's "Loci," where he says,—"*Non est, cur multum operae ponamus in locis illis supremis, de deo, de unitate, de trinitate Dei, de mysterio creationis, de modo incarnationis. Quaeso te, quid adsecuti sunt jam tot saeculis scholastici theologistae, quum in his locis solis versarentur? Hoc est Christum cognoscere, beneficia ejus cognoscere.*" In the subsequent editions he omitted this passage, and without doubt because he felt that it might easily give rise to a serious error—the error, namely, of constituting as the standard of Christianity the needs of men and their experience of its workings, instead of estimating the needs of individual men and human experiences by the standard supplied by objective Christianity: the error of being so greatly concerned for the "believer" and the state of his soul as to be indifferent to the "Faith" (*Fides quæ creditur*); of being so intent on edification as to forget the substance which is to edify, and the ground on which the building up is to be effected. This has shown itself clearly enough in Protestant Churches in times past, and manifests itself also in the arbitrary atomistic religiousness of the present day. Luther, whom no one can charge with being indifferent to the edificatory aspects of Christianity, drew a very sharp distinction between the thing itself and its application (*res ipsa et usus*); for example, between the sacraments in themselves and the use made of them ; and insists on the necessity of being clear about the doctrines which tell us what Christianity, what the thing itself is ; because otherwise our talk about the practical, about the application and use of the doctrines will be foolish. Now the aim of dogmatic theology is to exhibit the "fundamental form of sound doctrine" in such a way that it may be a guide to the public proclamation of the Gospel with due *reference to the special circumstances and culture of any particular age.* But besides this practical end, dogmatic theology is also an end in itself. For though we allow the perfect justice of the remark of Melanchthon adduced above, so far as it relates to useless speculations, which have nothing to do with life ; we still consider the knowledge of the mysteries of the kingdom of God to be in itself a good, and deem the knowledge of the glory of God to be a source of edification. Even if we make the acknowledgment that God's ways are unsearchable ; this very knowledge of the divine unsearchableness and the adoration of God's hidden wisdom will acquire greater force if we first traverse the path of human knowledge. The ignorance which remains after a man has attempted to know, is a very different thing from the ignorance of him who has never made such an attempt, who has never known the speculative impulse. As there is a knowledge peculiar to the theologian, to the *clerus* as distinguished from the laity, the *laici* (by which we do not mean anything at all like the gnostic distinction between exoteric and esoteric) ; so also must the theologian have a sense of ignorance which the layman has never experienced. *Per oppositionem* this may be seen from the circumstance that theological pride is as often associated with esoteric ignorance as with esoteric knowledge ; just as philosophic pride reveals itself as frequently under the mask of a Socrates as in the garb of a Paracelsus.

§ 33.

The task of dogmatic theology, therefore, is to set forth Christian views in the form of a connected doctrinal system. This process is primarily an *explicative* one, that is, its first business is to unfold the elements contained in Christian intuition, to develope the inner connection existing between them. But we cannot undertake to explain or unfold, without feeling also the impulse to speculate or comprehend ; in other words, we cannot be content merely with exhibiting the connection between the various parts of what we find given to our hand, but we desire also to understand the why and where-

fore : the goal of systematic theology is not merely the *ita*
but the *quare*.   A thorough explanation will be unable to
avoid antitheses of thought, antinomies, which require mediating, or reconciling ; for, as Jesus Sirach says, " all the works
of the Most High are two against two, and one against
the other" (ch. xxxiii. 16) ; and the essential feature of
speculation is to reconcile antagonisms in the higher unity
of the idea.   If our exhibition of Christian doctrine do not
rest on a speculative vision, it will either be a mere outward
thing, a thing of the understanding, or limit itself to its purely
practical significance and applications.   Many, therefore, as
may have been the doubts entertained by an Irenaeus and a
Luther too, regarding the efforts to attain a speculative *comprehension* of Christian truth, we find everywhere in their
works traces of the action of that contemplative eye which
views individual details in the light of the one fundamental
idea.   We grant too that the latter was right in asserting that
dogmatic theology as a *thetic* (positive) theology has to do in
the first instance with the *ita* and not with the *quare ;** but
must at the same time deny the possibility of separating the
explicative from the *speculative* action of the mind by any
fixed and impassable line of demarcation.   Every *ita* contains
a hidden *quare*, which, the moment we undertake a thorough
explication, is sure to come to light and summon us to seek
after the higher kind of comprehension which we designate
speculative.   We must never forget, indeed, that this speculative comprehension is precisely the fragmentary part of our
knowledge ; whereas faith embraces in its intuition the entire
fulness of the truth—a fulness which will never be exhausted
by any explicative or speculative efforts of the human mind.
But, just as they have always been put to shame who pre-
tended to have attained the comprehension of everything ; so,
and not less, have they been put to shame, who have sought
to set a limit once for all to human comprehension, to mark a
" *non plus ultra,*" beyond which no one could ever advance.
For it has always become evident subsequently that there was
a " *plus ultra ;*" and the boundary lines supposed to be fixed

---

* Luther often complains of the curiosity of the scholastic sophists with their
constant *quare*, and admonishes his readers to be content with the *ita*

E

showed themselves to be fluctuating, by being actually removed. A healthy mode of looking at things will recognize therefore that speculative comprehension is itself a very mobile and dialectic conception which cannot be settled with a mere dry Yea or Nay; with the assertion, that it must either be perfect or not exist at all, for it is itself a *growing* thing. Any conclusion arrived at in comprehending Christian truth will therefore never be more than relative ; each solution of the problem will be a new enhancement thereof; the conclusion to which we have brought our knowledge will contain a " divinatory " element pointing to another and still higher solution.*

§ 34.

The scientific method followed in systematic theology is partly *apologetic* and partly dogmatic, in the stricter sense. As *apologetic* it confirms and justifies Christian truth by the negation and overthrow of what is either non-Christian or un-Christian : as *dogmatical,* it investigates and exhibits Christian truth in its inner and essential richness. The first developments of Christian dogma, arising as they did out of struggles with Judaism and heathenism, bore a predominantly apologetic character, one might even say, polemic character ; for from the Christian point of view Apologetics and Polemics, defence and attack are inseparable from each other.† But, because the spirit of Judaism and heathenism encountered by the early church still continues under a variety of forms to stir in the world, it is necessary that systems of Christian truth should continue to overcome the world with their weapons of criticism. Besides, the distinction between the apologetic and the dogmatic, in the stricter sense, is merely relative ; for, as on the one hand, error and pretence can only be thoroughly laid bare in the

* Concerning the distinction between the explanatory and the speculative methods of development, and concerning what is merely relative and transitory in this distinction, see Sibbern's Treatise, Beidrag til Besvarelfen af det Spörgsmaal: Hvad er Dogmatik? (Philos. Archiv. und Repertor. Heft 3 und 4.)

† See 1 Peter iii. 15—" Be ready always to give an answer to every man that asketh you a reason of the hope that is in you with meekness and fear." 2 Cor. x. 5—" Casting down imaginations and every high thing that exalteth itself against the knowledge of God and bringing into captivity every thought to the obedience of Christ."

light of a positive knowledge of truth ; so, on the other hand, the full power of the truth is first revealed when it vanquishes contradiction.

§ 35.

We have finally to consider the relation between dogmatic theology and philosophy.   One thing is clear, that dogmatic theology is totally opposed to heathen philosophy which aims at arriving at truth by its own means.   As Christianity entered into the world with a call to repentance and conversion, and with a doctrine drawn from a source totally different from philosophy, its necessary influence was, of course, to lead away from the wisdom of this world.   But, having itself given birth to a new sum of knowledge, to a system of theology, the question arises whether there is room for a Christian philosophy alongside of Christian theology, and in what relation the two stand to each other ?   We take for granted at present that there is such a thing as Christian philosophy ; we take for granted, further, that it is subject to the same fundamental conditions of knowledge as theology, that is, that it must start with the *credo ut intelligam :* but we distinguish between the former and the latter as follows—*philosophy,* even when Christian, is a knowledge of the universe, a systematic view of the world as a whole ; *theology* is the knowledge of God.   The distinction is, it is true, merely a relative one, but still a distinction.   Philosophy directs its search to the divine law which pervades the universe, and is fulfilled by the various circles of the world of nature and the world of spirits ; and aims to understand Christianity as the fulness of the laws of the world.   Philosophy, therefore, begins with the manifold variety of objects contained in the world and reduces them to the kingdom of God as their one centre, in whose light they all become intelligible.   Theology, dogmatics, on the contrary, takes up its point of view from the very first at the centre, makes the one, the kingdom of God, as such the exclusive object of its investigations.   Even Christian philosophy must begin with the universe and its variety and endeavour to show in a series of general contemplations and enquiries, that Christianity is the highest force of existence and life.   Dogmatics, on the contrary, takes up its position in the *church ;* and seeks to exhibit the doctrines of the Christian Faith in their inner inherent connection with each other. So far, however, as dogmatic theology has the apologetic aspect to which reference was made above, it stands connected with the philosophy of religion. We may, therefore, say philosophy sets forth Christian knowledge in its universal aspects ; theology in its central significance. Philosophy is at home everywhere; the home of theology is the church.

Observations.—The peculiar distinction between theology and philosophy becomes clear also when we compare men who have a talent for philosophy with those whose talent is for theology. The talent for philosophy manifests itself in the discovery of categories which admit of application to all the various cycles of existence, and thus set forth the entire world in a new light. For example, the distinctive characteristic of the system of the first Christian philosopher, John Scotus Erigena, is its idea of the "*divisio naturæ*," the way in which he carries out the idea of the uncreated, creating, and created nature. In the system of Leibnitz, the Monad is the all-comprehensive category by which the entire world is set in a new light ; in Spinoza's system, "substance ;" in Fichte's, "the Ego and the non-Ego ;" in Schelling's, "the Absolute ;" in Hegel, "the Idea." Every new system of philosophy presents us with new general definitions, by means of which the thinker hopes to find his way through the labyrinthine edifice of the world ; and the reality of his philosophy depends on the force and efficiency with which he is able to carry out his design. The productiveness of the theologian lies in a totally different sphere. It manifests itself, not in the discovery of new categories of the world, but in the development of the old categories of revelation with new vigour into a complete system of religious and ecclesiastical knowledge. Take, for example, the categories, "sin and redemption," "law and gospel"—how they became to Augustine, to the Reformers, and to Schleiermacher, the source of a new view of Christianity. Or take the doctine of the Trinity, "the Name of the Father, the Son, and the Holy Ghost;" how it opened to Athanasius, and indeed, to the theologians both of the middle ages and of modern times, the possibility of giving a new representation of Christian truth. Or think of the expressions, "this is," "this signifies," connected with the doctrine of the Lord's Supper, and the dispute about the real presence: what a determined influence they had on the entire character of the Lutheran and Reformed Church, at the age of the Reformation. Doctrinal or dogmatic productiveness is at home in this central sphere ; philosophic productiveness bears a more encyclopædic character.

§ 36.

Dogmatic theology enters into a reciprocal relation, not only to Christian, but also to non-Christian philosophy. As the church exists in the world, the mind of the church must develope itself in connection with and relation to the culture and wisdom of the world ; the relation of dogmatic theology to philosophy must be not merely a polemical relation, but also one of recognition ; in other words, it must seek to appropriate and work up the elements of truth, which every real system of philosophy contains. But in entering into such a relation to philosophy, theology is very liable to fall into an error—an error which made its appearance at a very early period of the church's history and which constantly re-appears —the error, namely, of Syncretism, of concluding a false Concordat and unholy alliance with philosophy. The result of such an alliance has always been that theology has borrowed its light from philosophy, that a non-Christian was a substituted mode of looking at questions, and that to dogmatic theology might truly be applied the words, " *Aristotelem pro Christo vendere.*" We find an uncritical mixture of dogmatic theology and philosophy, for example, under various shapes in the works of the Alexandrian divines, where the categories of Platonism are frequently substituted for Christianity. The same experience was repeated during the middle ages in the case of divines under the influence of Aristotle. And we all remember how the categories of the modern Aristotle, Hegel, exerted a similar influence. These false modes of mediating, this show of effecting a reconciliation between faith and knowledge, reminds one of Augustine, who says in his " *Retractationes* " that during his Platonic period he found Plato in the gospel, and supposed himself, in this way, to have effected the reconciliation of religion and philosophy. When Christianity spoke of the wisdom of this world he interpreted it to refer to a wisdom which rests in the sensuous, in the κόσμος αἰσθητός, and does not rise to the κόσμος νοητός. When Christianity spoke of the kingdom which is not of this world, he interpreted it to refer to the kingdom of ideas ; and the man who lived in the kingdom of ideas was the spiritual, regenerated man, in opposition to the psychical, natural man, and so forth. Relatively to such modes of reconciling philosophy and theology, which in all essential features have been frequently resorted to again in our own day, we cannot insist earnestly enough on the necessity for theology to rest content with the "foolishness" of the Gospel ; on the duty of not sacrificing its own wealth for the mere semblance of clearness ; on the danger of trying to secure premature clearness and ripeness. For by anticipating in this manner that true, inner development from the inherent central principle of Christianity, it will lose both substance and form, both the truth and true clearness ; seeing that such true clearness is born of the darkness of mystery. Luther says truly, " he who means to philosophize with profit in Aristotle, must first become a fool in Christ." We must, therefore, lay down the canon, that it is the duty of theology in the first instance, and predominantly, to treat philosophy *sceptically* and *critically.* But such a sceptical and critical relation to philosophy necessarily involves conscientious efforts to penetrate really into it, and thoroughly to investigate it ; it is as different as possible from the relation recommended by some who treat the two as clean and unclean food ; who say, concerning the latter, " Taste not, touch not," without reflecting that their own theology, which, whether they call it biblical or ecclesiastical, is in many respects a word of man, may perhaps contain many impure elements, of which philosophy might cleanse it. When they say, indeed, that nothing can be learned from a philosophy which is not pervaded by the spirit of Christianity ;—it is true, that such a philosophy can give them no direct information regarding the kingdom of God ; but indirectly, it may instruct them, so far as every real system of philosophy throws a new light on the kingdom of nature, which is the preliminary condition of the kingdom of grace. They forget that it is the same Logos who works in the kingdom of nature and in that of grace ; that the germs of the latter lie scattered about in the domain of the former. The logical and ontological investigations, pursued by philosophy, in the various forms which it has assumed in the course of its historical development, supply a foundation of preparatory instruction for all science. Logic and ontology are contained in theology, and *condition* its development; as was shown with peculiar clearness during the important conflict that took place in the Middle Ages between the Nominalists and Realists ; a conflict which has reappeared in every form of modern philosophy. But every system of philosophy of any profundity, supplies the intellect in a pneumatological respect, with a fermenting element which theology must in its own way assimilate and work up ; notwithstanding, that when the same propositions are found occurring both in philosophy and theology, frequent occasion will be found for reiterating the old saying, " Two may say the same thing, and yet it is not the same." Those who try thoroughly to follow out the injunction, " Touch not, taste not," will soon fall into the danger of contenting themselves in false security with their traditional theological systems ; and repeat as often as they may, that Christian knowledge must be living and not dead, their Christian knowledge will be one, between which, and the natural life of man in its highest utterances, there is no vital reciprocity. As our motto, therefore, we will take, instead of the words, " Touch not, taste not," those others addressed by Paul to the Corinthians (1 Cor. iii. 22), " All things are yours, whether Cephas or the world ;"—which may surely be taken as equivalent to, " whether the wisdom of the Apostles or the wisdom of the world, whether Peter and Paul, or Plato and Schelling, or Aristotle and Hegel ;" although certainly it is also meant that we should draw a clear distinction between the wisdom of the Apostles and the wisdom of the world.

THE CHRISTIAN IDEA OF GOD.

THE NATURE OF GOD.

§ 37.

The God of revelation is not a hidden God; He is not that indefinite θεῖον, which is but another name for the dark root and cause of finite existence, and a mere blind force: nor is He the thought which orders the worlds, and which, being incapable of thought or resolve itself, is really identical with the order of which it is the source. The God of revelation is a SPIRIT, (John iv. 24). Being a Spirit, He reveals Himself in the first instance as " the Lord; " but considered in the fulness and truth of His nature, He is not merely "the Lord," who keeps Himself distinct and apart from the world, but eternal " LOVE," which reconciles the world with itself, (1 John iv. 16.) We have no intention here of proving the existence of the revealed God; we propose simply to glance at the conceptions formed of God apart from revelation, in which man gave expression to the knowledge of Deity which he arrives at by nature, —a knowledge related to revelation as the elements of a science (στοιχεῖα τοῦ κόσμου) are related to its full development. The representations of the Divine nature given by revelation will thus gain in clearness and certainty: and by considering the "proofs for the existence of God," we shall be furthering the knowledge of His nature.

§ 38.

The various proofs for the existence of God, though generally acknowledged to be formally invalid in a syllogistic point of view, are profoundly significant as indicating the general starting points for the development of the idea of God primarily dwelling in the human mind. They mark in a general way the principal stages of the knowledge of God arrived at by man independently of the positive revelation contained in the Scriptures. The manifold witnesses for God which man finds in and around himself are here reduced to certain general principles, and the various and intricate ways by which the human mind is brought to God, are indicated by the summary results of thought. Man rises to God and to the knowledge of the divine nature in two ways—by the contemplation of himself and by the contemplation of the world. The latter method is embodied in the cosmological and teleological arguments; the former in the ontological and moral. But no one of these methods conducts man to a true knowledge of the nature of God so long as he is ignorant of the revealed testimonies which Christianity awakens around us and in us.

Observations.—Whatever be the point of view from which the subject is considered, God is defined to be the God of the "world" and of "man;" the knowledge of His nature, therefore, is conditioned by the knowledge possessed of that world and that human spirit, for which He appears as God. Hence, also, whatever the point of view, the substance of the idea of God answers to the significance attributed by man to himself, and the world which he inhabits. A superficial knowledge of the world and self leads to an equally superficial knowledge of God. Where the world is treated as a mere seeming, and human life as an empty play, it is impossible that a true idea of God should spring up; only where the world and man are recognized as having in a relative sense, being, life, and freedom in themselves, as this is first brought properly to light by Christianity, can we think aright of God.

§ 39.

The cosmological argument or the "*argumentum e contingentia mundi,*" takes for its starting point, the finitude, transitoriness, contingency of the world, without paying attention to the internal distinctions between the various kinds of existences, and especially without regarding the essential distinction between the kingdom of nature and the kingdom of freedom. The world here is merely the domain of external antagonisms of contingent, changing phenomena, whose forms come and go in an eternally revolving circle. Everything is transitory—man no less than the flower of the field. But so certainly as finite existences dissolve and perish ; even as certainly does the eternal ground into which they are dissolved, and out of which they issue remain ; so certainly as the world has no real existence in itself, but merely the show of an existence, even so certainly is its existence not its own existence, but that of another being, of the Divine Being. This is Acosmism, κόσμος ἄκοσμος. The fundamental idea of this line of argument, to wit, the idea of God as universal being, is distinctive of pantheism in all its forms ; and the feeling of the transitoriness of the world which corresponds to the above idea, is the characteristic and fundamental feeling of every form of pantheistic religiousness. But the God of this argument and this religiousness is a hidden God, about whose nature, though we live and move and have our being in Him, nothing is known save that He is power and *necessity*. This is the idea which lies at the basis of Oriental pantheism, which regards the Deity as the life of the universe, eternally giving birth to and eternally annihilating existences. Spinozism was its philosophical revival.

What the cosmological proof is in relation to the outer world, such is the ontological in relation to the inner world of self-consciousness ; the result is the same, to wit, acosmism. Reflecting upon itself, and shutting out every determinate form of thought, every determinate subject of thought—reflecting on thought simply as thought—the mind falls back on God as the eternal ground of thought, the eternal possibility of self-consciousness with its changing variety of thoughts. Thought itself is inconceivable, save on the presupposition of a spiritual being as its inner ground and inner source. Consciousness can only be conscious of itself—consciousness can only be self-consciousness—as it is the consciousness of truth, or of God. Thought can separate itself from every determinate idea, save that of existence. The mind may entertain doubt as to any and every determinate form of being, but not as to being in itself ; for in the very act of laying down a proposition—which is an impossibility without the copula *is* (*esse*)—it is compelled to affirm being in general. The mind may be sceptical as to every determinate form of the idea of God, but it cannot call in question the idea of God as the first being, which is the principle of thought itself. Self-consciousness and God, thought and truth, are therefore inseparable. But because the ontological proof of the existence of God treats God simply as "pure truth," it establishes merely the general possibility of a knowledge of God ; it does not give us any actual knowledge of Him. That form of religion whose object and nourishment are "pure truth" is pantheistic mysticism. In mystical self-contemplation the soul seeks to free itself from all shews and unrealities, by regarding itself as the point of revelation for deity, as the "pure light" in which all finite thinking is consumed and swallowed up.

§ 40.

The cosmological argument conducts us, as we have seen, to a God who is mere power and necessity ; the teleological argument glorifies this power and necessity into freedom and intelligence. Whilst the cosmological argument takes as its starting-point the transitoriness of the world, the teleological begins with the consideration of its glory. This latter point of view is peculiar to the western mind ; to which has been given an insight into the domain of history as distinguished from that of nature. The world is not mere shew and seeming ; it is a *reality*, rich in meaning, and subserving a great design ; it is a grand combination of inner rational ends and means ; to this feature of the world life owes its value and significance. Finding, however, that every one of the various ends subserved by the vital forces of the world limits some other end, and that every end becomes in its turn a means, we are led to regard all these limited ends as means to one great, ultimate, self-realizing end, to wit, the absolute Idea or God. The contemplation of nature from the teleological point of view reveals God to us as the indwelling, formative activity of the world, as its organific soul (*natura naturans*) ; the contemplation of the human mind, from the same point of view, reveals to us God as the all-ruling Spirit of the world, who, by the dialectical process of history, evolves Himself as His own result. This is the theology of pantheism, or of the immanent God ; which has found expression in some recent systems of philosophy. The teleological spirit of the world is here identical with the teleological order of the world. God and the world are but two *sides* or aspects of one and the same unity ; there is in reality no relation of contrast.

The *moral* argument for the existence of God is the subjective aspect of the teleological one. As humanity cannot be satisfied with a God who is merely the God of nature and not the God of history, so is it unable to find rest in the ontological God to whom we are led by pure thought :—humanity yearns for the God apprehended in CONSCIENCE. In contemplating our ethical nature, we find that the law which raises its voice in the human breast requires unconditional submission of the will, and we are led to believe in a moral government of the world, whose aim is the good and the progress thereof onwards to complete victory over evil. Fichte, in particular, carried out this thought, looked at from the pantheistic point of view, in his doctrine of God as the moral order of the world. The religion of those who take this view consists in a mystical surrender to the moral rule to which mundane affairs are subject ; in a self-sacrificing readiness on the part of individuals to give up their life in the service of the idea. So long as God and man are not viewed as distinct from each other in the manner of the Scriptures, the existence of personal relation of love between them is impossible. On the view first referred to, God has real existence only in so far as we ourselves by our moral endeavours produce Him ; what the God-inspired man does is God ; God and the kingdom of God are one.

Observations.—The TELEOLOGICAL is the fundamental category of thought in its developed stage. It is the category of freedom ; indeed, in its deepest significance it is the category of Christianity itself. The ripest thinker of the Greek world, Aristotle, regarded "the idea" as having a teleological character. Thought, during the middle ages, was guided and ruled by this category. The battle between Leibnitz and Spinoza was a battle for its validity. Existences must be considered as standing in relation not merely to *causae efficientes*, to their immediate causes, but also to *causae finales ;* indeed the *causae efficientes* themselves must be conceived as moved by the *causae finales*, or in other words, by the eternal rational ends meant to be subserved by created objects—which ends, although in one respect yet awaiting realization in the future, must in another respect be supposed to be already *operative.* We cannot fully understand present realities unless we look forward to the result intended finally to be attained. Present actualities thus acquire a double significance, and receive a double explanation. The natural explanation recognizes solely *causae efficientes,* and looks upon everything as the product of the next working forces : the spiritual explanation finds everywhere a deeper significance (ὑπόνοια) ; it gives another turn to the natural, empirical explanation, by showing that the phenomena of nature and history have an end other than themselves, an end fixed by Divine wisdom, which, whilst lying out beyond, is now working in them as their motive principle. The whole of modern speculation has a teleological character. But the antagonism between pantheism and theism manifests itself the moment a deeper view is taken of the teleological principle according to which the world is created and ordered.

§ 41.

The teleology of pantheism is self-contradictory ; for, according to it, God, as a Spirit, is the result, without being at the same time the presupposition of the world's development. So far as pantheism recognizes in God the foundation of all existence, He is simply the slumbering thought, which does not think itself, but with instinctive necessity unfolds itself in successive developments in the kingdom of nature and the kingdom of history. As a Spirit, therefore, God is merely the God εἰς ὄν, but not the God δἰ οὗ τὰ πάντα. But such a God is not the absolute, the all-perfect Spirit ; for the marks of a creature cleave to Him. He is not truly the eternal Spirit ; for his spirituality is acquired in time, and He presses forward in the finite Spirit of man, through a *progressus in infinitum,* after real existence, without ever actually attaining it in fulness. In Him power and wisdom are disjoined ; for as a creative force the world-spirit is blind ; and as seeing wisdom He is incapable of creating. Only through the medium of the spirit of man has He some remembrance of that which He produced as the dreaming spirit of nature ; "how He then

ordered the heavenly bodies, formed the earth with its various
substances, gave animals and plants their organisms ;"—this
also is "the reason why man, or God in man, is now able to
understand the laws of nature ;" although, with all His knowledge He is not able to affix one leaf to a common nettle.*
Not only is this conception of God unsatisfactory, as opposed
to the true idea of perfection, but it does not supply a sufficient explanation (*ratio sufficiens*) of the existence of the
world.   For to trace back the marvels of nature and consciousness to a νοῦς working instinctively, or a *natura naturans*,
is to give an explanation, that itself very greatly needs explaining ; and one is involuntarily reminded of Lessing's words
that "many persons leave off reflecting where they ought properly to begin."   We too recognize in nature an unconscious
activity of reason—we trace it in crystals, in plants, in the
artistic impulses of animals ; in history too we recognize an
unconscious activity of reason, the highest individual embodiment of which, we designate genius; this is all matter of fact ;
but it is *by no means a matter of course* that it is so, and
this is, therefore, precisely the point at which that θαυμάζειν,
that *wonder* ought to be excited, which Plato calls the
beginning of philosophy.   For the very question with which
we have to do is—How is a rational instinct *possible*, that
works plastically, like a *blind* force, and yet carries out the
plans of wisdom ?   We, for our part, are unable to conceive
such a blind rational activity, save as a *natura naturans*,
which is itself *naturata*, as grounded in a *creative and wise
will*, revealing itself in the laws by which the vital operations
of creation are everywhere ordered.   The variously complicated concatenation of rational means and ends which co-
operate both in nature and history, to the realization of some
purpose, necessarily implies a self-reflective principle, which
determines itself and all other things.   But the only principle
which really *implies* its own existence, and which postulates
everything else *for* itself, the only principle which has power
over itself, which does not lose itself in the product of its
activity, which returns more profoundly into and on itself

* Compare Strauss, *Dogmatik* I. 351; where we cannot but be reminded of
the old saying in the book of Job (xxxviii. 4) " Where wast thou, when I laid
the foundations of the earth ?"

every time that it goes forth from itself, is WILL, personality. God is a PERSON, that is, He is the *self-centralized* Absolute, the eternal fundamental being, which knows itself as a centre, as the *I am* in the midst of its infinite glory (Isaiah xliv. 6.), which is conscious of being the *Lord* of this glory. He is not the undefined θεῖον, but θεός ; He is *seeing* omnipotence, in the depth of whose wisdom the end which the world is destined to serve, and of which the creature only becomes aware in time, was eternally contained in the form of a *counsel.* The world is accordingly not merely a system of eternal thoughts, but a system thoroughly worked out from eternity, and the signs of the presence of reason which we find in nature and history, viewed in their inmost significance, must be pronounced to be revelations of the will of the God of creation and providence, of Him who makes known in the world His eternal power and Godhead (Romans i., 18 ff.)

The ontological and moral view thus acquires profounder significance. That eternal something, without the presupposition of whose existence human thought is an insoluble riddle, is the thinking energy, the true God (*Deus verax*), who pervades all spirits, leads them to wisdom, and scatters all deception and mere seeming. And the obligation which we feel we are under to fulfil the law written in our hearts (Romans ii. 14 ff.), is in its deepest roots an obligation to obey the personal Will, the holy Being, who speaks to us through our conscience, and thus reveals Himself as the invisible One, in conjunction with whom we know what we know (CON-*sciens*).

§ 42.

Against the belief in the personality of God, pantheism has always objected that the ideas "absolute" and "personal" contradict each other. " As the absolute, unconditioned, unlimited being, God must be one and all ; as *a person*, He can only be conceived as limited, bounded by a world which is not part of Himself ; and this is opposed to the idea of the absolute." We cannot allow, however, that this contradiction really exists. The existence of created beings distinct from God, is not such a limit as to clash with the idea of a perfect being. When pantheism calls the omnipotent Creator of heaven and earth a limited being, it forgets that the limitation in question, so far as it deserves the name, is self-limitation, and that self-limitation is inseparable from a perfect nature. The inward fulness of the divine essence is reflected in the inner infinitude of the divine self-consciousness, and God thus has possession of Himself and the fulness of His being. An all-perfect being, which should be unaware of its own perfection, would lack one very essential element of perfection. God limits His own power by calling into existence, out of the depths of His own eternal life, a world of created beings to whom He gives, in a derivative manner, to have life in themselves. But precisely in this way above all others—that He is omnipotent over a free world—does God reveal the inner greatness of His power most clearly. That is no true power which refuses to tolerate any free movement outside of itself, because it is resolved to be and to do everything directly and by itself: that is true power which brings free agents into existence, and is notwithstanding able to make itself all in all. In other connections, Pantheists are fond of laying stress on the idea of inner infinitude; but they forget it the moment they allude to God. To Him they apply the idea of external infinitude, of extensive absoluteness—instead of the idea of intensive central absoluteness; and all the objections brought against the personality of God, converge at last in the irrational requirement that God shall be Himself the Universe (*unum versum in omnia*), instead of being its LORD.

Observations.—The apostle Paul traces the rise of heathenism to the circumstance that men did not worship God as God, but served the creature more than the Creator. In a certain sense, indeed, they were serving God; for it is the power of His Godhead which moves in created things; the objects of their worship were divine powers, divine ideas. But they did not worship God himself; they did not worship Him as God, as the Lord. They were blinded, as the ancient author of the Book of Wisdom says, by the beautiful forms of mundane things, and did not consider how much more beautiful must the Lord of these things be in whom beauty takes its rise. They marvelled at the might and force working in created objects, but considered not how much mightier

F

He is who prepared them (Wisdom xiii. 3, 4). In other words, they accepted the derived, instead of the underived Absolute. For in a sense, to wit, so far as it is a divine fulness, a totality of divine forces and ideas, the universe can be designated the Absolute; only it is the derived, and not the original Absolute.

In reality, therefore, there can be only two religious and two scientific systems—the Pantheistic and the Theistic;—the former having for its highest, the derived absolute, the universe; the latter based on the original absolute; that is, on God as God. The antagonism between pantheism and theism, is not merely an antagonism of science, of schools, but in its deepest roots, a religious antagonism; it cannot therefore be fought out alone in the domain of science. Our deciding for pantheism or for theism, depends not merely on thought, but also on the entire tendency of our inner life; depends not merely on the reason, but also on the conscience, or, as Scripture terms it, on the hidden-man of the heart. Where the mind is unduly absorbed in physical or metaphysical pursuits, the tendency of the inner life is pantheistic; where, on the contrary, the *ethical* is recognized as the fundamental task of existence, the tendency of the inner life is theistic. We are aware, indeed, that among pantheistic thinkers there have been men who must be counted not only amongst the greatest intelligences, but also amongst the noblest souls, of the human race; but we find precisely in these profoundest and noblest pantheists a something reaching out beyond their pantheism; we think we can discern in them a yearning and a striving, of which they themselves are unconscious, after an ethical, personal God such as their system denies. In their moments of greatest enthusiasm they have experienced a need of holding intercourse with the highest idea, as though it were a personal being. Even in Spinoza a certain bent towards personality is discernible; for example, when he speaks of intellectual love to God, and styles it a part of that infinite love with which God loves Himself. Schelling, Fichte, and Hegel too were stirred by a religious, an ethical mysticism, which contained the germ of a personal relation to a personal God.

Very different from these esoteric thinkers—who, wandering in a mystical twilight on the loftiest heights of pantheism, confounded their deep love to the idea with love to God, and who were prevented from seeing the frightful consequences of their system by the ideal brilliancy which suffused the kingdoms of the world and the glory thereof from the point of view they occupied— widely different from these men are those who have latterly begun to preach pantheism from the housetops. " Young Germany " has the sad glory of having reduced the negative consequences of pantheism to a system, for which it has tried to secure acceptance with the multitude. Instead of Schelling's or Hegel's intellectual, poetical, logico-mystical view of the world, we have at last been presented with an ordinary and vulgar " système de la nature." In the rough hands of this generation, the wings of the pantheistic butterfly have lost their mystic dust ; once it shone with great brilliancy ; now it presents itself in all its prosaic nakedness, or even with a death's head on its wings. We hear it now proclaimed without circumlocution, in all the simplicity of prose, that there is no God ; the name " God " is now a tedious word, to which no clear meaning can be attached ; let us therefore speak of " nature " instead of God ; of the " forces " and " laws of nature," instead of the divine attributes ; of the " course of the world " or the " progress of the age," instead of divine providence ; and so forth ; for we can understand that. This popular pantheism is working like leaven in the minds of the masses, and has played a most active part in the most recent movements of the time. The antagonism between pantheism and theism, which was once discussed in the schools of philosophers or in the esoteric conversations carried on in the higher walks of literature, has now become exoteric, and is taking hold of our populations in the form of a conflict between the denial of God and the belief in God.

43.

If God is personal, we should expect Him to reveal

Himself in the domain of personality, in a sphere of created spirits, by whom He can be believed in, known, and loved; we should expect Him to prepare for Himself, in the midst of the kingdom of nature, His own holy kingdom. The personal God is not merely the God of all creatures, but in a special sense the God of His *Church,* of His saints. The idea of the God of the Church, who, as such, reveals Himself to humanity, in its heathenish,—that is, apostate condition, in its condition of bondage to the world and its elements, as the new creator, as the REDEEMER, is inseparable from the idea of a special, *supernatural* revelation—of a sacred history in the midst of the ordinary profane history of mankind—of personal organs of revelation—of a Word of God and of divinely founded institutions. In the creation and sustentation of the Church under the Old and New Covenant we find the most complete and living testimony to the existence of a personal God, of " the Lord," whose essence is love ; and the various routes by which men arrive at a knowledge of their creator converge on this great highway of light. The cosmological and teleological evidences of God's existence are first seen in their full force in the light of that kingdom which stands immoveably firm in the stream of time, of that divine household which was established in Christ in the fulness of the times. The ontological and moral evidences acquire full significance from *" testimonium spiritus sancti,"* from the witness borne by God's own Spirit, the Spirit of truth and holiness in the hearts of believers.

Observations.—Theism owes its vitality, vigour, and fulness to the idea of God as the God of the Church. It is possible, indeed, to speak of a theism which is the natural religion of man—natural, so far as it arises in human nature through the contemplation of the works of creation. The Apostle Paul tells us that even heathens *ought* to have had this kind of natural religion, inasmuch as the eternal power and Godhead of God are clearly seen from the creation of the world and are understood by His works (Romans i. 20). But judging from experience, pantheism would rather appear to be the natural religion of man. For the myths, the *cultus* and the philosophical notions current amongst the heathen, have their

root in pantheism. Experience shows us that apart from
a positive revelation, natural theism has not only lacked
the power to form a community, a Church, but even
lacked the power vitally to possess, fill, and animate individual men. The God of theism is known amongst
heathens merely as "the unknown God," (Acts xvii. 23).
Nevertheless, the unknown, that is, in this instance, the
true God, did not leave Himself without a witness
amongst heathens. For, both in their religions and their
philosophy, traces are discoverable of a holy influence
exerted by conscience—scattered indeed, flashing in on
the surrounding darkness like *lightning*, quickly dis-
appearing again, but yet distinctly bearing this character;
we find interwoven with the woof of pantheism a weft of
theistic elements concerning which none can say whence
they have come. It is the unknown God who revealed
Himself by these flashings out of a higher region, and by
the holy forebodings and motions which were traced to a
daimonia:—an admonitory warning force which quietly
counteracted and restricted men's corrupt tendencies, and
by awakening a deeper sense of need and deeper seekings
(what Paul calls a ψελαφᾶν, a *feeling*) after God, prevented
their being completely lost in the beggarly elements of the
world. We need here only refer to Socrates, who, though
himself a heathen, was a powerful corrective of the carnal
and worldly tendency of heathenism. We, who have
grown up under the influence of Christianity, are accustomed to regard theism as a natural religion, for
we find many who, whilst refusing to believe in
Christianity as a positive supernatural revelation, still
cleave to the living God, who reveals Himself in the
works of nature and the course of human life; but it is
difficult to say how much of this theism is due to the
influence of Christianity, and how much has a purely
natural origin. Clear it is, however, that this undefined
theism—apart from Christ, apart from the Church—which
is professed by many of our contemporaries, produces
but a very vague sort of piety. It is of great importance,
indeed, as preparing the way for the belief in a positive
revelation, as a principle of conservation, by which the

soul is raised above the world and conducted towards the
kingdom of God ; but on no man can it confer the fulness
of truth and life after which we all yearn. Amongst
philosophers, no one has expounded this natural religion
of theism, as we may perhaps venture to term it, with
greater clearness and force than F. H. Jacobi. The
strength of conviction and eloquence with which this noble-
minded man asserted his faith in a living God will never
be forgotten by those who listened to him ; and his testimony was in truth a beneficent corrective, a protest in
the name of truth against the worship of the universe, the
deification of the idea and the apotheosis of the Ego
which were then so much the fashion. When he protested against making the self-consciousness of man
absolute, and said—" My watchword and that of my
reason is not my Ego,* but one who is more than I,
better than I, one who is entirely different from me, to
wit, God—I neither am, nor care to be, if *He* is not ;" or
when he resisted the doctrine of natural philosophy concerning an impersonal absolute, and inculcated with the
whole force of his thought and feeling the truth—" He
who hath planted the ear shall He not hear ? He who
hath formed the eye shall He not see ?"—he undoubtedly
gave utterance to a testimony which was written from
the creation of the world in the hearts of men ; although
the original characters of this sacred inscription were
afterwards darkened by the hieroglyphics of pantheism:
and this is the testimony which we can call the testimony
of natural religion. His religion, however, was merely a
movement towards, not a resting in, the kingdom of God.
It lacked a Mediator between God and man, One to
bridge over the infinite gap between the creature and the
Eternal, after whom our hearts yearn (" he that seeth Me
seeth the Father ") ; it took no notice of the problem of
sin, and its solution in the Gospel of the Cross. And
much as this theism may speak of faith, in the fullest
sense of the term, it was not a religion of faith ; it was
rather the religion of those yearnings and forebodings

---

* See his " *Sendschreiben an Fichte.*"

which stir the souls of many in our days, but which can never reach their goal, save in the God of the Church.

"The word *God*," says Luther, in a passage where he attacks the pantheists of that age, "the word *God* has many significations ; the true, the right God is the God of life and consolation, of righteousness and goodness." These words, however, did not flow forth from a vague, undefined religion of yearnings and premonitions, but from the clearly-defined religion of faith. For Luther believed that the God of life and consolation, of righteousness and goodness, had assumed a determinate form, had vouchsafed His presence in a determinate manner as the God of the Church. Luther was quite as well aware as the philosophers that God is omnipresent, that He is not shut up in temples ; but he knew also that God is only present for us where He vouchsafes His presence in a special, determinate manner. "Although God is omnipresent, He is nowhere ; I cannot lay hold of Him by my own thoughts without the Word. But where He himself has ordained to be present, there He is certainly to be found. The Jews found Him in Jerusalem at the throne of grace ; we find Him in the Word, in Baptism, in the Lord's Supper. Greeks and heathens imitated this by building temples for their gods in particular places, in order that they might be able to find them there ; in Ephesus, for example, a temple was built to Diana, in Delphi one to Apollo. God cannot be found in His majesty—that is, outside of His revelation of Himself in His Word. The majesty of God is too exalted and grand for us to be able to grasp it ; He therefore shows us the right way, to wit, CHRIST, and says, 'believe in Him, and you will find out who I am, and what are my nature and will.' The world meanwhile seeks in innumerable ways, with great industry, cost, trouble, and labour, to find the invisible and incomprehensible God in His majesty. But God is and remains to them unknown, although they have many thoughts about Him, and discourse and dispute much ; for *God has decreed that He will be unknowable and unapprehensible apart from* CHRIST."*

* See Luther's "Table Talk."

§ 44.

To know God as the Spirit who is not only the God of all creation, but has revealed Himself in Christ as the God of His church, is the aim of Christian theology. When Dionysius the Areopagite and John Scotus Erigena teach that God is absolutely incomprehensible, not merely for us, but also in Himself, on the ground that if He were known, the comprehension of Him would subject Him to finitude, antagonism, limitation ; when they assert God to be an absolute mystery, above all names, because every name drags Him down into the sphere of relations ; when they refuse to conceive of God save as the simply one ($τὸ ἁπλῶς ἓν$), as pure light, which does not differ from pure darkness, in which neither way nor path is discernible ; when they object to calling God anything but " pure nothing," not because of His emptiness, but because of His inexpressible fulness, in virtue of which He transcends every " something,"—on which ground also they define Him as super-essential ($ὑπερούσιος$) :—they give utterance, no doubt, to their sense of the unfathomable depth of the mystery ; but still such a mystical, neo-platonic mode of looking at the subject is an error—is a falling back on the indeterminate absolute of pantheism. By excluding the idea of understanding the Divine nature, mysticism excludes also the possibility of a revelation. For to comprehend a being is to know it in its relations ; and if it did not pertain to the nature of God to enter into relations, to make Himself intelligible, He would not have revealed Himself. God possesses His absolute " deity" in the inner relations of self-consciousness alone, and it is only as He enters into a variety of relations to the world which He has created, that He reveals to it His nature. Mystical theology commits the error of supposing pure " deity" to be better than " God," the living God, who reveals Himself in a variety of ways ; like pantheism in all its forms, it overlooks the significance of limitation as a condition of inner, intensive infinitude.*

Now, as God is in Himself knowable and comprehensible, so does He make Himself relatively discoverable and comprehensible to the creatures made in His image. Kant, indeed, maintains that divine things are totally incomprehen-

* Compare Martensen's "Meister Eckart."

sible, because human thought is bound to finite forms, which have merely subjective validity ; but this is only true of reason as it has fallen away from God and is left to itself, but not of human reason as enlightened by the word and Spirit of God.   Christianity recognizes both a searching (ἐρευνᾶν, 1 Cor. ii. 10) and a comprehending (καταλαβέσθαι, Eph. iii. 18).

§ 45.

But the idea of a revelation is utterly inadmissible, whether we hold, on the one hand, that God is wholly unsearchable and incomprehensible, as do many Christian apologists ;* or, on the other hand, go to the opposite extreme of asserting Him to be completely searchable and comprehensible.   Even in the light of Christianity, what the Son of Sirach said is still true, " To no one hath the Eternal given perfectly to declare His works.   Who can comprehend His great marvels ? Who can measure the greatness of His might ?   Who can tell out His great mercies ?   A man, when he hath done his best, hath scarcely begun ; and when he thinks he hath finished, there is still much lacking" (Ecclus. xviii. 4–6).   Not merely because of the limited extent of our outward experience—for when we look at the works of creation, we must say again with the Son of Sirach, " *We see but the fewest of His works :* for much greater are still hidden from us ;" not merely on this account is our knowledge imperfect, but also because of the inner, inexhaustible riches of the Divine essence.   We are warranted indeed in saying, that as Christianity is the perfect, final revelation of the nature and will of God, it must be possible to arrive at a fundamental knowledge of the perfect truth, at a fundamental idea of the truth.   But revelation points back to the mystery ; and it is only in God himself that the mystery ceases ; for before Him all things stand revealed with perfect clearness.   He alone has a perfect knowledge of the eternal *possibilities* of the revelation ; whereas the inner connection between mystery and revelation, between possibility and actuality, can only be relatively, not absolutely known by created spirits.   When, however, the claim is raised to a speculative comprehension of God, to an insight into the mystery, that is, into the ETERNAL

---

* For example, Mansel, in his " Limits of Religious Thought," a book which, however well meant, is quite anti-Christian in its tendencies.—Tr.

POSSIBILITIES of revelation, then may be applied with full truth
the words :—" When a man has got to the end, then he is
just beginning ; and when he ceases, he is still full of questions." Even the profoundest speculative knowledge must
be supplemented by a believing ignorance ; and the deepest
attempts to fathom the mystery of God reveal to us unfathomable abysses which no eye can search. But this unfa-
thomableness it is which is the source of reverence and ad-
miration—of that element of vague anticipation which is
the condition of all true knowledge. For this reason the
empty intellectualistic tendency which made its appearance
in the ancient church amongst some of the Arians (the Euno-
mians), who maintained that God must be as transparent as a
logical or mathematical truth, was repudiated by the church-
teachers of that day. But Gnosticism also was repudiated,
because it claimed, by an intuition of the speculative fancy,
that direct vision of God face to face which is really reserved for the future life. The error of the Gnostics consisted in cutting away the stem of knowledge from the root
of faith, in breaking down the wall of separation between
this world and the next ; in overleaping the historical and
cosmical conditions by which knowledge is at present bound ;
in aiming to occupy in this world the point of view which is
peculiar to blessed spirits. Though it is true that the kingdom
of God is come, that the perfect is revealed, it is also true that
it has still to come, that it still remains to be revealed. When
existence, when life has been made free with the freedom of
its ideal, then also will knowledge be free. If, then, we wish
our teachings regarding the knowledge of the Divine nature
to be true, we must combine the apparently opposite declarations of the Scriptures :—" We know all things" (1 John
ii. 20,) and "now we know in part" (1 Cor. xiii. 12) ; we
know Him now, and yet we shall not see Him as He is till
yonder world (1 John iii. 2) : We search the depths of Deity,
and yet no man hath seen God at any time (1 Cor. ii. 10 ;
1 John iv. 12), seeing that He dwelleth in light to which no
man can approach," (1 Tim. iv. 16).

What has been here advanced may be summed up in the
formula, that we can have a TRUE, though not an adequate
knowledge of the nature of God. We cannot have an ade-

quate knowledge of God, that is, a knowledge co-extensive in every feature with its subject.   Such a knowledge would be that vision of Him face to face, which cannot be ours till the last change is accomplished and everything partial shall have ceased.   We can, however, have a true knowledge, that is, a knowledge true in principle, true in its tendency, and true in the goal at which it aims;—true because it goes out from and leads to God.   This distinction between a true and an adequate knowledge of God hovered before the minds of our elder theologians when they distinguished between a " *theologia viatorum et beatorum.*"

The Attributes of God.

§ 46.

The nature of God reveals itself in His attributes.   If God were the simply One (τὸ ἁπλῶς ἓν), the mystic abyss, in which every form of determination is extinguished, there would be nothing to be known in the unity.   But the living God reveals the unity of His nature by a variety of *determinations* of His essence, or attributes.   His attributes express the different aspects of the same essence ; they are different fundamental utterances of one and the same nature.   They are therefore not separate from each other, but in each other, penetrate each other, and have their common centre of unity in the same divine Ego.   Although, therefore, they are distinctions which in the act of acknowledging we are compelled again to deny, they are by no means to be taken for human modes of looking at the nature of God ; they are not man's modes of apprehending God, but God's modes of revealing Himself.   We are unable, therefore, to agree with Nominalism when it represents ideas and general conceptions as merely ours, and consequently treats the conceptions which we form of the divine essence as nothing but forms in which we express our religious need of the world, lacking anything objective corresponding thereto in God himself.*   Distinctly

* For remarks on the merely subjective view of the divine attributes set forth by Kant and Schleiermacher, see my treatise on "Die Autonomie," §§ 14, 28.

as we must allow that the idea of God ought to be purged
of everything merely human, of all untrue anthropomorphisms,
we cannot but raise our voice against Nominalism as
incompatible with the idea of revelation. To say that we
are bound to conceive of God as the Holy and Just One,
whilst He in Himself is not holy and just, to call upon God
by this name, whilst He does not thus make Himself known
to us, is to brand the inmost of truth, of faith, a lie. We
teach, accordingly, with Realism, that the attributes of God
are objective determinations in His revelation, and as such
are rooted in His inmost essence.

Observations.—Not Nominalism alone, but one form of Realism also is chargeable with denying the reality of the
divine attributes. Realism assigns, indeed, objective
validity to ideas and general conceptions. But when
it has a pantheistic basis—as is sometimes the case—
the attributes of God assume the character of a mere
system of objective ideas. The ideas of omnipotence,
of righteousness, of goodness, are recognized, and validity is ascribed to them independently of our thought;
but their centre of unity is merely the formal ground
of mysticism, and not a personal subject. This form of
Realism, which looks upon personality itself as a mere
anthropomorphism, takes a false view of that idea which
is the inmost light of all other ideas. For the idea of
omnipotence, of holiness, of justice, is a mere blind
thought, unless there be One who is the Omnipotent,
the Holy, the Righteous.

§ 47.

In treating of the subject of the divine attributes, our older
theologians adopted the division into "*attributa absoluta,*" and
"*attributa relativa;*" that is, into attributes which express
the relation of God to Himself, and such as express His relation to the world. This division, however, is attended with
the difficulty that there are no divine attributes, which, if
conceived as living attributes, are not transitive, that is, do
not express a relation of God to the world;—nor are there
any which are not reflexive, that is, which do not go back on
God himself. We gain a more determinate principle of division when we consider the twofold relation which God holds

to the world. The relation of God to the world, namely, is on the one hand a relation of *unity*, on the other hand, a relation of diversity or *antithesis*. Indeed, our religious life, with all its morals and states, moves between these two poles— that of unity and that of diversity, that of freedom and that of dependence, that of reconciliation and that of separation. In our treatment of this subject, therefore, we shall have to give prominence now to the one and then to the other of the *momenta* of unity and diversity.

§ 48.

As the Being who has life in Himself (John **v.** 26), in whom is contained all fulness (πλήρωμα), God is THE ETERNAL. In the eternal God are all the possibilities of existence, all the sources of the entire creation. The eternal is the one who is, the I AM, who is *a se*, the unalterable and unchangeable. But His unchangeableness is not a dead unchangeableness; for it is to produce Himself with infinite fruitfulness out of Himself. His eternity, therefore, is not an eternity like that of the " eternal Hills ;" it is not a crystal eternity, like that of the " eternal stars ;" but a living eternity, blooming with never-withering youth. But His self-production, His Becoming [*Werden*], is not the fragmentary growth or production we witness in time. Created life has time outside of itself, because it has its fulness outside of itself. The Eternal lives in the inner, true time, in a present of undivided powers and fulness, in the rhythmic cycle of perfection. The life He lives is unchangeably the same, and yet He never ceases to live His life as something new, because He has in Himself an inexhaustible fountain of renovation and of youth. For this reason the Church magnifies the " Ancient of Days," as the " incorruptible " (ἀφθάρτῳ) and eternal King, who alone hath immortality (1 Timothy i. 17 ; vi. 16 ; Psalm xc. 2.)

The eternal God is OMNIPRESENT in His creation. Creation as a mere possibility without reality lies in the depths of the Eternal Being ; as an actuality, possessing any existence different and separate from that of God, it " lives and moves " in the omnipresent One. Everything is filled by God ; but that which is filled is different from that by which it is filled. The omnipresent God is the inmost fundamental being of everything that exists ; He is the life of all that lives, the

Spirit of all spirits. And as He is all in all, so is all in Him.
As the bird in the air, as the fish in the sea, so do all creatures live and move and have their being in God. The world
of time and space, of nature and history, is contained in Him,
as in the uncreated τόπος τῶν ὅλων. But although creation is
contained in God, God is not contained in His creation
(Psalm cxxxix. 7). Although the omnipresent One is essentially present in every leaf and every grain of wheat (ἐν πᾶσι),
He dwells and moves freely in Himself, in virtue of His
eternity. He is above and outside of all His creatures, and
governs all the possibilities of their existence (ὑπὲρ πάντων).
Omnipresence, therefore, must be conceived as the free, self-
determining presence of God with His creatures, to each of
whom He wills to stand in a different relation. The fundamental error of pantheism is the notion that God is omnipresent of necessity. God is present in one way in nature, in
another way in history; in one way in the Church, in another
way in the world; He is not, in the same sense, present alike in
the hearts of His saints, and in those of the ungodly; in Heaven
and in Hell (James iv. 8). That we live and move and have
our being in God,—an idea which pantheism sets forth as the
profoundest and loftiest wisdom,—is one of the most
elementary truths of Christianity, and was comprised in the
first instruction given to its Catechumens (Acts xvii. 28).
But they were also taught by no means to stop there; for
that which chiefly concerns us is the special presence of God
in His church, and not merely that universal presence by
which all creatures alike are embraced, and in which there is
nothing to bless the soul.

The eternity and omnipresence of God are one in His
absolute KNOWLEDGE. None but a God who knows is able to
live at once in Himself and in His creatures.

§ 49.

The OMNISCIENT God is the self-manifest God, whose own
essence is clear to Himself and to whom all other beings are
naked and open. His eternal being is transfigured into
eternal thought; in Him the life is light. The life of the
creature is never completely laid open to its intelligence;
there always remains a mystery which it has not fathomed;
God on the contrary knows the entire fulness of His being;

He is completely transparent to Himself. Hence the custom from of old of representing God under the figure of an eye ; not that He *has* an eye, but that He *is* eye ; His essence is knowledge. Relatively to the creature omniscience is an omnipresent, all-searching, all-penetrating vision (Heb. iv. 13 ; Matt. x. 30). In that he knows all things in their eternal unity, He knows them also in their inner diversities and distinctions. It was God who divided between light and darkness ; He knows substance as substance and appearance as appearance ; He knows the possible as possible and the actual as actual (Matt. xi. 23 ; 1 Sam. xxiii. 11) ; He knows the necessary as necessary, and the free under the conditions which He has Himself imposed on freedom.

The omniscient God is *eo ipso* OMNIPOTENT ; " *Scientia et potentia in unum coincidunt.*" The omniscient God has complete dominion over Himself, and in affirming His own being He acts with the most complete freedom and with thorough will. But omnipotence can only reveal itself *as* omnipotence by revealing itself as power over beings other than itself, by realizing its eternal thoughts in a world, different from God. If God is to have power over all and in all, He cannot Himself *be* all. Omnipotence as thinking, reveals itself in the rational order of existences, in the laws which pervade and regulate history and nature ; but it is by no means confined and shut in by this course of laws. Pantheism recognizes only an omnipotence which, as it were, is encompassed by the laws of the world ; theism, on the contrary, recognizes a God who had the beginning of the world in His power, and who is able to commence a *new* work of creation in the midst of the already existing order of nature. We discern, therefore, the Divine omnipotence with special clearness, when we look to the supernatural commencement of the world. By faith we know that the visible world was produced, not by a mere force of nature but by the Word of God ; and in the economy of redemption we recognize the God of marvels who is able to create a new thing on earth (Ps. lxxvii. 15 ; Jer. xxxi. 22). The declaration, "With God nothing is impossible," (Luke i. 37, Matt. xix. 26), is in this respect the great canon of faith, in revelation ; and has no limitation save the internal one, that it refers to *the God of revelation,* who can-

not deny Himself, but must necessarily act in harmony with
His own eternal thoughts. With this exception, however, it
teaches that the divine omnipotence is absolutely unlimited;
it sets before us the idea of the wonder-working God who
has not expended His creative power in the laws and forces
of nature, but still contains within Himself, in the depths of
His being, an inexhaustible fountain of possibilities of new
beginnings, new revelations, new signs. To profess that the
Divine omnipotence expended all the possibilities open to it
when it created the present order of nature, is to represent
Him either as not a creator at all, after the manner of pantheism, or as having exhausted His power as creator in producing the world, after the manner of deism.

Omniscience and omnipotence are combined in the Divine
WISDOM, in the practical, teleological knowledge of God.

§ 50.

The only WISE God is not merely a God of knowledge, but
also a God of action—a God of decrees, of providence, of fore-
sight,—who directs His efforts to the realisation of the infinite design of His will. The subject of the divine wisdom
was the eternal image of the world, which was to be realized
in time. In the Holy Scriptures, accordingly, wisdom is regarded not merely as a divine attribute, but also as the divine
thought, which the Only Wise God "possessed in the beginning of His ways." What speculation calls the idea, the
world-forming thought, is called in the Holy Scripture *wisdom*, which was with the Lord, and "daily His delight,
rejoicing always before Him" (Prov. viii. 30). It is described
not merely as the inner reflection of the divine mind, but
also as operative, all-moulding thought. For wisdom (the
idea, the divine σοφία, the heavenly maiden, as theosophists
have styled her,) is the "worker of all things" (Wisdom
vii. 22). This artist was with the Most High when He prepared the heavens, when He set bounds to the depths, when
He established the clouds above and laid the foundation of
the earth. But in man alone can it complete its work. It
sought rest in all things: it received an heritage amongst all
peoples and Gentiles, but in Israel alone (Ecclus. xxiv.), in the
Church of God, did it receive an abiding place, where "she
entereth in all ages into holy souls, making them friends of

God, and prophets." (Wisdom vii. 27). Under the Old Covenant, the Church learned the wisdom of God from the law and the prophets, and from its works in the visible creation. But the riddle of wisdom is first solved in the New Covenant, where prophecy finds its fulfilment, where the topstone is put to the manifestations of wisdom in creation, and the wisdom that is in Christ is all in all. The glorious descriptions of nature, which throughout the Old Testament proclaim the glory of the Creator, are in the New Testament thrown into the shade by the wisdom displayed in the work of redemption.* Solomon in his wisdom "spake of trees, from the cedar-tree that is in Lebanon, even unto the hyssop that springeth out of the wall" (1 Kings iv. 33); but his wise discourse is cast into the shade by the words of Him in whom "all things are to be gathered together in one" (Eph. i. 10); and the Pauline wisdom was 'to know nothing among men save Christ alone' (1 Cor. ii. 2).

The power of wisdom is RIGHTEOUSNESS. What omnipotence is in relation to omniscience, that righteousness is in relation to wisdom. In saying that God is a righteous God, we expressly postulate omnipotence as *moral* power. A complete revelation of righteousness is therefore possible only in the world of Freedom. That of which we find the type in nature, where a power may be discerned reducing to order its wild and irregular forces, and setting bounds and limits—which says, " hitherto shalt thou come, and no further; here shall thy proud waves be stayed," (Job xxxviii. 11)—shows itself in its full significance in the domain of the Will. Righteousness is the organizing power in wisdom—it is that *distributive* energy which assigns to each creature in the divine state its ordained place. But this distributive power is also *discriminative;* it *maintains intact* the distinctions it has established; it brings to light the difference between good and evil, and reveals itself in judgment and retribution.† In righteousness, wisdom has an eternal guarantee against all human arbitrariness : for the

---

* Eph. iii. 10: "To the intent that now unto the principalities and powers in heavenly places might be known by the church, the manifold wisdom of God." Rom. xi. 33: "O the depth of the riches both of the wisdom and knowledge of God!"

† Gal. vi. 7; "Be not deceived; God is not mocked: for whatsoever a man soweth that shall he also reap." See also Romans ii. 6—8.

G

just and righteous power of God is present wherever man works unrighteousness, and causes that it hastens with unavoidable necessity onwards to its crisis. There is nothing hid that shall not one day be brought to light, sifted and judged, and in this sense we can say that the world's history is a continuous self-judgment. It is due to righteousness that wisdom continues to be wisdom, notwithstanding the folly of the world; that the wisdom of this world is shown to be folly in the light of the Gospel; that the might of the world is brought to nought by the Word of God. Whether righteousness be considered as distributive or judicative, we must hold fast the canon that, inasmuch as its manifestations are manifestations of the eternal wisdom, every such revelation has a teleological bearing on *the highest good.* Separated from wisdom, the idea of divine righteousness or justice is a blind levelling power, nothing more nor less than the heathen *Nemesis* or Fate; rent asunder from the idea of the good, we are landed in the principle—"*fiat justitia, pereat mundus.*"

The wisdom and righteousness of God are combined in His GOODNESS. So far from righteousness standing in irreversible antagonism to goodness, it forms in point of fact a constituent element of goodness.* Goodness which does not do justice, which does not uphold laws, is not goodness; for precisely in executing justice, nay, even in executing punitive justice, does goodness reveal itself; for in that way it seeks to conduct creation to, and educate it for itself. We may characterize the goodness of God in a general way by saying that He has constituted the great end of creation His own end (τέλος), that in constituting creation a means of revealing Himself, He makes His own revelation of Himself a means for the furtherance of the good of creation. It is the nature of goodness to possess its own fulness only in communication, to have only as it gives. But no one is good save the one God (Mark x. 18). As every good and perfect gift comes down from the Father of lights, so also do we derive our *susceptibility* for these gifts from the same source. To the end that He might be

---

* 1 John i. 9; "If we confess our sins He is *faithful and just to forgive* us our sins, and to cleanse us from all unrighteousness." Romans iii. 26; "To declare his righteousness, that he might be just, and the justifier of him which believeth in Jesus."

" *Communicativum Sui* " God has brought forth a creature whose nature it is to be " *indigentia Dei.* "   He has created the need and the yearning, in order that He might be able to be its fulness and satisfaction.   Susceptibility to the communication of the Divine life we find at all stages of creation, but in man alone does it exist in a perfect form—to wit, as susceptibility for God Himself.   On this very ground man is the most perfect creature, because he is created to stand in absolute *need* of God.   It is in man that the goodness of God first reveals itself as love.

§ 51.

Considered in relation to the universe the communication of the Divine life is goodness; considered in relation to personality, it is LOVE.   All creatures participate in the goodness of God; but personal creatures alone can be constituted partakers of His love.   God *is* love (1 John iv. 16).   He neither can nor will be without His kingdom— the kingdom which is constituted by " I and Thou," in which not merely Divine powers and gifts, but the Divine personality itself dwells in the soul and the soul in it.   All the Divine attributes are combined in love, as in their centre and vital principle.   Wisdom is its intelligence; might its productivity; the entire natural creation and the entire revelation of righteousness in history are means by which it attains its teleological aims.   When the fulness of the time came love revealed its true nature to the object beloved, and prepared itself in Christ a Church for eternity.   And as Christ in His gospel made known to our race the inmost thoughts of His wisdom —" if He had had a better gospel, He would have given it us "—so does He make those who believe partakers of His own divine *nature* (2 Peter i. 4).   This unity is more than a moral union; it is one of essence; it is more than the mystical unity of pantheism, for it is one of holiness.   Viewed in relation to sin eternal love is compassionate *grace ;* viewed in relation to the education of sinful man, it is *longsuffering ;* viewed in relation to its promises and the hope which it awakens in the hearts of men, it is *faithfulness* (1 Peter iv. 19 : " As unto a faithful Creator.")

The kingdom of love is established on the foundation of HOLINESS.   Holiness is the principle that guards the eternal

distinction between Creator and creature, between God and
man, in the union effected between them; it preserves
the Divine dignity and *majesty* from being infringed by
the Divine love; it eternally excludes everything evil and
impure from the Divine nature (Isaiah vi. 3: "Holy, holy,
holy, is the Lord of Hosts." See also Deut. vii. 21; James i.
13; Heb. x. 27; xii. 29). The Christian mind knows nothing of a love without holiness. Error has been fallen into
relatively to this subject, both in a speculative and practical
direction. The *speculative* error we find embodied in pantheistic mysticism, which converts the free moral necessity which
moved love to create man, into a mere metaphysical, natural
necessity. For example, Angelus Silesius says :—

> "God has as much need of me, as I of Him;
> His nature I help Him to guard and He guards mine.
>
> I know that without me God cannot live a moment,
> If I should perish, He too must needs give up the Ghost.
>
> Nothing there is save I and Thou; if we two cease to be,
> God then is no more God, and heaven falls to ruin."

These mystical paradoxes are true indeed, so far as they
give expression to the element of *necessity* in the divine love
—the necessity under which it lies of willing to reveal itself
by an infinite communication of itself. But the position that
God needs man as much as man needs God, is true only so
far as it is accompanied by the recognition of the majesty of
God as revealed in His holiness; so far as *reverence* is guarded
in the midst of love. The holy God testifies to us in our consciences, that He has no need of man, in order that He may
be able to say to Himself "*I*." The holy God testifies to us
in conscience, that love is not an indefinite flowing over of the
nature of man into that of God, but a community of *persons*,
the purity of which depends on strict regard being paid to the
limits separating the one from the other. The *practical* error
is *antinomism*, which consists in rending asunder gospel and
law, and in pouring contempt on the law and God of the Old
Testament,—a contempt which we find expressed by several
Gnostic writers, who, supposing that love gave something of
the license commonly awarded to genius, set at naught the
idea of duty as something appropriate solely to subordinate

beings. We acknowledge, indeed, that holiness without love, as embodied in the Pharisees, is no true holiness; that mere duty, the mere categorical imperative "thou shalt," apart from the promises of the Gospel, is not the spiritual law of Christ; but we must at the same time maintain with equal distinctness, that a gospel of love without law, is a false and impure gospel. The true Gospel confirms and is itself the fulfilment of the law.

The reflection of the rays of love back on God, after passing through His kingdom, is BLESSEDNESS. Blessedness is a term expressive of a life which is complete in itself. It is the eternal *peace* of love, which is higher than all reason; it is the sabbath of love in its state of eternal perfection (Heb. iv. 3). But the sabbath of love must not be compared with the εὐδαιμονία, with the idle enjoyment attributed to heathen gods; love's eternal rest is eternal *activity*. "My Father worketh hitherto" (John v. 17). In the more exact development of the idea of blessedness this difficulty arises, that on the one hand God must be conceived of as self-sufficient, and needing no one—"not having need of anything" (Acts xvii. 25)—and on the other hand that His blessedness must be conceived of as conditional upon the perfecting of His kingdom; because divine love can satisfy itself only as it is bliss-giving, only therefore as it becomes all in all. The only way to solve this contradiction, is to assume that God has a twofold life—a life in himself of unclouded peace and self-satisfaction, and a life in and with His creation, in which He not only submits to the conditions of finitude, but even allows His power to be limited by the sinful will of man. To this life of God with His creation, must be referred the Biblical ideas of divine grief, divine anger (Eph. iv. 30; Rom. i. 18), and others which plainly imply a limitation of the divine blessedness. This limitation, however, is again swallowed up in the inner life of perfection which God lives, in total independence of His creation, and in triumphant prospect of the fulfilment of His great designs. We may therefore say with the old theosophic writers, "in the outer chambers is sadness, but in the inner ones unmixed joy."

THE DIVINE HYPOSTASES.

The Triune God.

§ 52.

We have seen that the divine attributes find their harmonizing completion and unity in LOVE ;—love, which is not merely one single aspect of the divine essence, but that essence in its fulness. Indeed, all the divine attributes are but more precise definitions of love. Taking love as the starting point of a new contemplation, we are introduced at once to a new cycle of relations in the divine revelation. We have now to speak not only of single " aspects " of the relation between God and the world, but of that relation in its *entirety ;* and the same Gospel which teaches us that God is Love, teaches us also that the one love reveals itself in a threefold personality as Father, Son, and Holy Ghost. Although the Christian mind rests in the purest monotheism, it can only attain to a knowledge of the one Love through the medium of the three Persons. Christian worship calls men away from the altars of polytheism, and elevates their souls to the one God, but it does so in a threefold direction ; for we know by faith that eternal life streams down to us out of three personal fountains of love—from God the Father who has created us ; from God the Son who has redeemed us ; and from God the Holy Ghost who sanctifies us, and makes us the children of God :—in this TRINITY alone do we possess the whole of love. Father, Son, and Spirit are not qualities, not powers or activities of the nature of God ; they are *hypostases*, that is, distinctions in the divine nature expressing not merely single " aspects," single " rays " of that nature, but each expressing by itself the entire essence ; they are momenta each of which for itself at the same time, and in equal degree, reveals the whole of God, the whole of love, though each in a different way. All the divine attributes are in the Father, who created the world by His divine word, and from eternity formed the decree to establish His kingdom. All the divine attributes are in the Son, the eternal Word, who was in the beginning with God and was Himself God, through whom all things are created, and who, when the time was fulfilled,

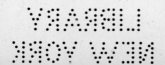

became Flesh and dwelt among men (John i. 14 ; Philippians ii. 6 ; Hebrews i. 3 ; Matt. xi. 27). All the divine attributes are in the Holy Spirit, through whom we know what is given us by God, and search the depths of the Father and the Son (1 Cor. ii. 10 ; Matt. xxviii. 19 ; 1 Cor. xii. 3-7 ; 2 Cor. xiii. 13; Titus iii. 4-6). For each of these is the whole of love, though each in a different relation.

The Christian doctrine of one God in three centres of revelation, each of which by itself reveals the whole of God, has not been merely the offspring of metaphysics, but has grown out of faith in the *facts* of revelation. The first simple, historical faith in Father, Son, and Holy Ghost is expressed in the directest possible form in the apostolic formula which is still used by the Church in the performance of the rite of baptism. In rearing on this apparently scanty foundation its clearly defined doctrine of the Tri-unity, of one God in three persons or hypostases, the design of the Church was to secure the Christian conception of God from every sort of adulteration, whether coming from Judaism or Heathenism. The contest waged by the Church against Arianism and Sabellianism was a struggle for Christianity as the *perfect revelation of the Love of God,* which excludes both Deism with the yawning gulf it interposes between God and the creature, and Pantheism with its commixture of the two.

§ 53.

Arianism, which calls the Father alone God, and considers the Son and the Spirit to be subordinate beings, is an apostacy to unbelieving Judaism with the insurmountable wall of separation which it raised between God and the creature. Only in the reflection of glory of the Most High, as it shows itself in His works, only through the medium of divine powers and workings, only by the law of his will, is man able to attain a knowledge of God. God (according to Arianism) sits on His throne above the world in incomprehensible majesty; never does He show Himself to man, who in nature sees only the hem of the garment of the Most High, and in history only His finger, but can never see Him face to face. In opposition to such a doctrine, the Church replied that it is true the Father did not come into the world, but that God would not be love if the Son did not proceed from the Father; if the

God, who, as the Father, is *above* the world, were not from
the beginning in the world as the Son, as God of God, who
is the Light and Life of the world, and who, when the time
was fulfilled, became Flesh in Christ. If Christ is merely a
Demi-god; or if He is a mere man, who raised Himself up
to the highest degree of resemblance to God possible to man;
if He is merely an Arch-angel, or the greatest of all the
Prophets, that is, after all, merely a creature; then is
Christianity not the perfect revelation. For no creature, no
man, no angel, but God alone is able to reveal God as He is;
the God-man alone, who unites in Himself the created and
uncreated natures, is able to fill up the gulf between Creator
and creature, to be the perfect Mediator of love between the
two. The same remarks apply also to the doctrine of the
Holy Spirit. As God can only be revealed through God, so
can He also only be appropriated and loved through God.
The God who is the object of knowledge and love must Himself be the principle of knowledge and love in the human
mind. If the Holy Spirit is a mere divine force or activity,
it is not God himself who dwells as the Holy Ghost in His
Church as in His temple; consequently, the love and self-
communication of God to the human soul are not a reality.
When, therefore, we keep firm hold, with Athanasius, on the
oneness of the nature of the Son and Spirit with the nature
of the Father (ὁμοουσία); when we maintain that they are not
mere divine gifts or forces, but God himself, who is revealed
in Christ, and God himself, who is the Spirit in His Church,
we are asserting the immanence of God, His holy presence in
creation.

§ 54.

But as the Christian conception of God differs from unbelieving Judaism, so also does it differ from Heathenism,
with its pantheistic commingling of God and creation. The
Sabellian heresy is chargeable with this same commingling of
God and creation. Sabellianism designates Father, Son, and
Spirit God; but it takes Father, Son, and Spirit to be only
three different modes of the manifestation of the divine
essence, so far as it shines into the world; not inner, eternal
distinctions in God himself:—in other words, the Trinity
first comes into existence with the world. Prior to the

existence of the world, or independently thereof, God is not triune, but pure unity, impersonal deity, raised above every distinction and every determination. The Unity broke out into a Trinity when the world came into being; or, to put the matter more correctly, the manifestation of the essence of God as triune, is coincident with the *development of the world,* nay more, with the development of the *religious consciousness.* So far as the divine essence is viewed as the originator of the world, it appears to the religious consciousness in the light of a Father; in Christ we represent to ourselves the same essence as a Son; in the Church, as the Holy Spirit. God did not, however, become Son till the fulness of the time was come; and He first became Spirit in and with the Church. The Trinity, therefore, denotes here merely the different momenta of the *history* of revelation, the various steps in the self-upholding of the divine essence in the world. In opposition to such a doctrine, the Church had no alternative but to object that it no less than Arianism denies Christianity to be the perfect revelation of God as love. For we cannot speak of a revelation of love, where God in Himself is mere impersonal deity, which first became conscious of itself as an Ego in Christ, and first knows itself as Spirit in the Church. If God is love, He must have been able freely to resolve on revealing Himself in the world; and *revealing Himself eternally to Himself,* He must have lived an inner life of love. If God reveals Himself to us in a threefold personal form, as Father, Son, and Spirit, He must also be from eternity manifest to Himself, and must love Himself, in the threefold relation of Father, Son, and Spirit. If, then, we are able to say that the one God looks into His world, as it were, with three faces (τρία πρόσωπα), we must also say that these faces are turned not merely outwards toward the world, but also inwards, toward Himself, that they behold themselves in mutual reflection. Otherwise, they would be deceptive masks, and not the revelation of the true inner being of God. According to Sabellianism, however, Father, Son, and Spirit are mere masks, which simulate a revelation of love, whilst in reality there is nothing behind them but an impersonal essence which can neither love nor be loved. And as Sabellianism does away with the revelation of love, so also does it deny

the majesty of the triune God as *independent of the world.*
The same charge may be brought against every pantheistic
explanation of the doctrine of the Trinity, from Sabellius down
to Schleiermacher and Hegel. For this reason, following the
example of the Church, we draw a distinction between the
revelation of God to the world (*ad extra*) and His eternal
revelation to Himself (*ad intra*): in other words, between
the *œconomic* Trinity and the Trinity of *essence* (τρόπος
ἀποκαλύψεως and τρόπος ὑπάρξεως.)

Observations.—Although the Holy Scriptures consider the
divine Trinity principally in connection with the historical economy of redemption—in connection with the
eternal counsel of the Father to redeem, with the coming
of Christ, with the work of the Holy Spirit in the
Church; still there is by no means a complete absence of
hints that this economic Trinity, this Trinity of revelation expresses not merely God's relation to man, but also
His essential relation to Himself. When we read in the
Gospel of John that the Word was in the beginning *with*
God, and was itself God, we are introduced to an inner
distinction between God and God, to an inner relation of
God and God. And when Paul says that the Spirit
searches the depths of God, he teaches that the Spirit is not
a mere activity of God directed to the world, but also an
activity directed inwardly, in other words, that the Spirit
of God, who is Himself God, searches God. In these and
similar expressions, the Church necessarily found the
clearest summons to trace back the economic to an essential Trinity. Indeed such a demand arises in general out
of the idea of God as revealed to Himself.

§ 55.

A full living knowledge, a comprehensive intuition of
the essential Trinity is impossible to created minds; for we
are unable to represent to ourselves the esoteric glory of God,
and in this connection we may say, " The triune God dwells
in light into which no man can approach." A living and
clear intuition of the triune essence of God is only possible to
us, so far as it has revealed itself in the economy of the universe, in the works of creation, redemption, and sanctification.
Still we must be capable of a shadowy knowledge, that is, of

an *ontological* knowledge of the essential Trinity. The idea of the Trinity of essence is one with the idea of the Divine personality; and, therefore, to have an ontological conception of the essential Trinity is to have a conception of the form which is fundamental and necessary to the personal life of God; is to have a conception of those momenta of the essence of God, without which personality and self-consciousness are *inconceivable*. It is true, both ancient and modern Arianism is of opinion that God may be a personal God without being a Trinity, and that the personality of God is sufficiently secured if we represent to ourselves a " God the Father," to whom we attribute self-consciousness and will. But we ask, —is it possible for us not merely to imagine to ourselves, but to think, that God could have been from eternity conscious of Himself as a Father, if He had not from eternity distinguished Himself from Himself as the Son, and if He had not been as eternally one with the Son in the unity of the Spirit? Or, in other words, Is it possible to conceive of God as eternal self-consciousness without conceiving of Him as eternally *making Himself his own object* ? When, therefore, following in the footsteps of the Church, we teach that not merely the Father, but also the Son and the Holy Spirit eternally pre-existed and are independent of creation, we say that God could not be the self-revealed, self-loving God, unless He had eternally distinguished Himself into I and Thou (into Father and Son), and unless He had eternally comprehended Himself as the Spirit of Love, who proceeds forth from that relation of antithesis in the Divine essence. In thus following the analogy of the human consciousness,—which we conceive ourselves justified in doing, seeing that man is created in the image of God,—we are liable to be met by the objection that the distinctions in the human mind are merely ideal, not real, not hypostatic distinctions. This objection, however, rests on a misapprehension of the distinction between the created and uncreated self-consciousness. For the circumstance that the Trinity as conceived of in the human mind, is merely an ideal and not an hypostatic trinity, is due to its being created. As created, the human mind is bound down by the antithesis between being and thought, and its self-consciousness can only develope itself in relation to and connection with beings, with a world existing *outside* of itself. In God, on the contrary, thought and being are one, and the movement by which God completes His self-consciousness is a movement not merely of the divine subject, but also of the divine substance. So certainly as God could not but open Himself to Himself in all the blessedness of His being; so certainly must a πλήρωμα be laid bare in Him, a kingdom of essences, of ideas, of powers and forces, an inner uncreated world (κόσμος νοητός). Inasmuch as, in the cycle of self-consciousness, the triple relation of the divine Ego to itself is conditioned by its triple relation to the uncreated heavenly world, the three Ego-centres become not merely ideal, but hypostatic distinctions, not merely forms of consciousness, but forms of subsistence (τρόποι ὑπάρξεως).

§ 56.

As the Ego arising out of its primal natural ground, revealing itself to itself, and unfolding its fulness in the form of distinct thought, God is the eternal *Father.* Looking on the heavenly image of the world as it arises out of the depths of His own nature, God sees the image of His own essence, His own Ego in a *second* subsistence. The heavenly ideal world, which is born out of the depths of God, and discharges the same function for the divine self-consciousness as the *outward world* for the human mind, would not be a system, but rather a chaos, would be split up into a variety without order, if the birth of this heavenly ideal had not been at the same time the birth of God Himself as the *Logos,* as the *principle of thought* in the living world of light which dawned on the Father, as the ordaining, all-embracing, and all-sustaining principle in that objective manifoldness which presents itself to the Father's gaze. The apostle John says, " In the beginning was the Word, and the Word was with God, and the Word was God." He thus describes the eternal Word, in which the Father perceives Himself, not merely as the spoken, but also as the *speaking,*—not merely as the revealed, but also as the revealing Word. Here, in the doctrine of the inner revelation of God, lies the distinction between Christian and Jewish theology. The Old Testament represents God as becoming manifest to Himself in Wisdom, which was with

Him from the beginning, and before the creation of the world acted its part, and "rejoiced always" before His face. In the Old Testament, however, Wisdom is merely the eternal image of the world, the idea which, though uncreated and supernatural, is not God Himself, but something between the Most High and the created world. The same may be said of the Religious Philosophy of Philo, where Logos is merely another term for the heavenly world ($\varkappa \acute{o} \sigma \mu o \varsigma$ $\nu o \eta \tau \acute{o} \varsigma$), which, though uncreated, is subordinate to God. Jewish theology represents God in His inner revelation as occupied solely with the thought of the world, and makes the Father the Father merely of the idea of the world, and of the creature. But in order to become conscious of Himself, God required not merely to think something other than Himself, but to think Himself as another; in order to know Himself as the Father, He must think of Himself not primarily as the Father of the creature or of the idea, but as the Father of the thinking Logos, who is the vehicle of the idea, and without whom no single thought would present itself to the Father as an *object* different from Himself.

When therefore we say that God knows Himself as a Father, we say that He knows Himself as the ground of the heavenly universe, which proceeds eternally forth from Him, solely because He knows Himself as the ground of His own outgoing into this universe, in which He hypostatizes Himself as Logos. When we say that God knows Himself as Son, we say: God knows Himself as the One who from eternity proceeded forth from His own Fatherly ground, He knows Himself as the $\delta \varepsilon \acute{u} \tau \varepsilon \rho o \varsigma$ $\Theta \varepsilon \acute{o} \varsigma$, who objectively reveals the fulness wrapped up in the Father. Without the Son, the Father could not say to Himself *I;* for the form of the Ego, without an objective something different from the Ego (a non-Ego, a Thou), in relation to which it can grasp itself as Ego, is inconceivable. What the outward world, what nature, what other persons are, for us,—to wit, the condition of our own self-consciousness,—the Son and the objective world which arises before the Father in and *through* the Son (δi $\alpha \grave{u} \tau o \tilde{u}$) are for the Father,—to wit, the condition of His own identity.* But if the

* Compare the treatises of Nitzsch and Weisse. "Von der Wesentlichen Dreieinigkeit Gottes."

inner revelation were terminated in the Son, God would be manifest to Himself merely according to the *necessity* of His nature and thought, not according to the *Freedom* of His will. It would be merely in intellectual contemplation that God would stand related to the heavenly world which by a necessity of nature proceeds forth from Him in the birth of the Son ; but He would not stand to it in the relation of a free formative cause. It is only because the relation of God to His world is that of a freely *working*, moulding, creating agent, as well as that of a natural logical necessity, that He constitutes Himself its *Lord*. If then the "birth" of the Son out of the essence of the Father denotes the momentum of necessity, the "procession" of the Holy Spirit from the Father and the Son, denotes the momentum of freedom in the inner revelation. The Spirit proceeds from the Father and the Son, as the *third* hypostasis ; whose work it is to transform and glorify the necessary subject of thought into the free act of the will, and to mould the eternal kingdom of ideas into a kingdom of inner creations of free conceptions. The fatherly πλήρωμα which is revealed in the Son as a kingdom of ideas, of necessity proceeding out of the depths of His being, is glorified by the free artistic action of the Spirit into an inner kingdom of *glory* (δόξα), in which the eternal possibilities are present before the face of God as magical realities, as a heavenly host of visions, of plastic architypes, for a revelation *ad extra*, to which they desire, as it were, to be sent forth. Only on the basis of such a free procession of the Spirit, which is at the same time a free *retro*cession, can the relation between the Father and the Son be one of love. In the Spirit alone is the relation of God to Himself and to His inner world, not merely a metaphysical relation, a relation of natural necessity, but a free, an ethical relation. But notwithstanding that the Spirit is a distinct hypostasis, the perfecting completing momentum in the Godhead, the entire Trinity must also be designated Spirit. "God is a Spirit," says Christ; and this is the comprehensive designation of the true, that is, of the Trinitarian God.

There are therefore three eternal acts of consciousness, and the entire divine Ego is in each of these three acts. Each hypostasis has being solely through the other two. Here there is no temporal first or last.   The entire Trinity stands in one present Now, three eternal flames in the one light.

§ 57.

In His inner glory the triune God knows Himself as the *Lord* of the heavenly world, of the inexhaustible variety of ideas and forces, of the heavenly host of visions. But the glory (δόξα) of God would not be perfectly revealed, if He shut Himself within Himself, content to reveal Himself to Himself alone. The personal God can be truly self-sufficient only in one way, to wit, by manifesting Himself as the Lord of an actual world of spirits, of a kingdom of personal beings, by whom He can be known and loved. A perfect dominion is a dominion over free beings ; and perfect love is not merely the love of God to Himself, to His own perfection, but must also be conceived as love to what is imperfect ; in other words, it must be conceived as the will to create a world, one of whose essential features is the need of God ; a world of finite person-alities in whose midst He purposes to establish the kingdom of perfect love. The magic visions which play in His inner self-revelation before the face of God, must be conceived therefore as determining themselves to *counsels* relating to creation and to the economy of the kingdom of God amongst created things — counsels which even as counsels possess reality, in so far as their fulfilment is eternally anticipated in that Will to which alone belong the kingdom, the power, and the glory. In the execution of these eternal counsels, or in the revelation of God *ad extra,* the same momenta find expres-sion as those to which we have referred in considering His inner self-revelation. God creates the world through the Son ; He reveals Himself as Father and Creator only so far as, in His character of Logos, He is at the same time the immanent principle of the creation—the principle which, when the ful-ness of the time was come, became the actual Mediator be-tween the Father and the manifold variety of the universe. The eternal counsels relating to the kingdom of God in the world are revealed in Christ. But these eternal counsels revealed in Christ are carried into execution by the Holy Spirit alone, who proceeds from the Father and the Son, and whose work it is to glorify the Son and to give the kingdom of heaven reality in the world ; so that the Spirit is the plastic, consummating, completing principle in the divine economy. But that which in the inner revelation manifests itself in one eternal Now, manifests itself in the economy of history under the conditions of time. Through the Law and the promises of the Prophets God revealed Himself as the Father ; in the fulness of the times He revealed Himself as the Son, when the Word became flesh and dwelt among us; and by the miracle of Pentecost He constituted Himself the Spirit of the Church. These main points of the economy of revelation are repeated during the first half of the Church's year, and are brought to a close and summed up in Trinity Sunday, as a testimony to our belief that the Trinity of History has its foundation and roots in the supra-historical Trinity of the divine essence.

As the revelation of God in the world presupposes His eternal self-revelation, so must the former conduce to the fuller and richer unfolding of the latter. God loves Himself in His Son ; but through the creation and the Incarnation the relation between Father and Son becomes not merely a relation of antithesis between God and God, but also a relation between God and the *Firstborn of all creation,* between God and the *God-man,* between the Father and Christ. In consequence of the relation of love between Father and Son becoming subject to the conditions of time and of finite creatures ; in consequence of God in Christ taking up created finitude into His own essence, the relation between Father and the Son is not merely an intellectual relation of love, but becomes —we know no better expression—a pathological relation of love, in which God moves agreeably to His heart as well as to His majesty. It is when His glory is reflected back to Him, not merely from a kingdom of ideas, but from a kingdom of actual spirits, a kingdom of souls, all united together under Christ and all witnesses, not merely of the eternal power and Godhead of God, but also of His saving grace, and then only, that the divine blessedness becomes in the full sense perfect. It then for the first time becomes perfect, in so far as it is the will of God not merely to rest in His eternal *majesty*—for in this the Triune God was able to rest independently of the world, before the foundations of the world were laid ; but to rest and be blessed in the completed work of *grace* and *love*, in the glorious liberty of the children of God,—a goal which will not be reached until, in the words of the Apostle Paul, God shall be all in all. Then first, in the new Economy (in the new Heavens and the new Earth), will the glory of the triune God be perfectly revealed—the glory which is reflected from His perfect communications of love to the creature.

§ 58.

As the doctrine of the Trinity embraces the entire Christian view of Revelation, there being no point in the economy of revelation capable of being understood without it; the following exhibition of systematic theology will necessarily be a development of the economic Trinity, a development of the doctrine of the Father, Son, and Spirit, as they have revealed themselves in the works of creation, regeneration, and sanctification. In the present treatise, therefore, we shall pursue the path marked out for us in the earliest ages in the Apostles' Creed.*

---

* Amongst recent dogmatic theologians to Marheineke belongs the merit of having revived this division. Amongst the Reformers Calvin adopted it in his " *Institutio Christianæ Religionis.*"

THE DOCTRINE OF THE FATHER.

CREATION.
§ 59.

In the act of creation God brings forth that which is not God, *that,* the essence of which is different from His own essence; He brings forth free finite beings, whom He purposes to fill with His own fulness. Because God is Love, it is impossible for Him to shut himself up in himself, as a mere God of "ideas;" on the contrary, He cannot but constitute Himself the "Father of Spirits," the Ruler of the manifold variety of "the Living," the Spirit in the realm of spirits and souls, in which he purposes to prepare for Himself a dwelling. The idea of creation is, therefore, inseparable from that of the incarnation of God in the world (taking this latter expression in a general sense). In a certain sense one may say that God created the world in order to satisfy a want in Himself; but the idea of God's love requires us to understand this want as quite as truly a *superfluity.* For this lack in God is not, as in the God of Pantheism, a blind hunger and thirst after existence, but is identical with the inexhaustible riches of that liberty which cannot but will to reveal itself. From this point of view, it will be clear, in what sense we reject the proposition, and in what sense we accept it, "without the world God is not God."

§ 60.

As Love is the ground of creation, so the *kingdom* of love

is its end and aim (*causa finalis creationis*).   But in the
kingdom of love God and His creatures are reciprocally means
and end to each other.   As God himself alone can be the final
goal of His ways, we must undoubtedly say, " *creat sibi mun-*
dum."   But as God glorifies His love to Himself through His
love to the world, we may equally say, " *creat nobis mundum*."
A God who should have created the world purely for His own
glorification (*in gloriam suam*), without constituting it an end
to itself, would be a mere egoistic power, but not eternal love.
This hard thought occurs in the theology of Calvin, who represents even individual human beings as mere dependent
vessels for the honour of God, and as born and pre-ordained either to blessedness or to damnation.   It occurs also
in pantheistic systems, which treat individual men as mere
vessels for the glory of the idea, for the spirit of the world ;
about whose weal or woe that spirit is completely indifferent.
If the means by which God reveals Himself are mere means
and nothing more, the Divine will itself loses its significance,
because in that case it operates upon a worthless and insignificant
material ; whereas the eternal power and deity of the Creator
acquires fuller significance, the nobler the finite beings are
which He has brought into existence.   In agreement therefore
with the hints given by the Scripture we combine the two
formulæ, God has created the world " *in gloriam suam* " and
" *in salutem nostram*."*

Observations.—The reciprocal relationship of means and end
here described, we shall find recurring when we come to
discuss the doctrine of the new creation.   For Christ, the
incarnate Logos, came not to be ministered unto, but to
minister ; He came to make Himself a *means* for the
human race.   But the same Christ makes the entire
human race, and with it the whole creation, visible and
invisible, a means for the revelation of His glory, and is
therefore *an infinite end to Himself*.   The kingdom of
nature is merely a preparation for His coming ; human
souls are to be constituted vessels of the activity of the

---

* Eph. i. 12—14; " Unto the praise of his glory."   2 Cor. iii. 18 ; " We all
with open face, beholding as in a glass the glory of the Lord, are changed into
the same image from glory to glory, even as by the Spirit of the Lord'

Holy Spirit ; and all tongues are to confess that Christ is Lord to the glory of God the Father.

§ 61.

When God creates, He calls into existence that which has no being.   This is the meaning of the old doctrine that God created the world out of *nothing* (2 Maccabees vii. 28.) Not that the nothing out of which the world is created is literally nil,=0 ; regarding which the principle would apply, " *ex nihilo nihil fit.*"   The nothing out of which God creates the world are the eternal possibilities of His will, which are the sources of all the actualities of the world.*   But as God can only have power over the possibilities of His being, so far as He is open and manifest to Himself ; and as these eternal possibilities are only known to Him in the *Son ;* the proposition that God creates the world out of nothing, is inseparable from the other proposition that He creates the world through the *Son.* When we say that God creates the world through the Son, we mean that he lays hold on the thought of the world *not* immediately, but in the thought in which He conceives Himself as His Son ; that He conceives the creative thought of love alone in the love with which He loves Himself.   The Old Testament clearly teaches that God created the world by His word, by an omnipotent " Let there be ;" but it does not recognize the truth that the Word by which God creates the world is God Himself, that God himself is the immanent World-Logos, who causes one eternal thought of His wisdom after another to pass into reality.

CREATION AND COSMOGONY.

§ 62.

It is involved in the idea of creation that God brings forth, not something dead, but something living, to wit, a creature which, being endowed with independence, is able in turn to

* Heb. xi. 3 ; "Through faith we understand that the worlds were framed by the Word of God, so that the things which are seen were not made of things which do appear."

produce and develop itself.   We must accordingly conceive of
creation as laying the foundation of a *cosmogony*, or of
the self-development of the world, of its *genesis*.   The Mosaic
account of creation gives expression to the fundamental idea
of creation, when it tells us that the world was created by
the omnipotent word of God.   He spake, " Let there be
light," and there was light.   Each of the six days of creation, that is, each new epoch in the system of the world,
makes its appearance solely in virtue of the omnipotent word
spoken by the Creator.   But this same account contains also
the idea of a cosmogony, of a genesis ; for creation is represented as taking place progressively, as rising from the imperfect to the more perfect ; by which we are to understand that
the progress made by creation depends on the progress made
by the creatures themselves in the course of their natural
self-development.   Each new day of creation dawned when
the time was full ; when all the conditions and presuppositions of its dawn had been developed.   But notwithstanding
that the Mosaic account of creation contains in this way the
idea of a cosmogony, or of the natural birth of things, it was
not thoroughly followed up and unfolded by the later Jews.
On the contrary, one must say it was necessary that the doctrine of creation should here be set forth *exclusively* in its
opposition to and distinction from the naturalistic view of the
world that prevailed among the heathen.   In Judaism the
world is predominantly regarded as *creatura*, not as *natura* ;
as κτίσις, not φύσις.   But for this very reason, the Jews failed
to understand the full significance of creation.   For it is not
by the production of an impotent world, without independence, and which melts like wax before His breath, but by the
production of a world which is endowed with freedom and
a limited measure of independent power, that the Creator
reveals His power as the power of wisdom and love.

§ 63.

Whilst Judaism had no eye for the cosmogony of creation,
Heathenism had no eye for the creative element in the cosmo-
gony.   Whilst the Mosaic account of creation begins with the
Spirit as that which is original, with the Spirit of God that

moved on the face of the waters, with the creative word, at whose command light and all the forms of life entered on existence ; the heathen writers of Greece begin with the dark and formless chaos, in whose womb all beings slumbered in the form of dreaming and fermenting germs, out of which they develop themselves by degrees in a dark and instinctive manner. They view the world exclusively as κτίσις, not as φύσις, as *natura*, not as *creatura*. With them all is *birth ;* there is no creation. Light, for example, does not come into existence through the word of the Creator, but develops itself out of darkness, through which it breaks its way as through a dark womb, where its rays were originally imprisoned. The kingdom of the Spirit and of freedom is not called forth out of the night of possibility by the creative command of love, by the eternal Father of spirits ; it fights its way by its own power out of the depth of the life of nature, emancipating itself from the blind forces of nature, and wresting from them their sceptre. Accordingly, we find that the nobler and more beautiful gods of Greek mythology developed themselves through the conquest and overthrow of the Titans, of the rough and formless forces of nature. In the mythology of the North, the myth of the *Yetten Ymer*, whom the *Ases* kill,[*] and out of whose monstrous body they build up the world, is an expression for the process by which a higher teleology broke through into existence, both in nature and in history. But being a cosmogony without creation, and being impregnated with theogony, the cosmogony of heathens became an incomplete, imperfect thing. Failing to recognise a true *beginning* of the world, they found it impossible to arrive at a true *completion* of the world ; they were unable to get beyond a half organization, a world born before its time, a teleology in which unreconciled antagonistic elements eternally ferment. As they knew nothing of an omnipotent creative Word that orders all things, their view of the world supplies the spectacle of an unclear mixture, an unreconciled twofoldness of spirit and nature, of providence and blind necessity, of idea and formless matter (ὕλη), of *system* and *chaos*. In this way the world of the Greeks was developed into a kingdom of beauty ; but their moral

* See § § 101, 120, and notes.

and spiritual being remained bound by the chains of the flesh ; and over the beautiful world of light hovered blind fate, threatening to cast down men and gods again into the old chaos. If the fear of the old chaos is to be thoroughly banished, if the world is to be seen to be in very deed an orderly system, not chaos but mind must be conceived as the primal, original being, and the creative Spirit must be held to have brooded in the beginning upon the face of the waters.

Observations.——A faint presentiment of the fact of the world being a CREATION is contained in the idea of the Father of the All, and of the completion of the world by Ragnarokr, which we find in the mythology of the North. The Northern mind thus gave expression to the premonition that the world has not merely a cosmogonic but also a creatural origin, that the riddle of life cannot be solved in a merely natural way, but demands a supernatural solution, that is, a solution through a CREATIVE teleology.

§ 64.

The ideas of creation and cosmogony are combined in the Johannic view of the divine Logos as the immanent principle of the world, by whom everything that has had an origin has come into existence. John teaches, on the one hand, that the existence of the world has its ground in a creative PRODUCTION ; on the other hand, that the world exists in virtue of a TRANSITION from not-being to being, through a growth, an arising, a birth, a *fieri*, a γίγνεσθαι. The world, therefore, has had a twofold beginning, a cosmogonic and a creative, a natural and a supernatural beginning. The cosmogonic or natural beginning is the relative, the finite one, which as such is split up into a SPORADIC variety. Every species of organization appears in a sporadic form; accordingly, considered from the cosmogonic or natural point of view, the world may be said to have had an innumerable number of beginnings; each of the infinitely many vital germs, which, so far as they are regarded exclusively from the naturalistic point of view, have their sole common centre of unity in *chaos*, constitutes a new beginning. But the innumerable natural

beginnings, all have their ground in the one, creative, supernatural beginning, in the will of the divine Logos, who has in
Himself the source of life and light, and causes the entire
variety of vital forces to issue forth to the exercise of the
power of free and independent motion.   It is only because
this supernatural beginning, this creative will, continues to
stir in the many finite beginnings ; and, in virtue of its free
omnipresence, permeates with light and activity the natural
development; that the agitation of chaos can be thoroughly
overcome, and the sporadic antagonistic elements be united to
form one organic, systematic, and harmonious whole.   The
world, therefore, at every moment of its existence, must be
regarded both as *natura,* or an organism developing itself,
and as *creatura,* or continuous revelation of the divine *will;*
and it is the *one,* solely *because* it is also *the other.*   Whilst,
then, we meet everywhere in the New Testament with the
idea of creation, we no less clearly find the idea of *organism*
and natural development.   As an instance of the latter idea,
we may refer to the important position occupied by the
" *grain of seed,*" in the New Testament chain of thought,
whether the subject under consideration be the first creation
or the second.   The New Testament recognizes no seed-corn
without creation, and no creation, in the natural world or in
the spiritual, without a seed-corn or germ.

Observations.—In regard to the efforts made by philosophy
    to solve the problem of the rise and origin of things, we
    remark that it is in all cases limited to the choice between
    the type of mythology and that of revelation.   For
    although we do not overlook the distinction between
    intuition and conception, there is no denying the fact,
    that all that is *essential* in the knowledge possessed by
    humanity, and the fundamental features of its consciousness
    of these things are embodied either in myths or in revela-
    tion.   Nothing more can be *positively* known concern-
    ing these things than is furnished by mythology and
    revelation, by the mythological representation of *chaos*
    and the Mosaic idea of the *creative Word,* the profounder
    significance of which was first opened up by John in the
    prologue to his gospel.   The one or the other of these
    two types is necessarily followed by every logically

self-consistent system of philosophy. The most recent philosophical systems have received their fructifying element principally from the mythological type, especially from the Greek view of the world, and have endeavoured to explain the origin of things in a purely cosmogonic way, to the exclusion of creation proper. But the philosophical image of the world that has thus been produced is marked by the same defects as its mythical prototype. No pantheistic system of philosophy, be it developed with ever so great dialectic skill, is able to work its way thoroughly out of the old heathenish chaos. If mind or spirit had not been the original of all things, if the creative Spirit had not moved at the beginning on the face of the waters, the chaotic masses would never have been reduced to order. If nature existed before spirit, the Spirit can never be more than a mere Demiurge, or architect who works with materials which he finds ready to hand. He is but the half-conscious spirit of the world who works his way more and more fully to light as culture and civilization advance, but is never able to complete his work, because he is himself bound to the antagonism which it is his mission to overcome—the antagonism, to wit, between the conscious and the unconscious. Under these conditions mind can never attain to supremacy over the dark natural ground or root of things which lies beyond self-consciousness. That Spirit only, who is able in a perfect sense to commence His work of creation, has power also to complete it.

§ 65.

So far as the cosmogony, and with the cosmogony the "birth of time," has its ground in a creative will, which is independent of all the conditions of time, the creation of the world may be described as *eternal*. But so far as the activity of the creating will is conditioned by the successive growth of the creature, the world may be said to have originated in time. Time is neither a mere form of subjective intuition, as Kant defined it, nor a " thing in itself."

It is the form—as truly objective as subjective—in which the *teleological* development of creation is accomplished ; in which the various momenta, which in the idea constitute one inner undivided unity, necessarily enter on partial and progressive existence. Beginning and result, reality and idea, are not coincident in time ; on the contrary, they are *outside* of each other. It is in this *outward* relation between the teleological momenta, and in the successive movement through which they are brought to form an inner unity, that time has its existence. As teleological time has had a beginning, so must it also have an end. For the goal of the development must finally be reached, and that which is fragmentary must be done away with by what is perfect. Time, too, owing as it does its existence to the antithesis and discord between the finite and the infinite, between the ideal and the real, between the variety of life and its unity, must also ultimately be absorbed into *eternity*, that is, into the complete unity of the finite and infinite, into the undivided fulness of life.

§ 66.

The Christian dogma of the creation of the world in time does not relate merely, as has been frequently said, to metaphysical subtleties, but has a profound religious and moral significance. The inmost kernel of the dogma, namely, is the idea of a creative *teleology*, and what is closely connected therewith, of an *historico-prophetical* view of mundane life as a development, which points forward to a *fulness of the times*. As the Mosaic narrative teaches us that the natural universe was completed in a series of days of creation, that is, epochs of time, so too must we say that the kingdom of freedom is brought into existence in a like series of days of creation. No sooner does one epoch in the history of the world come to an end, than a new creative day dawns—the words "let light be" are spoken anew by the divine creative Word. But as the natural creation attained its consummation and rest in man, so also does the spiritual creation move onwards through a series of creative days or epochs, to that eternal rest or Sabbath which has a significance not merely for creation, but also for the Creator. The teleological, or historico-prophetical view of time as the gradual *passage* of the creature into eternity, is incompatible on the one hand with the representation of mundane life as a constantly and uniformly recurring *cycle;* on the other hand, with the idea of an endless progress (*progressus in infinitum*).

Observations.—If we represent time to ourselves as a series that never runs out, without beginning or end, to which, whithersoever we look, whether forwards or backwards, we can see no limit, we cease to take a teleological view of it and things. The objection raised by some, that the world cannot have had a beginning, because every space of time must be supposed to have been preceded by another space, rests on a forgetfulness of teleological principles. Time that precedes teleological time is a mere abstraction, which has meaning only when we make the experiment of conceiving of " pure," that is, empty time, of a naked Chronos without determinate contents; or, so far as we conceive it to contain something, to contain pure matter, the infinite nebulous world, " the waters " (Gen. i. 2), on which the creative spirit had not yet moved with his plastic energy. This sort of time, gazing into which we seem to be gazing into an immense mass of mist and cloud, where there is no separation between light and darkness, where the momenta of existence by which time *is determined,* are not separated from each other, where there is no measure for time,—this may fairly be termed limitless, immeasurable time. But from the moment the words were spoken, " Let there be light," words which brought the teleological development into action and inaugurated the epochs of organic creation and the history of creation proper, we can only speak of definite time, time which is *measured* in God's eternal wisdom, by which all the periods of the world, all the aeons, are determined. (" Thou hast ordered all things in measure, number, and weight."—Wisdom xi. 21). That time, according to its true idea, is not limitless, is indicated symbolically in the Holy Scriptures by the numbers employed both in the account of the creation of the world and in the prophetic announcements of its destruction and renovation. We cannot really form a conception or attain an intellectual intuition of a development which has no whence and whither, no beginning, middle, and end. And as we are compelled to assume a first day upon which the periods of the organic creation were inaugurated, so also are we compelled to assume a last day ; understanding by it the transition of the creature into eternity, that is, into the true, God-filled time.

The proposition, "Time has no reality *for God*,"—a proposition which is not seldom advanced even by theologians who suppose themselves to have taken their stand on divine revelation—is incompatible with the idea of creation, and leads to *acosmism*. If time has no existence for God, creatures too whose development takes place in time, have no existence for God. If it is not unworthy of God to create a finite world at all, it cannot be unworthy of Him to accept the consequences which necessarily flow from such a creation. If it be His will to establish His kingdom in creation, He must take part in the vital development of the creature, He must subject Himself also to all the conditions involved in the idea of creation. Not only is the creature subject to growth, but creative love also has made its revelation of itself subject to growth, to development.* For although God in His own knowledge anticipates the development of the world and the result thereof; although to Him a thousand years are as one day ; love, that is, in other words, the *living* fellowship of the Creator with His creature would lack perfection, if the opposition between thought and actuality, purpose and execution, *promise and fulfilment*, had not also significance. For it cannot surely be immaterial with God whether He merely loves and knows his creation, without being known and loved by it ; or whether in knowing He is known, and in loving He is loved. We cannot conceive it possible that the Son of God should become, not merely ideally present in humanity, but actually man, that He should suffer, be crucified, and reconcile the world with the Father, in the fulness of the times, without supposing a profound movement to have taken place in God's own life of love. And the fact that the world lives and

---

* Compare Sibbern's " Speculative Kosmogonie,"—p. 113.

moves in God as eternal power and righteousness, and
that God as the source of sanctification and blessing is all
in all, must affect not merely creation, but God Himself
also. Taking, therefore, for our starting point, the idea of
creation as a free revelation of the love of God, we exclude
the dead conception of the divine unchangeableness, which
represents God as too exalted, too lofty, to come into contact with time, that is, with the actual life of His creatures ; too exalted, one ought indeed to say, to create at
all. We also equally exclude the idea of a God who is
Himself sunk and lost in the great stream of time. For
as God has subjected Himself to the conditions of *History*,
not from any necessity of nature, but from free love, He
remains at every moment of His mundane life the " Lord
of the Ages."

§ 67.

So far as the divine will brings into existence new *begin-*
nings, and inaugurates new stages of development and epochs,
—new days of the world,—God reveals Himself as the transcendent, the supra-mundane principle, as the supernatural
principle in nature, as the supra-historical principle in history.
For new stages of development, whether in nature or in history,—although the way is prepared for them, and their
appearance is conditioned by already existing forces,—can
never be explained by or derived solely from such forces. In
nature we find no direct transition from the inorganic to the
organic ; by no continuation of the process of self-development can the animal world ever produce a man ; nor can a
new epoch in the history of the world,—the epoch in which
a new and essentially higher form of the ideal of the freedom
of the human race finds realization,—be shown to be the
mere prolongation and onward movement of the preceding epoch. Interruptions of the unfruitful "*progressus*
in infinitum" are in all cases due to a movement from the
centre, to an act of creative freedom, out of whose fulness new
beginnings of life are established in nature and fruitful
momenta in the history of the world. The movement in
question cannot take its rise in the creature itself, it is an
act of God in nature, and an act of God in human freedom.
But the divine will does not merely institute the beginning

of higher forms of life in nature and history ; God continues also His activity through the medium of the activity of the creature as *regulated by law ;* He confines His activity within the limits of the *laws* of development, of the manifold variety of finite causes and their reciprocal action.   So far, His workings are not transcendent, but immanent.   It is this antithesis between the transcendent and immanent activity of God that gives rise to the distinction between creation and *sustainment.* Creative work passes on into sustaining activity so far as the creative will assumes the form of *law,* so far as it works at every stage of development under the form of the *order* of the natural and spiritual world, in, with, and through the laws and forces of the world.*   But the creative power again breaks forth out of the sustaining activity, passes out beyond the order of the lower world, constitutes itself the principle of a higher mundane order, to which the first stands in the mere transient relation of a means or a basis.   Hence this higher order is a *miracle* relatively to the lower.   The animal is a miracle for the plant ; man is a miracle for the whole of nature.   For the true idea of a miracle is that of an effect in nature which cannot be explained by the laws of nature, which can only be explained as the result of a thoroughly *original* movement from the divine centre.   Divine providence unites and glorifies the creative and sustaining activities ; for it involves the idea of the goal and perfection of the world.   But as the ultimate end of the world is first revealed in man, the true character of providence can never be known till the position of man in the world is understood.

Observations.——The antithesis between creation and sustainment shows itself not merely in the relation of the different stages to each other, but also within one and the same stage of development.   For so far as we regard the individual creature as a continuation of the series of development of the genus or species, it is merely an expression of the *sustainment* of the said genus or species. So far, however, as the individual creature is not a mere repetition of what had gone before, but something new and original ; so far is it a revelation of the *creative*

---

* Gen. viii. 22 ; "While the earth remaineth, seed-time and harvest, and cold and heat, and summer and winter, and day and night, shall not cease."

activity of God. The less the independence possessed by
a creature,—the more destitute it is of peculiar characteristics,—the more inclined shall we feel to regard it as a
mere link in the maintenance of the species. The more
independent and free, on the contrary, a creature is, the
more truly can we say of it, it is an individual, it has
life in itself; the more shall we feel called upon to see in
it the finger of the Creator, and to regard it, not as a
product of nature, but as a product of God.

MAN AND THE ANGELS.

§ 68.

That part of the creation which we call nature attains its
culminating point in man, in whom God and the creature
meet and become united. It is for this reason that Christian
thought has contemplated man both as a microcosm and as a
microtheism, as an image of the world and an image of God.
But besides man, Revelation takes notice of another class of
spiritual beings, namely, THE ANGELS. Whether the utterances
of the Holy Scriptures respecting the angels be regarded as
an expression for a higher cosmical empiricism, or as a religious
symbolism ; in either case they express the truth, that man is
the central point of the creation. The angels are to be regarded
as among the *presumed conditions* for the existence of man ;
as would appear indeed from the Scriptures,* according to
which they shone like spiritual morning-stars at the very
beginning of the Creation, and before the appearance of man
upon the Earth.

According to the intimations which Scripture and ecclesiastical teaching afford us respecting the nature and essence of
angels, we must represent them to our minds as pure spirits,
and not, like men, attached to bodies and limited by the conditions of space. Their home is heaven, but not heaven in
the astronomical meaning of the expression, but rather heaven
in the intellectual and spiritual sense. If, on the one hand,
they are entirely unshackled by the conditions of space, just

---

* "When the morning-stars sang together, and all the sons of God shouted
for joy."—Job xxxviii. 7.

as little, on the other, are they subjected to the conditions of time. An angel cannot become old. Youth and age are antitheses which have no meaning as applied to them. Although they have an origin, and indeed may be said to have a history in so far as a falling off from God has taken place in the angel-world, yet have they no history in the sense of a continuous development, a continuous progress and advance to a state of maturity. For, from the beginning of their existence, the angels have ranged themselves either on the side of God or against him, and it is only in so far as they enter into the world of mankind that they have any part in a progressive history. Passing out of that heavenly kingdom in which the good angels sing the praises of the Most High, the angels enter the world of man, and work as spirits of light for the furtherance of the kingdom of God upon earth.

If we now combine these characteristics in one general view—characteristics which the older theologians have deduced from the Scriptures, and strive to grasp them and place them clearly before our mind—we shall find that the world of angels will almost involuntarily suggest to us the world of ideas. The whole description of the angels in its fundamental features conforms exactly to the Ideas, those intermediate existences, those mediators between God and the real world, those bringers of light, who bear their messages from God to men, those heavenly hosts, who encircle the throne of the Most High, to reflect his glory back upon himself. It is not ideas as they are presented to our abstract thought, but rather ideas as they are presented to our intuition as living powers and as active spirits ($\pi\nu\epsilon\dot{\nu}\mu\alpha\tau\alpha$) which are to be regarded as angels. The Apostle Paul calls the angels principalities and powers,* and he thus describes them as reigning in certain definite departments of the economy of God, as rulers to whom different regions in the Creation are subjected; and when we regard them from this point of view, we

---

* "For by him were all things created, that are in heaven, and that are in earth, visible and invisible, whether they be thrones or dominions, or principalities, or powers: all things were created by him and for him."—Col. i. 16. "Far above all principality, and power, and might, and dominion, and every name that is named, not only in this world, but also in that which is to come." —Eph. i. 21.

are naturally reminded of the gods of mythology. What philosophy calls ideas, and mythology calls gods, receive in revelation the name of angels ; but it is the peculiar characteristic of the angels to be ever active for the kingdom of God. Ideas, the divinities of life, operate as angels then, and then only, when their tendency is, not in the direction of the kingdom of this world, but in that of the kingdom of God, as their main object—when they are mediators for the kingdom of holiness.

Observations.—In Deut. xxxii. 8-9, we find in the Septuagint: "When the Most High divided to the nations their inheritance, when he separated the sons of men, he set the bounds of the heathen according to the number of the angels of God, but he himself took up his abode in Israel." This passage contains an intimation of the tendency suggested above. It was in Israel, therefore, that the Lord himself took up his abode, but over the heathens he placed his angels. It was not in his immediate personal presence, but only through finite mediators, through subordinate deities, that the Highest revealed himself in heathendom ; and it was his goodness to heathendom, that, although it was left without GOD in the world in the highest sense of that name, it was still not left without ideas. It was through the instrumentality of ideas that God revealed himself to the heathens, although the heathens did not acknowledge *Him* to whom the world of ideas belonged. In so far, therefore, as the deities of mythology may be regarded as the ministering spirits of that Providence which preserves the human race from sinking into an utterly unspiritual state, in so far as they operated in the fallen race as a *protecting* and *maintaining* power, until the time was fully come in which God decreed to reveal himself as the God of the heathens also, to this extent must they be regarded as angels, even from the higher point of view which is occupied by revelation. But in so far as these deities are idols, in so far as they draw men away from the true God, and incite them to fight against the kingdom of God, to this extent they are demons. It is in this light that

I

they are regarded by the apostles* and the first teachers
of the Church. For the hostility of the gods necessarily
ensued upon the first appearance of Christianity ; a war
between the gods of heathenism, and the one true God.
It will moreover be evident at once from the foregoing
remarks, that the fundamental conception which must be
taken as the original starting point is the conception of
powers and spirits. Whether these are to be regarded
as angels or as demons, depends entirely upon the relation in which they stand to the kingdom of God. And
as heathenism has a side which is turned towards the
kingdom of God, as well as one which is turned away
from it, we are perfectly justified in asserting, in the
language of revelation, that angels as well as demons
have been active agents in heathenism.

§ 69.

If we start from powers and spirits as the fundamental
conception, we shall see at once that the question respecting
the *personality* of angels must receive different answers.
For all that is of an unfixed and dialectical character contained in the conception of " spirit," is equally applicable to
the conception of " angel." From the tempest which executes
the behests of the Lord, to the Seraph who stands before His
throne, there exist a very great diversity and variety of
angels. There are many sorts of spirits under the heavens,
and for this very reason also many degrees of spirituality and
spiritual independence ; and we may therefore very properly
assert that the angels are divided into classes, without being
obliged on that account to acknowledge the further development of this thought, as we find it in the work of the
Areopagite, respecting the *heavenly hierarchy.* If we contemplate the angels in their relation to the conception of personality, we may say : there are powers, whose spirituality is
so far from being independent, that they possess only a *represented* personality ; in short, are only personifications. Of such
a character are the tempests and flames,† which execute the
commands of the Lord, and the angel who troubled the water of

---

* " Ye cannot drink the cup of the Lord and the cup of devils: ye cannot be
partakers of the Lord's table, and of the table of devils."—1 Cor. x. 21.

† " Who maketh his angels spirits, his ministers a flaming fire."—Ps. civ. 4.

the pool of Bethesda,* in whom we recognize nothing more than the personification of one of the powers of nature. There exist other powers in the creation which possess a higher degree of spirituality, an intermediate state of existence between personification and personality. Under this category may be classed the spiritual powers in history, as for instance the spirits of nations and the deities of mythology. He is but a very superficial thinker who can recognize in the spirit of a people nothing more than a mere personification, a mere generic *expression* for the aims and aspirations of individuals. If, on the one hand, we must not hypostasize such a national spirit, or attribute to it an independent existence, just as little, on the other, shall we be justified in regarding it as a mere personification ; for whatever can impart soul and spirit to other things, must also in a certain degree contain *spirit in itself.* It is only a Sadducean view of mythology which can desire to contemplate its deities as the mere products of human imagination, as mere personifications of human feelings and passions, without attributing to them a certain kind of spirituality of their own, quite independent of the human individuals who may feel themselves governed, animated, or inspired by them. But if in this manner we find powers in history, which hover in the region lying between personality and personification, it is no less certain that revelation recognizes a third class of cosmical powers which constitute a free and personal spiritual kingdom. Our Lord and His apostles have borne testimony to this representation among their followers, by whom its correctness had been expressly called in question, in as much as the Sadducees asserted that there was neither angel nor spirit.† If to this assertion, which we are constantly meeting at every turn, we oppose the authority of the scriptural doctrine, we must at the same time observe, that no speculation will ever be able to decide how far there may be powers existing in the creation, possessing such a degree of spirit-

---

* " For an angel went down at a certain season into the pool, and troubled the water : whosoever, then, first after the troubling of the water stepped in, was made whole of whatsoever disease he had."—John v. 4.

† " For the Sadducees say that there is no resurrection, neither angel nor spirit ; but the Pharisees confess both."—Acts xxiii. 8.

uality in themselves, as to be able to serve their Creator, or to resist His will, with a personal consciousness of the act. Speculation can neither affirm nor deny anything on this point, but should rather take to heart the words of the poet : " there are more things in heaven and earth than are dreamt of in your philosophy." Revelation tells us, that at the beginning of the creation the shouts of joy of the children of God resounded at the same time as the songs of the morning stars ;* and when in our daily prayer we say, " Thy will be done on earth, as it is in heaven," our thoughts will naturally revert to the heavenly hosts, the perfect instruments for the carrying out of the holy will of the Father.

§ 70.

If we now endeavour to determine the relation between the nature of angels and human nature with a somewhat greater degree of precision, it will be evident that in one respect the angels are higher than men, whereas in another they occupy an inferior position : higher because they are powers and energies, the strong, the mighty ones,† who execute the commandments of the Lord, elevated above all earthly limitations : inferior, because they bear the same relation to man as the universal to the microcosmical ; for which reason they are also represented as spirits waiting and tending upon human life, as a firmament of stars ministering to the life of earth in its historical convulsions. Although the angel, in relation to man, is the more powerful spirit, man's spirit is nevertheless the richer and the more comprehensive. For the angel in all his power is only the expression of a single one of all those phases which man in the inward nature of his soul, and the richness of his own individuality, is intended to combine into a complete and perfect microcosm. If we contemplate the revelations respecting the angels in the Scriptures, we can obtain no definite outline of their personality, but only a vague and hazy picture which always remains enshrouded in the undefinable brightness and splendour of their spirituality, while, on the other hand,

---

* " When the morning-stars sang together, and all the sons of God shouted for joy."—Job xxxviii. 7.

† " Bless the Lord, ye his angels, that excel in strength, that do his commandments, hearkening unto the voice of his word."—Ps. ciii. 20.

Christ and the apostles stand before us as clear and sharply defined figures. It is precisely because the angels are only spirits, but not souls, that they cannot possess the same rich existence as man, whose soul is the point of union in which spirit and nature meet. This high privilege, which man enjoys above the angels, finds its expression in the Scriptures, where it is said that the Son of God was made not angel, but man. He does not take on Him the nature of angels, but He takes on Him the seed of Abraham.* He was willing to unite Himself with nature alone, which is the central point of the creation. The saints will judge the angels,† in conjunction with Christ they will judge all the powers of existence, all the energies and spirits which have moved under the heavens. When the apostles speak of the angels as desiring to look into the mystery of the redemption, in order that the wisdom of God in the gospel might be made known to principalities and powers,‡ the nature of these spirits is expressly stated as that of *witnesses* to the glory of man, while they themselves cannot, like man, be made partakers of Christ in any real manner. As man is that point in which the spiritual and corporeal worlds are united, and as humanity is the particular form in which the Incarnation has taken place, it follows that men are capable of entering into the fullest and most perfect union with God, while angels, on account of their pure spirituality, can only be made partakers of the majesty of God, but cannot, in the same immediate manner as man, be made partakers of His revelation of love, the mystery of the Incarnation, and the sacramental union connected with it.

§ 71.

If we pursue our investigations still further, and inquire into the nature of the activity of angels in human affairs, we

---

* "For verily he took not on him the nature of angels, but he took on him the seed of Abraham."—Heb. ii. 16.

† "Know ye not that we shall judge angels? how much more things that pertain to this life?"—1 Cor. vi. 3.

‡ "Unto whom it was revealed, that not unto themselves, but unto us they did minister the things, which are now reported unto you by them that have preached the gospel unto you with the Holy Ghost sent down from heaven, which things the angels desire to look into."—1 Pet. i. 12. "To the intent that now unto the principalities and powers in heavenly places might be known by the Church, the manifold wisdom of God."—Eph. iii. 10.

shall find intimations that they are the ministering spirits of
Providence.   Just as the Son of God is the primary Mediator between God and man, the angels are relative mediators,
and appear especially as ministering spirits for Christ and
the kingdom of Christ.   Christ's entrance into the world
and departure from it, His birth, resurrection, and ascension,
are all accompanied by the ministry of angels; and clear intimations are to be found in the Book of the Acts, that angels have
also been co-operative in the extension of Christianity.   Roman
Catholicism has developed the doctrine of the active interfer-
ence of angels to such an extent as to cast the mediatorial
office of Christ completely into the shade ; but later Protestantism, by speaking of angels as if they had long ago entirely
ceased to take any active part in human affairs, has been no
less guilty of taking a one-sided view of this question.   When
Christ says, "Hereafter ye shall see heaven open, and the
angels of God ascending and descending upon the Son of
man" (John i. 51), we are to understand this as signifying,
that through the whole course of history angels will continue
to be active ; that when Christ comes with His kingdom,
"ministering spirits" will be ready, in the fullest and most
comprehensive sense of the expression.   In our days, indeed,
the belief in angels has been too much thrust out of sight,
even in the consciousness of believers ; but in spite of this,
the generally accepted representation of the " powers of this
earthly life" offers a point of connection to which this belief
may be attached, and through which it may attain a firmer
footing, a representation indeed which is constantly expressed
in a worldly sense, but which it is of great importance to
conceive also in a sacred one.   When we give utterance to
this representation in the light of the Christian doctrine of
Providence, we have already entered upon the ground apper-
taining to the belief in angels.   For the essential and distinguishing marks in the conception of an angel are not
personality, but spirit and power, operating as instruments
for the fulfilment of the holy designs of Providence in the
lives of men.   May we not then in this sense assert,
that the angels of the nations were active among them in
the introduction of Christianity ?   May we not say that
the spirits, the ideas, to the dominion of which the people
were of course subjected, have been the natural approaches

for the admission of holiness,—mediators, who have prepared the way of the Lord in the heart of the people, and have thus been the determining conditions of the particular adoption of Christianity by that people ?   And when Christ says that He will send out His angels on the day of judgment to call together His elect from the four corners of the world,* does not this signify, that just as the demoniacal powers will make their influence felt, more especially in the later periods of history, so also will all good powers display their might and sovereignty by leading men to Christ, and by striving to bring about the consummation, that the separation between light and darkness be completed.   On that day will the Lord deny the wicked, not only before His Father, but before all the holy angels.†   The ungodly shall be deserted, not only by God, but by all the gods, by all good powers.

Observations.—Schleiermacher is of opinion that there is no essential difference between the belief in angels and the belief in the existence of rational beings in other planets, inasmuch as the angels owe their origin to no other source than the necessity which man feels for peopling the universe with rational beings different from himself. But this manner of regarding the subject rests upon an utterly erroneous conception of the nature of angels.   For even if we accept the very doubtful hypothesis, that there are also inhabitants upon the other heavenly bodies, we can only imagine them to ourselves as in some measure analogous to man, consequently as rational beings, whose existence is a certain form of union of body and spirit ; and these individuals, therefore, will again require angels, and stand under the influence of universal powers.   On every heavenly body in which we image a human race to exist, the metaphysical opposition between heaven and earth will also manifest itself, and consequently the opposition between a human life moving on in a succes-

---

* "And he shall send his angels with a great sound of a trumpet, and they shall gather together his elect from the four winds, from one end of heaven to the other."—Matt. xxiv. 21.

† "Whosoever therefore shall be ashamed of me and of my words, in this adulterous and sinful generation, of him also shall the Son of man be ashamed, when he cometh in the glory of his Father with the holy angels."—Mark viii. 38.

sion of historical events, and those universal powers and energies of Providence to which human life stands in a certain relation, will be apparent.

MAN CREATED IN THE IMAGE OF GOD.

§ 72.

While the angels are pure spirits, and the objects of the natural world are imprisoned as it were in a state of unconscious corporeity, man, on the other hand, is the free, personal unity of spirit and nature, a *spiritual soul,* which is not held captive in corporeity, like natural objects, but intended to manifest itself with freedom through the instrumentality of the body, as a temple of the Spirit.   In this temple the whole corporeal world finds its central point, illuminating and glorifying everything, just in the same manner as the spiritua-world collects its rays in the inner being of man, as in a focus in which all things converge.   The dignity of man is entirelyl lost sight of in the heathen view, which endeavours to explain the manner in which he first came into existence as purely cosmogonical, and conceives man as nothing more than the spirit of nature, which has come to a consciousness of itself.   But the view of man's nature as presented in revelation is, that he has been created after the image of God, and is as copy, and in a state of created dependence, what the divine Logos is as pattern, and as itself creative.   And it is only upon this supposition that we can explain that man, although a limb of the great body of nature, although unwinding himself from out of the swaddling-bands of the natural life, although subject to the natural laws for the development of his species, is nevertheless free of nature, and free of the world, and that in every human individual there exists something unconditioned, by means of which he is independent of the entire macrocosm.

Observations.—The heathen view of man is very significantly expressed in the mythical Sphinx, in which the human countenance rises out of the savage form of an animal. It is the cosmical fermentation which is represented in this mixture of animal and man, of nature and spirit.

Man here endeavours to disentangle himself from the coil of natural life, but he is chained to it, and imprisoned, and not allowed to rise to free and independent human existence. As is well known, it was the sphinx which proposed to men the riddle; What animal is that, which in the morning goes on all fours, in the day-time on two legs, and in the evening on three? And although it was the Greek who solved the riddle, when he answered that it was man, yet did he by no means succeed in finding a true answer to the riddle of liberty. For even Greek humanity itself may be represented under the image of a sphinx, the upper part of which is a beautiful virgin, a form fair to behold, but the lower part of which is a monster. While Greek humanity presents us with an image of freedom in its social and moral life, in its art and in its science, this image of freedom arises out of the dark ground of its natural life. In the background of the bright world of freedom stands blind fate, an evidence that man is not yet emancipated from the macrocosm. And if the Greek was unable to solve the riddle of freedom, the Roman Stoic also met with no greater success. For the Stoic only endeavours to get out of the difficulty by sacrificing himself to the great monster with the defiance of resignation, with the courage of despair. From whatever side we look at Heathenism, it always appears that man has only the world for his principle, and therefore can never in reality be free from the world. It is true, the free spirit is seen to emerge from out of the natural life, just as the countenance of the sphinx rises from the animal body, but it never really becomes free. It is only when man, the creative freedom (*libertas liberans*) takes the holy will of love for his principle, only when he is the free and immortal organ of this will, that he is free with regard to the world, free with regard to nature, although himself constituting a member of the world.

§ 73.

The conception of humanity therefore consists in this, that two principles, the cosmical and the holy, are intimately combined together in man into a free and personal unity. It is the vocation of man to be lord of the earth; but as a free organ for the holy will of the Creator, it is his vocation to glorify and raise his freedom into a dependence on God, his life in the world into a life in God, his ideal of the world into the ideal of the kingdom of God. The conception of man is by no means exhausted by the definition, that man is a free rational being. His humanity is founded on this, that as a free rational being he is a religious being, that his reason and his freedom are determined by the laws of conscience. Conscience is the seal and pledge of man's freedom and inward independence of the universe ; but it is so only in so far as it is also the token of his dependence upon his Creator. The nature of man in his relation to conscience is such, that he is lord in so far only as he is at the same time servant,— that he is in spirit and in truth his own, in so far only as he is in spirit and in truth the Lord's also.

Observations.—The world of modern culture regards it as its greatest honour that it has developed the idea of humanity, and that its leaders and teachers, its thinkers and poets, are heroes of humanity. Humanity has become the universal watchword of modern times, a synonyme for *freedom*, and *all-sided* development, in opposition to bondage and barbarism. Indeed, with a great many of our contemporaries every positive characteristic in this conception has been entirely lost ; and it has been very aptly remarked that the modern world, instead of the old saints of Catholicism, has procured for itself a new saint of its own, namely the *humanus*, whom it seeks after at all times, among all nations, and in all religions and churches. But in this *humanus* we are only too often reminded of heathenism, rather than of man created in God's image.

If we wish to institute a somewhat closer comparison between the Christian and the heathen conceptions of humanity, we may start from the position that the opposite of humanity is *barbarism*. But what is barbarism ? Barbarism is not only opposed to *culture*, is not only a want of education, but is just as much opposed to a true uncorrupted *nature;* it is indeed a perversion of the original relations of nature. In history, in the moral world, barbarism is precisely that which *chaos* is in nature, a disorder in the fundamental elements of human nature

Heathenism considered in its cosmological relations can never get beyond the old chaos, and similarly, in its anthropological and ethical relations, it is equally unable to liberate itself from the *principle* of barbarism, because it is tainted with disorder and confusion in the ethical foundations supplied by nature. *Culture* is the highest expression for the heathen humanity, which overlooks the fact, that human liberty itself requires to be cultivated by divine grace,—requires to be made free by a higher *libertas liberans.* Heathen humanity develops only the autonomic, the independent element in human nature, it seeks only to make the earth subject to itself, and man the centre in a kingdom of world-ideals. The relationship of dependence arising from creation, the recipient, submissive relationship to the divine love, the yearning after God as a need of man's nature, and the holy liberty arising from it, are all wanting in the heathen humanity. The barbarism of it appears in this, that there is a whole region in the soul, which lies fallow and uncultivated, that the noblest seed of the spirit does not grow in this soil, that the deepest feelings and emotions of the mind, religious humility and love, divine sorrow, and joy in God, cannot germinate in the coldness and hardness of the heart. Instead of these genuine human feelings a wilderness of coarse feelings and profane thoughts grows up in this heathen world of cultivation, and is but very ineffectually concealed by the glorious blossoms of art and science. Many men of cultivation in modern times, display a certain coarseness of feeling with reference to matters of religion, and to the more delicate moral relationships, which is little in harmony with their scientific and æsthetic culture. Greek humanity, while it quite ignores all dependence on the Creator, cannot preserve itself from lapsing into a very pernicious dependence on the world. And, however high it may place the human individual, it does not escape entertaining barbarous views of the human individual touching his glorification. This barbarism has manifested itself in our days in the denial of the immortality of the soul, as also in the position, that it is the highest vocation of the individual to become the organ of the idea or of the spirit of the world. This

world-spirit does not trouble itself about the individual,
but only about the work which it intends to perform
through his instrumentality. The worth of the individual
is, therefore, only to be estimated according to the extent
to which he is adapted for executing the works and performing the acts which have to be executed and performed
in the name of the idea; according, therefore, to his genius
and talent; and great *genius* is the highest representation
of humanity. But this is precisely the nature of barbarism,—to estimate the humanity of the individual according to his talents and his deeds, instead of according to his
conscience and his *will;* to make the personality merely
a vehicle for the talent, the will merely a vehicle for the
act, instead of making the act a means for developing
the inward man. This same barbarism manifests itself
in such propositions as the following: every individual is
nothing more than the work which he does, and his significance is precisely equal to what he accomplishes and
makes known during his phenomenal existence.*

Both Roman Catholicism and Protestantism acknowledge
man to have been created in the image of God, but the
idea of humanity is very differently viewed in the two
confessions; because the relationship between nature and
grace is differently conceived. Catholicism regards grace
as a *donum superadditum,* as a higher gift which the
Almighty added after He had created man; but, at the
same time, it maintains that human nature would still
have been a true human nature even without Divine
grace. Protestantism teaches, on the other hand, that it is
an essential part of the conception of human nature not to
be nature entirely left to itself, not to be the so-called
"merely human," but for the human to manifest the
Divine, in liberty to manifest grace. The barbarism
of Catholicism consists in its combining the two fundamental factors of human life in an outward and
mechanical manner, a barbarism which manifests itself
not only in its dogmas, but also in its life, in as much as
throughout Catholicism we meet everywhere with a

* Compare Zeuthen's Humanität, Betragtet fra ent Christeligt Standpunct,
p. 19.

certain dualism between the Divine and the human, the holy and the profane, the religious and the moral, the aims and objects of the church, and the aims and objects of the world. Protestantism, on the contrary, proposes to itself as the problem of true humanity, that the relation of man to God, and his relation to the world, should permeate each other in a free and spiritual manner.

§ 74.

When we assert that the Divine image or the essence of humanity must be recognised as present in every human individual, this must not be understood to signify that human individuals are distinguished from each other only externally and with reference to differences arising from sense and time, while the inward man is the same in each individual. If the essence of the individual were only the *universal* abstract man, if it possessed no inward and eternal *peculiarity*, it would be nothing more than a meaningless repetition of the genus, but no real individual. Just, therefore, as each human individual must be regarded as a link in the succession of the development of the genus, it is also at the same time a particular form of the Divine image, a particular and a new point of manifestation of the Divine will. These considerations supply the answer to the question, whether human individuals are *born* or *created*,—the question respecting the soundness of Traducianism or Creatianism. The truth to which Traducianism may lay claim consists in . this : that every human individual is a product of the natural activity of the species, just as this is determined by the peculiarities of the race, the family, and the parents. But the truth of Creatianism lies in this: that the universal natural activity, by means of which the species propagates itself, and new souls are formed, that this mysterious natural activity constitutes the instrument and means for the individualizing activity of the Creator, that each single human being therefore is a new manifestation of the Divine will, which thus prepares for itself a peculiar form of its own image. Each of these views is only true, when it affirms its own antithesis. According to the one-sided view presented by Traducianism, the individual is reduced into a condition of utter dependence upon the *species*, and its whole existence is thus entirely determined by the preceding series. An eternal particularity, an infinite germ of freedom is perfectly inconceivable on the hypothesis of Traducianism, because the latter can never get beyond the notion of the *species*, and the *naturalistic* conception of the individual which is implied in it. According to a one-sided Creatianism, on the other hand, every individual proceeds from the hand of his Creator as pure and undefiled as the first Adam ; and the apparent dependence of the individuals upon the preceding members of the series, the notion of inherited qualities, and especially the phenomenon of natural *sinfulness*, become quite inexplicable. The Scriptures acknowledge both points of view——"Behold, I was shapen in iniquity; and in sin did my mother conceive me " (Ps. li. 5), are the words of the Psalmist confirming Traducianism. But at another place the Psalmist also bears witness, that the providential eye of the Creator watches over the birth of the individual, when he says: "I will praise Thee; for I am fearfully and wonderfully made." "My substance was not hid from Thee when I was made in secret, and curiously wrought in the lowest parts of the earth. Thine eyes did see my substance, yet being imperfect" (Ps. cxxxix. 14-16). And the Lord says to Jeremiah, "I *formed* thee in the belly" (Jer. i. 5). Even if it remains a mystery, how in the secret laboratory wherein man is formed nature and creation merge in one another,——how the activity of the Creator, and the conditions of nature mutually set limits to each other,——for birth has its secrets even as death has,——still must each individual be regarded at once from the point of view offered by Traducianism, and also from that of Creatianism, or, in other words, as a continuation and a member in the series, and also as a new and original beginning. We cannot assign any other signification to the representation of the *pre-existence* of souls than this: that souls have pre-existed as *possibilities* in the depths of the Divine creative power, a position which may easily be reconciled with another, namely, that souls have been laid down as possibilities in the depths of the nature of the species.

Observations.——If in the contemplation of the creation of the world generally, we have advanced the position, that the world must be regarded from the point of view of natural development as well as from that of the creation, this position meets with its highest application in *man*. Man is the most perfect creature, because he is the most perfect *nature*, and he is the most perfect nature, because he is the most perfect *creature*. He is the most perfect nature, because he is the individual, or nature in itself ; but it is precisely for this very reason, that no other nature points so directly to the Creator as its originator, for the individual cannot be explained out of a merely general activity of nature, which can only produce individuals in semblance or patterns. " That is a nature," is the expression we use, when we wish to say of anybody, that he is a real man, a genuine individual who has originality and character in his soul, and cannot therefore be understood by general categories of species and kind, but by the study of himself alone. But to whatever extent it can be predicated of any one that he is a nature in himself, just to that same extent does he appear before us as a *new* and original point of commencement in the series, that is to say, just so far as he appears as *natura*, to the same extent does he also appear as *creatura*. Now, although every human individual must be contemplated as well from the point of view of creation as from that of propagation, there is a relative difference which nevertheless must not be disregarded in the contemplation of human individuals, a difference which is the same as that which we have treated above as the difference between creation and preservation. The more primitive and the more original human individuals are, the more readily do they allow of being conceived from the point of view of creation, and the more does the question respecting the manner of their first coming into existence, admit of an explanation on the Creatian hypothesis. On the other hand, the less primitive they are, the more do they appear as mere shoots or offsets from that which has preceded them, and therefore only as members or links in the preservation of the species, of the people and of the family, just as also in the economy of the life of the community, they appear as if intended only to preserve, continue, and prolong, what others have commenced and established. The representation of the divine activity of the Creator then takes a far more subordinate place, and the Traducian explanation obtains the pre-eminence, always remembering, however, that this opposition is only a relative one, because we must always presuppose a *creation*-moment in every individual, if it is to be a true individual in the image of God, and not a mere individual in semblance. It is just this Creatianism in the sense given above, by which the creation of the world of mankind is distinguished from that of the world of nature. Strictly speaking, it is only the genera and species which are created in nature. Individuals come into existence through continued Traducianism, while the individualizing activity of the Creator manifests itself here only in hasty and prefigurative intimations. Every human individual on the other hand, contains in itself an eternal idiosyncrasy, and therein, a talent given and entrusted to it by God, which, although remaining in many individuals in a latent and inactive condition, must nevertheless be supposed as existent, if they are to be regarded as creatures created in the image of God.

Although there are many individuals in whom the Creatian-moment is not to be discerned, it nevertheless forces its necessary recognition upon us through the teleological contemplation of history. If, for instance, we cast a glance at the groups of talents which rise upon the horizon of history at critical epochs, like new clusters of stars, and which are evidently ordained to solve the problem of a particular age, we shall find that the original natural destination of these individuals can only be explained on the supposition of Creatianism. For even if we were to assume that talents are welling forth in one uninterrupted stream from the fruitful womb of nature, —an assumption, by the way, in direct contradiction to the law of economy which history teaches us in this respect,—it would still be a matter of chance *what* talents Nature produced at any given epoch, because every historical period is perfectly indifferent to Nature, considered purely as such. On the other hand, the greater the influence which real talent exercises upon its time, the more evident does it appear, that it was ordained precisely for this particular historical period, that indeed, as

the Prophet says, it was already fashioned in the womb
for its peculiar work. According to purely pantheistic
views, it is nothing but the historical spirit of the age
which causes the individuals to become what they are.
But even if we grant that this view is a correct expression for one side of the problem, it is still necessary to
add, that the new period, the new historical dawn first
breaks in upon us in great *individuals*, and that these
bringers of light, these children of the dawn, are not mere
empty vessels, which can be filled with any sort of spirit
indifferently, not mere clay out of which the particular
epoch can mould whatever it may please ; but that they
are original natures with a particular stamp upon them
from the first, which contain within themselves the source
of a determined form of activity, by which they themselves determine the form and colour of their time. But
in this manner we find ourselves obliged to assume Providence as operating not only in the world of consciousness, but also in the hidden fundamental nature of the
species. For, if we regard Providence only as a *governing*
providence in history, but not at the same time as a
creating Providence in nature,—if we do not recognize
the comprehensive signification of the words spoken by
the Lord to the Prophet : " Before I formed thee in the
belly, I knew thee ; and before thou camest forth out of
the womb I sanctified thee, and I ordained thee a prophet unto the nations" (Jer. i. 5), how are we to explain
this coincidence between talent and the problems of history ? If it is only a blind genius of nature who in its
hidden workshop forms the tools of history, how comes
it, that it never makes mistakes, producing a Dante
when history requires a Luther ? Whence comes it that
it does not produce philosophical and contemplative
natures, when history requires practical and heroic
natures, and *vice versa ?* The harmony between the
natural vocation of individuals and the requirements of
history admits of no other sufficient explanation (*ratio
sufficiens*) than that to be found in the conception of a
creative Providence, which wields a power at once over
both nature and history.

K

In the meantime, however, we cannot help presuming the presence of the creative force, even where it cannot be recognized. Christ says : " A woman when she is in travail hath sorrow, because her hour is come : but as soon as she is delivered of the child, she remembereth no more the anguish for joy that a man is born into the world," John xvi. 21. This joy that a man is born into the world is conceivable as a spiritual joy on the hypothesis of Creatianism alone. The spiritual joy at the birth of a child is not merely the joy at the preservation and continuation of the species or family, but the joy that a really *new* existence has come into the world, an existence which has never been before, and never will come again. But that there exists a relative difference between different individuals follows at once from the very conception of a kingdom of man. For a kingdom must contain a variety of differences and degrees. The activity of the Creator cannot manifest the same abundance at every point ; and is, moreover, subjected at every point to the determined conditions of the relatively independent activity of nature, or of the Traducian force. Even here then the conception of *election* already manifests itself—a conception which will appear again in a higher form in the kingdom of grace—for even in the kingdom of nature we must already begin to distinguish between the elect and favoured natures, and those which, relatively speaking, have been overlooked and placed in the shade. But it must be especially observed here, that this NATURAL ELECTION, as we will designate it, decides nothing respecting the personal merit of individuals. The personality of man depends on the free union of talent with will, and we here regard this union only as a possibility. From which it follows, that he who has in himself the greater possibility, is by no means on that account the greater personal reality ; on the contrary in this respect, as Christianity teaches, the last may become the first, and he who is faithful over a few things may be placed higher than he who is unfaithful over many things. And hence it also follows, that the importance of a talent considered merely with reference to its influence *on the course of historical events* is by no means a measure of its ethical worth ; because it is easy to imagine the development of a talent up to a certain degree of activity as necessarily determined by nature, and of a merely instinctive character, without its being sanctified by the operation of the will.

What has here been stated with reference to individuals, respecting a natural election founded in the circumstances and conditions of their creation, is equally true of the idiosyncrasies of nations. Although it is the vocation of each nation to represent one side of the divine image, we must nevertheless distinguish between such natures as are more primitive, and such as are more derived, between such as express more decidedly the idea of creation, and such as express more decidedly the idea of maintenance and preservation.

§ 75.

The entire diversity of individuals created in God's image, of nations, of tongues, and of races, finds its unity in the divine *Logos*, the uncreated image of God (*imago dei absoluta*), who in the fulness of times himself becomes man. If the divine Logos did not Himself become man, the Ideal of humanity would not be realized ; for each of the created individuals represents only an imperfect, a relative union of the Logos and man, of the uncreated and the created divine image. The Logos having become man, reveals the whole fulness of the ideal according to which human nature was originally planned, but which can be realized only imperfectly in each finite individual. If the divine Logos did not become man, humanity would be without any real point of unity and without a *head*. It would want the *actual* Mediator, who can lead the species out of the created relations of dependence into the spiritual relations of freedom, who can raise it from the level of the natural life to the level of perfection and true being. We therefore accept the essentially Christian belief, that the Son of God would have been made man, and would have come into the world, even if sin had not come into the world,*—the belief, that when God created man after his

---

* See Irenæus adv. haer. Book 5, Ch. 16.—" That in the dispensation of the fulness of times he might gather together in one all things in Christ, both

own image, He created him in the image of his Son, in the image of the Son who was to become incarnate, so that even at the creation of man the image of Christ was present to the mind of the Creator, and was the prototype according to which man was created.

THE FIRST ADAM.

§ 76.

The Church answers the question respecting the origin of the human race and of history, by pointing to a first pair of human beings,* and she recognises in the first Adam the natural pattern of the second Adam, who was to come in the fulness of times ;† but there is another view which has obtained advocates in all times, and which asserts that the human race has developed itself from several centres entirely independent of each other. As the question here at issue lies entirely beyond the limits of our present experience, its answer must also ultimately depend on the general fundamental view which we take of the vocation and condition of man. The naturalistic point of view, which does not recognise *revelation* as the necessary presupposition for the development of human freedom, regards the origin of human life entirely under the type of natural development. It supposes that in different

which are in heaven, and which are on earth ; even in him :" Eph. i. 10. "Who is the image of the invisible God, the first-born of every creature : And he is the head of the body, the church : who is the beginning the first-born from the dead ; that in all things he might have the pre-eminence :" Col. i. 15 and 18. "And that ye put on the new man, which after God is created in righteousness and true holiness :" Eph. iv. 24. "And have put on the new man, which is renewed in knowledge after the image of him that created him : Where there is neither Greek nor Jew, circumcision nor uncircumcision, Barbarian, Scythian, bond nor free, but Christ is all and in all." Col. iii. 10, 11.

* "And the rib, which the Lord God hath taken from man, made he a woman, and brought her unto the man :" Gen. ii. 22. "And he answered and said unto them, Have ye not read, that he which made them at the beginning made them male and female :" Matt. xix. 4. "And hath made of one blood all nations of men for to dwell on all the face of the earth, and hath determined the times before appointed, and the bounds of their habitation." Acts xvii. 26.

† "Wherefore, as by one man sin entered into the world, and death by sin ; and so death passed upon all men, for that all have sinned :" Rom. v. 12. "And so it is written, The first man Adam was made a living soul ; the last Adam was made a quickening spirit." 1 Cor. xv. 45.

regions of the earth, the Aborigines (οἱ αὐτόχθονες) sprang out of the slime of matter.   At last in the midst of their struggling and wrestling with the powers of nature, the Promethean spark of genius flashed up in some of these children of the earth, and these it is who have become the heroes of culture and humanity, and have led their brothers further on the road of "self-liberation."   Whether this view establish itself on a foundation of Deism, which, it is true, recognises a Creator above the stars, but a creator who having given His world the first impulse towards its further development, remains for ever after an inactive spectator,——or whether it endeavours to establish itself on a basis of Panthism, and regards the spirit of man as a self-developing power of the Godhead——on either hypothesis it has entirely perverted the true conception of the nature of creation, and of man created after the image of God.   For if man is a creature after the image of God, the creating principle must also be the principle of his *development ;* and the true development of man can never be imagined as left entirely to itself, but only as guided by revelation and grace.

§ 77.

If we allow that the significance of history is to be found in its representation of the mutual relations between the human and the divine wills, between self-consciousness and revelation, that its ultimate object is the perfect union of God and man, it follows that these mutual relations and this union must have been present in the beginning of history as in a fruitful germ.   Humanity is not to propagate itself corporeally alone, it must also propagate itself intellectually by means of sacred tradition.   And as surely as revelation and sacred tradition constitute the foundation of the history of the development of man in God's image, just so surely can this history have only *one* starting-point, because this is the condition for the propagation of the sacred tradition from one generation to another.   The representation of Paradise and of the first Adam is founded, therefore, not only in the letter of Christianity, but also in its spirit ; and the opposite view must be rejected as Pelagian, because it makes liberty begin without divine grace, self-consciousness without a divine word.   And just as the human race, regarded from the point of view of a spiritual propagation, must be conceived as having only one starting point, the same assumption will appear as a no less necessary logical consequence if we regard it from the point of view of natural propagation. For as man is the unity of spirit and nature; as the development of mind and soul is conditioned by a corresponding constitution of nature, the intellectual unity of the race is also conditioned by its natural unity, or by the fact that the whole human race has sprung from "*one blood.*" To a certain extent we may recognize this in the relations between parents and children, in families and in races, in which the intellectual relationship is not to be separated from the blood-relationship; but we are also obliged to regard this natural relationship as transmitted to the race in its entirety. And although this view of the matter is the more obscure, it is at any rate clear, that only on the supposition of "first parents" can the hypothesis of the universal innate sinfulness of man, in its *Christian* sense, be maintained. On the hypothesis of αὐτόχθονες, or of many original starting-points of the human race, independent of each other, the universal sinfulness of man must be regarded as something which belongs to the original arrangement of the creation. But only on the supposition of "first parents" can it be regarded as something which was introduced afterwards, and which has penetrated through to all.

Observations.—It is in the first Adam that Creatianism attains its fullest significance. The first Adam was *created* in a sense in which we cannot predicate creation of any of his posterity. His is a miracle for the whole of nature, which can only supply the conditions necessary for his existence, but which cannot effect his existence of itself. It is this miracle which Naturalism endeavours to avoid by assuming that mankind has come into existence through a *generatio æquivoca*, that the fluid-element has been impregnated in the very beginning with germs of life, which, through the accidental concurrence of certain physical conditions (temperature, electricity, galvanism, &c.,) have developed themselves into human organizations. In this manner everything appears to go on in conformity with natural laws, and miracle seems to be most successfully got rid of. For if the fact of a miracle were con-

ceded at only one point of the system, it might, of course,
recur again at other points, more especially at the appearance of the second Adam in the midst of mankind. But is
the miraculous really disposed of by this hypothesis? This
most remarkable coincidence of natural conditions requisite
for the development of the germs of man, supposed to be
dormant in the depths of nature, this predetermined harmony,—is not this indeed a teleological miracle? And is
it not a contradiction to what we generally designate as
the *eternal* laws of nature, *i.e.*, to the laws of our ex-
experience *as it is at present*, if we imagine men to arise
out of the " fluid element," at different parts of the earth,
whether it be in the form of children or of adult human
beings? Is, then, this solution of the enigma of the origin of mankind more conceivable than that offered by the
Mosaic tradition, and the representation that the Lord
God formed Adam of the dust of the ground, and breathed
into him spirit of His own Spirit? Something inexplicable, something beyond the domain of our sensible perceptions, remains on either hypothesis; because on either
hypothesis we are carried beyond the present conditions
of experience and of sensible perception. But the difference is this : in the former case we arrive at a supposition which is perfectly monstrous, because the miracle is
effected by blind powers ; while, on the other hand, the
latter representation awakens feelings of awe and admira-
tion, because the miracle is effected by the Spirit, by holy
wisdom.

It does not fall within the province of dogmatic theology
to enter into any minute and lengthy investigations respecting the differences between various races and nationalities, based upon either physiological or philological
considerations. It is well known that sometimes points
of difference have been regarded as the original element,
and sometimes differences have been developed out of
the presupposed unity. Both explanations are supported
by the authority of scientific men of high repute. For
the world of experience is ambiguous on this point, and
one evidence is opposed to another. But we have not to
do here with a mere question respecting the variety of

reasons for and against, but rather with the question as to which is the one sufficient and decisive reason for our judgment. However great importance may be attached to the investigations of natural science, they can never bring us any farther in this question than to a supposition, an assumption, which they endeavour to raise to "*the highest probability*" by the consideration of the facts. And although there are great scientific authorities for the hypothesis of the descent of the whole human race from a single pair, which we can oppose to other equally great authorities, who assert the contrary, dogmatic theology cannot support itself on conjectures and assumptions of natural science. It must know that the final decision in these investigations must depend upon the views we hold respecting creation, revelation, and sacred tradition, and also respecting the relations between spirit and nature. And here dogmatic theology is in its own peculiar province, and must decide the question according to its own laws, leaving the investigations of natural science to go their own way ; yet in the confident expectation that the *ultimate* conclusions arrived at by natural science can never contradict revelation.

§ 78.

The real relation to God in the first Adam cannot have been a state of perfection, neither, on the other hand, a mere disposition, but rather a living *commencement* which contained within itself the possibility of a progressive development and a fulfilment of the vocation of man. It is the one-sidedness of Augustinianism to confound the conceptions of innocence and sanctity ; to attribute to the first man a purity of will and a perspicuity of knowledge, which can properly be conceived only as the *goal* of a free self-development. The Augustinian dogma has not been able to escape from a Docetic conception of the first Adam ; inasmuch as his true human nature becomes mere appearance, if his innate innocence is to be conceived as real sanctity. (Compare 1 Cor. xv. 45-47, where it is expressly intimated that the first Adam stood only upon the level of the natural life, whereas the kingdom of the Spirit as such only came into the world with the second

Adam*). Pelagianism, on the other hand, confounds innocence with animal rudeness, and regards the original image of
God in Adam only as a dormant *capacity*. But when man
is abandoned to a mere capacity or talent, he can never arrive
at real religion ; as may be seen in the case of savages at the
present day, among whom, it is true, we must presume the
bare capacity, but who nevertheless display utter religious incapacity ; for they never get even as far as the commencement
of the development of their capacities, but always require some
impulse from without. As, therefore, we can be just as little
satisfied with the hypothesis of the mere capacity as with
that of a developed state of perfection, we say that the first
Adam has had in him the LIVING BEGINNING of a true relation
to God. This *beginning* of a blessed development of life in a
created dependence, this starting-point for liberty, so pregnant
with life, containing in itself a blissful future, is the true conception of PARADISE.

Observations.—It is precisely because Paradise lies outside
   the conditions of our present experience, that it is so
   easy a task for criticism to prove the impossibility of our
   forming for ourselves a picture of the first Adam. There
   is a certain analogy between the representation of Paradise, of the first conditions of human life, and the representation of the last conditions of human life, that is to
   say, of a future life. Both lie alike beyond the conditions of present experience ; which is the reason why
   there are so many persons who esteem them as mere pictures of the fancy. But because we are not able to have
   any empirical intuition of the Paradise of our past or of
   our future, we are not on that account the less obliged to
   think of it, as we also see it in faith, as in a glass darkly.
   Although, therefore, the first Adam stands like a figure in
   the background of the human race, shrouded in a cloud,
   and with an undefined outline, a dim memory, as indistinct as the recollection of the first awaking to self-consciousness in each individual ; yet does the consciousness

---

* "And so it is written, The first man Adam was made a living soul; the
last Adam was made a quickening spirit. Howbeit that was not first which is
spiritual, but that which is natural ; and afterward that which is spiritual. The
first man is of the earth, earthy ; the second man is the Lord from Heaven."

of the species, when directed upon itself, necessarily return to this dim memory; because without it the consciousness of the species would be entirely wanting in unity and connection.

It is a just remark of Steffens, when seeking some analogy to Paradise in our present experience, that this is to be found in the first enthusiasm, the first love to the Eternal, the first meeting of the human and the Divine spirit. The history of all great actions, of all great thoughts, has begun with a fruitful enthusiasm, with a moment which, though unconsciously, contained within itself, as a pattern, the fulness of a whole future. Comparatively speaking, a paradise may be discovered in every highly gifted man, and in every eventful epoch of history. Only that which has germinated in such a beginning can eventually become fruit, and that development alone is healthy which remains true to the beginning that it has received from God. This *first* enthusiasm, this inspiration, is the moment of *creation* in the kingdom of self-consciousness. No intellectual creation can ever be perfected by dint of a mere psychological possibility,—it must first be fructified and awakened by a higher inspiration. The faculty of reason is the common property of all mankind; but he alone possesses the spirit, who can embody reason in a progressive development; and the gift of being able to make a beginning has always been the peculiar characteristic of genius. Just as the history of every important individual and of every important nation points back to such a beginning of the spirit, the first Adam must also have had a beginning of the spirit for that development which was to *prepare the way for* the entrance of the second Adam, with whom a new creation, a new kingdom of the Spirit, the kingdom of the perfection of the world, was to come into force. And the human spirit, which has lost its connection with its first love, with its god-inspired primæval time, is a fallen spirit, which has at the same time lost its future.

MAN'S FALL FROM GOD.

§ 79.

If the divine likeness was not to be a mere gift, but rather a self-acquired attribute of humanity, it was necessary that the paradisaical condition should come to an end. The liberty of man had therefore to be brought within the range of temptation. The possibility of temptation lies in the fact, that there exists a world outside God, which can be mistaken for God,—a resplendent glory, which can be preferred to God, and that this two-sidedness repeats itself in man's own nature, inasmuch as he has been created both in the likeness of the world and in the likeness of God. Considering the nature of temptation from a psychological point of view, we may say that in temptation the opposed fundamental impulses of human nature seek to bias the will. If, on the other hand, we contemplate temptation from a metaphysical point of view, we must say that superhuman powers, namely, God and the cosmical principle, seek man through his affections, in order to tempt him, and to force him to a decision. That there must be temptation, may be deduced as a necessary consequence from the conception of created liberty ;* but that its issue should be the fall of man can only be known by means of an historical and psychological experience.

Observations.—In the Mosaic account of the fall of man (Gen. iii.), we meet with a combination of history and sacred symbolism, a figurative representation of an actual event. The fact of the fall is there represented by a consciousness to which both paradise and the fall are transcendental and *prehistoric;* for which reason there can be no immediate knowledge of it, but only a mediate and an allegorical one, as in a glass darkly.

In our attempt to find the significance of this dark image, we will first call attention to the mystical TREES which stand in the garden. That the tree of life designates life in God appears self-evident; the tree of know-

---

* Compare Sibbern's Pathology; p. 67.

ledge on the other hand is ambiguous. That it should signify nothing more or less than *knowledge*, and that this should be in and for its own nature forbidden to man, cannot be the true explanation; for God himself leads man to contemplation, by showing him the opposition between the two trees,—God himself indeed awakens the consciousness of the difference between good and evil, by imposing the prohibition. It is for this reason that we would say: It is not the thought of the opposition and difference between good and evil,—for the mere thought of evil indeed is represented in the Holy Scriptures as existing in the consciousness of Christ, the second Adam,—but it is the *experience of evil*, that knowledge of good and evil which arises from man having taken evil into his very being, which brings death with it. Man, therefore, ought to know evil only as a possibility that he has overcome; he ought only *to see* the forbidden fruit; but if he *eats* it, his death is in the act. If he attains the knowledge of evil as a reality in his own life, he has fallen away from his vocation, and frustrates the very object of his creation.

But man would not have eaten of the tree of knowledge if its *fruit* had not possessed a peculiar charm for him, and if it did not, in a certain sense, appear to him to dispute the palm with the fruit of the tree of life. "And the woman saw that the tree was good for food, and that it was pleasant to the eyes, and a tree to be desired to make one wise." The attractive fruit is the glorious *world-phenomenon*, and by eating of this fruit, man can become *as* God, because, in his freedom, he can conceive himself as lord of the world. The tree of life on the other hand, is the tree of the gifts of grace; and if man eats of this tree, he may eat gladly of all the other trees of the garden (Gen. ii. 9) may gladly appropriate to himself all created things, because he receives all as a gift from the Lord. But on the mystical tree of knowledge the created fruit shines in its *own* splendour in its *own* glory. The entire history of heathendom offers a commentary upon this fact. The heathens allowed themselves to be infatuated by this fruit; they gave their hearts to this world, they loved the creature better than the creator. The lovely form of created things beguiled them ; and they loved the visible more than the invisible.

Besides the tree of knowledge there is another mystical figure which attracts our attention, namely, the SERPENT. Man is not tempted by himself to eat of the tree of knowledge, but by the serpent. Thus much is evident, that we are led away from the natural serpent to a *principle,* —a principle which forms an opposition not only to man, but also to God himself. For the serpent says exactly the opposite of that which the Lord says,—opposes a direct *no* to the divine *yes.* "Ye shall *not surely* die " if ye eat of the fruit. Besides God and man, there is also a third actor in this scene. The Judaic revelation of the Book of Wisdom has interpreted the serpent as the devil.* As, moreover, we shall return to the serpent, when speaking of the doctrine of the devil, we may pass over this difficult and complicated question for the present, especially as the Mosaic account itself does not actually name the devil. The principal question still remains, namely, what is that principle in the creation, which can tempt man to fall away from God ? or,—if we wish here to introduce the representation of the devil,— what is that principle in the creation by which the devilish becomes possible ? We answer, it is the cosmical principle itself considered in its relation of opposition to God, the principle of the autonomy of the world, of the self-subsistence of the world. Just as the creature has one side turned towards God, it has also another side turned towards itself, a tendency to live for itself and of itself, a tendency to move in its peculiar and individual way. It is the law of the cosmical principle to be subordinate to the kingdom of God ; but in order to become the foundation upon which service may rest, it must first act as an exciting power, must throw itself in man's way, and shew him the possibility of rebelling against God, of saying no, when God says yes. According to the moral explanation, the serpent is to be regarded as the symbol of this *impulse* towards

* Wisdom ii. 24, "Through envy of the Devil death came into the world."

independence becoming active in man, and inciting him to become free apart from his Creator. But this impulse towards independence could most assuredly never become active in man, if it had no foundation whatever *in the constitution of the creature*,—if it had not its deeper root in a principle which is active in all created things. The serpent is the outward expression for this principle which creeps up to man to obtain an entrance, and which, notwithstanding its approaching man through his impulses, may yet be said to be external to man, and to be a superhuman power, because it is active throughout the whole creation. Finally, there is a natural connection between the serpent and the forbidden fruit. The fruit is the glittering world-phenomenon, which invites man to enjoy it, and to make himself its possessor. The serpent, on the other hand, is the worldly principle, which gives the world-phenomenon a significance for the human consciousness. Without showing man the fruit, the serpent could never have obtained access to man ; for a tempting principle, which is not able to point to any corresponding reality, which has no splendours to offer, is only a feeble shadow. But, on the other hand, the fruit could not have allured man if the serpent had not brought it into connection with the human impulse towards independence ;—if it had not represented to man, that by partaking of the fruit he would attain the enjoyment of his own freedom. All the splendours of the world would have failed to tempt man, if they had not at the same time shewn man his own image in a tempting light. The two momenta here described recur in every act of sin. No sin is committed without the presence of both fruit and serpent, an alluring phenomenon which attracts the sense, and an invisible tempter who holds up before man an illusory image of his freedom.

If we consider that the condition of the first man was that of unprotected innocence, and that although we do not accept the literal interpretation of the fruit and the serpent, we have nevertheless recognized in them tempting powers different from man himself, we must also acknowledge the truth of the representation that man has been *seduced.* Should this be alleged as an extenuating circumstance for fallen man, it must also be remembered, on the other hand, that he was only seduced, because he *allowed himself* to be seduced ;—and with respect to the result of the temptation, we can by no means admit the application of the position, that the actual is also the reasonable. It is true, Jehovah says, " Behold, the man is become as one of us," from which it has been concluded that the serpent did not lie, but that the fall was necessary in order that man might attain his true distinction as a free and independent being. But the context shows distinctly, that although in a certain sense man had become " as God," it was in an unrighteous manner, and " the Cherubim with the flaming swords " shew that the independence and liberty which man attained through the fall, stand in irreconcilable contradiction with *holiness*, a quality which is indispensable in any true resemblance to God.

THE MYSTERY OF THE FALL.

§ 80.

Although the fall of man is a true history, which having happened once has become universal history, it is nevertheless not eternal history ; this would involve as its necessary consequence that sin is inseparable from the conception of man, and that sin was absolutely indispensable if the created spirit were to attain its destination. The speculative view, which conceives evil as a necessary principle in the conception of the world, may refer partly to nature, partly to history, partly to the supernatural and superhistorical, to the divine decree, for the necessary origin of evil. But it is neither from the relationship of liberty to nature, nor from the conception of the world-historical development of liberty, nor from the divine decree, nor from the created nor the uncreated, that the necessity of evil can be deduced ; it is only the *possibility* of evil that admits of demonstration. But evil is just that possibility which ought to have remained a possibility for ever ; its realization, therefore, can only be conceived as arising from the free will of the creature, whose self-obscuration must in so far remain inconceivable, as it is precisely a falling off from the divine necessity of reason. For the fuller development of this position it will be necessary to consider the relation of evil to nature, to history, and to the divine decree.

§ 81.

To make nature itself the evil principle is just as great an error as to make freedom itself the evil principle, and belongs only to the Oriental Manichæism. On the other hand, Western speculation has endeavoured in various ways to derive the necessity of evil from the relation of liberty to nature, and to conceive the fall as the expression of the necessary transition of the human race from the state of nature to that of culture. While a state of nature is the normal state for the animal, it is for man one in which he ought not to remain, one which must be got rid of, because man is a thinking and a free being. Man must make himself free from nature by means of his thought, his freedom. The earliest outward expression of self-conscious thought and will, must (it is argued), be tainted with the rudeness of nature, with the finiteness of impulse, with the fortuitousness of desire. The first act by which it disengages itself from its unity with nature, the first independent act of liberty, can only manifest itself as arbitrariness, as the lowest form of free self-determination. But in an arbitrary act the Ego places itself in contradiction to its own conception, to the universal liberty necessary for reason. It has become evil, because it has opened up within itself the contradiction between its individuality and its *universal* essence, between its subjective arbitrariness and the *necessity* of reason. This experience of its double essence, of the contradiction in its own innermost nature, is the bitter fruit which man has plucked from the tree of knowledge. But just as it is the faculty of thought that expels man from that paradise which animals can never lose, so is it also the faculty of thought which contains the deliverance from that disunion, by leading the will to resignation and to the renunciation of its egotism, and by offering it a reconciliation in the world of culture, of morality, and of religion. Thought here is the arrow which wounds, and also cures. The fall and the reconciliation thus supply the eternal type for the finite development of freedom, a type which is repeated, not only in the different epochs of history, but also in the life of individuals.

Observations.—This theory of the necessity of evil has been more especially developed by Hegel. The fundamental idea, however, has also been propounded in various other systems of modern times. Thus, for instance, Fichte makes the ego begin with being held in bonds by the non-ego, because the ego, from its very conception, must first conquer for itself its own liberty ; and he makes evil the *vis inertiœ* in consequence of which the ego inclines to remain in its original state of nature, instead of under-taking the labour of going out of and beyond itself. When Schleiermacher propounds, as an explanation of sin, that the sensuous consciousness has obtained a *start* before man's consciousness of God, this must be understood as involving the position, that the higher intellectual consciousness of man is in bondage to the state of nature, which must at last appear to man himself as a false relation, as something from which he must strive to be released. Kant and Schiller interpret the fall as the necessary transition of reason from the state of nature to that of culture, and a poetical illustration of this thought has been given in Baggesen's Adam and Eve.

§ 82.

While the doctrine of Christianity represents Paradise as the cradle of the human mind, around which guardian powers hover protectingly, Paradise is regarded here as nothing more than a garden of animals. That man is wicked by nature, is accepted as an unconditioned, an eternal truth ; for the natural state of liberty is a contradiction to the ideal, and as such is in itself a fallen state. It must, however, be denied that the bad, to say nothing of evil itself, is already to be found in the conception of the state of nature. The conception of innocence as of immediate goodness, as of the unconscious life of the soul in the good and the true, contains no other contradiction than that which lies in the conception of *childhood* itself, namely, that it is as yet only the imperfect age of man, and not that which has become clear to itself. But that the thought and will which lie concealed in the form of nature

L

should be in themselves not only an imperfect but also a
false spirituality; that childlike reflection should be not only
the imperfect but also the false liberty, by which we first attain
the conception of evil,—these are positions which have never
been proved. For in whatever measure the consciousness of
self and the consciousness of the world progress in their development, in that same measure must also the consciousness
of God in the normal state be imagined as developing itself as
the dominant principle in the soul, which has been created
after the image of God. If indeed it must also be allowed,
that holiness from the very beginning can only be present
under the form of the *feeling* of conscience, as religious impulse and child-like representation, yet the conception of a
good *nature*, as of the good *beginning* of the right development of liberty will always preserve its validity. We do not
complain of the child because it has not the consciousness of
the man, but we do complain of the *naughtiness* of the nature
in the child, and thus express both the requirement and the
want,—not of the conscious but of the unconscious good,—of
the good nature. Unconscientious arbitrariness does not
lie in the conception of the first reflection of liberty, although
the latter undoubtedly contains the possibility of a self-determination in opposition to the conscience. If experience shows
us the present state of nature as rudeness devoid of all spirituality, as desire devoid of conscience, this only proves that the
natural has lost its original unity with the ethical, which
unity must not be imagined only as that which is still
to be produced, but must be no less *presumed* as the real
starting point, if it is ever to be produced at all. The
denial of the good nature contains a concealed Manichæism,
an eternally irreconcilable conflict between nature and
mind. If it is the conception of nature to be not only that
which has to be formed, but to be no less that also which has
to be combated and overcome as a hostile principle, or to be
separated from the bad and the fortuitous, the mind, which
cannot be without nature, must to all eternity have its desires
against nature, and nature its desires against the mind, and
every reconciliation must be of such a character as to bear
concealed within it the slumbering germ of a new conflict.
Observations.—The denial of the sinlessness of Christ is a

necessary logical consequence of the view above described, which is therefore utterly irreconcileable with Christianity. For if it is a part of the conception of innocence to be base, if it is an *eternal* truth that man is evil by nature, this must also be true of the second Adam, who begins his development with the natural step of childhood. His sinlessness is only a relative one. Christ has then to combat with the reality of evil, the bad nature, in himself, in order to become the spiritual redeemer—a position which does not find many adherents at the present day. In order to avoid the division involved in this Dualism, evil is brought within the range of the base, the unreal, the eternally evanescent, and the fortuitous. But thus the power of evil is underrated, and in another point of view—by raising it into an indispensable co-worker in the realm of spirit—it is overrated.

§ 83.

Inadmissible as it is to deduce the necessity of evil from the idea of the state of nature ; equally inadmissible is it to derive it from the idea of the *history of the world* as an actuality :—indeed, the latter view or mode of explanation is closely connected with the former. Considered from this point of view the necessity of evil is supposed to arise from the circumstance that the history of the world can only be conceived as a life developing itself through antagonism and conflict. The various powers must needs come forth separately ; and in consequence of each of the historical spirits seeking to secure reality and prevalence for its peculiar characteristics, there necessarily arise concussions and *confusions,* the existence of which is inseparable from injustice and sin. The onesided forces and powers cannot but mutually exclude each other, and thus, notwithstanding that each by itself has a justifiable existence, they become unjustifiable and unjust. National individualities and personal individualities, which represent historical ideas and are capable of doing so only in as far as they manifest a vigorous onesidedness—for no great thing can be accomplished without a measure of suffering— must come into conflict with each other ; and this conflict is the development of the eternal tragedy of humanity, of which we can form no conception apart from guilt and sin. Considered, however, from a higher point of view, this tragedy bears the aspect of a *divina comœdia*. For it is by means of the conflict and ruin, by means of the many onesidednesses, which go to make up the tragedy, that the spirit of the world succeeds in fully revealing its contents. Looked at in a higher light, the history of the world assumes the glorified character of an eternal work of art. That which, from a lower point of view, is a moral dissonance, is found in a higher position to subserve the harmony of the whole. That which, from a lower point of view, appears to be ugly, assumes when looked at from the higher, the character of a shadow, which gives effect by way of contrast to the lighter parts of the picture. In the perfect world, all the forms of existence that are possible, must also acquire actual existence ; whilst the idea, as queen over them all, must be recognized as positing them for the purpose of being elements of her own glory. Thus considered, evil becomes an indispensable element in the optimistic picture of the world.

Observations.——In the church this view of evil and its functions was hinted at even by John Scotus Erigena. The principal Protestant thinkers by whom it has been set forth are, Leibnitz, Schleiermacher, Schelling, and Hegel; in a popular form it is pretty generally entertained by educated people of the present time.

§ 84.

The truth in the view above delineated is that we are unable to form any conception of a living spiritual development save as a development through antagonisms. But so far from evil being necessary to the process of development, it is involved in the very idea of evil to be at once a false antagonism and a false reconciliation of antagonisms ; to be an untrue dialectic and an untrue solution ; consequently its influence is to hinder and *disturb* all true development. Evil cannot be regarded as an immanent feature of the idea of the world; but must, on the contrary, be treated as an *interruption* of the course of its immanent development. Evil is a *false extreme* and must not therefore be confounded with the antitheses or oppositions which are grounded in the nature of the idea. It is the piercing discord which disturbs the harmony of the creation, and as it cannot be resolved into it, it must necessarily be cast out. Evil is not involved in the conception of individuality, but is rooted in the perversion of the conception of individuality; in the breaking loose of individuality from its inner limits, from its innate peculiarities; in the unwillingness of the individuality to be what it is, in its desire and aim to be other than as it has been constituted by its Creator. In a healthy vital development, on the contrary, individual antitheses or oppositions must seek, confirm, and complement each other in the unity of *love*. For this reason we must allow it to have been possible that history should have pursued a normal course of development, a course of development in harmony with the ideal, without being saddled with those "caricatures of holiness" which now everywhere make their appearance, in the life as well of entire nations and ages, as of individuals. To deny this possibility is nothing, but, after the manner of the Manichaeans, to make evil eternal. For if evil has once been constituted a necessary factor of the life of the spirit, it can never be expelled therefrom ; and the Christian idea of a future life of blessedness, must be pronounced an image of the fancy. If, as that doctrine teaches, human life and goodness cannot have actual reality, save as there is an uninterrupted conquest of the evil, they will need evil as a spur and incitement throughout eternity and without it will lack real existence. Those, however, who entertain the opinion that the good would lack vigour and reality unless accompanied by the evil, must have but a faint conception of the inner power of the good, of the fulness of positive forces which it contains within itself.* They look upon good predominantly as a critical power, and overlook its productive, *plastic* power. They forget also that the critical power and inward excellence of the good are evinced no less forcibly in resisting evil as a *possibility* in temptation, and thus rendering evil impossible, than in vanquishing evil when it has acquired actual existence.

Observations.—Although we are unable to form any conception, based on experience, of a history of the world that is in full harmony with the ideal; and although, on the

* Compare Julius Müller's "Doctrine of Sin."

contrary, the only idea we have of the history of the world is of a history which has not merely *not yet* attained its ideal, but presents many features *contrasting* with and opposed to the ideal, which require to be set aside ; still the relationship subsisting between believing Judaism and. Christianity presents us with a pattern for sinless development. Believing Judaism closed its mission like John the Baptist, who testified concerning Christ—" He must increase, but I must decrease;" it departed in peace like old Simeon, who rejoiced at the birth of the Child. This supplies us with the normal type of the relation of the different epochs of the world to each other. If history had run a sinless course each epoch would have regarded itself as preparing the way for the next following, would have fostered and cherished the germs of the future which it contained within itself, and in hope and promise reaching forwards towards the fulness of the times. The opposite type, on the contrary, has embodied itself most distinctly in unbelieving Judaism. It treated the stage of development which really bore merely a preparative character, as though it were conclusive and perfect, and thus put itself into a false relationship both to the past and to the future. This falsity, in its relation to the past and to the future, which caused the momenta of development to be thrown out of their healthy connection with the entire organism, is the characteristic mark of sinful history. Neither the history of nations, nor that of individuals, is characterised by harmonious progress ; on the contrary, at one time we find a false tendency to movement which leads to the fruit being plucked before it is ripe, and the goal being reached forward to ere the development is complete ; at another time spiritless stagnation, when life seems to have been brought to a close just where it ought to begin. How often, too, do we find the progress both of peoples and individuals interrupted by their falling back into old and long-discarded errors. The conflicts constantly taking place in social life between the old and the new, bear witness to the existence of this disorganization, which chokes the germs of the future and denies the past, instead of seeking to secure for its spirit and substance a continuous and progressive life. The sinful type of history has come, however, to be regarded by man to such an extent as the only one possible, that some pronounce the utterance of John the Baptist referred to above, concerning his relation to Christ, to be a later poetic fiction, on the ground of its being inconsistent with the idea of a real history of the world, that an earlier point of view should allow itself willingly to be absorbed by a later one. We are quite ready to allow that it is not an *ordinary* case for the earlier thus cheerfully to submit to being swallowed up by the later; but no one has as yet been able to show that the thing is essentially impossible. It is at the same time very obvious, that we have not here assumed the possibility of a development of the world different from the one actually existing, in order that we may be able to give ourselves up to fantastic dreams regarding its more precise character. On the contrary, to assume the possibility of a sinless development of the world, seems to us necessary, in order to ascertain theoretically as well as practically, our whereabouts in the actual world. We are quite willing to allow that it is impossible for us to form an experimental conception of a world different from that which we find existing; but we must at the same time maintain that they are blinded who assert that the world, as we now find it, is the only world which is *metaphysically* and *ethically* possible.

§ 85.

The doctrine of the necessity of evil, traces it back from nature and history to the divine decree. If the revelation of God in Christ is the expression of an eternal divine decree, and if, as the perfect revelation of God, it is a revelation of redemption, then must redemption be conceived necessarily to presuppose sin as its condition. If the eternal decree of God is conceived to be *unconditioned,* sin too must be conceived as one of the objects of its determination. God must be conceived as having ordained sin as the condition of redemption : He must be supposed to have ordained sin that He might show grace. Sin thus becomes indispensable to a system of religious Optimism, and redemption is seen to be the true Theodicy. And when the mind turns its gaze on the source of love and compassion which is opened up in redemption, and on the deep and intense humility which the consciousness of sin develops in man, it is driven to exclaim, "*O felix culpa Adami quæ meruit talem et tantum habere redemptorem!*

Observations.—This *supralapsarian* view was set forth in particular by Calvin. God allows man to fall in order to bring him to the conviction of his natural impotence and nothingness, that the need of grace may become profounder. Leibnitz in his Theodicy develops Calvinism from the point of view of religious optimism, and tries to set forth the fall as a *felix culpa.* The same idea was introduced in an aesthetic form in later times, amongst the educated, by Novalis, who described Christianity as the "Religion of Pleasure," in which the union with God acquires a piquant character through sin.

§ 86.

When the supralapsarian theory describes the fall as a *felix culpa* it is forgotten that, coming from such a quarter, this saying loses all its meaning. If sin be pre-ordained of God, it must have formed part of the original world-plan, and accordingly it loses its moral sting, even as redemption also loses its ethical reality. If sin may claim to belong of necessity to the idea of the world, the consciousness of guilt is weakened, and the consciousness of redemption, as that free act of love whereby it shows mercy to the lost, is enervated. The moral relation is thus evaporated into a relation merely metaphysical; and this has actually taken place in the more modern philosophy of religion. Thus the Hegelian philosophy adopting the comparison of the Mystics, describes the Atonement as "the play" of Divine love with itself. But if sin be the negative force indispensably necessary to the completion of this eternal game, it ceases to be sin; what appears to be sin in a finite point of view, would, if seen in its true light, turn out to be only a necessary step in the realization of the plan. Schleiermacher also suffers the ethical in this doctrine to disappear in the metaphysical; because he teaches that sin is not ordained of God as sin, but as limitation, and that *for God sin does not exist.* But if with God there is no such thing as sin, it follows that with God redemption in its proper sense has no reality. What presents itself to the finite consciousness as sin and as redemption, is, according to Schleiermacher, the antithesis only between the first and the second creation, between the stage of imperfection and perfection in humanity. It is certainly important and even necessary to find a means of reconciling the ethical and the metaphysical view of the world. But surely a true reconciliation is not attained when the moral is destroyed by the metaphysical. The doctrine which explains sin to be a necessary means towards the perfect revelation of God, can do so only by sacrificing the moral for the sake of the speculative; in a word, it can only congratulate man upon the fall, because it explains that sin is not sin, and that redemption is not redemption. It cannot solve the religious problem, because it destroys it.

§ 87.

The fundamental view, upon the supposition of which alone the reality of sin and of redemption can be maintained, is that which recognizes the Divine Decree as at the same time unconditioned and conditioned, and thus embraces the truth both of the supra-lapsarian and of the infra-lapsarian theories. When we say that the divine decree is not only unconditional but also conditional, we mean that it is not only a decree determined from eternity, but that it is also determinable by the freedom of the creature; it is not a perfected decree, concluded already for all time, but one continually coming into existence and being realised,—" becoming,"—determining itself according to an historical movement of life; it does not establish its eternity by merely repeating itself in time; but as it enters time it enters upon a new stage of life, and receives new determinations. In other words, it is not merely a logical but an ethical decree, the decree of the divine will for a *free* world-manifestation. It is included in the counsel of God's holy will that there shall be a creature apart from Him who in a derived sense shall have life in himself, shall possess a self-movement independently of God, which as a free self-determination in the man belongs to consciousness. But hence the human will obtains a discriminating, a determining force, in the revelation of the divine will, and together therewith. In the divine counsels, moreover, there is something *undecided*,—in so far as they are viewed in their pure essence as above history, and in their eternal pre-existence, — something undecided, which attains its decision in a following stage, when the divine decree passes out of the stillness of eternity into the movement of freedom in time. Not only has man a history, but eternal love has a history too. The divine will submits itself to the conditions of history, it makes its definite and active manifestations contingent upon the free self-determination of the human will. The divine will must abdicate its natural, its unconditioned power, in order to reveal itself as the holy power of love.

§ 88.

The difficulty involved in the position, that the divine decree submits itself to the conditions of history, is removed by the consideration that it does not after all belong to the *essence* of God's decree that it be unconditional; and that all forces in the ideal of humanity necessarily *must* be taken into account and realised. For as true freedom involves the possibility of the fall, and hence the perversion of the ideal, the possibility of redemption is thus eternally established. Although man, in virtue of his actual will, may fall from God, according to his *essential* will, in the innermost kernel of his freedom, he is indissolubly united to the divine λόγος as the holy world-principle, who has power to subdue and triumph over the world by His own free movement. It is, therefore, only upon the supposition of the Son, that God can venture upon human freedom; for redemption from a possible fall is eternally presupposed in the Son. But it arises not from an unconditioned, but from a conditional, an *economic* necessity, that the divine manifestation of love should appear in activity as a revelation of redemption. Since, that is, the will of man determines itself as a will to sin, the divine will of love must assume another, a new relation to the human,—it must determine itself as a punishing and redeeming will. As darkness has come upon the creation, the light which streams forth from the Creator, and which cannot help shining in the darkness, must indicate a new refraction. No idea, no eternal truth, is destroyed by the fall of man. But the relation of the ideal to human consciousness is altered. Not the eternal ideal, but the *way* to the ideal, the divine method in the guidance of man, is different.

§ 89.

The supralapsarian view, which refuses to recognise anything conditional in the divine counsels, thus distinguishes itself as the *unhistorical* view, because it makes history merely a dependent reflection of the divine will. If the divine decree be not conditioned by the self-determination of man, the idea of history is annihilated. For the essential idea of history is to give expression to the living reciprocal relation between the divine will and the human, between eternity and time, between the ideal and the actual: the aim of history is to bring the undecided to a decision. But in consequence of the pure unconditional decree history becomes only the carrying out of that, which has been already decided from eternity; and the moral world advances only after the pattern of the world of nature. As the supralapsarian theory does not recognise the independence of created freedom, it cannot conceive of history as a living reciprocal movement of the divine and human wills; of the Creator, and created spirits. Yet it contains a deep truth; namely, that the advent of Christ, the revelation of the highest good, cannot be viewed as a mere *means* towards something else, but must be looked upon as *its own end;* that all things, all nature and all history, must be looked upon as means for Christ. This undeniable position, however, is satisfied by the truth contained in the proposition: *Etiamsi homo non pecasset, deus tamen incarnatus esset, licet non crucifixus.* The supralapsarian view finds both its truth and its limitation in this statement—a statement which includes the necessary realization of the eternal ideal of humanity, together with that of the kingdom of God. The supralapsarian view is right in maintaining that the Incarnation of God in Christ was an unconditional necessity; but it errs when it demands the same necessity for the crucifixion, the sufferings and death of the incarnate Son.

§ 90.

The infralapsarian view maintains the sacred reality of the

consciousness of sin, and the necessity of the coming of Christ
as conditional upon sin; it gives freedom and history their
due : but as the manifestation of Christ is thus willed only
on account of sin, it becomes only a means, it is not its own
object.   In this way the world becomes entirely a world of
relativity; and there is no absolute, no unconditioned point
in the course of history wherein the economic and the eternal
necessities coincide.   The *infra*lapsarian hypothesis can find
this unconditioned point only in the principle which we have
adduced as involving likewise the truth underlying the *supra*-
lapsarian theory.

Observations.——The proposition, *Etiamsi homo non peccasset,
deus tamen in carnatus est—licet non crucifixus,* has been
maintained in the Lutheran Church by Andreas Osiander.[*]
If orthodox theology has not ventured to adopt this proposition,——which by many is regarded as *nova inutilis et
impia,*——this may be explained as arising from a fear,
unreasonable here, of being led astray by an unscriptural
Gnosis regarding the facts of revelation.   A closer examination of such passages as the first chapters of the
Epistles to the Ephesians and the Colossians will lead to
the recognition of this doctrine as an inner and silent
exponent of the teaching of Scripture.

§ 91.

From what has now been developed it is clear that the true
optimism and the true Theodicy are to be looked for in the
blending of the *supra*lapsarian and the *sub*lapsarian views.
Christian optimism recognises the unconditional necessity of
the Incarnation, and as upon this principle it regards human
nature in the light of redemption, it can adopt the exclamation
felix culpa!   For, though sin was not willed by God, it
could not occur beyond the range of His counsels; though
God has not ordained it, it becomes a teleological force for the
revelation of God's love.   " God hath included all in unbelief,
that He might have mercy upon all."[†]   As the manifestation
of Christ is the unconditional design of revelation, for which

* Professor of Theology at Königsberg: born 1498; died 1552.   His son and
grandson were also eminent theologians.
† Romans xi. 32.   See also Luke xv.

the whole creation must serve as the means, the freest self-abnegation of His love appears in his making Himself the means of man's redemption, in His becoming a servant, for our sinful as well as imperfect race. "God commendeth His love towards us in that, while we were yet sinners Christ died for us," (Rom. v. 8). As the world-subduing, world-redeeming love of Christ reveals its infinite power in putting an end to the most deep-seated and real contradiction that can be conceived,—the contradiction, that is, between the will of the Creator and that of the creature,—the world must be viewed as the fittest sphere in which divine love and wisdom have centred in order to accomplish that victory, (Rom. xi. 33—36). Christian optimism thus regards history as the living drama of freedom, wherein all points are affected by the movement, not only of divine thought, but also of holy will. And though Christian consciousness must recognise the possibility of a development of the world without sin ; yet taking redemption into consideration, the desire for a development of the world, other than the actually existing one, must vanish. The pessimist views and subjective ideals regarding the world, belong only to the stand-point of sinfulness itself.

HUMAN DEPRAVITY OR ORIGINAL SIN.
§ 92.

The first man was not only one in a series of individuals constituting the human family, he was the personal starting-point likewise for the development of the whole organism of the race; and in like manner sin, which was introduced into the world by the first Adam, was not only a single instance, but an active *beginning*, exercising a disturbing influence upon the entire development. "By one man sin entered into the world and death by sin; and so death passed upon all men, for that all have sinned " (Romans v. 12). The sinful determination of will in the first Adam cannot certainly be looked upon as leading to a transformation of the substance of humanity, yet it must be regarded as necessarily involving a disturbance of the whole mode of human existence, *modus existendi*. The original condition of human nature is, for instance, *formability ;* it is not essentially perfect and complete, it is not determined, but *determinable*. The things in relation to which the first Adam had to determine itself as the beginning personality of the *race*, were superhuman powers, the universe, and God, the cosmical principle, and the principle of holiness. When man gives way to the cosmical principle and imparts to it an activity which does not belong to it, he is no longer master of the development, but has yielded to the universal power which he has suffered to overcome him. The perversion of principles which took place in the first Adam had a moral bearing upon the entire organism which has in him not only its historical, but also its natural, starting-point.

§ 93.

All the descendants of the first Adam are by nature that which the first Adam made himself by a free act of will. Human beings cannot certainly be looked upon merely as the offspring of their parents, or as created by them; every individual is a creation of God, as well as a self-development of its own point of life. But the ethical *basis of nature*, which is not only in but *born with* the individual, is conditioned for each succeeding generation by the generations going before. Individuals and races are organic points in that sum total of development which has its starting-point in the first Adam, and they by nature repeat the Adamic type. Every individual begins from his birth an abnormal development of life whose universal characteristic is the conflict between the flesh and the spirit. " The flesh lusteth against the spirit, and the spirit against the flesh ; and these are contrary the one to the other" (Gal. v. 17, see also Romans vii.). This discord first appears in the natural life as the dominion of worldly impulses and carnal appetites, the impulse towards the kingdom of God being thereby hindered. In the spiritual life it shows itself as a development of the world-consciousness, whereby the consciousness of God is limited. As this worldliness involves the alienation of the will from God it is clearly a false *autonomy*, the contradiction of the true *theonomy*. And as this universal phenomenon of sinfulness, which is presented in a multitude of psychological forms, has its foundation deep-seated in the perversion of the due relation between these two factors which make up human life,—the cosmical and the spiritual principles, whose normal union ought to be complete in man,—it is evident that he

cannot redeem himself from evil, because evil has its foundation in the dominion over him of a universal principle, which
anticipates his free self-consciousness. But as, on the other
hand, the principle of good is *essentially* present in human
nature, a principle which unceasingly strives against sin, this
implies that human nature has in it the *possibility* of being
redeemed. Humanity still possesses the *idea* of the excellency
and glory of freedom. But this idea of freedom, this possibility of sanctity would be a poor consolation for man if *power*
was not given him from above, in the fulness of time, to develop this possibility; if a turning-point had not occurred in
the fulness of time, when the original and true relation
between the principles was restored. Carrying out the
explanation now given, Manichaeism and Pelagianism are
alike excluded. Original sin is neither a substance nor an
accident ; it is a false relation of existence.

Observations.—The doctrine has been advocated in modern
   times, chiefly by Rousseau, that there is no such thing as
   inborn sinfulness, but that sin is only the product of a
   false culture, which has forsaken the sure guidance of nature,—an imperfect education, distorted reflection,—and
   so forth. But when Rousseau thought that man could
   be redeemed by returning to a state of nature—*retour-
   nons à la nature*—his opinion can only be regarded as a
   fanciful aspiration after a lost paradise. That our present state of nature is not one of innocence but is affected
   equally with our state of culture by the sinful principle,
   has been perceived and stated by the acute Kant in
   his doctrine of radical evil, or of the *inborn tendency* to
   prefer the motive of egoism to that of the law, even as
   a means towards pure moral obedience. Nothing more
   plainly witnesses to the depravity of human nature, than
   does the consideration of the so-called state of nature.
   So far from this being the pure, uncorrupted childhood of
   humanity, the pure unbiassed germ of development in
   freedom, we find that this principle of development is
   wholly wanting, and that nations in such a condition
   lead on for centuries a stationary existence—a sort of natural history. So far from these men of nature presenting an immediate harmonious equilibrium of being, we

find whole masses given up to the consuming fire of the
wildest passions, or sunk in a slow indifference to existence, like petrifactions in the world of mind. So far
from manifesting the unconscious yet unerring dominion
of pious instincts of reason, they display wildnesses of
natural impulse that indicate, not merely defect of culture, but actual mal-formation, and which in the world
of humanity correspond to monstrosities in nature. The
more we consider the *state of culture* among nations, the
more shall we discover marks of a perversion of *nature*
akin to these ; so that the vices of a state of nature
sometimes appear in a state of culture. If, then, it must
be allowed that the wild appetites and passions move and
work in this case also out of a sinful nature, and are restrained only by the power of *the law,* it becomes clear
that the opinion is equally erroneous, which adopts the
opposite extreme to that of Rousseau in his commendation
of a state of nature,—the opinion, I mean, that culture is
sufficient to deliver men fundamentally from egoism.
The contemplation of the heathenism of Greece and Rome
is a sufficient witness against this. Goethe, in his *Schrift
über Winkelmann,* may speak of " an indestructible
health" to be found in the heathenism of Greece. But
this optimism is based upon an aesthetic and superficial contemplation, which fails to recognise the inner disease lurking in the spiritual core of life ; a disease which
at length broke out in an appalling mass of sinfulness,
such as that which the apostle Paul depicts in the first
chapter of his Epistle to the Romans.

In opposition to Rousseau's doctrine that man is by
nature good, all profounder forms of religion and philosophy have perceived evil to be a universal phenomenon
in humanity, the foundation of which must be sought beyond and before self-consciousness in the individual, because when this awakes it finds itself already beset by
the principle of sinfulness. The only real question in the
matter accordingly is, how this "radical evil" in human
nature is to be more accurately explained and defined.
In addition to the scriptural view here developed, there
are two explanations possible ; namely, that each indivi-

dual has pre-determined his own nature by an "intelligible" act done before time for him began : or, that man was so determined by *nature*, as an intelligent and free agent, that consciousness, developing itself out of the swaddling-clothes of naturalism, is, *eo ipso*, sinful ; Adam being only an instance of this naturally sinful development of the race.

Schelling in his treatise upon human freedom, and Steffens in his Religious Philosophy,—both following the example of Kant in his doctrine of radical evil,—explain inborn sinfulness as the result of an intelligent mystical act committed by the individual before his entrance upon this natural world of experience. This is an opinion involving the idea of the pre-existence of the soul, and it had an advocate within the Church in Origen ; but it is beset with insurmountable difficulties. If man in a pre-existent state brought himself into the depraved condition in which he finds himself in his present life, this present life and everything in time is deprived of significance, and we are brought to another form of supra-lapsarian one-sidedness. The fall of Adam in this case becomes only the necessary *manifestation* of a pre-existent fall, and his freedom in time has no reality. This doctrine is moreover inconsistent with the organic progress of human development. The theory that each individual has already pre-determined itself independently, is opposed to the undisputed fact of experience that distinctive types of character, family and national, impress themselves on individuals ; that the peculiarities of parents reappear in their children ; an experience which is confirmed by the scriptural representations of a pre-determination arising out of the organic progress of human development. The Church adopts this experience as her own when she teaches that individuals receive at birth a spiritual *inheritance* which has no foundation in their own self-determination.

Hegel and Schleiermacher, notwithstanding the great difference in their views regarding freedom, coincide in explaining inborn sinfulness as *natural* to human existence, because man who, in the very conception of him as

man, is a reasonable being, is bound at his birth by the
blind impulses of nature, so that the will cannot but determine itself in an egoistic direction. This is certainly
a *description* of the opposition universally felt, and confirmed by experience, between the flesh and the Spirit;
but to represent this phenomenon as necessarily involved in
the idea of human development, is, as we have endeavoured
to show, wholly inadequate as an explanation. The difference between good and evil dispositions is overlooked; it
has not been proved that it necessarily enters into the
idea of human nature to lust against the Spirit, or that
action assumes *only* the form of self-consciousness, and
never of natural genius. In Christ, the second Adam, we
behold a human life of which we cannot suppose that it
began with this discord, but throughout whose course
there was clearly a rhythmical harmonious movement of
the factors of life. As the theory of original sin now
mentioned teaches that sin did not enter into the world
by one man, but is originally in the world, and that the
first Adam had radical evil in him as a natural possession,
it cannot abide by the definition that sin is *inborn* in
man, but must say that it is not only inborn but *innate;*
and thus we are brought to the verge of Manichæism.
For it is equally the doctrine of Manichæism that sin is
innate in man and not only inborn, or in other words,
that it not only *has arisen*, but is in itself original.

Each of these modes of explanation, the mystical as
well as the natural, makes evil *eternal :* the one because
it carries it back beyond the limits of time to a pre-
existent state, the other because it makes it an essential
part of human existence; and neither method has any
thought regarding an actual deliverance from this natural
corruption. We cannot see, for instance, how it can be
possible for man to *convert himself* in time, when before
all time he had chosen a state of sinfulness. As little can
we understand how the prayer " Deliver us from evil" can
ever be fully accomplished if evil be given a place in the
very *conception* of life and activity, not only as a possibility, but as a necessity; if it be indispensable to the
very movement of life and manifestation of good. Simi-

larly we cannot understand how Christ can be the Saviour, if this radical evil must have been in Him also, though only in a *minimum* degree. The Scriptural view, which teaches that " by one man sin *entered into* the world," and has thus passed upon all men, admits of a well-grounded belief that it may be taken away *out of* the world, if the world is brought back to its true ideal. We explain the universal phenomenon of sinfulness on the ground of an act of human freedom, which was done in the beginning of the development of the race, by that individual who must be looked upon as the first representative of the race. And we do not base this doctrine upon the authority of Biblical tradition alone. A spiritual contemplation of the phenomenon of evil, as it lies before us in human life, necessarily leads us back to the fall ; so that even supposing this fact were not related in the Bible, we should postulate it as a necessary truth. For if we exclude the supposition of a fall, the only alternative is, either to deny sin as a universal phenomenon, and to make it something merely individual and fortuitous, or seeing it to be a universal phenomenon, to recognize it as an eternal principle in human life, as an inherent element in the idea of the world. But thus we blunt the sting of sin, and can never pronounce the sentence of death upon it. The moment we pronounce sentence of death upon sin in any one of its forms, we must maintain the same judgment upon all sin : this is necessary to the essential and well-understood interests of good, and, as we have already shewn, the Christian idea of perfecting the world, by the total destruction of evil, must be given up. The true mean between the two extremes,—between that which makes sin merely individual and fortuitous, and that which makes it eternal,—is the view given by St. Paul in Rom. v. 12—" By one man sin entered into the world, and death by sin ; and so death passed upon all men, for that all have sinned."

§ 94.

When the Church in her Theology describes inborn sinfulness as *totalis carentia virium spiritualium*, and includes all " spiritual energies " as energies moral and religious in the

deepest sense, as energies of the kingdom of God, she by no
means denies that spiritual gifts of nature may be manifested
by sinful humanity in the sphere of this present life, or that
human nature possesses a susceptibility for the revelation o
love, and impulses towards the kingdom of God: she only
declares the total incapacity of sinful humanity to bring forth
of itself the highest good, its inability to realize the true ideal.
It is not the *receptivity*, but the *productivity* which is wanting to the natural man.   Man's *actual* will, while still without
the range of redemptive influences, even in its noblest outgoings, is lost in worldly aims; and the natural man, even
in his highest and most spiritual activity, is only *a man of
this world*, not *a man of God*.   Still, in a state of sinfulness,
he is estranged, not only from God, but from his own ideal
also, the ideal of moral freedom; and this defect of nature
may be called the inability of man, apart from redemption, to
attain his true personality; whatever is holy within him,—
and this is essentially the material of a true personality,—
being fettered and even crushed.   In heathendom, for instance,
the development of human consciousness was kept in bondage
by a frigid objectiveness,—by the tyranny of the senses.
Heathenism disappeared in the ideals of politics, of art, of
speculation; but these world ideals in their turn could never
become the means of attaining the ideal of personality and of
holiness.   Our Church further describes inborn sinfulness as
concupiscentia, or evil desire,* and this is only the positive
complement of the first definition.   Man seeks in the world
for self and not for God, and egoism is developed in various
forms, from sinful appetite to spiritual pride, in which man
extends his *I* to an autonomic *world-I*—making himself all
in all.   The more accurate description of these various forms
of selfishness, manifest in individual life, belongs to the department of Christian ethics.

Observations.—The doctrine that the unregenerate cannot
but sin, by no means excludes the fact of there being
many degrees of morality, many grades of moral character
among them.   Some may be described as *not far* from
the kingdom of God, and others as *very far off* (Mark xii.
34; Acts ii. 39).   Even outside the kingdom of God,

* Confessio Augustana, Art. ii.

there exists a relative distinction between the righteous and the wicked; there are various stages of preparation for and nearness to that kingdom. But all these differences, however great their importance in the departments of morality and of history, when individuals are *compared* one with another, utterly vanish when individuals are measured by the universal standard of sinfulness of *race* or *nature*. Judged in this way it holds true, they cannot but sin ; that is, they all alike contradict the true ideal of humanity ; even in their highest moral activity their ideals and their aims are of this world, and not for the kingdom of God. Viewed thus, the question is not one concerning different degrees of morality, but concerning the general tendency and aim of life. In the same way therefore the Apostle John says, concerning the regenerate, that *they cannot sin*. In this expression he does not deny a relative power of sin in those who are born of God, he does not exclude a great many stages and differences of virtue and holiness among them. We take his meaning to be, that the regenerate, notwithstanding their relative sinfulness, cannot but will the realization of the kingdom of God ; can never cease to strive after the true ideal of life.

§ 95.

Universal sinfulness assumes as many forms in *individuals* as there are peculiarities and idiosyncrasies among men. The sinful tendency of human nature is not only manifested generally ; when humanity is viewed as an unorganized body in a state of nature, or in separate associations of men, in families and in nations, all which present natural peculiarities, and various shades of contrast with the true ideal of humanity : the effects of its deranging activity appears also in the personal and distinctive character of each individual man. In his individual nature, in his peculiar temperament, in the characteristic tendency of his desires, each one possesses, not only an appropriate basis for the development of freedom, but a limiting and disturbing barrier. This barrier cannot be explained as if it belonged to the idea of individuality, for it is not moral freedom *in abstracto* which is limited, but the individual manifestation of freedom, the unfolding of the true

personality of the man, of the talent implanted in him, entrusted
to him by God.   The individuality of every human being is
thus originally perverted and biassed ; and every one is,—if
we may adopt an expression often used,—involved in a contradiction between " his ideal and his caricature."

Observations.—The consideration of human TEMPERAMENT is
closely connected with the doctrine of original sin.   Temperament is the natural groundwork of character, and
though the power of temperament may be checked by the
will, the individual activity of the will is in turn limited
by temperament.   In the true conception of it every
temperament is good, and is intended as the foundation of
a determinate type of personal character.   But inborn
corruption,—*vitium* or *morbus originis* in the language
of Church theology,—shews itself in the fact that the
human ψυχή has by nature a *bent* or tendency to separate
itself in its distinctive temperament, and to exclude those
contrasts which must be maintained in order to the preservation of inward health.   Not only is the melancholic
temperament the natural foundation of a profound and
contemplative character, but the melancholic ψυχή has
also a tendency to waste itself in fruitless speculations, in
dreamy broodings and dissatisfied longings after subjective ideals, and in groundless sadness about existence ;
and accordingly the older theologians regarded melancholy
as the result of original sin.   The choleric temperament,
again, while it may be the groundwork for energetic
action, for a vigorous prosecution of the battle of life,
leads also to a one-sided zeal, an inner restlessness of soul,
an inquietude, which hinders its possessor from attaining
the satisfaction of life's fulness.   The sanguine man,
further, possesses in his temperament not only a natural
basis of a pure satisfaction and enjoyment of life, but a
natural propensity to fritter life away, to squander his
energies upon a changeful multiformity of fortuitous,
momentary, and transitory aims.   And he who is of a
phlegmatic disposition, while he possesses a natural
groundwork for a harmonious equanimity, for a self-
possessed peace of mind, which remains unshaken by the
storms of life, is at the same time liable to fall into a

superficial contentment with the state of things around him, and to *trivialize* life by a careless acquiescence in the course of the world. Such dispositions and tendencies to pervert individuality into one-sidedness are, in the present state of human nature, not only possibilities, which it rests with free will to discard, they have essentially the impress of a bias which the pious will must fight against and root out. But man does not obtain any true *ability* to conquer inborn partialities until he is brought within the range of redemption where the Spirit who proceeds from Christ, the second Adam, glorifies all natural characteristics in the universal system of the gifts of grace.

SINFUL HISTORY.
§ 96.

If we now consider the effects of the fall upon the course of historical development, not only in the case of individuals, but of the race collectively, the term WORLD ($\varkappa\acute{o}\sigma\mu o\varsigma$) bears a special meaning, different from that which it would have were the development of humanity normal. The cosmical principle having been emancipated by the fall from its due subjection to the spirit to a false independence; and the universe of creation having obtained with man a higher importance than really attaches to it; the historical development of the world has become one in which the advance of the kingdom of God is *retarded* and hindered. As the created universe has, in a relative sense, life in itself,—including, as it does, a system of powers, ideas, and aims, which possess a relative value,—this relative independence, which ought to be subservient to the aims of the kingdom of God, has become a false " world-autonomy." Hence arises the scriptural expression " *this* world," $\acute{o}$ $\varkappa\acute{o}\sigma\mu o\varsigma$ $o\mathring{\jmath}\tau o\varsigma$, whereby the Bible conveys the idea that it regards the world not only ontologically, but in its definite and *actual* state, the state in which it has been since the fall. " This world" means the world content with itself, in its own independence, in its own glory; the world which disowns its dependence on God as its Creator. " This world" regards itself not as the $\varkappa\tau\acute{\iota}\sigma\iota\varsigma$, but only as the $\varkappa\acute{o}\sigma\mu o\varsigma$, as a system of glory and beauty which has life in itself, and can give life. The historical embodiment of "this world" is heathendom, which honoureth not God as God. In the consciousness of heathendom the visible and invisible κόσμος is taken to be the highest reality ; and the development of this consciousness, displayed in heathen mythology, is a reflexion of the universe, not of God, an image of the world, not the manifestation of the true image of the LORD. The darkness of heathen consciousness does not consist in the total absence of any enlightening idea of what is really true and universally excellent, but in the fact that it does not see that idea reflected in God. It is not the contrast between the idea and the want of it,—between the spirit and the spir'tless,—which must guide us in judging of heathenism ; it is rather the contrast between idea and idea, between spirit and spirit, between the holy aim and the world's aim, between the holy spirit and the spirit of the world. Ὁ κόσμος οὗτος is not confined exclusively to the old heathenism ; it is wherever the kingdom of God is not, wherever that kingdom does not exercise its guiding influence. This world is ever striving after an earthly state which does not make itself subordinate to God's rule ; it developes a wisdom which does not retain the living God in its knowledge ; it forms for itself an excellency which is not the reflection of His glory. And this glittering pantheistic world-reality is not a mere imaginary thing, for the powers of the universe are really divine powers. The elements, the materials with which this world builds its kingdom, are of the noblest kind, their want of genuineness lies in the *ethical form* given to them ; or in the false relation between the glory of this world and the will of man.

§ 97.

As the expression *this world* implies the negation of the true ideal of the world, its condition may be described as one of *unrighteousness.* The conception of true righteousness is applicable not only to the deliberate act of commission or omission, but to the entire being and capacity of man. The true δικαιοσύνη includes the coincidence of man's actual life with his true life, the harmony of real existence with the *essential law* of existence, with its eternal pattern. But as the true δικαιοσύνη is by nature wanting in the individual man (Romans iii. 23), it is also wanting in the historical life of the race, wherein worldly objects are sought at the sacrifice of man's true relation to God; and the world as it is continually contradicts the true. Not only are individuals egoistic, but the entire organism, historically viewed,—with its aims whether of state, of art, or of science,—is beset with a general world-egoism. In proportion as these aims have become powers in "this world," they work in peripheric one-sidedness, in separate circles, the true centre, the kingdom of God, being outside of them; and thus we may speak of an egoism of *ideas.* Accordingly sinful history indicates an ἐχθρα (Eph. ii. 15), an enmity between the spirits of nations who mutually exclude one another, or equally shut themselves up from one another. Thus each of the various worldly aims developed in sinful history seems to advance its sway with absolute effort at the expense of all the rest. Thus each individual, even if he widen his personal *I* to a general *I,* which includes others besides himself, even if he devote himself to some more general aim—giving his life to the realisation of an idea—cannot attain true δικαιοσύνη, for in the highest act of individual self-sacrifice—as in the self-sacrifice of the heathen for their country—we find the egoism of the cosmical idea of which the man makes himself the organ. The same hold true of sacrifices made in behalf of the ideals of art and science. The true δικαιοσύνη is unattainable by *this world.*

§ 98.

As the development of this world is thus a development of unrighteousness, TIME also receives a new import for man as the form of the development; and as the world becomes ὁ κόσμος οὗτος, time becomes ὁ αἰὼν οὗτος. *This* time stands in *contrast* with the *true* time. The true time expresses for the normal development of life, its undisturbed advance towards the goal of eternity. *This time,* on the contrary, means a time of conflict and suspense during which the forces of life come continually into *collision* with each other; a season of pain and restlessness. But the troublousness of this time does not arise from the fact that the fulness of life has "not yet" been reached, but from the fact that life is parcelled out and divided, that the holy unity which should harmonize the various forces in the progress of life, and give peace and rest thereto, is limited and retarded. The designation ὁ αἰὼν οὗτος gives the impress of profanity to the history of the world. It is profane, not because it realizes what is not holy, but because it embodies the opposite and contradictory to holiness. In the fact of its separation from the kingdom of God, the history of the world is a history without a centre, and it therefore can never attain its end. Profane history progresses in a vicious circle, a *progressus in infinitum*, yet continually repeating itself; according to the complaint of the scoffers of whom St. Peter writes, "Since the fathers fell asleep all things continue as they were from the beginning of the creation," (2 Peter iii. 4). In *this* αἰών, experience continually repeats the old tale how many things are born only to come to nought, how beauty dies and truth grows old. Notwithstanding all the praise of this world's glory, the complaint continually is heard in this present αἰών, that the world is vanity, that there is nothing new under the sun, and that in all things there is only sorrow and vexation of spirit.*

Superhuman Evil: Dæmoniacal Powers; and the Devil.

§ 99.

Although evil has no true reality in itself, yet it works as a kingdom of negations, limited in its advances by the kingdom of goodness, and of true activity. The sinful world of mankind, however, is not as such the kingdom of evil. " The whole world lieth in wickedness;"—ἐν τῷ πονηρῷ κεῖται (1 John v. 19) ;—but it is not wickedness, it is not evil in and for itself. The sinful world of humanity includes in it a germ of good; it possesses *essentially* a tendency towards the kingdom of God, and reveals a relative goodness in every stage of the development of its history. But a disturbing, disorganizing principle ever manifests itself side by side with that which forms and organizes. There is a kingdom of principalities and powers, which, while in conflict within itself, conspires against the kingdom of good; principalities and powers in creation who, originally good, have become evil, by entering the service of that principle which seeks to defeat the end of God's creation. We can certainly as little say of the kingdom of evil

* See Ecclesiastes, *passim.*

as of the kingdom of good, " Lo, here ! or Lo, there !" yet the former, equally with the latter must be viewed as uninterruptedly progressing, continually *coming,* endeavouring to organize itself as if the true reality, and finding its *instruments* in this sinful world of men, who in their thoughts and in their lives follow demoniacal influences, and labour for demoniacal tendencies. The demon is evil, as a super-sensual, and purely spiritual power. In the world of intelligence *falsehood* has its prophets, and in the world of practice there are men who have so initiated themselves into the mysteries of wickedness, that they have brought themselves down to a *disinterested love* of evil. The warfare of this kingdom against the good, runs throughout history, and thus all its possibilities must be exhausted in order that it may be overcome in all.

§ 100.

The contrast between good and evil is described in Holy Scripture as a conflict, not only between good and bad men, but between good and bad powers, superhuman powers ($\dot{\alpha}\rho\chi\alpha\iota$ $\varkappa\alpha\iota$ $\dot{\epsilon}\xi o\upsilon\sigma\dot{\iota}\alpha\iota$) in whom the life of man is with freedom complicated. These demoniacal powers not only appear in the struggle of Heathenism and Judaism against Christianity, but even in sacred history the demon appears as a power to which man, as far at least as the body is concerned, stands in a passive relation. Demoniacal possession, as it is called, which is referred to in the Gospels, may indeed be interpreted as natural infirmity or sickness, but it is essentially of such a nature as to affect alike the physical and the psychical. The ultimate sources of these sicknesses are super-sensual, are of a moral nature, and this it is which gives them a demoniacal character. And as Scripture speaks of a demoniacal kingdom, the church in like manner continues to bear witness that we have to wrestle not only with flesh and blood, but with invisible principalities and powers, " against the rulers of the darkness of this world, against spiritual wickedness in high places " (Eph. vi. 12). The central head of this demoniacal kingdom is called the Devil, Satan, Antichrist, the prince of this world. The Christian doctrine of evil terminates with this doctrine concerning the devil, because the anthropological and historical consideration of the subject becomes at this point metaphysical rather than religious. The Devil is not merely evil in this or that particular relation, it is evil in and for itself, the evil spirit as such. The Devil is not merely one evil creation, not one demon among many, but the evil principle itself *in persona.* The notion that the doctrine of the Devil has only of late been imported into Christianity,—that the question as to his existence should not, as Schleiermacher thinks, be the subject of Christian or theological discussion,—must vanish and disappear before every deeper consideration of the nature of evil, and of the essence of Christianity. We must, on the contrary, go so far as to affirm, that the way and manner in which any one speaks of the devil may be taken as a test and criterion of his views regarding evil generally. Theology must therefore assert the necessary connection of this doctrine with the entire range of Christian ideas, and must represent the doctrine of the Devil as the doctrine of the evil principle, in accordance as far as possible with the presuppositions of Christianity.

§ 101.

A closer analysis of this idea of the Devil will show that the Christian view of the reality of evil is thus expressed. The conception of a Devil as a superhuman, yet created spirit, who originally was good, but fell from his station, and in pride became the enemy of God, involves the clearest contrast and opposition to the dualism of heathendom, which either makes two fundamentally distinct existences, as in the Persian religion, or makes evil the dark and mysterious source from which good developes itself, and which existence conquers,—the view adopted by the Greek and Northern mythologies. (The Titans are opposed to the gods, and the giants to the *Ases.**) The Christian view is also contrasted with that explanation which makes evil to consist in sense, in matter, or which reduces evil to a mere privation, a limitation, a μὴ ὄν. The Devil is a highly-gifted, a powerful spirit. This doctrine concerning him involves the most obvious antagonism to *Acosmism.* Pantheism with its ἕν καὶ πᾶν has no

---

* Odin the Scandinavian god, and Frea, " Mother earth," his wife, correspond to the Jupiter and Apia of the Scythians, the Saturn and Ops of Greece. Their children were called Ases, and were as gods engaged in conflict with the Jö tuns, the giants. See § 120, Obs. and note.—Tr.

place for the Devil. The free God of creation that Theism recognizes may not only endure another than Himself,—a world which is a *non deus,* but even a contrast to Himself, which contradicts Him, an *adversarius dei,* without encroaching upon His almighty power. Whether Acosmism is fundamentally subdued is best tested by this doctrine ; wherefore Luther, when he would test a Christian teacher, asked, " Does he believe in death and devil ? or is it all mere joy and pleasure ? "

If, again, we view the devil in relation not only to God but to man, he appears a spirit external to and distinct from man, yet who insidiously has crept upon him and has brought him under his dominion. Evil, accordingly, is alien to human nature, and is excluded from the true idea of humanity. In and for itself it must be looked upon as a spirit hostile both to God and man ;—the enemy of both. But while existing in creation, it cannot itself be a separate creation, because the individual creature can only be *participant* of evil. Evil in and for itself can be looked upon only as a universal *principle.* Hence we attribute to the devil a sort of omnipresence, for wherever *this world* is, there is also the devil. Those attributes which appear in special activity in the evil spirit are power and cunning. The former expresses the positive character of evil ; for positive powers are at his command, and as ' Prince of this world ' he could offer Christ " the kingdoms of this world and the glory of them." But his kingdom is at the same time a kingdom of falsehood and deception ; for his power is only *temporal ;* viewed in the light of eternity he is ever the rejected and condemned, and it is only by lying and delusion that he succeeds in obtaining entrance among men. The evil spirit, therefore, can only be *Satan,* the Titanic power, because he is at the same time διάβολος, the deceiver, the *father of lies ;*—who belied the Creator, who sowed tares among the wheat, and who transforms himself into an angel of light. Thus the devil embodies the idea of evil as it must be viewed according to the presupposition of the creation-dogma, and of the given relation between God and the world.

§ 102.

But the true doctrine concerning the devil is not presup-

posed in the dogma of the creation alone; it has its deepes
presupposition in the dogma of the "Son of God." Althoug
Judaism rests upon the Creation-dogma, it has no continuou
Satanology, the doctrine of an evil spirit is not evolve
throughout it; and this arises from the fact that it failed t
apprehend the immortality of the created spirit, and the fal
also in its infinite consequences. In its demonology th
later Judaism was led on to a profounder perception of th
workings of evil; but evil for and in itself, the *depths o_*
Satan were not recognised. The idea of the Son of God a:
the principle of creation was not propounded in Judaism. I♦
was not perceived that the destiny of the created spirit wa:
to be an organ of revelation for the Son,—to be in a copy
what the Son is originally, to become by grace what the Sor
is by nature. In Christianity it is first perceived that evi
is that which opposes the revelation of the Son, that which
instead of becoming the organ of the Son, endeavours to
usurp His place. Evil is essentially *the cosmical principle*
in so far as this belies its character as created, and in false
independence opposes itself to the true and holy world-principle who is the Son. Jacob Böhme thus expresses this :
" Lucifer (the fallen star of the morning) imagining himself
in himself—contemplating his own beauty as self-contained
—envied the glory of the Son. His own beauty deceived
him, and he sought to sit upon the throne of the Son." The
doctrine of the devil does not obtain its full exposition until
it is viewed in connection with the holy *Trinity;* in the light
of this doctrine the world is seen to be a force which is not
God, in the Godhead, the negative of the Son, *Alterum dei*
filii; and thus we recognize a certain shade of truth in the
paradox which Schelling in his *Satanologie* adopts as the tenet
of an heretical sect in the Middle Ages, that the devil is the
brother of Christ. We cannot agree with the Bogomili* and
Schelling in calling the devil the *elder* brother of Christ; we
must inversely call him the *younger* brother; for the Son of
God is older than the world, is the eternal presupposition of

---

* A sect of the *Cathari*, in Thrace, in the twelfth century, who held a modi-
fied form of Dualism. Their name is supposed to have been derived from a
Bulgarian pope named Bogomil. See Herzog's Real Encyck., Article *Katharer.*
—*Tr.*

the world, and does not develop himself from it as from a
dark source. Lucifer, as the embodiment of the cosmical
principle, must therefore be figuratively called the younger
brother, because he is the *second*, who comes after the first-
born; because, moreover, the existence of the world, and
therewith a centre which is not God, rests with the Son as
"the first-born of all creatures." Lucifer is only the devil,
Antideus, because he would not be second, but first; because
instead of being the reflecter of light, he would be light himself, and have light in himself. Thus the idea of the devil
coincides with the idea of the cosmical principle, hypostasized
—*i.e.*, personified—as a negative spirit; and thus it may be
perceived how the devil must not in the first instance or
chiefly be apprehended as an individual, a personal creature.
Whether there be diabolizing creatures, whether among these
there be one creature in whom the evil principle is so centralized, and has attained so personal a form as to be called
"the Prince of the devils;"—this question can have no meaning for us until we have recognised the devil as a principle.
We must first and chiefly apprehend the devil, not as a creature,
but as a god, as Paul calls him *the god of this world* (ὁ Θεὸς τοῦ
αἰῶνος τούτου, 2 Cor. iv. 4). Schelling acutely observes, that
the devil in order to be the equally born antagonist of Christ,
must be more than an individual creature, against whom it
would not have been necessary to make so great preparations.
And we certainly must confess that an individual creature
who is not in the first instance a principle, who is not a god,
would only have made himself ridiculous when he offered to
Christ the kingdoms and the glory of this world. The entire
history of temptation obtains quite a new and fuller meaning
when the devil is taken as the embodiment of the cosmical
principle itself, which, with its wide dominion, opposes itself
to Him who is the personal revelation of the principle of
holiness. The contrast between Christ and the devil is, in
its inmost import, the contrast between the two great principles wherein all the contrasts of life have their foundation.
It is the contrast between God and the world, which here
appears as the pure contrast between the holy centre and the
world centre, asserting itself in a false independence.

§ 103.

As good does not become active till it assume a *personal* form, so is it with evil likewise. The evil principle can only be conceived of as a *will*, which is the foe of God and man. If evil be taken as impersonal, its sting is taken away, and it sinks into a mere power of nature. But what must we suppose its personality to be ? The evil principle cannot certainly be personal in the same sense as the good principle, as God, is personal. The evil principle cannot be personal in itself ; it can only obtain personality in a creature who is endowed with will. Were we to imagine the evil principle as a personal anti-god, who existed in the fulness of his own being apart from God's creation, we should fall into Manichaeism. Evil can only obtain personal existence surreptitiously ; the negative principle can be helped to personality only by the will of some creature. In other words :—the devil, understanding thereby the cosmical principle, can only become personal in the creatures who submit to become its instruments ;—it can only become personal in its kingdom. The personality, moreover, which pantheism attributes to its God —as it can become active only in finite spirits, in the human consciousness, in the moral order of the world,—this kind of personality is all that can be assigned to the Devil ; because he must be conceived of not as an individual creature, but as a universal principle. But such a personality is not a real existence, a being resting in itself, it is only a *becoming*, something that hovers half way between existence and nonexistence, between personality and personification, between reality and possibility, between " it is " and " it seems." The conception of the Devil as the god of *time* throws us back upon the notion of a personality continually becoming personal. The devil, as the evil principle, ceaselessly strives after existence, which it can obtain only in time, only in this world ; it therefore unceasingly lays snares for men, in order to obtain existence in them, in order, like the *vampire*, to procure for itself fulness, by sucking their heart's blood. Whereas the Manichaean theory makes the evil principle a perfect and complete existence, an actually existing god opposed to the God of good ; according to the principles of Christianity we must teach that the evil principle *exists* only in so far as it continually *generates* itself in God's creation, as it *smuggles* its kingdom in, like tares among the wheat. The devil of Christianity endeavours to make himself what the evil spirit according to Manichaeism actually is,—namely, a god who divides the government of the world with the God of goodness.

Observations.—Schleiermacher, in his celebrated criticism upon the doctrine of the devil, endeavoured to prove that the expressions of the New Testament upon the subject cannot be harmonized in one conception, but have been blended together from various constituent parts ; that the doctrine of the devil accordingly subverts itself ; and that Jesus and his Apostles must only have availed themselves incidentally of the popular belief, without intending to develop or to ratify any doctrine upon the subject. It is however a more profound and worthier task to shew that these various declarations are only different aspects of the same conception, and that they are essentially connected together and explain one another. Though we by no means hold (as will be seen in what follows) that the doctrine of Scripture is exhausted by the representation of the devil as the principle of evil, this is withal the fundamental definition which we must in the first instance fully grasp ; and the enquiry regarding the devil as a personal evil being, has no real import till this is recognized as the fundamental idea. We shall now endeavour to confirm the chief points above developed out of holy Scripture.

If we look to the Old Testament our attention is specially directed to two points, namely, to the *serpent* in the Book of Genesis, and to *Satan* in the Book of Job (Gen. iii.; Job i.). Orthodox theology has often asserted that the serpent in paradise was the devil. The Old Testament does not say so, and therefore we may in the present connexion pass by the question whether the serpent was led by an evil spirit, or whether an evil spirit assumed the form of a serpent. If we abide by the original narrative, we may say that the serpent is the allegorical designation for the cosmical principle which opposed itself to man in a temptation. So far as *tempta-*

tion is necessary to man, paradise cannot be without a serpent, and so far as Satan is only the tempter who evokes human freedom, bringing it into action and manifestation, we may say that he has a function to perform in the divine economy. This, moreover, is attributed to him in the Old Testament, in the Book of Job, when he appears in heaven among the Sons of God, and obtains permission to tempt Job by means of various plagues. Here he is not only the neutral tempter, but evil subjectivity comes to light in him. He is not yet indeed the Satan of the New Testament, who is driven from the presence of God, because he wills evil as such ; but he takes a malicious pleasure in undermining and deceiving human virtue. His joy consists in spying out the weaknesses and sins of men, and in bringing men by his temptations to manifest these ; and then he returns back to the Lord as the accusing angel to prove the untrustworthiness of human virtue. He does not yet appear, strictly speaking, as the evil spirit, for he practises a certain kind of justice, namely, the negative justice of irony, but he is without goodness or tenderness. That Satan which appears in heaven among the Sons of God reminds us of the *Loke** of Northern mythology,—not *Utgardeloke* but *Asaloke,* who, notwithstanding his wickedness, lived upon a trusted footing in the Walhalla with the gods. Goethe has conceived his Mephistophiles after the same pattern. This idea of Satan appears in the New Testament in the

---

* The Scandinavians seem to have regarded Loki or Loke as the evil principle, whom notwithstanding they ranked among the gods or Ases. The Edda (Mythol. 26) calls him "the calumniator of the gods, the grand contriver of deceit and frauds, the reproach of the gods and men. He is beautiful in his figure, but his mind is evil, and his inclinations inconstant. Nobody renders him divine honours. He surpasses all mortals in the arts of perfidy and craft." The older form of his name, Lodur, denotes *fire,* as his brothers Kari and Oegir denote the elements of *air* and *water.* They were the sons of Feriot "the old giant." As Odin and Honir gave man reason and soul, Loke gave him the warmth of life and sensual feelings. Hence "the flesh" is allied with the evil principle in this mythology. Loke gained access to the Ases in consequence of their innocent play with gold being transformed into a lust for gold (Mammon). Hence he was called the Asaloke. Utgard was a city of the giant Skrymner visited by Thor, and Utgardloke "the demon from without" was the King of this city. See Mallet's transl. of *the Edda*, and Herzog's Real Encyck. Art. Mythologie.—*Tr.*

words of the Lord to Peter : "Simon, Simon, Satan hath desired to have you that he may sift you as wheat !" (Luke xxii. 31). The Lord prays for Peter that his faith may not fail him, and exhorts him to strengthen his brethren. The accuser desires to sift the believers in order to spy out their weaknesses, and to tempt them ; the superficial and unstable in faith and in life cannot hold their ground against his temptations ; the unstable are marked out to be surprised by his cunning machinations. Sincerity and stability are needed if one is not to be brought to shame and ruin.

This representation of Satan is, according to Schleiermacher, one of the elements which go to make up the New Testament doctrine of the devil : the other element, which is far different from this, must have been derived, he thinks, from the Persian Dualism, so far as the essential existence of an evil being could be adopted by a monotheistic people. But the idea of the devil, as the evil one, ὁ πονηρός, the enemy, (Matt. xiii. 19, 39,) may easily be explained as arising naturally out of the expansion of the first element. Its affinity with the evil being whom the Parsees believed in may have been the occasion of its development in the consciousness of the nation, but revelation itself has not borrowed the idea from any external source. Satan having first been looked upon as negative irony, without positive righteousness or goodness, is now recognized further as one who not only takes pleasure in the ruin of men, but who makes evil in and for itself, evil as such, his object and aim. The activity of evil appears in the New Testament partly in the form of *cunning*, and partly in that of *power*. In the form of cunning he works as the enemy who sows tares among the wheat, who perverts the true doctrine, and in the form of an angel of light, spreads a false wisdom (2 Cor. xi. 14.) In this way he is specially dangerous to the faithful and to the spiritually awakened. Power, on the other hand, is the main feature of his influence over those who are beyond the range of the true faith, or who have fallen therefrom. Thus he "taketh the word out of the hearts" of the ungodly, (Matt. xiii. 19,) so that they do not understand, and are not converted. The heathen world is accordingly spoken of in the New Testament as the kingdom of Satan, and " to deliver a person over to Satan," (1 Cor. v. 5), is, in the phraseology of the New Testament, to excommunicate him from the fellowship of God, to give him over to heathenism. The New Testament gathers up the various points of the idea of the devil in the designation *Antichrist.* (1 John ii. 18.) Antichrist is that historical expression for the devil, the meaning of which is gradually declared in the historical development of religion in the world. The super-historical and metaphysical import of the idea is indicated in the designation " the prince of this world" (John xiv. 30.)

The most appalling outgoings of satanic power are in those *possessed,* of whom the New Testament speaks. Demons are not only the mere sinful propensities of the man ; they are spirits, powers, by which the man is enslaved. When Christ addresses himself to the possessed, He does not speak to the man, but to the demons ; and the man possessed answers, not in his own name, but in theirs. But the consideration of demoniacal possession shews us that the evil spirit seeks possession of man in order to procure an activity for itself, because it has in itself only an abstract existence. When the demons go out of a man, they betake themselves to the wilderness, and to dry places, (Luke xi. 24) ; apart from humanity, they have only an empty, unproductive existence ; and accordingly they lie in wait continually for the opportunity to return again to the world of man, and to set up their abode there. Or they remain in the air, (Eph. ii. 2 ; vi. 12,) in the undetermined, unformed element ; and this mode of expression in like manner shews that, apart from the world of man, they have only an empty being. Or again, they go into the swine, (Matt. viii. 32,) they are sent back into nature, into the world of unclean animals, from whence they had before insinuated themselves, into the human world, in order to contaminate souls. The idea of the wilderness as the abode, the retreat of evil spirits, reminds us of Peter's comparison of the roaring lion—" Your adversary the devil, as a roaring lion goeth

about, seeking whom he may devour," (1 Peter v. 8.)
Here again it is implied that the devil hungers after fulness of life, and must come for his substance, for the
material on and in which he works, and for his means of
nourishment to the world of man.

§ 104.

Thus far we have considered the devil only as a principle.
But as this negative principle can obtain for itself personality
only in free creatures, a question arises which is not of a
speculative but of an empiric character, namely,—Did this
principle enter *first* into *mankind*, or had it entered into
creatures of another order before its coming into the world of
man ? Abiding by the assumption that the devil has personal
existence *only* in the world of man, we may conclude our consideration of the subject according to what has already been
developed, by saying ;—the devil is originally the cosmical
principle, which as such is not yet evil ; it is moreover the
tempting principle that seduced man in paradise, because
it shewed him the reality of the world, which he can prefer
to the reality of God. But still it is not evil, still it is only
the possibility of a devil ; and the temptation accordingly
assumes the form of a natural impulse only which man can
repel if he will. In the serpent the evil spirit only glimmers
or dawns; in the serpent Satan is, so to speak, still in swad-
dling clothes. He becomes the actual devil—the personal evil
—for the first time, when man has allowed him entrance into
the sphere of consciousness. It is man, therefore, who gives
the devil being ; but it by no means follows from this that
man is only his own devil. It is another, a superhuman
principle to which existence is imparted by man, a tempting,
seducing, making-possessed, and inspiring power, to which man
lends himself, as to a *non-ego*. And though the existence of
the devil has from the beginning been dependent upon man,
man on the other hand has been subdued by his dominion,
and by his demoniacal workings since he has obtained
entrance into the human world. The devil is a spirit that
man has conjured to himself, and is not able to cast out. He
cannot accomplish the exorcism which is needed, by his own
power ; he requires the higher help of Him who is the Master
and Lord of the spirit-world.

The view of the devil here developed may be described as
that obtained from the stand-point of *immanence*, inasmuch
as no personal reality is attributed to the devil, *beyond* or
apart from the world of man. Speculation concerning the
doctrine of the devil has usually terminated here, as may be
seen, for example, in Schelling's *Satanologie*, which is the
latest important treatise upon the subject.

§ 105.

Although it must certainly be affirmed that the negative
principle has no personality in itself, but can only obtain personality in living creatures, it by no means follows that this
principle has obtained personality in human creatures alone.
Biblical tradition and ecclesiastical teaching recognizes a personal *fall* from God, which took place *in the angel-world* before the fall of man. The term *angel* indeed has the same
indefiniteness and width as lies in the idea "spirit," and it is
not, therefore, necessary when we speak of an angel always to
understand a personal spirit : there are angels mentioned in
Holy Scripture that are clearly mere personifications, or mere
intermediate beings, hovering between personality and personification : but the fundamental usage of Scripture teaches
us that such an explanation does not apply to all cases, and
that there are among angels, personal spirits ; and among these
again some who have fallen from God;—"angels who kept
not their first estate, but left their own habitation" (Jude 6),
(the place assigned to them, and their due rank in the order
of creation);—angels "that have sinned" and "are reserved
unto judgment" (2 Peter ii. 4). Among many demons Revelation speaks of one, who is called "the chief of the devils"
(Luke xi. 15), who is the *originator* of the fall, and of falsehood. This beginning of the fall our Lord gives us a hint of,
when He says "he abode not in the truth," and when He calls
him "the father of lies" (John viii. 44). As this evil angel,
the chief of the devils, the head of the kingdom of evil, is described in Scripture as the evil principle itself *in persona*, as
not only a devil but as *the* devil, we may explain this upon
the supposition, that this creature is the one, among all creatures, who, on account of his position in the realm of creatures,
succeeded in making himself *the central manifestation* of the
cosmical principle (as of the evil principle); the creature in

which that principle attained perfect personality, so that he is the most perfect representative and supporter of it.   We must accordingly define more accurately what we have already developed, thus:——The evil principle has in itself no personality, but attains a progressively universal personality in its kingdom ; it has no individual personality, save only in individual creatures, who in an especial manner make themselves its organs ; but among these is one creature in whom this principle is so hypostasized that he has become the centre and head of the kingdom of evil.   And as in the foregoing section we said that the declarations of Scripture regarding the devil had no deeper meaning than this, as they do not speak of *more* than one single creature, as they do not speak of a universal principle ; this acknowledgment must be supplemented by the corresponding or additional truth.   It is clearly the witness of the closest investigation of Scripture, as the most eminent doctors of the Church have perceived, that the declarations of Scripture regarding the devil, the *enemy*, speak of him as *more* than a principle, more than a universally evil *volition*, speak, that is, of an active personal *will;* although, of course, sometimes the one, and sometimes the other aspect, sometimes the altogether spiritual, sometimes the personal element is that which appears more prominently.   The conflict of Christ with the devil is certainly a conflict with a universal principle; yet it does not obtain its full import, until it is realized as a personal *will* whom He repels and overcomes.   And when the Church in baptism renounces the devil and all his works and all his ways, she does not renounce the evil principle only, which surrounds us on every hand, but the personal enemy of God and man, the evil will who appeared in the creation, the will which opposes God and his kingdom, who says *no* to every *yea* and *amen* that Christ utters.

§ 106.

Beyond the world of man, evil has had a mysterious beginning ; it had a history before it received a history upon earth ; and we are reminded of the mythical dream of the conflict of the Titans against the gods before the origin of man.   We have now reached that side of the subject which transcends speculation : for the conception of angels and fallen angels, the *conceivableness* of a creature that is the central manifestation

of evil, and that in a special sense may be called *Evil*—this no
speculation can reasonably deny. It has been said, indeed,
that the idea of such an absolute evil creature would be
Manichaean, but this rests upon a misconception ; for it cannot be supposed that evil is the essence of this creature in a
metaphysical sense, but that it is so only in an ethical sense ;
and the centralizations of evil which we already find in the
world of man, are the only types thereof, shewing how evil
in an ethical sense may become the element of a creature's
life. As little inconceivable will it be found that the human
world should be open to the influence of a higher and personal
spirit-world. We suppose, in accordance with revelation, that
both angels and demons are pure, *i.e.*, bodiless spirits ; they
are not, therefore, subject to the conditions of corporeity and
of space, they may be in the universe where they will ; and,
accordingly, ecclesiastical symbolism has represented both
angels and demons as *winged* beings. And as, according to
the representations of Revelation, it belongs to the definition
of an angel to be a ministering spirit for the development of
the kingdom of God among men, we must also allow it conceivable that demons in like manner seek the theatre of their
activity in the world of man, endeavour here to organize their
kingdom, here to obtain fulness and substance for their empty
being. Against the conceivableness of the devil as an evil
creature there is no objection, but it must certainly be confessed that this being can neither be handled nor seen, comprehended nor perceived. For to comprehend how a single
creature can become the central manifestation of evil, requires
an insight into the cosmical position and import of this creature, which lies beyond our experience. And we are equally
unable to discern the real possibility of this evil creation, its
power and influence upon the world of man ; we are equally
unable to perceive it in its absolute wickedness, because
absolute wickedness, when we contemplate it, transforms
itself into an abstraction. In poetry, therefore, when the
devil is presented in a visible individuality, it is necessary
always to conceal somewhat of its absolute wickedness, to
present only satanic characters (as, for example, Mephistophiles
by Goethe) instead of the satanic essence itself, which, as the
pure unnaturalness, resists personation. But it is not the less

a *fact*, for which the Word of God is our authority, that there is a father of lies ; there is an enemy of God and man ; there is a superhuman evil will, whose kingdom and dominion we strengthen and further by our sins.*

But although we cannot comprehend this enemy, though every attempt to do so is ἐμβατεύειν εἰς ἃ οὐχ ἑώρακε, (Col. ii. 18), we can nevertheless understand that it is only when will resists will that any mention can in truth be made of spiritual conflict. While we conceive of the kingdom of evil without a personal head, we have to fight only against a principle, against an impure world-spirit, against an active force more or less blind, a force which is half nature and half spirit,—a definition which has certainly a comprehensive reference to evil, but which does not exhaust the full conception of it. The expression, " father of lies," refers to an intelligence, a personal self-consciousness, and through him the struggle against evil becomes a really spiritual struggle. And although there are implied depths of spiritual wickedness (βάθη τοῦ Σατανᾶ, Rev. ii. 24) which cannot be fathomed in the present earthly stage of knowledge, yet the consciousness of a demoniacal kingdom and of its chief—that dark, gloomy background of Christian consciousness—and the dread of the devil, the profound horror of demoniacal fellowship—form the dark basis for the Christian fear of God. However much the history of superstition may show us what errors arise, when what can only be comprehended spiritually is taken in a literal and fleshly sense ; and however often we are content with such expressions as " the power of evil," " the evil principle," " the impure spirit-world," in our expositions of Scripture, yet the more profound consideration of Scripture, of life, and above all of the stern conflict against evil, will ever lead back our thoughts to the doctrine of an EVIL WILL. " However often the reality of the devil be turned away from in life and science, and be explained as a mere chimera, the earnest inquirer will ever again come back to it, and the doctrine of his existence will continually become anew the subject of investigation."†

§ 107.

If we now, in conclusion, inquire as to the teleological re-

---

* Compare Nitzsch, *System der Christl. Lehre.* 5 *Ausg.* 237.
† Daub in *Judas Ischarioth*

lation of the devil to the economy of the kingdom of God, we
must reject the view, which has of late been put forth by
Schelling, that the existence of the devil is relatively necessary ; that he is a participating factor, recognized by God, in
the divine economy ; because he is, in a negative sense, the
moving principle in history, which without him would come
to a stand.   It must on the contrary be said, that we may
certainly recognize the necessity of the cosmical principle for
the revelation of God, but not in the form of the evil principle and the evil will ; we may certainly recognize the necessity of temptation, but not of the fall; in a word, that the
thought of evil is a necessity, but not the *evil thought.*   As,
however, the devil, having once attained an illegitimate existence, must necessarily be an instrument in the realization of
God's designs, we may explain his teleological relation and
import thus :—he is the *unwilling medium* for the revelation of God's righteousness towards the human race.   Thus
Scripture describes him as the angel of death, who fills sinful humanity with the fear of death ; "That through
death He might destroy *him that hath the power of death,*
that is, the devil ; and deliver them who through fear of
death were all their lifetime subject to bondage" (Heb. ii. 14).
The dominion which he exercises over man, in virtue of his
all-embracing world-egotism, weighs like a fate upon the sinful race of man ; he is, to adopt a mythical comparison, the
serpent Midgard,* "the earth-encompassing torment."   His
dominion is established as the just punishment of the race
who have given themselves up to him.   But by Christ his
power is broken ; and the relation of the devil to the Church
is therefore different from his relation to the world.   For the
faithful his power is not a fate, to which they must in suffering submit, it possesses only the force of a tempting power
against which they must watch and pray, but which may be
overcome by the aid of the Holy Spirit.   As, on the one

---

* The serpent Midgard was, according to Northern mythology, the product
of the marriage of Loke (the evil principle) with the giantess Angrboda ("mes-
senger of anguish").   At the request of the gods, who feared the new monster,
Odin the universal Father cast him into the sea.   As the sea compasses all
lands with its troubled waters, the serpent was called Midgardswurm, "the
earth-encompassing torment."   See *Mallet's* Northern Antiquities, and *Herzog's*
Real Encyk. article Mythologie der alten Germanen.—*Tr.*

hand, he implies a fatalistic power which is subservient to
the revelation of God's righteousness, yet, in the same degree
as this power is recognized by man it loses its sting, because
men, in proportion as they recognize sin as a calamity, are
brought to redemption ; so, on the other hand, as he is the
tempter, who against his will operates on the faithful to
strengthen them in the Spirit of God, his universal significance is simply to be the dark ground for the divine revelation of light, to minister towards the glorification and
triumph of the Divine love. But his existence in and for itself is not a necessity in the divine economy of creation ;
were this so, he could not be as he is the eternally damned.
Were the devil necessary to the perfection of the universe, he
might at the Day of Judgment adopt the conclusive plea
which the apostle combats, "If the truth of God hath more
abounded through my lie unto His glory ; why yet am I also
judged as a sinner?" (Rom. iii. 7.) But this false plea is
already conclusively condemned in the Word of God.

GUILT AND PUNISHMENT. DEATH ; AND THE VANITY OF ALL
CREATURES.

§ 108.

In so far as mankind in virtue of their birth become partakers of the sin of the world, their inborn sinfulness must be
looked upon as their *fate;* but in so far as the sin of the race
is converted into the actual sin of the individual, it is his
guilt. That man's allotted heritage should become his guilt ;
or that inborn sinfulness should be *imputed* to the individual ;—this has its foundation in the mystery of the will, in
the nature of the *I.* The imputation is conditional upon the
appropriation. The Augustinian idea, that the sin of Adam
is imputed to his posterity as guilt, is certainly severe and
fatalistic, so long as it is not explained, and resolved into its
necessary middle terms ; but the relation is not to be con-
strued as an outward mechanical one, as though an absent sin
were imputed to the individual ; neither is it to be imagined
that sin and guilt are separable from each other. Individuals
stand in an *organic* connection with their Adamic parentage.

The Adamic nature is the distinctive nature of the individual ; sin is not foreign or alien to the individual. Were we to abide by the definition that sin is the lot or fate of the individual because he now inherits this nature, the individual could only be the object of compassion ; and the individual who maintained an absolutely passive relation to sin, as to an infirmity of nature only, who preserved a state in which he himself in no sense acquiesced, he might be described as suffering innocence. But here comes in the saying of Augustine : *Non inviti tales sumus.* Fate is, in the will,—in the person's self,—turned into guilt ; the merely organic relation is converted into a spiritual one, the natural into a moral relation. This double-sidedness of sin is presented even in the birth of man. For the birth of the individual is not only the result of a preceding parentage, it is also the beginning of a new distinct and independent life. The man is not only born as a being of nature, but as a *beginning ego,* a germinal self. His development is subject to the indispensable demands of the law of *holiness,* and the law asks in the first place, not what the man *can* be according to his activity afterwards— but what he now *must* be according to his nature. On this ground it is that the apostle says : "We are by nature the children of wrath" (Eph. ii. 3), and that the heathen have no excuse, "because they worshipped and served the creature more than the Creator" (Rom. i. 20) ; for though their consciousness of God was certainly fettered by the powers of this world, yet the true knowledge of God is what they are really appointed and called to ; the holy law has a claim upon the will which is not fulfilled, for which no satisfaction is given ; and the sinful will is concluded under that condemnation which is hidden in the depths of consciousness. The Evangelical Church accordingly, in her teaching defines original sin, not only as *morbus,* or *vitium originis,* but as *vere peccatum.** Whereas Catholicism recognizes only an inborn *weakness* of nature, and only the actual, the *manifest* sin as sin, the Protestant view penetrates into the *mystery* of the will, into the union of fate and guilt, of the natural and the moral, of necessity and freedom.

Observations.—It is on the ground of this unity of guilt and

* See Confessio Augustana, Art. ii.

destiny that the sinner becomes the subject not only of punishment and of the stern judgment of righteousness, but especially of *sympathy*, not only the object of the divine wrath, but also of the divine *compassion*. On this account it was that the Redeemer of the world wept over Jerusalem (Luke xix. 41), when he pronounced the judgment of righteousness upon it ; and on the same ground the apostle Paul, when he conducts us down into the depths of personal knowledge of sin, depicts not only the strong self-accusation, but self-accusation which includes the feeling of deep pity upon man's part towards himself, a sadness on his own account : " O wretched man that I am ! who shall deliver me from the body of this death ?" (Rom. vii. 24). The more we view the individual according to the relations of race, and in the light of his sinful nature, the more do his sins present prevailingly the aspect of sufferings, having their origin in the sinful development of the race ; and so much the more also is the aspect of pity laid stress upon ;—childhood, and tempted innocence, and inexperience, being for the most part the objects of compassion. And in like manner, on the other hand, the more completely the individual has separated himself from the life of the race, and made for himself an independent and personal life, and is contemplated from this point of view of self-determination, so much the more does he become the object of condemnation. Personal guilt grows in proportion as the individual, instead of enduring the opposition of his sinful nature, appropriates this as his own and develops it ; and instead of laying hold upon the proffered grace of Christ, which will free him from his sinful nature, opposes Christ and rejects Him. In proportion as the sinner knowingly hardens himself against grace, knowingly rejects the Saviour, in that proportion he goes beyond the range of pity and comes as if home to judgment ; he is no more the object of compassion but of horror ; for in the same proportion he is approaching the stand-point of the devil. Hence it follows that original sin, as such, never brings with it damnation to any individual ; and that those theologians who, in the strongest sense, have taught this, and upon this ground have prejudged regarding the salvation of the heathen and of unbaptized children, do not sufficiently distinguish between the condemnation which rests upon the sinful life of the race, and the personal condemnation of each separate individual. Nothing can, strictly speaking, be pronounced regarding the condemnation of the individual, unless he himself has made a personal decision, exercising freedom of choice in relation to divine grace, which will redeem him from the power of original sin. But beyond the range of Christ's revelation no judgment whatever can be pronounced absolutely upon any individual, for it is Christ, who, as He 'is set for the rising again' of man, so in a final relation 'is set' also for his *fall*.*

§ 109.

The knowledge of sin and guilt depends upon the knowledge of the law ; "for by the law is the knowledge of sin" (Rom. iii. 20 ; vii. 7) ; and the depth of a person's knowledge of sin is proportionate to the extent of his knowledge of the law. All knowledge of the law which views it either in undefined generality merely, or with the perception of particular commands only, brings with it an inadequate knowledge of sin. The true idea of the law is the idea of an all-embracing rule of personality, the union of the general and particular. But this knowledge, again, cannot be truly living, so long as the law does not come before the man *in personal form*, in a sinless human life which in its entire being reveals the *fulness* of the law. Hence the true knowledge of sin is attained first in Christ, who in this point of view must be regarded as the incarnation of the law, the incarnate conscience of the race. For it is only where this holy picture, 'full of grace and truth,' has shined into human souls who were far from truth, that the knowledge of sin has been living ; for there the righteousness of the world grew pale, and the demands of the law and of conversion were perceived in their full range. When the moment came for the revela-

* It is only upon the presupposition of the distinction here indicated that we can appropriate the *formula* of the Augsburg Confession upon original sin ; *Damnans et afferens nunc quoque æternam mortem his, qui non renascuntur per Baptismum et Spiritum Sanctum.*—*Confessio Augustana*, Art. ii.

tion of pure humanity in the second Adam, in whom the possibility and reality of a sinless human life was presented, sin was recognized as a violation of nature, as a perversion of the will in its root. The Jews perceived that they, as well as the heathen, were wanting in true righteousness ; and the heathen looked upon sin not only as ignorance, and the want of enlightenment, they considered their earlier state not only as a misfortune but as a hidden guilt. The history of missions shews that the heathen themselves have recognized the truth of the apostle's word that " they are without excuse." For though they certainly have looked upon the state in which they sat in darkness and in the shadow of death as a hard destiny, the result of the universal guilt of the race, and so far as though they were not without excuse ; as even the apostle, indirectly at least, excuses them when he says : " How shall they call on Him, on whom they have not believed ? and how shall they believe in Him of whom they have not heard ? and how shall they hear without a preacher ?" (Rom. x. 14, 15)—yet they have not only accused the gods whom they gave up for Christ, but they have accused themselves.

§ 110.

With the knowledge of sin and guilt there arises the just view of pain, of misfortune, of the contradiction between the course of this world, and the true ideal of human life. The view of life which is presented in the law of holiness and in the God of conscience, recognizes in the discrepancy between the course of this world and human endeavours, in the oppression of nations, and in the sufferings of the individual, the revelation of the righteous judgment of God against sin, (Rom. i. 18.) The religious character of the various views of life is embodied in the different ways of regarding and of explaining the miseries of this world. The merely naturalist view takes misfortune to be only the expression of a dark objectless *necessity*, the unavoidable lot of this finite life. The ethical view looks upon misfortune as in close connection with conscience. Even in the heathen world misfortune was considered as *punishment*, arising from the wrath of the gods, but as yet the true idea of conscience and of sin was not fully perceived. The *Nemesis* of the Greeks not only punished the pride of men, but was a levelling power which envied men their good fortune. The God of Hebraism, on the contrary, is a zealous God, who in righteousness visits upon the sinner his sins; and misfortune is the punishment of transgression of the law of holiness and violation of the Divine will. But as the full perception of original sin as the common sin of the race does not appear in the Old Testament, there was a tendency to the belief that whatever suffering befalls the individual, it bears a strict proportion to his personal sinfulness; that excessive suffering must lead to the conclusion that the subject of it is a sinner above others. This notion appears in the book of Job, for instance. Although this idea is in part contradicted by the teaching of the Old Testament itself, it is not fully exploded except by Christianity. Christianity, by its doctrine of original sin, leads us to view individuals as developed by the sufferings of the race. Those sufferings, which have their cause in the common guilt of the human race and of society, may be accumulated in extraordinary measure upon certain portions of the community, or upon a few individuals therein, without there being any reason to suppose that these are sinners above the rest because they suffer these things. "Suppose ye that these Galileans were sinners above all the Galileans because they suffered such things? I tell you, nay," (Luke xiii. 2.) And though the sufferings of this present time, brought about by sin, are divine punishments, they are nevertheless in their final intent *divine kindnesses*, means of healing and means of nurture in the hand of everlasting love, discipline, and wholesome chastisement, παιδεία, (Hebrews xii. 5-12; Rev. iii. 10), occasions and means for the manifestation of God's salvation, (John ix. 3.) Both ways of viewing misfortune hold good in human life; but which of them must be adopted as the more prominent, in any particular case, can only be decided by the relation in which the times in question, or the individuals in question, stand and have been standing to the law of holiness. The external suffering is not the standard whereby we are to measure the moral state, but, on the contrary, the moral state is to be the measure for the outward suffering. There is no outward sign that can adequately be relied on as a means of deciding whether the calamity be mainly a deserved punishment, or a moulding discipline and a fatherly chastisement: the final standard of judgment rests in the mystery of individual conscience. The old ascetics, therefore, rightly spoke, not only of the *revealed* judgments of God, which are obvious to all who contemplate the course of this world in the light of God's Word ; but of God's *hidden* judgments also, known only to the individuals themselves in their own consciences.

Observations.—The proposition that sin is itself the punishment of sin embodies the truth that man, by sin, subjects himself to a moral fatalism, a *misera necessitas mali*, expressed by our Lord in the words, "Whosoever committeth sin is the servant of sin," (John viii. 34.) When it is said of God that He hardens the hearts of men, that He gives them over to spiritual blindness, and makes them incapable of understanding His Word, it is not thereby implied that God wills sin as such, but that He permits the *manifestation* of sin ; He wills that sin shall be left to accomplish its own results ; and that He has included sin in the necessary law of development to which everything is subject.

§ 111.

Holy Scripture sums up all the disturbances of human life which are the result and punishment of sin in the designation *Death.* "The wages of sin is death," (Rom. vi. 23 ; James i. 15 ; Rom. v. 12.) There are various kinds of death ; and Revelation means by the term not only the death which concerns the inward life,—the spiritual semblance of life, the mock being which the sinner leads apart from God, not only the divided state of the inner man, the breaking-up and dismemberment of the spiritual powers, which is the result of sin ; but also the death which embraces the outward life, the whole array of sicknesses and plagues, which visit the human race, and "all the various ills that flesh is heir to," which are consummated in death,—in the separation of the body and the soul.

In calling the death of the body the wages of sin, we give expression to a doctrine belonging to that department of our knowledge which is the darkest. We find the doctrine in Revelation, and it is naturally associated with the horror that we feel in the thought of death as something which is unnatural in nature, as "the last enemy that is to be destroyed," (1 Cor. xv. 26). This is not a feeling to be condemned as merely sensual ; in its inner essence it is of a spiritual and moral kind, and is found not only in the rude and natural man, but is confirmed in the most spiritual of all religions, in Christianity itself. In itself it seems very natural for man to die, and it is not difficult to prove death to be a universal law of nature to which every living thing is subject. But when a man argues from the analogy of nature that death belongs to the natural development of the race the inference is one which will not stand proof. For in such an analogy the essential difference between natural existence and man is overlooked. Granting that death is natural for existence generally it by no means follows that it is natural for an individual *personal.* For natural existences to die seems to involve no contradiction ; they are not individuals—persons—but only exemplars, points of transition in the life of the species, in their very conception they are transitory and mortal. But that the personal and immortal individual—who in the very conception of him is a union of spirit and nature—that this being should die, that the immortal soul should be separated from its body, this in itself is by no means natural ; it is a riddle, a mystery. The modern doctrine of immortality may indeed comfort us with the notion that it is only the body which dies, that death is a liberation for the soul, its freedom from a limiting bondage. But how will this doctrine, which seems to harmonize so well with the problem of death, solve for us the problem of birth ? For what purpose is the soul born in this corporeity, if its union with the body is not only unreal, unessential, but even a hindrance to its freedom ? And how shall we as Christians, on this ground explain the great importance attached in Christianity to the resurrection of the body as the final achievement of the work of redemption ? "We ourselves," says St. Paul, "groan within ourselves, waiting for the adoption, to wit, the redemption of our body," (Rom. viii. 23). Christ indeed died though He was without sin ; and as He says that the corn of wheat must fall into the ground and die, in order to bring forth fruit, (John xii. 24). He seems to describe mortality as naturally pertaining to the normal life of man. But looking at it more closely, we find the true explanation of the passage to be, simply, that the Redeemer was made in all points, sin excepted, like unto us ; that He took upon Himself the likeness of sinful flesh (Rom. viii. 3), that He submitted Himself to all the present conditions of human life and development. While we, therefore, maintain the doctrine of our church that death was not a necessity in man's original state (*potuit non mori*), we would not have it believed that it was the original destiny of man to remain for ever on earth ; we would only suppose that another mode of departure, another kind of transformation, would in that case have been natural to man,* not that painful dissolution, that violent unclothing of the soul, that decease of the body through the fainting of the spirit.

However dark this doctrine may be when we contemplate closely the natural side of the subject, it appears clear again when we consider it in a moral point of view. For even were we to take it for granted that death belonged to man's primeval state, it is clear, notwithstanding, that death by sin must have for man another and a moral import, that as the form of human life was altered by the fall, the form of death must also have been changed. As the world by the fall became *this world,* as time became *this time,* so also must death have become *this death.* This death, which awaits man in this present world as an inevitable fate, as a destiny whose fulfilment is unconditional, though so uncertain as to its hour, this death, with its impenetrable darkness, with its gloomy demons of doubt and fear, is not natural to man created in the image of God. For the *sting* of death is sin, (1 Cor. xv. 56). This thought lies at the foundation of that sadness which we find expressed in the Old Testament regarding "the shadow of death," and the mournful abode in Sheol, (Psalm vi. 5 ; xxiii. 4). But Christianity at length unveiled the darkness of death, and fully revealed to the worlds the terrible spectre, because it has introduced another, a new death into the world. For though the sting of death is certainly felt in secret by the natural man, heathenism shuns the thought of it, and endeavours to hide from itself the monster.

* Compare Genesis v. 24, "Enoch walked with God : and he was not ; for God took him."

Observations.—The relation between the Christian and the heathen view of death is apparent in Christian and heathen art. While Grecian art represents death as a genius with inverted torch, Christianity pictures him as the skeleton with the scythe and hour-glass. The worldly, eudemonistic man cannot bear to ponder over the thought of death. He endeavours to withdraw from the terror of death, to soften the thought of it as that which is inevitable, and thus he throws an æsthetic veil over it in art ; and the Greeks are, as Herder remarks, in this respect like children who hold their hands over their eyes in order not to see the dangerous and frightful. More closely viewed, the Greek genius with inverted torch is only a poor and meagre consolation ; for it is a picture without hope or comfort, it only points to the end of life in calm yet hopeless resignation. Christianity on the other hand strips death of that softening adornment, for it looks at death with the eye of conscience, as the death of the sinner, before which this world vanishes. Its *memento mori* is not only a remembrance of the transitoriness of life, it is not an æsthetic, mournful lamentation, but a remembrance of the death of the sinner, of guilt and judgment. And the Church can with confidence represent death thus, because she can plant the cross upon the grave, and shew to the believer the hopeful symbols of redemption and resurrection.

§ 112.

According to the representations given us in revelation, it is not only man's own nature which has felt the disordering effects of sin, but nature itself which surrounds him : nature not only within us but about us, bears witness (to use an expression of Pascal's) of a lost God. This representation has often in modern times been rejected as a mere poetical phantasy, without any foundation in fact. It is not difficult to show in how unsatisfactory a manner the entrance of evil into nature has been explained, whether it be by presupposing that nature is subject to the curse for the sake of man, or (according to Jacob Böhme, Baader, and Steffens), by assuming that evil was made to penetrate nature by some supernatural and superhuman power which, having generated in itself the principle of disturbance, generated it in those ranges of creation into which it obtains access.   It is not difficult to show that such explanations explain nothing, because they need explanation themselves.   But it is very difficult to deny that there are phenomena in nature which call forth the problem of the entrance of evil into nature.   We will not appeal only to the manifest tokens of moral evil which we so often meet with in nature, we merely refer to the sad truth that asserts itself in the darkness of the human soul, that whispers in the leaves of the forest, in the coiling of the serpent, that howls through the desert in the bloodthirstiness of the wild beasts.*   But we especially appeal to the fact that there is manifest in nature an enigmatical contradiction of the inner and true teleology of nature, a contradiction of its own inner conformableness to the end designed.   Nature not only presents to us a sound and normal display of its powers, but a range of limited, broken off, and distorted developments ; it shows us a death which is too early ; it shows us the blossoming life on the point of its development, when its beauty and its glory should be displayed, struck to the ground by the destroying worm.   This frustration of the proper object of nature cannot be looked upon as having its foundation in a *true* necessity.   Appearances in nature which contain in themselves a destructive principle cannot be viewed as normal.   We doubt not that there may be given an adequate physical explanation of such appearances as the desolating pestilence, hurricanes, and earthquakes ; we doubt not that a theodicy which starts from an outward and finite teleology is able to prove that such phenomena as destroy the life of nature, the life of man, and his noblest works, may in another light be regarded as useful, especially because they hinder other destructive powers in their progress, but we very much doubt whether they can fairly be derived from the true *conception* of nature itself.   A theodicy which would satisfy us with the general statement of finiteness, and of the necessary development of life by contrasts, only evades the problem. For the false as well as the true development proceeds by means of contrasts ; and the very question is, whether all the

---

* Compare Munster's *Abhandlung von den Trieben.* (*Schriften der wissenschaftl. Gesellschaft*).

contrasts which the life of nature presents to us are normal. And though a full and satisfactory explanation of the dark sayings of nature may be impossible in the present limits of our experience,* yet a spiritual, a moral view of nature will always be led back to the words of the Apostle that the creature (ἡ κτίσις) is subject to vanity and sighs for redemption (Rom. viii. 20).

Even the person who cannot be convinced that destruction has penetrated the creation which has no freedom nor will, who yet allows that it has penetrated the world of freedom, must perceive that the *relation* of nature to man has been altered by the fall. For nature does not attain its final design unless it be mirrored in the spiritual view of man, unless it be glorified in freedom, and by freedom be reflected back to God. It must therefore be confessed in the deepest sense that the true *revelation of nature* has been injured by sin. For instead of nature being thus moralized—given a moral import—spirit has been naturalized—has been given a false dependence upon nature. And so long as human redemption is not complete, nature subdued by destiny and "subject to vanity," cannot realize its true moral import ; with all its beauty it is but a broken piece of mechanism, because by the fall of man it has lost its crown its highest ornament ; because its development has been perverted in the last and finishing point, just when its whole beauty and glory should be unfolded into a temple of the Spirit.

THE PROVIDENCE OF GOD.

§ 113.

As the contradiction which ensued upon the fall, finds its solution in redemption, redemption itself has its general groundwork or pre-supposition in divine Providence. The idea of Providence is the development of the idea of creation. It expresses the principle that God creates and sustains the world in order to accomplish His great end, the highest good. Al-

---

* Pascal's words continually are fulfilled regarding the destruction which prevails in nature, as well as regarding the prevalence of death in human life : *Ce sont choses, qui se sont passées dans un état de nature tout différent du nôtre, et qui passent notre capacité présente.*—Pensées de Pascal.

though every created thing is only what it is in relation to the highest good (*providentia generalis*), that good can be realized in the kingdom of freedom only, and Providence can therefore be revealed, strictly speaking, not in nature but in history only (*providentia specialis*). Goodness must be realized in history as the development of the freedom of the race. But as good requires a personal appropriation, the individual man is the proper subject of divine providence (*providentia specialissima*), not in the minute atomistic division of the race, but as a member of the great spiritual love. This is expressed in the idea of the *kingdom of God* wherein the highest good which does not differ from God himself, is realized in a system of divinely blessed individuals. In consequence of sin, the kingdom of God has to be manifested as a kingdom of redemption, and active Providence must be revealed in the *economy* of redemption.

The Free Course of the World and the Manifold Wisdom of God.

§ 114.

The purpose of divine Providence is in its nature simple, because it wills only one thing—the good, the kingdom of God ; but in its manifestation it is manifold, not only because He is a *living will,* but likewise because He reveals himself not by a merely necessary law of nature, but in the free progress of the world, in a *world-course* which itself includes an endless variety of independent world-forces and energies, which presents an innumerable manifold and complicated play of free causes, and which therefore by no means excludes sin and human spontaneity. And the manifold wisdom of God (ἡ πολυποί-κιλος σοφία θεοῦ) (Eph. iii. 10), is revealed in the fact that these movements and complications of freedom *must* unavoidably manifest the eternal counsel of God, and *must* work together for its accomplishment. The divine counsel is the *proper determination* or limiting principle of created freedom ; and amid the entanglements of this world's life created freedom cannot but become the instrument of this counsel and subservient thereto, *either* for the fall *or* for the rising again of itself.

§ 115.

The supposed contradiction between the course of the world, whose ways are not God's ways, and the absolute dependence of the creature upon divine power, arises from a mistaking of the truth that in its essence omnipotence is a moral and self-limiting power. Considering only the *natural* dependence of the creature upon God, the world appears to be the bare and immediate expression of the divine will; for there is not a moment in the life of any creature in which it is not dependent upon God, who penetrates it with His all-pervading power and gives it "life and breath and all things" (Acts xvii. 25). "Thou takest away their breath, they die, and return to their dust. Thou sendest forth Thy breath and they are created" (Psalm civ. 29, 30). In this sense, we may, with our older theologians, recognize a *concursus dei et creaturae* in every movement of life and freedom, and grant that God works together with the creature even in evil, so far at least as the power of life which works evil is, in its essential nature, a power derived from God. But this natural dependence upon the divine Omnipotence is only the ground-work of a moral and religious dependence, which allows ample room for the exercise of self-determination. In the moral order of the world God's power does not reveal itself merely as natural omnipotence—as the all-generating, world-creating, and world-sustaining will—but as a *commanding* and reminding will, speaking to us "at sundry times, and in divers manners," by the law and the prophets within us as well as without: and likewise as the permissive will (*voluntas permissiva*), which permits even "darkness" to have its hour and its power (Luke xxii. 53). Viewed then in the light of the *holy law* of God, the course of this world is not only a working together with God, but a working against Him also; and the words of Scripture are realized, "man's thoughts are not God's thoughts, neither are man's ways God's ways" (Isaiah lv. 8): "the people imagine a vain thing;" the truth is held "in unrighteousness;" the spirits of time and the powers of the darkness of this world oppose God and the kingdom of His holiness (Psalm ii. 1-3; Rom. i. 18; Eph. vi. 12). It is only a false optimism which regards the actual as in and for itself necessary. Nevertheless it must be maintained that God's holy

will fulfils itself in the course of the world ; it fulfils itself κατ'
οικονομίαν, in harmony with nature and with human freedom.
What worldly wisdom calls the "stratagem of reason," whereby
it hides itself beneath the unreasonable and even the criminal
acts of men, and makes use of these in the fulfilment of its
aim, we recognize as "the manifold wisdom of God," His all
pervading, all *directing*, all *governing will*, which has entwined
its thread in the course of the world.　　This will of divine
wisdom does not forcibly prevent the divers failings and sins of
men ; it introduces new unforeseen developments whereby it
makes use of the devices of men *indirectly* to accomplish its
own holy plan.　　The true Theodicy cannot undertake the
thankless labour of tracing the course of humanity towards its
goal in a natural and continuous line of development, as the
exact and therefore the shortest way between two points.　　It
rather recognizes that the course of human development resembles the wandering of the children of Israel through the
wilderness to the land of promise, which they did not reach
by the exact and shortest route, but by a very circuitous jour-
ney, with many delays and retrogressions.　　The true Theodicy
does not shut its eyes to the judgments of God upon races and
individuals ; it looks upon these as the *reaction* of divine
righteousness against the transgressions of men ; but it takes
its stand upon the perception that the primitive revelation of
God's righteousness is one of the conditions necessary to the
coming of God's kingdom, and that demoniacal powers also
must work, even against their will, for the advance of that
kingdom of the Spirit and of Love, which is the final end of
the creation.　　It is in that kingdom of God wherein the freedom of grace is fulfilled, wherein God's will is done, not against
nor even *apart from* the will of His creatures, but wherein
His free creatures are knowers together and labourers together
with God (John xv. 15 ; 1 Cor. iii. 9), that it recognizes a
concursus in the fullest sense of the word, regarding which it
may be said, *ut idem effectus non a solo deo, nec a solo creatura,
nec partim a deo, partim a creatura, sed una eademque effici-
entia totali simul a deo et creatura producatur.**

Observations.—A *true* Theodicy must take Christianity as its
　　basis, and may be raised upon it, but the *perfect* Theo-

* Quenstedt i. p. 531.

dicy cannot be attained except in the perfected history of the world. There are phenomena in the misfortunes of the species and of individuals, whose economic purpose cannot be understood at our present stage of knowledge, but which must be accepted in faith. To demand a perfect Theodicy during this temporal life, would be to require us to see through the course of this world in all its parts, and to expect that the manifold wisdom of God shall be exhausted in this present life. The idea of the partial, of the contrast between mystery and revelation, between faith and sight, the idea and the actual, is inseparable from the temporal, especially from this present time, which is limited by the conflict of light with darkness :—a dispensation wherein the victory is already won, yet wherein the actual necessarily bears the impress of the undecided, a twofold aspect wherein signs stand opposed to signs.

§ 116.

The contradiction which has been supposed to exist between the idea of the free progress of the world and the *omniscience* of God, rests upon a one-sided conception of omniscience, as a mere knowing *beforehand,* and an ignoring of the *conditional* in the divine decrees. An unconditioned foreknowledge undeniably militates against the freedom of the creature, so far as freedom of choice is concerned ; and against the undecided, the contingent, which is an idea inseparable from the development of freedom in time. The actual alone, which is in and for itself rational and necessary, can be the subject of an unconditional foreknowledge ; the actual which is not this, cannot be so ; it can only be foreknown as possible, as eventual. But such an unconditional foreknowledge not only militates against the freedom of the creature, it equally is opposed to the idea of a freely working God in history. A God literally foreknowing all things, would be merely the spectator of events decided and predestined from eternity, not the all-directing governor in a drama of freedom which He carries on in reciprocal conflict and work with the freedom of the creature. If we would preserve this reciprocal relation between God and His creatures, we must not make the whole actual course of the world the subject of His foreknowledge, but only its eternal import, the essential truth it involves. The final goal of this world's development, together with the entire series of its essentially necessary stages, must be regarded as fixed in the eternal counsel of God; but the practical carrying out of this eternal counsel, the entire fulness of actual limitations on the part of this world's progress, in so far as these are conditioned by the freedom of the creature, can only be the subject of a conditional foreknowledge; *i.e.*, they can only be foreknown as possibilities, as *Futurabilia*, but not as realities, because other possibilities may actually take place. In thus asserting that God does not foreknow all that actually occurs, we by no means imply that every event is not the subject of his all-penetrating cognizance. God is not only *before* His creatures—" before the mountains were brought forth, or ever the earth was made,"—He is also *in* and *with* His creatures, in every moment of their development. While God neither foreknows, nor will foreknow what He leaves undecided, in order to be decided in time, He is no less *cognizant* of and *privy to* all that occurs. Every movement of His creatures, even their most secret thoughts, is within the range of His all-embracing knowledge. "Thou compassest my path, and my lying down, and art acquainted with all my ways. Whither shall I go from thy Spirit? or whither shall I flee from thy presence? If I ascend up into heaven thou art there: if I make my bed in hell, behold thou art there" (Psalm cxxxix.). His knowledge penetrates the entanglements of this world's progress at every point; the unerring eye of His wisdom discerns in every moment the relation subsisting between free beings and His eternal plan; and His almighty hand, His power, pregnant of great designs, guides and influences the movements of the world as His counsels require.*

§ 117.

We must distinguish between the *immanent* and the *transcendant* in the operations of the providence of God. We call those of its workings immanent wherein the divine providence encloses itself in the laws of this world's progress, and reveals itself in the form of *sustaining* power in the

* Richard Rothe's Theologische Ethik, i. 124.

moral order of things. We call those of its operations transcendant, wherein the course of history is interrupted, and the
divine will breaks forth in creative or commanding manifestations, more or less resembling and corresponding to " the
lightning that lighteneth out of the one part under heaven,
and shineth unto the other part under heaven," (Luke xvii. 24.)
When we speak of "*the finger of God*" in the lives of individuals, or of the race, our meaning is, that the combination
of circumstances necessary to a certain *turning-point* in
human history, or whereby some *epoch* is begun or terminated, is brought about, not by these circumstances themselves, but by an overruling will manifesting itself in the
course of events. It is the idea of *wonder*, of a miracle, which
in these cases takes possession of us. And yet it is a miracle
only relatively to us ; it is the expression of creative power
either in history alone, *or* in nature alone, apart from the
perfect union and perfect working together of both, as they
usually appear. We cannot distinguish *sacred history* from
the perfect miracle ; it is a miracle, for it not only reveals the
creative agency of Providence in general, but its special
workings,—those special workings whose object is to establish the true belief in Providence among men ; and it unfolds
itself in a series of acts which serve as " signs and wonders,"
i.e., witnesses that the God of history and of conscience is Lord
also of nature's laws.

Observations.—He who truly believes in continual acts of
creation, and in a living Providence, must believe also in
miracles, *i.e.*, in new manifestations of the divine will,
both in nature and in history. But we are apt to stop
short at the relative miracle, because we regard nature and
history as two distinct ranges running side by side, each
of which has its own laws and its own miracles. We
forget that there are stages in the work of creation when
the perfect union of nature and history is revealed, *i.e.*,
when the perfect miracle takes place. A man readily
allows, for example, that the birth of Christ is a miracle
in history, but he will not grant that this birth is a profound miracle in nature,—the miraculous conception.
Or, again, he allows that the working of the Gospel in the
heart of man is a spiritual miracle, whereby the spiritually

blind and deaf are made to see and to hear; but he denies
that the Gospel can accomplish the same things as miracles
of nature.   Now, Revelation unites both in one; it places
miracles of nature and of history side by side.   "Go and
tell John again," said our Saviour, "what ye have seen
and heard.   The blind receive their sight, and the lame
walk; the lepers are cleansed, and the deaf hear; the dead
are raised up, *and the poor have the Gospel preached unto
them*," (Matt. xi. 4, 5.)   Could the idea of Providence,
could the idea of a free-creating God be entertained, if He
were limited in His revelations by the contrast between
nature and history?—if nature, which is a fettering limit
to the struggling human spirit in history, and to the freedom of the creature, were also a limit to the holy will of
God?—if the dominion of God were divided, so that when
He reveals Himself as Lord of the spirit-world, he must
abandon His claim to reveal Himself as Lord of nature;
and when He reveals Himself as Lord of nature, he must
conceal His spiritual Majesty?   Is it not the grossest
anthropomorphism,—the grossest transference of our
limited weakness to the great Creator,—to describe Him
as a God who makes the kingdom of His holiness His
highest aim, and who yet finds an insuperable barrier in
those laws of nature which are opposed to the law of
holiness, and who has no power to reconcile these, though
both were alike ordained by Him?   If a miracle be impossible to God, He is Himself fettered by the contrast
between the law of freedom and the law of nature, whereby
every created spirit is fettered,—a bondage which is the
inextinguishable mark of created dependence!

There is a mysterious harmony between the natural
and the moral, between facts of nature and facts of history, manifest in what we call the "wonderful" (*mirabile*),
as distinct from what is properly called the "miraculous"
(*miraculum*).   While the miracle, properly speaking, implies a violation of the laws of nature, the wonderful,
which is closely connected with it, is such a coincidence
and working together of nature and history, as reveals a
supernatural result to the religious perceptions, while the
natural explanation still holds good for the understand-

ing.   The march of Napoleon into Russia, pregnant with
results, and the severe winter, the invincible Armada of
Philip the Second, and the sudden storm (*afflavit deus et
dissipavit eos*), serve as examples of the "wonderful" in
the sense referred to.   There is in these things a sur-
prising and unaccountable harmony of nature and history, and yet all is natural ; no law is broken, but the
coincidence is inexplicable.   Wonders such as these continually present themselves to us both in the world at
large and in the lives of individuals.   There is, generally
speaking, an unaccountable power of nature which plays
its part in the historical and moral complications of human life ; and it cannot escape the notice of the careful
observer that wonderful coincidences often occur, which
to reason may appear only as an extraordinary, inexplicable *chance ;* to the poet as a profound *play* of the spirit
of the world, and an active presence of a divine phantasy
in the world's progress ;—combinations which lie beyond
the range of rational computation, and which, like genii,
scorn the narrow laws of human knowledge ;—but in
which the Christian discerns the *finger of God.*   But he
who truly recognizes the finger of God in these strange
coincidences must be led on to a recognition of the actually miraculous.   The wonderful is only the half-de-
veloped, unperfected miracle.   The wonderful possesses
that ambiguous character, half chance, half Providence,
half natural, half divine, just because the coincidence of
the holy and the natural is external only ; and faith
must still demand a revelation wherein nature and freedom—separate in the usual course of events—shall not
only seek one another in wonderful configurations, shall
not only approach one another, but be immediately and
essentially united; faith must still long for an unequivo-
cal sign, of which it can say, Here is God, and not nature.*   This sign is given in the sacred history of Christ ;
a sign which is spoken against, and which is set for the
fall of many, and for the rising again of many.†

* Compare Mynster : Vom Begriff der Dogmatik.   (In the *Studien und Kritiken.*)

† Luke ii. 34 : Ἰδού, οὗτος κεῖται εἰς πτῶσιν καὶ ἀνάστασιν πολλῶν ἐν τῷ Ἰσραὴλ
καὶ εἰς σημεῖον ἀντιλεγόμενον.   [A favourite quotation of our author ; see §§ 108.]

§ 118.

The perfect revelation of the wonder-working Providence of God is presented in the incarnate Logos, in the world-redeeming, soul-saving manifestation of God in Christ. Human history finds its *centre*, its true meaning, in the revelation of Jesus Christ. It is only in the light which comes from Him that humanity can look back upon a past which is full of meaning, can look forward to a future full of promise, and can contemplate its development as an organic whole. Human history, which moves on apart from Christ, without desire for or belief in Him, knows neither beginning nor end, it is objectless, it has no centre. The Christian doctrine of Providence, accordingly, finds its full expression in the doctrine of the election of grace, of the creation and nurture of nations and individuals for the kingdom of God : a nurture that is begun, continued, and perfected, not only by inward spiritual awakenings and movements of soul, not only by the efficacy of God's word and sacraments, but also by the outward circumstances of life and destiny.

Belief in the providence of God in individual life (*providentia specialissima*), finds its true foundation in the revelation of Christ. As it is evident in the history of mankind from the time that Christ came into the world, so is it also in each particular life. As the ways of Providence may sometimes be inscrutable in the life of the individual,—because man's earthly life is only a fragment, which finds its final explanation in the pregnant future awaiting man beyond the grave,—the believer must nevertheless seek after a partial knowledge of the Divine wisdom and will in this life ; and there never was a truly Christian life without some knowledge of the leadings of God's providence, although true faith is not careful to show this palpably.

The germ of Christian experience regarding Providence is individual conversion and the experience of the grace of God in Christ, whereby the believer is brought to the very centre of all the divine counsels. As the minuter circumstances of life, inward and outward experiences—even the smallest and most insignificant thing, which, like a blade of grass, has only a casual and transient import,*—gather round this germ of

---

* Matt. x. 30 : "The very hairs of your head are all numbered."

life, and are of importance in its development, the believer traces in all the leading and drawing will of God. And in the divine counsel, which fulfils itself in individual life, and which appoints the hour not only of our birth but of our death, the believer recognizes no unconditional decree, no fatalistic determination, but a conditional ordainment (2 Kings xx. ; Psalm cii. 25), a decree dependent upon the free action of the individual, who is directed to labour and to pray ; and conditioned also by that economic necessity in which God has put the individual life, intertwined as it is with that of the race generally.

But while the manifold wisdom of God in the individual life disappears from our view in its immortality ; while this department of knowledge belongs to the faithful experience of each one ;—to the inner life which is hidden from the world, which the believer lives with his God, and which is embodied in words in Christian biography alone, as for example in the Confessions of St Augustine :—the fundamental facts of that wisdom are written in the history of the race in coarser and more generally legible characters, and Christian thought has from the beginning of the Church, endeavoured to read this in the light of God's holy word. In the next part of our enquiry, we shall consider the leadings of Divine wisdom in Heathendom and among the children of Israel, or in *the economy of preparation.*

HEATHENDOM.

§ 119.

Heathendom seems to be beyond the realm of Revelation and even of Providence in its narrower sense ; with its many mythologies it presents the aspect of a Babel (Gen. xi.), wherein the languages are confused and the people cannot understand one another, having lost the common bond of union in the Word and Spirit of God. God nevertheless works in Heathendom according to His eternal wisdom, placing it under a necessary law of development, whereby the Babylonish confusion of myths regulates itself into a significant whole, in which the thoughts of God's providence are hidden. Viewing heathendom as the Apostle Paul does in relation to Israel

as humanity left to itself, as the *wild olive tree ;* viewing also mythology according to Schelling's happy comparison, as "religion growing wild ;" we find that though it
may want the divine worship, it must follow the necessary
law of *natural* development. While mythology in itself
cannot be considered God's work, as little can it be looked
upon as merely man's. And while the history of heathendom cannot be called the history of God's revelation as little
can it be designated the history of human errors. It is the
history of the *world-idea,* embodied in the nature-bound
spirit of peoples who are its spiritual instruments. What
would have been a free development of ideas in man's normal
condition, now breaks forth out of the chaos of consciousness
as a process of theogony, as the birth of a world of Gods.
The plastic natural security peculiar to mythology arises
from the fact that consciousness is *fettered* in a life of nature,
it is taken with its own inner vision and gives thereto an
outward reality. As a man in a dream or in a state of somnambulism can imagine only what he performs himself, so
mythology by a natural psychological necessity pictures itself
to itself, not as an incoherent, but as a connected methodical
dream. The mythical consciousness must go through all the
manifold forms in which it is possible to take the world-idea
instead of God. It must roam through various ranges of
existence, and make each a form for the divine. It sees the
highest powers of life in the stars, in the heavenly lumin-
aries ; it surmises the secret of the All-living in the silent
vegetable world ; it regards the animal creation as a sort of
hieroglyphics, the mystical disguise of the deity ; until the
sphinx of nature is thrown down, and man himself is recognized as the true form of God ; a perception which gives to
the myths of Greece and of the North a loftier spirituality
than that of the nature-myths of the East. As therefore this
long wandering which the heathen consciousness must go
through presents a progress from the natural to the spiritual,
from the impersonal to the personal, and thus a dark feeling
after (ψηλαφαν, Acts xvii. 27), the unknown God ; we cannot
but discern in this law of development both the eternal power
of the Creator and His overruling Providence.

P

§ 120.

If it be asked, Why has God left men to dream this long dream? Why has He left the Heathen to wander their own ways without a true revelation for thousands of years?—we find the answer already given by the earliest doctors of the Church, by the author of the epistle to Diognet, Irenaeus. He replies, Because God would show men what by their own power they could accomplish; because heathendom, like the prodigal son in the gospel (Luke xv.), must know by experience the vanity of the world. In other words, the kingdom of this world must be revealed in its full range in order to the manifestation of God's kingdom in spirit and in truth. Revelation is the object of existence; and as the world by the fall has become *this* world, it must accomplish its own revelation, so as fully to display itself in all its glory and in all its worthlessness, in all its glitter and in all its emptiness. In order that the victory of the true God may be a spiritual a *righteous* victory, heathendom must exhaust all its possibilities, must work out and fill its pantheon, and thus it will be manifest, that what is small and despised of the world, that the still light which shone in the depths of conscience, though the darkness comprehended it not (John i. 5), which shone amid the despised people Israel,—that this alone has power and glory. In the historical fate of heathendom we must therefore recognize not only the power and the wisdom of the Highest, but His righteousness likewise. Righteousness demands that unrighteousness should reveal its own condemnation, and that the wages of sin should be seen to be death. The mythical world of Gods comes to naught in a spiritual *Ragnarok*,* in the doubt of the understanding and

---

* Odin, the Scandinavian god, the Prince of the Ases, "Gods" or "Asiatics" (?) who were his children by Frigga or Frea, "mother earth," dwelt with them in the palace of Walhalla. This palace was the *present* heaven. At the end of the world Ragnarockur or the Ragnarok, "the twilight of the Gods" is to occur. It is preceded by the utter desolation of nature, the breaking loose of Loke, and the raging of the serpent Midgard. In a conflict upon the plain Wigrid, the gods are defeated, but the powers of evil are also slain, and the earth itself is burnt up. After this catastrophe, there is to follow the renovation of the Gods and of the World,—the second or *future* heaven called Gimle, "the palace covered with gold." See Mallet and Herzog as before, and the Observations at the end of this Section.—*Tr.*

in unbelief. The idea loses its glitter, the vision fades, and the kingdoms of this world sink down into an historical chaos, as a sign that "the great Pan is dead." The Prophets of Israel declared these judgments of God and this revelation of righteousness upon heathen kingdoms. A lamentation is heard from the people of the sea, a mournful lamentation sounds on account of the departed glory of this world, the gods thrown down, with whom is no salvation ; a lamentation on account of the song and the stringed instrument, which now are dumb.* But the revelation of redeeming love shall at last break through that manifestation of righteousness, a revelation not only foretold in Israel, but longed for in Heathendom. Weak expectations and longings after redemption appear embodied in the various myths, which, however, are hidden from this world's sight, until at last the impulse towards the kingdom of God appears, forming for itself a perfect expression in the northern myth of Ragnarok, in that apocalypse of mythology, which may be regarded as the consummation of the entire scheme. The mythical consciousness herein proclaims its own defeat, and the victory of the principle of holiness. Behind the twilight of the gods, Vola perceives the glow of the morning of redemption, a new heaven and a new earth.

Observations.—Among the various attempts to give a connected picture of the religious systems of heathendom, those of Hegel (in his philosophy of religion) and of Schelling (in his newer system) are the most worthy of note. Without entering here into particulars, we must explain our decided preference for that of Schelling, because he has endeavoured to draw a distinct line of demarkation between Mythology and Revelation, between the wild and the noble olive tree ; whereas Hegel looks upon all religions as branches of one and the same stem, whose top and crown is Christianity. The fact that Hegel, in his philosophy of religion, looks upon the Greek, the Jewish, the Roman religions, as ramifications of the same development, clearly shows that he overlooked the decided divergence of the history of religion in two separate directions.

* Compare Isaiah and Ezekiel generally.

The omission of any reference to, or description of, the Norse Mythology, is a more serious defect, common to both the treatises named. Without this the mythical pantheon is wanting in its true consummation ; for without the knowledge of the Northern Gods, we have only an imperfect apprehension of the economy of Providence in regard to heathendom, and of the hidden connection between Mythology and Revelation. It has been customary to regard the Greek Mythology as the most elevated ; and this may indeed be true in an aesthetic point of view, and in relation to historical culture ;—for in these respects Greek Mythology, and the art and science associated with it, may be called " the Old Testament of the world of culture." But it is not difficult to prove that in a religious point of view the Northern Mythology stands higher, because it is the only mythology which is positively preparative for the faith of Christ. It foretells its own *Ragnarok,* whereas this overtakes the other heathen " who have no hope," as a sudden and unexpected dawn. " The inhabitants of the North," says Grundvig, in the first edition of his Northern Mythology, " readily yields the palm to the Greek, if the question be concerning definiteness and adornment of figures ; but when we enquire as to inner depth and power of thought, the Norseman calmly refers to Ragnarok, and the Greek must keep silence." While the Greek Gods stand before us in the unchanging rest of an aesthetic eternity, as a world of perfect natures resting in themselves, the doctrine of *Asa* unfolds a progressive drama, beginning with the birth of time, and concluding with the renovation and regeneration of all things on the other side of Ragnarok. The full import of the Norse Mythology is not to be found only in the conflict of the *Ases* with the Yettes ;—although it must be confessed that a life devoted to action even in circumstances of tumult and restlessness is truer than a life spent in aesthetic satisfaction, whose perfection is only a shadow, because it is reconciled too soon to the riddle of life :—its highest import does not lie in the opposition which the Ases meet with from without, but in the contrast which they experience within. The antithesis between the holy and the

worldly principle as recognised by the mythical consciousness, appears in the contract between *Balder* and *Thor*,
between the *Gimle* and the *Walhalla*. The tragical myth
of Balder's death, to which Oehlenschläger's* immortal
poem has given new life, expresses the profound sadness
which Gods and men feel in the contemplation of that
existence from which the holy principle has departed, and
in the loss of innocence and piety. Balder's death is the
result of the indiscretion and fault of the *Ases* themselves.
It is because Balder, because piety is excluded from Walhalla, that the Ases must go down into Ragnarok; for
"Balder was the bond which held together the society of
Walhalla," the point of union for the various powers of
life. But *Gimle* breaks forth out of Ragnarok, a kingdom of joy and redemption, in which Balder returns, and
the *Ases, i.e.*, the fundamental energies of life, rise again
purified and glorified. Now, we recognise the economy
of Providence in the fact, that the Romantic principle
should thus assume a mythical form among those heathen
who had been destined, in contrast with the old and lifeless world, to afford a fresh spiritual soil for the holy seed
of Christianity; and that the impulses towards the kingdom of God should become strong in the North, because
the light had already died out in the East. We discern
herein more than a merely worldly impulse, which led the
hordes of Northern nations to wander out, and, like birds
of passage, to seek a milder climate.

THE CHOSEN PEOPLE.

§ 121.

While heathenism, the wild olive tree, was in its development subject to the law of *nature*, the law of *holiness* was

---

* Adam Gottlob Oehlenschläger, born at Vesterbo, a suburb of Copenhagen,
1779, died 1850. He is esteemed the greatest poet of Scandinavia, and one of
the greatest European poets of the 19th century. The work of his referred to
above, is his "Nordens Guder" the "Gods of the North" (published in 1819),
combining in a convenient whole all the scattered legends of the Eddas. A
translation of the work into English verse by W. E. Frye was published in 1845.
See *Penny Cyclop.* Supp. 2.—*Tr.*

made known to the people of Israel. In their case we have
not human nature feeling after and moving towards the unknown God, with instinctive aspiration and dark questionings;
but we behold the LORD himself moving towards man in revelation, and a fundamental principle is presented to us which
forms, so to speak, the opposite pole to mythology. In mythology the world-idea, which spreads itself in manifold forms, is
the all-determining principle. Israel, on the contrary, begins
with the fear of the Lord, and bears witness of ONE, the true
God, the invisible Creator of the heavens and the earth, who
has made a covenant with man. What conscience is in the
inner world of the sinful heart, Israel was in a sinful world,—
the silent witness for truth amid the prevailing unrighteousness ; and, therefore, they were a people overlooked by heathendom, and despised. They were not distinguished for the
realization of any world-idea, in politics, in art, or in science.
Their vocation was exclusively a religious one ; their appointed
office was to embody and illustrate the education of sinful
humanity by the agency of God's word and Spirit for His
kingdom. The warfare which this people were to carry on
throughout their history was the warfare of *faith,* the spiritual
conflict between God and the world, between Jehovah and
false gods, between the law of the Lord and idolatrous life, in
order to the final establishment of the kingdom of God upon
the earth. The Old Testament represents the heathen gods,
partly as sham-divinities, weak creations of the imagination,
and partly as actual powers with which Jehovah is at war.
Jehovah is great above all gods (Exodus xii. 12 ; xviii. 11).
Mythical divinities are mere shadows and shams, in so far as
they are put in the stead of Jehovah ; otherwise they are
spiritual powers (ἀρχαὶ καὶ ἐξουσίαι) which have a realm of their
own and can strive against Jehovah. The contrast between
the Lord and the false gods is one between the holy will of
the Creator, whose exclusive right it is to reign, and cosmical
powers in their false dominion over the souls of men ; and this
is further expanded and explained into a contrast between the
kingdom of God (the Theocracy) and the kingdoms of this
world by which Israel is surrounded, and which are not justified in the sight of Jehovah. This principle of Israelitish belief explains the history of the chosen people. The necessity

for such a people has its foundation in the economy of salvation. As in sinful human *nature*, conscience and contrition of heart prepare the way for God's redeeming grace, so in sinful human *history* this people, with the law and the prophets, prepare the way for the realization of salvation, and provide the conditions thereto. Despised and neglected of the world this nation was searched out and chosen of God as a people separated from the other nations, the teleological people, the people of Providence and of the future. "For salvation is of the Jews."

§ 122.

The chosen people are emphatically the people of *miracle*, not only because sensible signs and wonders appear from time to time in their history, but because that history is itself miraculous, historically and psychologically. It cannot be looked upon as a merely natural creation and development, it is a *new a moral creation*. In the call of Abraham the command was given, " Get thee out of thy country and from thy kingdred, and from thy father's house into a land that I will show thee ;" and herein is expressed the interruption of this world's ordinary development and of natural ties, the breaking off from heathen associations and the entrance upon a new beginning, a new supernatural development. Of themselves no people can produce anything beyond what the spirit of the nation naturally suggests, and accordingly the mythologies are *ethnical* religions, their gods are esteemed as national divinities. In Israel, on the contrary, we behold a single man and a single people made the stewards and preservers of a principle which overlies the spirit and genius of nations. God is the God of Abraham only so far as He is believed in as the God of all the families of the earth ; what is individual or particular is only the vail for the universal. It cannot be looked upon as an arbitrary or capricious act that this particular people should have been the one chosen. God's supernatural choice indicates and is based upon a natural distinction, upon an *innate* foundation of faith, a natural religious basis, which characterized and fitted this people above other nations and races, to be the appropriate preservers of the sacred tradition and the instruments of its development. The growth of Israel, however, did not consist solely in a natural religiousness, in a

merely instinctive religious development. Natural development may, indeed, suffice to explain a mythical element which
is marked by holiness, but it can by no means produce a sure
word of prophecy progressively unfolding itself from one degree of clearness to another; it may explain manifestations of
holiness appearing here and there, but it cannot give rise to a
continuous chain of tradition in which each succeeding link
is organically connected with the preceding; it may show
itself in longings and " feelings after the unknown God," but
it cannot beget any definite faith in the invisible God nor any
steady growth of faith.   The religion of Jehovah is not a religion that grows wild.   The children of Israel themselves
were continually falling away from Jehovah and wandering
after false gods.   This proves that the God of Israel was not
like the gods of the heathen, a god after the natural heart. A
continual warfare was being waged between Jehovah and the
gods of the nations, between the true prophets and the false.
Israel delighted in the law and word of the Lord after the
inward man, but he lusted for the mythical image worship
after the carnal man, and went after strange gods.   The fact,
therefore, that the Jehovah-principle triumphed, that by a
gradual progress His kingdom was established, that amid all
commotions and conflicts, a holy chain (Hebrews xi.) of faithful witnesses stretched itself in unbroken line from Abraham,
the father of the faithful, who in spirit saw the future salvation, onward to the aged Simeon, who with bodily eye saw its
fulfilment in the Temple (Luke ii. 30),—all this cannot be
explained upon the ground of a religious development merely
natural, but upon the higher principle of a divine *election*,
of a *covenant* made by God himself with this particular people.
Although criticism, therefore, may throw doubt upon certain
sensible miracles, it cannot explain away the fundamental
miracle of this election.   The faith of Abraham, the giving of
the law upon Sinai through Moses, the sacred kingdom of
David, and the building of Solomon's temple; the second
temple, and the preservation of Messianic hopes onwards to
their fulfilment;—these undoubted facts can be explained only
upon a principle which forms the opposite pole of the contrast
with mythology and with every form of natural religion.*

* See Grundvig's Dannevirke, 3 Bd. p. 281.

§ 123.

As the history of Israel expresses the progressive realization of fellowship between God and His people, it is also the anticipation and pattern of that economy which God was to establish with all nations in the fulness of time. The chosen people were thus the *typical* people. We must not distinguish between a typical development and one teleological, wherein the present is impregnated with the future, and the final end is interwoven in all its pre-suppositions. As the realm of nature abounds in types of the kingdom of the spirit, as every more important mythology is the pattern and presage of the nation's future, so the history of Israel is the sacred type of the kingdom of grace which is to be realized in the fulness o times. The history of Israel represents the destiny of the true church in the world and God's condemning and redeeming government thereof. " All these things," says the Apostle, " happened to them as ensamples (τύποι), and are written for our admonition, upon whom the ends of the world are come " (1 Cor. x. 11). The Israelitish law and ordinances were " shadows of good things to come " (Hebrews x); and the distinguished characters in the history were types or representatives of Him who was to appear on earth in the fulness of time. Prophecy developes itself out of the type, and thereupon a new contrast appears in Israelitish history. Prophecy not only declares the contrast between Jehovah and false gods, it expresses the consciousness of a duality in the revelation of holiness, of a twofold covenant. The prophetic consciousness recognizes that the old covenant is essentially preparatory and temporary ; and it has accordingly to argue with the people who hold fast to the type, and forget the invisible in the visible, and the future in the present. The prophets of the old covenant already bear witness of the new, a heavenly Jerusalem and a newer Temple hover before their vision above the earthly Jerusalem, and the prophets, priests, and kings of the earthly Israel point to the Messiah as the eternal Priest, the great Prophet, and the true King.

Observations.—Moses with the tables of the Law, the tabernacle and the Levites, gave to the earthly Israel its essential form, so far as it is looked upon in the light of the present and the actual ; and the image of Abraham the

father of the faithful, plays the part in the history as it is
regarded in the light of the future, of the *promise* and the
ideal. It is Abraham's faith which spreads its wings in
the Davidic psalms, and soars in the eagle flight of the
prophets. As Abraham believed in God who can make
the barren fruitful, and create life in death (Rom. iv.), so
the prophets do not look for help from the natural course
of the world, but discern in unfruitful times the coming
creative crisis, the wonderful birth in history. The
coming of the Lord will renew the face of the earth, the
wilderness will blossom as the rose, and the dry bones
covering the valley will be raised to life by the Spirit of
the Lord (Isa. li. 3 ; Ezek. xxxvii.). A holy shoot shall
grow forth out of the dry stem of Jesse, and all the heathen shall flock to Mount Zion (Isa. xi. ; Jer. xxxiii. 15 ;
Isa. ii. 3). And it is in the faith of Abraham who hoped
against hope, that in the fulness of time a daughter of
Abraham bears a Son whose goings forth were of old,
from everlasting ; in whom the economy of Israel reaches
its goal because the wild olive tree may now be engrafted
and Jews and Gentiles may be gathered together in one
in Christ. In the recognition of the *possibility* of prophecy the truth is confirmed " that the present is pregnant
with the future," and that the prophet discerns the ideal
of the future in the *larva* of the present. True prophecy
takes its rise in the history ; the same divine Spirit who
manifests Himself in any given event or fact, declares
Himself in the prophetic word which points out and explains the typical in that fact. The perspective of the
future widens and extends before the Seer's vision in proportion as the historical types and prefigurements extend
in range and in copiousness. The several indications of
the future ideal are from time to time unfolded in a
fragmentary manner, and are not gathered into symmetri-
cal unity until their fulfilment. The Messianic hope
assumes one form in the days of the patriarchs, another
in the Mosaic period, a third in the Davidic period, and a
fourth amid the oppressions of the exile. But these
various prefigurements are blended together in Christ, in
whom they all are fulfilled ; in Him they are harmonized

in one. He who would find in the Old Testament a full
and complete Christology, forgets that what is true of the
types is true also of the prophecies, namely, that they are
only σκία τῶν μελλόντων (Heb. x. 1); and that as the types
are prophetical, so the prophecies themselves are typical.
Prophesy represents the Messianic hope in its fragmentary
development, and on this very account there must always
be a certain want of conformity between the prophecy and
its fulfilment. Thus we are reminded of the apostolic
saying that all prophecy as well as knowledge is " in part,"
ἐκ μέρους (1 Cor. xiii. 9), an expression which denotes
what is *relative* in the idea of prophecy, its *historical*
limitations. Without this limitation we should have to
suppose that God could unconditionally allow the human
spirit, at any time He pleased, and under any circumstances He pleased, to look into the future and to see
what it might be, to see a future which was still contingent to Himself, contingent by His ordainment upon
human freedom ;—a supposition which would require the
surrender of the idea of the *economic* God. In opposition
to such a theory we recognize the inseparable connection
between prophecy and history, and accordingly we perceive that the types and prophecies were looked upon in
the Old Testament itself as progressively fulfilled ; but
every partial fulfilment afforded yet again a new type,
and became the material and occasion for a new prophecy
until it found its final and perfect accomplishment in the
New Testament. We must not, therefore, interpret the
ἵνα πληρωθῇ of the New Testament as if it meant that
the prophecy or the type was now for the *first* time fulfilled, but that it was now fulfilled according to its full
and *pregnant* meaning, not moreover as though the thing
denoted had passed before the eye of the Prophet with
the same distinctness as before the Evangelists and Apostles. It is clear from the nature of the case, that the
fulfilment, the perfect realization, must contain much
more, many greater and richer things than any preceding
fragmentary knowledge of it in expectation or hope.

Prophecy stands in striking contrast alike with heathen philosophy and with the heathen oracles. Heathen

philosophy isolates itself from facts and from popular life. It unfolds an ideal realm of shades above the ruins of reality, and it is only in this twilight according to Hegel's comparison, that Minerva's owl begins its flight. Prophecy, on the other hand, hovers over the popular life and leads this on and up, not into a sphere of mere ideas but into a higher and more wonderful activity. The heathen oracle is as ambiguous as its dialectic; but Jehovah is no Loxias, the prophetic word clearly and unambiguously points to the one thing. The consciousness of Pythia was veiled in the dense vapours which issued from the hole in the earth, her inspiration was an unconscious inspiration of nature as in magnetic vision; it is, on the contrary, "the hand of the Lord" which comes upon the prophets of Israel, they are the sanctified of Israel, whose lips are cleansed by the touch of a live coal from off the altar (Isa. vi. 6, 7); their vision is not that of somnambulism but that of the Spirit, the con-knowledge of the human spirit with the Holy Spirit of Providence and prescience. The heathen soothsayer divined by means of entrails and the flight of birds: the prophets of Israel on the contrary looked into the mirror of history and prophesied according to the signs of the time.

§ 124.

The heathenism alike of Greece and of Rome terminated in a negative result, in lamentation over a lost ideal of life; in a brazen age, when the golden age was thought of only as a dream of youth long since passed away; Israel ended in the realization of Abraham's hope, "When the fulness of time was come, God sent forth His Son, made of a woman" (Gal. iv. 4). The people of hope and of the future reached their appointed goal like John the Baptist, who prepared the way of the Lord, saying, "He must increase, but I must decrease" (John iii. 30), like the aged Simeon in the Temple when he took the child JESUS in his arms, and said, Lord, now lettest thou thy servant depart in peace according to thy word; for mine eyes have seen thy salvation!" (Luke ii. 29, 30). They reached their destination in THE HOLY FAMILY, and in the chosen remnant of Israelites indeed, who became the APOSTLES and DISCIPLES of CHRIST.

THE DOCTRINE OF THE SON.

THE INCARNATION OF GOD IN CHRIST.

§ 125.

THE manifestation of the Son of God in the fulness of the
times points back to His *pre-existence;*—by pre-existence,
understanding, not merely that He had being originally in
the Father, but also that He had being originally in the world.
As the mediator between the Father and the world, it appertains to the essence of the Son not only to have His life in
the Father, but to live also in the world. As " the heart of
God the Father," He is at the same time the " eternal heart
of the world," through which the divine life streams into
creation. As the Logos of the Father, He is at the same time
the eternal Logos of the world, through whom the divine
light shines into creation.* He is the ground and source
of all reason in the creation, be it in men or angels, in Greek
or Jew. He is the principle of the law and promises under
the Old Testament, the eternal light which shines in the darkness of heathenism; and all the holy grains of truth which
are found in heathenism were sowed by the Son of God in
the souls of men. He is the eternal principle of Providence
in the tangled web of human life; for all the powers of existence, all ideas and angels, are instruments to carry out the
will of the all-ordering, all-controlling Logos. During His
pre-existence, however, He was merely the essential, not the
actual, mediator between God and the creature; for the antagonism between the created and the uncreated was as yet

* John i. 4—" In Him was life, and the life was the light of men."

done away with merely as to the essence, not as to existence (*essentia, existentia*) ; the strife between God and the sinful world was healed merely in idea, not in life and reality. In His pre-existent state, therefore, the Son regards Himself as the *One who is to come* in and through history ; who prepares beforehand the conditions under which the revelation of His love can take place, His incarnation in the fulness of the times can be effected, and the manifestation be made by which the idea of Him as the *mediating* God will first attain complete realization. The announcements and delineations of Christ contained in the Old Testament were the continuous unfolding of His self-announcement and His self-delineation ;—they were a continuous coming. It was the divine Logos Himself who presented Himself to the vision of the prophets in the form of His future incarnation ; it lay in the nature of the Mediator to assume human nature as His own, and on that account to show Himself to the prophetic eye as a Son of man ; it was the divine Logos Himself, who imaged Himself forth beforehand in elect sons of men under the Old Covenant, who moulded human personalities to a limited extent after His own holy nature, and thus realized beforehand some features of the image whose entire divine and human fulness He purposed to express in His revelation as the Christ. Nay, more, in the sons of the gods of Heathendom, and in the men who stood forward as witnesses of a noble, God-related humanity, we may trace individual features of His image, which He has stamped on them, although the heathens mis-apprehended them, and did not lay hold on the promise they contained.

Observations.—The doctrine of the Logos contained in revela-tion has been often compared with the doctrine laid down in the Alexandrian philosophy ; nay, more, it has often been asserted that John borrowed his ideas of the Logos from the Jew Philo. But there is the most decided an-tagonism between the two. Teleology, time, history, and corporeality are totally foreign to the Alexandrian Logos ; whereas they are inseparable from the Logos of revelation. Philo converted the history of men into a world of shows ; historical facts into an allegorical vehicle of general thoughts and ideas. To his mind there seemed to be a yawning gulf fixed between "Word" and "Flesh" (λογος and σάρξ); for he regarded sense and nature as the person of the Spirit, and deemed it impossible for the thinker to attain to union with the divine reason, save by being mystically or ecstatically lifted above realities, and by the mortification of sense unto death. The Logos of revelation, on the contrary, who came through the medium of history, type, and prophecy; ended by making corporeality and nature a part of Himself, and thus revealed the unity of nature and history. Here sounds in our ears the joyous message, "the Word became flesh, and dwelt among us: we have heard it, we have seen it with our eyes; we have handled it with our hands," (John i. 14; 1 John i.)

§ 126.

That the Incarnation was historically accomplished in Jesus Christ, who was "born of the Virgin Mary and suffered under Pontius Pilate;" that Jesus Christ is the real Mediator between God and the world, has been confessed and testified by the entire Christian Church:—Jesus Christ, glorified in the Spirit, as set forth and delineated by the Evangelists and Apostles of the Church. The living image handed down to us by them, constitutes the fixed presupposition and sure polestar for all human reflection on the mystery of the incarnation. As the Son of God came into the world, we are to receive Him; as He revealed Himself, so are we to know Him.

Observations.—We take for granted here that the image of Christ, handed down to us in the four canonical Gospels is genuine. If the Christ is the real and proper substance of Christianity, there must exist a correct representation of His personality; for to say that the true image of Christ has not been given to the world, is equivalent to saying that Christ is not come into the world as the Truth. The assertion, therefore, which is made ever and anon by modern critics, that our Gospels give a false and unaccurate, or, at all events, an extremely imperfect picture of the Christ who really came into the world, is indirectly a denial of the essence of Christianity. Christ, it is true, is not present in the Scriptures alone; it is true, the image of Christ lives in a manner relatively independent of Scripture, in the heart of the Church, and in the heart of each individual believer ; but the inward Christ of the heart, presupposes the Christ manifested in history, and without the latter, soon fades away into a mystic cloud. The manifold representations of Christ, which exist in the Christian Church as a whole, in the various confessions and sects, in the various forms of Christian art and science, all spring from the one grand fundamental form which is sketched in the Gospels; and they must all be judged and tested thereby. If we had not such a representation, no really essential feature of which is absent or incorrect ; if Christ were solely the half apocryphal person to which one-sided critics love to reduce Him, by enveloping Him in an impenetrable mist, we must give up speaking of a Christian revelation in the sense that Christ himself is its fundamental feature. But that Christ is Himself the very centre and essence of the Christian revelation ; that He came into the world as the Truth and the Life—this is the fundamental testimony, and the fundamental experience, of the Christian Church. And the assurance of the inner truth and original perfection of the testimony of the Gospels, is a prime experience, which is renewed in all ages by the church at large, and by every individual believer.

§ 127.

The new feature in the revelation of Christ is not that union of the divine and human nature, which is involved in the idea of man as created in the image of God. The new feature is such an union of the two natures, that a man on earth appears as the self-revelation of the divine Logos. Although the word "God-man" is not found in the New Testament, the thought expressed by it lies at the basis of its Christological representations. Christ describes himself as both the Son of God and the Son of man. In styling Himself the Son of man, He sets himself forth as the personal embodiment of human nature in its pure archetypal form—(as the second Adam, according to the explanation of the apostle.) And in styling Himself the Son of God, He assumes the position of the Only-begotten of the Father—(He is "the brightness of the Father's glory, and the express image of His person," Heb. i. 3).   To Him is given all power in heaven and on earth (Matt. xxviii. 18): He designates himself " Wisdom ; "* He ascribes to himself holiness by raising himself above the holiest in Israel ;† He proclaims himself the Redeemer and Perfecter of the world.   As He has the power to forgive sins (Matt. ix. 6), to send the Holy Spirit (John xv. 26), and to be present where two or three are gathered together in His name (Matt. xviii. 20); so will He also be the future Judge of the world, and His coming is of significance not merely for humanity, but also for the entire spiritual and natural universe (Matt. xxiv. ; Luke xxi.) Whilst announcing Himself as the One who will come at the end of the world, He also represents himself as the One who was from the beginning, who had glory with the Father ere the world was (John xvii. 5).   It has often been asserted that the conception of the God-man contained in the gospel of John is different from that contained in the synoptical gospels ; some indeed maintain that the two are incompatible with each other, on the ground that the latter do not clearly mention the Logos and the doctrine of the pre-existence of Christ, which is connected therewith.   The only real difference, however, is, that John gives distinct expression and prominence to that which is really present in the other gospels, though in undeveloped fulness.   The first three gospels present the divine glory of Christ essentially from the prophetic and eschatological point of view ; or, if we may so express ourselves, the point of view of His *post-existence* They regard His glory principally as the glory of the One who, having already come, will henceforth continue to come ; on whom depends the *future*, not merely of the human race, but also of the universe ; who is the Judge of the world and its Redeemer, to whom all spiritual and natural forces, all heavenly and earthly powers must finally submit.‡   In this way they not only characterize Him as a prophet endowed with divine gifts, but also attribute to His person as such a

---

* Luke vii. 35: "Wisdom is justified of all her children."

† Matt. xii. 6: "I say unto you, that in this place there is One greater than the temple."

‡ See especially our Lord's discourses concerning the destruction of Jerusalem and the end of the world.

metaphysical and cosmical significance. Now, such a view of Christ involves in it the thought—a thought to which John gives clear expression—that He who is the LAST, who in His future will be exalted to power over all things in creation, over all things in heaven and on earth, must also have been the FIRST, must have existed before all creatures ;—the thought that He to whom we must ascribe post-existence in such a sense, must also have been pre-existent. In other words, because the principle that wills the world must be identical with that which creates the world ; He who is the personal revelation of the principle that completes the world must also be the incarnation of the principle that created the world, of the Word which was in the beginning with God and was itself God (John i. 1, 14). Each of the representations, therefore, derives its colouring from a different aspect of the glory of Christ ; and the two, so far from excluding, mutually require and supplement each other. The first three gospels look forwards ; they have a prophetico-historical character ; they contemplate Christ from the point of view of the future, of the teleological end and goal. The Gospel of John, on the contrary, looks backwards, not only into time past, but into eternity ; contemplates Christ predominantly from the metaphysical point of view, from the point of view of Christ's pre-existence, of the eternal commencement of teleology.*

§ 128.

The idea of an union of the divine and human natures was not unknown to *Judaism ;* for it recognized the existence of a communion between the Spirit of God and the spirit of man, which manifested itself plainly in the case of pious men and divinely-endowed prophets. But that God himself should become man—this was an idea totally foreign to Judaism, one which it was prevented from entertaining by its rigid view of the antagonism between Creator and creature. The Messiah presented Himself, it is true, to the prophetic eye in human shape ; but still the anticipations of the full union of the divine and human essence were but very vague and feeble ; and as a general rule, the Jewish mind

† Compare *Dorner*, Entwicklungsgeschichte der Lehre von der Person Christi, 2d ed. vol. i. 234.

regarded it as a blasphemy that Jesus, being a man, should
wish to make himself God (John x. 33).   Nor was the idea
of the union of the divine and human natures foreign to
Heathenism, for, on the contrary, it presents us with a whole
world of divine-human ideals.   But that the Divine Logos
should become Flesh—this was something new to heathenism.
For, confounding as it did God and the world, it had in reality nothing but men who regarded themselves as divine.
The unity of the divine and human natures acknowledged by
it had no real existence, had existence merely as an ideal of
the imagination, which hovered before the mind as the goal
of effort, but which could never attain more than an extremely imperfect realization.   In heathenism, therefore, the
divine-human ideal has merely a mythical existence, an existence in the world of shows, of fancy, of poesy.   A Christ in
idea ; a Christ, who was a picture of the Divine glory painted
by the human mind, would have been accepted by heathens.
Nay, more, at the time when Christianity made its appearance, heathens would readily have accepted the doctrine of
an omnipresent, Divine Logos ; such a doctrine would have
found a point of contrast in the theory of ideas laid down by
some of their philosophers—a theory into which the mythology of their fathers had at last resolved itself.   But that the
Logos had become flesh ; that a man had come into the world
who was not merely a revelation of that union between the
divine and the human, which is by nature the proper portion
of us all, and which has manifested itself in the deeds of heroes
and in the thoughts of the wise ; but being perfectly united
in essence with God was the personal manifestation of the
Divine sanctity and righteousness on earth, belief in whom
is the condition of blessedness or damnation ; that this God-
man should have actually and truly allowed Himself to be
crucified as a propitiation for the sins of the world—the proclamation of this was foolishness to the heathen ; for to them
the true God was an unknown God, and the idea of holiness,
sin, and damnation, foreign.

It was natural that when the new Gospel with its power
on the one hand to attract, and on the other to repel, was
published in the world, there should be found men who sought
to appropriate such elements of Christianity as fell in with

their previous views and wishes, whilst they endeavoured to cut away those elements which were offensive to them. Amongst the confessors of the new faith both Jews and heathens were to be found who framed a Christ for themselves in agreement with the impulses of their own hearts. This was the source of the various heresies and false representations of Christ that arose. The idea of God himself being in Christ was offensive to the Jewish mind; and, therefore, it reduced Jesus to the rank of a divinely-endowed man, of the greatest of all prophets, of the most perfect of all that had hitherto appeared. The stumbling-block was thus removed; but the excision of the "offence" was the denial of the new feature peculiar to Christianity; thus constituting Christianity the mere blossom and flower of Judaism. On the other hand, the heathen mind found it incredible, that God and man should really form one essence; that their union should be more than one of thought and image, and therefore it maintained that Christ had a body merely in appearance; in other words, heathens converted His history into a myth; Christianity thus lost its "foolishness," that is, its miraculous character; but it also lost its novelty. For the thought of a merely ideal unity of God and man is one which may be found at little cost in nearly all systems of philosophy. Christianity would, on this supposition, be the mere crown of the great mythical tree; and must, therefore, be assumed to have root and stem in common with the various other myths produced by the mind of man. The former is the Ebionite (the meagre, common-sense moral) view of Christ; the latter is the Docetic or Gnostic (the speculative, phantastical) view. These are the fundamental forms of all heresy; the prototypes of all false images of Christ, that is, of the images which in leaving out what is "offensive," leave out also what is new and original. They make their appearance ever afresh; and as often as they present themselves the Church repels them.

Observations.—In the present day Docetism has been revived again in the mythical treatment of the sacred history. Of such a treatment Schelling gave the first practical sketch; and his sketch recent critics have carried out in the prose of common sense. Docetism, it is true, has frequently protested, that whilst rejecting the mere history as the

transitory husk, it preserves the permanent and indestructible element of Christianity, to wit, the idea ; but we
answer, that to make a mistake relatively to the Gospel
history, is to misapprehend the fundamental thought of
Christianity ; that to view Christianity as a mythology is
to form a false conception of the fundamental problems of
all religion—those problems which are the starting-point
of Christianity, and whose solution is presented in the
person of Christ. These fundamental problems are the
problems of creation and sin. As the antithesis between
God and the world is not a mere semblance ; and as there
are created beings outside of God, which yearn for, and
struggle backwards towards, life in their Creator ; the
antithesis demands reconciliation—reconciliation too, not
merely in thought and image, but in life and reality. As,
further, the antagonism between the sinful world and the
Holy God is not a mere pretence, but a solemn reality,
not merely a hindrance and disturbance in thought, but a
hindrance and disturbance in reality, the deliverance to
be effected must be more than a deliverance of thought
from semblance, it must lead back existing being to its
true fundamental relations. A mythical solution of these
problems would contradict the inmost substance of Christianity ; it would be a mocking irony of the deep, moral
earnestness involved in the relationship of creation to its
creator and in the consciousness of sin. " If the Son of
God," we may say with the Apostolic fathers (for example,
Ignatius), " has been crucified for me merely in appearance, then am I bound down by the chains of sin merely
in appearance ; but those who thus speak are themselves
a mere show" (that is, they live in a dreamy condition
which prevents them seeing the earnestness of life and
estranges them from true actualities). The mythical
theory, therefore, is an attempt to reduce Christianity to
an aesthetic or art religion, in which realities in the ordinary sense are not necessary, but merely such realities as
are supplied by thought and fancy ; in which no corporeality is requisite but that of image and appearance ; in
which the relations of man's personal existence find no
recognition. And criticism can succeed in cutting off piece

after piece of the Gospel history only on one condition—
to wit, that it enter on the examination of every separate
miracle with the denial of a creation and of the fall of
man from his Creator. For our part, therefore, we consider it only natural that the solution of the riddle of life
offered by Christianity, both in word and deed, should
fail to content those who deny altogether the existence of
the riddle. We find it also quite in order that this criticism should direct its weapons of destruction not merely
against the doctrine of the person of Christ, but also
against revelation as a whole, and that it should seek to
supplant the Christian by the heathen view of life.

Quite ready as we are to acknowledge that it is out of
our power to force on any one the view of Christianity
which prevails in the Church ; we are equally unable to
allow that the mythical view is the only one deserving of
the name of philosophical or scientific. When we ask
what the critical writers just referred to have advanced in
particular against the view entertained by the Church, we
find that it may be reduced to the following three principal points :—

I. The first is, that *the ideal and the real can never
be reconciled or made one in actuality, but solely in thought
and imagination.* These critics say—precisely because
everything in the Gospels is poetically true, it cannot be
historically true. The world of realities is a hard mass,
difficult to penetrate ; a material that resists spiritual
influence ; a domain of conflict and pain ; and it is in the
sphere of philosophic thought alone, which may be regarded as the perfume and spiritual essence of these hard
realities, that the reconciliation has taken place. Accordingly, the more practical, the more profoundly symbolical
the narrative which is presented to us, the less credible
must it be considered in an historical point of view. For
the poetic imagination is accustomed to blend together
into one image, features which in the actual world never
occur otherwise than singly and sparely ; and what the
spirit in its poetic workings builds up in a moment by one
magical stroke, requires long and weary ages for its actual
realization ; and even then attains it only in a fragmentary
and sporadic shape.

The contradiction between the ideal and the real, which these critics take every opportunity of insisting upon, arises from the want of a true conception of creation and providence. Gnosticism here passes over into Manichæism. So long as finite objects are regarded merely as a condition of the life of deity, they must necessarily appear, at one time, as unreal shows without independence; at another time as a restrictive limit which can never be fully overcome; nay, more, which must necessarily remain, in order that the divine life may not fall into stagnation. Whereas, if we recognise the existence of a *created* mundane life, destined to be transformed and glorified by becoming a life in God; if we recognize the presence of a creative *providential* thought in history, then must the end of life be to reduce this thought to reality—in other words, to constitute thought and life a living unity. History supplies, it is true, evidence enough of the fact, that the real world is a material which resists permeation and animation by spirit; but still we find also that history in general, and the life of every great man in particular, is marked by a *plastic* tendency—a tendency that is to blend and combine the ideal and real, the internal and external, freedom and fate. Who, for example, does not find in the events of the life of Napoleon or Luther an historical symbolism, through which expression is given in a plastic manner to the ideal? It has been justly remarked that on the method and principles adopted by modern critics, it would be easy to show that Luther and Napoleon were mythical persons—that the account of the series of brilliant victories and conquests gained by the latter in so short a space of time is more a fairy tale than a reality; because the real world is a hard mass, hard to penetrate, and because really to carry out such labours would require a long and weary period:—it would be easy to show that the reports of Napoleon's death on St. Helena, a remote island of the ocean, can only belong to the world of fancy, because they symbolize so strikingly the fall and humiliation of the mighty monarch. But that plastic, symbolical procedure of providence, which we can trace more or less clearly at all the principal turning-points of history, found perfect revelation in the life of Christ ; for His life was the *fulness of creation and providence,* and therefore the perfect unity of the real and ideal, of nature and history, of fate and liberty. Like all poetry and art, the myth is merely the subjective solution of the contradiction between the ideal and the real—that contradiction which is the source of the conflicts and sufferings of the human race. In this middle region alone has poesy any significance. But what reality can be ascribed to poesy unless it be a true dream, a true reflection pointing to a realization of the ideal higher than that which itself claims to be ?

II. The second point is contained in the well-known proposition :—that *the idea does not exhaust its fulness in one exemplar.* The idea never realises itself in one individual, but distributes its fulness over the whole race. On this ground, Christ can neither be the perfect revelation of the divine nature, nor the perfect revelation of human nature. For God can only be perfectly revealed by the entire kingdom of spirits ; and the full idea of man can only be perfectly revealed by the entire human race.

The proposition, that the idea does not exhaust its fulness in one exemplar, is correct if we take it to mean that the idea does not communicate itself to any one individual in such a manner, that he may possess its full wealth in a selfish manner for himself, without others becoming participators therein. But in the sense in which these critics lay it down, it is not true. In all spheres of life we find centralizations of the idea such that we are compelled to say—here has the idea poured its whole wealth in one individual. All the individuals who have played in history the part of *heads* and *representatives* of circles of men, may be said to have contained within themselves, in a compressed form, the wealth of the idea. Hence the favourite designation of such individuals at the present day, is *Incarnations of the Idea.* And as the works of art, which we term classic, (for example, Homer's Epic poems), owe the position thus assigned them to the circumstance that they are fitted to serve as eternal representatives in their particular kind ; so also are there men of whom the same thing may be affirmed. The position

that a single individual cannot embrace in itself the
infinitude of the idea, but that a world of individuals is
necessary thereto, rests on an *external* and false conception of the infinite. Rightly understood, the doctrine of
the God-man does not require us to suppose that the
divine essence in the external infinitude by which it fills
the universe was in Him, but merely that the fulness or
the powers of deity were intensively concentred in Him.
When we say that man is the fulness of the natural
creation, we do not mean that man possesses all the partial
perfections which we find in the animal world, for
example, the strength of the lion, the eye of the eagle, the
speed of the horse, and so forth ; but that all these relative perfections are taken up into the inner perfection of
the human organism. So is it with the second Adam.
It was not his task to unite in Himself all the relative
perfections and excellences which we find in the entire
world of men, but merely the fundamental form of all
these perfections. In like manner, we must look for the
accomplishment, not of all the tasks of human life, but
merely of its great fundamental task in the work of
Christ. We might fairly meet such misconceptions by
the remark of Schleiermacher—if any one wants to be a
philosopher he must go to philosophers ; to be a poet, he
must go to poets; to be a painter, he must go to
painters ; but if any one desires to be a Christian he must
go to Christ ; for in Him is the fulness of the kingdom of
God, of the kingdom of heaven. Let us add, however,
that inasmuch as the kingdom of God is not merely a
higher stage of *consciousness,* but the highest stage of
existence and *life ;* we are warranted in saying regarding
Christ—in Him was the fulness of the entire creation ;
and all the powers and potencies which work separately
in nature and history, have found a place, and are transformed and glorified, in the fulness of the vigour of His
love and sanctity.

III. The third point is contained in the position—
*that the first link in a chain of development cannot
possibly be the most perfect.* All development, say these
critics, begins with the lower and advances onwards

towards the higher.   First comes the state of ferment, a
groping after the truth ; and then a gradual progress
towards light and clearness, each successive stage being
an advance on its predecessor.   Applying this position to
Christ, our critics allow that He gave the first impulse to
the new development ; but deny that He was in perfect
possession of the new principle Himself.   Considered in
this light, the Holy Scriptures contain merely the rough,
fermenting elements of the Christian literature, of which
they constitute the first beginnings.   " To make these
books the norm and measure of the Christian is as per-
verse as to seek for the ideal of a human being in the
forms of a child."

Of this position we may say, what we said of the preceding one—that though it contains a relative truth, experience is totally opposed to the setting it up as a rule
without exception.   It rests on an uncritical, inaccurate
conception of the true nature of a commencement ; no
distinction is made between an approximative, merely
preparative beginning and a central, *creative* beginning.
To a beginning of the former kind, the position is perfectly applicable.   The individuals whom these critics
have in view, as the first links of the chain, are in reality
mere forerunners of the true beginning, of the link which
is veritably the *first*, they are the representatives of that
fermenting and groping which are in general characteristic of periods of transition as they are termed.   Indeed
the great misfortune of such periods consists precisely in
their incapability of taking the first step in the new development, whilst at the same time they feel the need of
doing so.   Such individuals indicate the general expectation of the dawn of a new creative era ; and, on the
other hand, make various attempts to bring about its in-
auguration ; these efforts fail not from lack of true creative
ability, for experience teaches us that the true beginner,
the genius as we term him, never arises in any sphere of
life, till the time is fulfilled.   Relatively, however, to the
beginnings inaugurated by men of genius, we are fully
warranted in saying—the *first* link in the chain of development is the most *perfect*.   Not as though the entire

work to be accomplished by the development were accomplished at once in them; but that by virtue of the fulness and variety of their inner life, they infold in themselves and prefigure the entire future development. Were then Plato and Aristotle, Schelling and Hegel, the most imperfect members of the philosophical schools, which date their existence from them? or were Shakespeare, Goethe, Raphael, Angelo the most imperfect poets and artists of the epochs inaugurated by them? or are we to suppose that Luther and Calvin were the most imperfect members of the communities to which they gave rise? Must we not rather say—they were the personal prototypes of the churches which bear their name; they, as the heads of their churches, possessed in fulness that of which their followers only possess fragments? The higher the sphere of life, the more fully does it hold good, that particular individuals must be many things to many men; that many may be called but few chosen; and that the many draw their supplies from the fulness of the few. This law of divine election, according to which the first link in the chain is the most perfect, is most clearly and fully exemplified in connection with the redemption, the regeneration of the race. The new Adam commenced a line of development which, instead of being destined to be supplanted by another, will remain the typical norm for all ages, races and individuals; whereas, others who have originated new creations in humanity, have been the mere heads of a movement or series of movements ending in time.

Let us now turn our attention to the historical soil out of which these myths grew; let us ask—what then really happened capable of producing an impression so mighty, that a new mythology arose into existence,—a mythology, too, which, when compared with the cycle of legends that subsequently sprang up in the Romish Church, fully confirms the truth of the proposition, that the first link in the chain is the most perfect? The answer we receive is as follows:—In the reign of Tiberius, a highly-endowed man, Jesus of Nazareth, made His appearance, and gave utterance to the word which became the watchword of

the new era. At that time, namely, all minds were in a
state of ferment. Heathenism and Judaism had alike had
their day, and the world needed something new. The
new principle by which the whole aspect and shape of the
world were changed may be described as the knowledge
of the oneness of God and man. " I and the Father are
one." This energetic affirmation of the infinite freedom
of the mind of man—an affirmation by which Jesus, as a
kind of Palestinian Socrates, drew men away from the
Jewish bondage to ceremonies, saved them from heathenish
absorption in this world (the political kingdom), and led
them into their own inner being, produced a great impression. The dominant party rose against Him, and in
consequence He was crucified; but after His death, the
thought which He had embodied continued to develop
itself with greater vigour. Still the human race was not
then ripe for regarding itself as the God-man; in consequence whereof the first believers attributed the entire
wealth of the idea to the individual who first gave utterance to it; ascribed to Him qualities which can only be
properly ascribed to humanity in its entirety. Out of
the dark and permeating depths of the religious mind
arose a cycle of myths which identified the person of
Christ with the idea, and thus presented Him to the gaze
of believers in supernatural and marvellous light.

We have here been able merely to indicate the fundamental features of modern docetism; but enough has
been adduced to enable us to judge how far it supplies
a satisfactory explanation of the rise of the Christian
Church, and of an entirely new history. One thing, at
all events, is certain : the basis must be as broad as the
subsequent edifice, the cause cannot be slighter than the
effect which it produced. The history of the Christian
Church and the history of Christendom cannot be explained by a reference to the pantheistic doctrine of the
unity of man and God; for in the form in which it is set
forth by the critics in question, it lacks all capability of
exercising a fructifying influence on human life. If such
a principle, such a doctrine of the infinite freedom of the
spirit of man, and of the invisible world of the idea, had

been fitted to infuse new life into the dying world, Neo-
Platonism would have been its regenerator.   Even if we
conceive the principle combined with a purified system of
morals, whilst it might have given rise to a school analogous to those founded by Socrates, it could never have
originated a religion for the whole world, or a new
humanity.   But we have also another question to
ask :—Is it conceivable that the age in which Christ
appeared should have produced a mythology ?   Our
answer is, No !   That age was an age of culture ;
an age of intellect, an age of unbelief and doubt.
Intentional religious fictions may indeed be issued
in such an age ; in point of fact writings of this character were promulgated by the leaders of individual
sects.   Fantastic and senseless superstitions, such as are
commonly found accompanying an age of unbelief, may
have made their appearance in that day.   Anecdotes and
particular traits of a mythical character, such as are accustomed to gather around great historical persons and events,
and to constitute as it were a border to realities, may
then spring up ; but the creation of a world of myths is
impossible in such an age.   Myths proper only arise
where the human mind still occupies the stage of nature ;
where the world of imagination has not yet been clearly
and consciously distinguished from the world of reality.
Only in its childhood is the human race capable of dreaming mythical dreams like those we find in the mythologies of Greece and the North ; in an age, whose predomi-
nant characteristic is *scepticism,* it is impossible for it to
cherish such *naive* faith in its own dreams of the " Reconciliation of the Ideal and the Real."   On the contrary,
it is one of the most marked features of age to give
prominence to the contradiction between the ideal and
the real ; and it totally lacks the inner force requisite to
the creation of a world of dreams, full of life and spirit.
That naked philosophical thought of the pantheistic unity
of the divine and human essence—a thought which
would have been worthy of the religious philosophy of
Alexandria—might have found expression in poetical
allegories of a value corresponding to their subject, but

never in living and breathing poetry like that of the gospels. Here, therefore, in asking us to conceive of Christ as a creation of the Church, instead of regarding the Church as a creation of Christ, as the temple built of living stones, Jesus himself being the chief corner stone, these critics have again offended against the "*principium rationis sufficientis.*"

Let us now direct our attention to their treatment of the Holy Scriptures. They maintain that our gospels were composed far later, and by quite different authors, than is commonly supposed by the Church. Critics maintain them to be productions of the second century ; the Church assumes them to have been written during the latter half of the first century. Such an assertion is absolutely necessary to the critical point of view : for otherwise the time would have been too short for the formation of a complete cycle of myths. But if we find that towards the close of the second, and at the beginning of the third century, all witnesses testify that our gospels existed in the *different* regions where churches were established, we shall be compelled again to charge our critics with advancing no *satisfactory* reason why precisely our four gospels were selected from the entire mass of apocryphal writings, and alone constituted canonical. Why just *these four ?* Whence the unanimous recognition which we find both in the Eastern and Western portions of the Church ? The only sufficient explanation of the phenomenon is, that there existed a tradition on the subject, which was derived from and was handed down through the whole of the second century.* The circumstance that our first written testimonies regarding the gospels are of a comparatively so late date will occasion no difficulty when we consider that the first generations, enjoying as they did the full tide of oral tradition, did not feel the same interest in written testimonies as later generations naturally must. But it is principally on *inner* grounds that these critics assert the unhistorical character of our gospels. "Even if we pass over the

---

* Mynster's " Kl. theol. Schriften." H. N. Clausen : " Udvikling af de christelige Hovedlärdomme," p. 120.

metaphysical and doctrinal difficulties which they contain ; even if we pass over the miracles ; there are so many other contradictions int he Gospels, that a scrutinizing eye cannot possibly regard them as genuine history." The examination in detail of this objection we must leave to the department of Biblical Theology ; one point only will we notice, the main one, to wit, the supposed want of agreement between the gospels and the course adopted by critics relatively thereto. It is well known that the old orthodox Harmonies started with the presupposition that every event must have taken place, and word have been spoken, precisely and literally as set forth in the gospels, *in the same order of place and time.* This notion gave occasion to the difficulties and artifices in which the old theologians, as is well known, got involved, the moment they endeavoured to reconcile the different Gospels with each other. Modern critics start with the same mechanical presupposition, but apply it in an opposite manner. They take for granted, namely, that every evangelist meant his work to be regarded as a literal reproduction of the life of Jesus, as, so to speak, the protocol of His words and deeds. Naturally enough, when they came afterwards to submit them to a cross-questioning, it was easy to show that they contradict one another. As has been justly observed, however, it was not the intention of the evangelists to give a daguerreotype of Christ, but to present a picture of the Redeemer in spirit. We have not to do with four daguerreotypes, which must in that case undoubtedly be false ; but with four free, spiritual reproductions of one and the same. It is needless to attempt to show that the person of Christ and His life might be set forth from four principal points of view. Each Evangelist was guided by one distinct and principal aspect of the doctrinal idea ; and his selection of historical material, of words and events, and his arrangement of what he decided on admitting, were determined by the general plan of the work. The individual words and events all served to throw light on that particular aspect of the great picture of Christ which had specially struck the author's mind, and which he

meant to delineate. Considered in this light, a harmony
of the general character noticed above becomes unneces-
sary. Still the main question remains, to wit, Do the
gospels agree relatively as to *the Gospel?* Can the different representations of Christ be combined in spirit to
form one fundamental image, whose inner fulness and
wealth are shadowed forth by the various forms in which
it appears? This question even critics must answer in
the affirmative. One might concede that mythical elements cleave to those portions of the gospel history
which relate solely to what is outward and contingent;
one might allow the existence of single historical details
relatively to which an investigator must exclaim, *non
liquet;* but this would only show that we are not justified in retaining the mechanical conception of inspiration laid down by our older theologians. In reality,
however, the traces of human limitation which we find
in these writings do but serve to bring more clearly
to view the grand phenomenon which characterises them,
the image of the person and life of the Lord; to throw
a fuller light on the immoveable, historical rock on
which the main fact is based. The holy, objective calm;
the clearly-defined physiognomy, and the essential identity of the main features of the figure drawn by each
several narrative, shows that it must have exercised unbounded sway over the individual minds in which it was
reflected; that it was possessed of a spiritual energy capable of surmounting the limitation of the letter. Nowhere are we left in doubt as to the character of the
Lord; no inner contradiction, no inconsistency, can be
pointed out in this pure, faithful image of the *essence,
will,* and *work* of the Only-Begotten, presented to us by
the various evangelistic narratives.

We are brought here to the consideration of a point
of great importance in forming an estimate of the critical methods and principles to which we are referring.
A proper estimate can never be formed of any personality,
merely from the aggregate of its single actions and the
events of its life, but solely from an intellectual intuition
of its inner essence and character; the acts must be un

derstood by the character, not by themselves.   It is true, this intellectual intuition, if it is not to have a mystical and purely subjective character, must find confirmation in every individual feature and trait; on the other hand, however, a right view of the fundamental character is essential to the right understanding and estimate of the acts.   Indeed, we may say, that to the right and full understanding of every great man a corresponding sense, a fitting spiritual organ is necessary; where such an organ is lacking, misapprehension is quite unavoidable.   This applies above all to Him who is the personality of personalities.   We must add, however, another consideration. Persons alone are able to understand persons; and the view we take of particular persons is necessarily determined by personal sympathies and antipathies.   It is a simple mistake for any one to imagine that his relation to human beings can be entirely independent of such influences; the more important the character of the individual in question, and the more distinctly he lays claim to recognition, the more will these influences make themselves felt.   The application of these remarks to Christ is obvious.   No one can receive a true impression of His personality unless his mind be prepared for it by a previous devotion of the *will.*   Hence the Lord constantly demands faith in His person; and precisely because Christ requires faith, unconditional self-surrender, therefore must every man, not utterly destitute of thought, who tarries spiritually in His neighbourhood, enter either into a *religious* or irreligious relation to Him.   We are willing to allow that the critics in question have displayed much learning and acuteness; but they have lacked one all-important condition of the fulfilment of their task, to wit, that spiritual intuition and sympathy without which no great man can possibly be rightly apprehended; and in their treatment of the life of Jesus they have been predominantly under the sway of personal antipathies.

Just one concluding observation:——A Docetical view of Christ inevitably leads to and changes into an *Ebionite* view.   The speculative mythical theory which we have been discussing, looks down with haughty contempt on

R

the old Rationalism; but at heart there is no difference between them. For when we have stripped Christ of the mythical garment in which the imagination of the Church is supposed to have clothed Him, His divine glory vanishes, and the real historical Christ is seen to be nothing more than a man of high endowments. He is a mere teacher, a great *prophet*, who gave utterance to a new form of consciousness; but for His high-priestly and kingly offices there remains no room—and this is a distinctive characteristic of Ebionitism.

The Union of the Divine and Human Natures in Christ.

§ 129.

Although the relation between God and man in general involves the possibility of an union of the divine and human natures, this possibility does not account for the glory of the Only Begotten of the Father. It follows, indeed, from the circumstance of man being destined to bear the image of God, that human nature is capable of becoming partaker of the attributes of the divine nature, of the divine wisdom, righteousness, holiness, and love, and thus also of the divine freedom. By a general unity of this nature, however, the capacity for which, at all events, we must suppose to be possessed by every being created in the divine image, we should only be led to the notion of a kingdom of individuals united with God, but not to the idea of a person like Christ. The basis thus gained for the Incarnation is too wide; for on it we all take our stand; accordingly there is no room left for the Only Begotten One. It is on this foundation that are built the theories of abstract speculation and the fancies of religious mysticism. So far as man turns away from creatures, and through God denies himself, he is more God than creature. For it is then not he himself that lives, but God who lives in him. To lay hold on God as He is in Himself, is in a certain sense to be God with God." Mysticism takes for granted that every soul united with God is essentially the same as Christ. The historical Christ was merely the first representation of a soul united with God; His history is full of quickening pictures and symbols for the pious mind; but the true Christ is the inner, mystical Christ whom we all bear in ourselves, although He does not stir with equal vigour in all. We have here a new form of the Docetism which denies the reality of the Incarnation. For the idea of the Incarnation is not that of a soul united with God (*unio mystica*); but that of a man in whom dwelt all the fulness of the Godhead *bodily*.

§ 130.

An understanding of the glory of the Only Begotten One can only be arrived at in one way—that way trodden by Christian thought from the very beginning of the Church's existence; to wit, by starting with the conception of a *Mediator* between God and man. The *redeeming* Mediator, whose destiny it is to restore the fellowship of the human race with God, interrupted by sin, must stand on the one hand in perfect fellowship with the human race, and on the other hand in perfect fellowship with God; otherwise He cannot form a perfect bond of union between the two. As the Mediator between God and the human race, it was necessary that He should, on the one hand, be a member of the race; and yet, on the other hand, stand above, or in a relation of antithesis to, the entire race; not merely because He alone in the midst of a sinful world was without sin, but because no one can come to the Father but through Him; because we all are to receive of His fulness, because He alone is the *giver*, whereas all others are *receivers*. But the fulness from which we are to receive is not merely the fulness of His human nature, but also the fulness of His divine nature. What we men need is the union of the two; and what the true Mediator has to do is to reveal this union, not merely under this or that finite form, in this or that finite connection, but in prototypical perfection, so that its fulness may be such as to meet the requirements of all. He must, therefore, set forth human nature in its purity, in its susceptibility to God, in other words, He must be the true *Adam*. At the same time, whilst revealing the depths of human nature, He must also reveal the depths of the divine love, that is, He must be the revelation of the perfect *self-communication* of the divine, to the human nature. God must be in Him, not merely relatively, in finite degree, but absolutely and fully. He must be the revelation

of the divine love itself in its deepest depths, the self-revelation of the principle which was from the beginning the life
and light of the world—the light which shone in the darkness
although the darkness comprehended it not. As the Person
who renders it possible, not merely for a single nation or a
single age, but for the entire human race and every separate
individual, to develope his humanity in the right relation to
God ; and whose activity is accordingly destined to surmount
every limit of time and space, Christ is more than the founder
of an historical religion——He is the world-redeeming Mediator
who must be conceived as holding a necessary and *eternal* relation both to the Father and to mankind.

§ 131.

If then the Redeemer of the world stands in an eternal
relation to the Father and to Humanity,—if His person has
not merely an historical, not merely a religious and ethical,
but also a metaphysical significance,——sin alone cannot have
been the ground of His revelation ; for there was no metaphysical necessity for sin entering the world, and Christ could
not be our Redeemer, if it had been eternally involved in His
idea that He should be our Mediator. Are we to suppose
that that which is most glorious in the world could only be
reached through the medium of sin ? that there would have
been no place in the human race for the glory of the Only
Begotten One, but for sin?* If we start with the thought of
humanity as destined to bear the image of God ; with the
thought of a kingdom of individuals filled with God ;
must we not necessarily ask, even if we for the moment suppose sin to have no existence,——Where in this kingdom is the
perfect God-man ? No one of the individuals by himself expresses more than a relative union of the divine and human
natures. No one participates more than partially in the fulness. All, therefore, point beyond themselves to an union of
God and man, which is not partial and relative ($\epsilon \hat{\iota} \varsigma \ \mu \acute{\epsilon} \rho o \nu \varsigma$), but
perfect and complete. If we answer, the entire number of
individuals, each of whom by himself is united with God to
but a limited extent, the entire *kingdom*, the totality as a
totality, is the perfect union of the divine and human natures,

* Compare *Mynster :* Vom Begriff d. Christl. Dogmatik. (In den Studien
und Kritiken).

is the true and complete God-man ;—even then we have not discovered the Perfect One. The perfect God-man would in this case be a mere personification ; He would be a mere representation or conception of our minds ; whereas the union of the divine and human natures demands realization in an actual personality. We are compelled, therefore, to look upon the Only Begotten of the Father as the Individual, who, as the centre of humanity, is also the centre of the revelations of God ; who is the point in which *God* and the Kingdom of God are personally united ; who reveals in fulness what the Kingdom reveals in manifold and divided forms and varieties. If we recognize that apart altogether from sin, the union of the human race with God is involved in the idea of the per- fection of the world ; if, further, we are convinced that this union is to be one not merely of sentiment and thought, but also of human nature in its entirety, that it must accordingly embrace the body of man, which is to be fitted to become a temple of the divine fulness ; we are led back again to the Only Begotten One, who appeared in the midst of the process of human development as the *Incarnation* of the divine nature, as the *beginner* of the *world's perfection*, and as the personal manifestation and embodiment of the goal of the ways of God with man ; and who, by continuing to work through the medium of the new economy of creation which He inaugurated, is still the Mediator of the completion of the whole kingdom, and of every individual member thereof.

This is the thought to which the Apostle Paul gives ex- pression when he describes Christ as the one in whom, " according to the good pleasure which God hath purposed in Himself, He would gather all things together in one," (Eph i. 10-12 ; Col. i. 15-17) ; a thought which was appropriated by the earliest teachers of the Church, for example, by Irenaeus, and employed to prove the *cosmical* significance of Christ. Unless we hold to Christ, who is the head (Col. ii. 19) ; unless we regard Him not merely in the light of the Redeemer of the world, but also in that of the perfecter of the world ; we shall never be in a position rightly to understand the proto- typical perfection of Christ in its distinction from the anti- typical union of God and man. What the appearance of the first man was for nature ; that is the appearance of the second

Adam for the entire human race.   As man was placed in the middle of creation, so that all the other forms of nature stand related to him as the parts to the whole, as the scattered rays to the focus in which they are all collected,—as the manifold variety of nature is destined to be embraced and constituted under man as its head and crown,—so is the human race with its variety of individual antitheses, activities, and powers, which find their point of union in Christ, destined to be constituted into one great body, under Him as the Head.   And as man is on the one hand a single member of the great whole of nature, whilst he is on the other hand not merely a microcosmic representation, but stands *above* all nature, being the mediator between the sensuous and the invisible holy order of the world ; so also Christ.   On the one hand He is an individual member of the human race, not merely setting forth microcosmically, but also standing above, the entire race, as the Mediator between the race and God.   His individuality stands in the relation to all other human individualities in which the centre of a circle stands to all the single points of the circle.   No otherwise than on the ground of this fundamental individuality can the manifold members of the race be organically combined and completed so as to form a kingdom of God, can every individual man attain possession of his proper peculiar characteristics, and his proper position in the entirety of humanity.

As the world-redeeming and world-completing Mediator, He must be recognized as the self-revelation of the divine Logos.   For the principle that brings about the perfection of the world, cannot be different from the creative principle by which all things were brought into existence.   As the incarnate Logos, He is the centre not merely of the world of men, but also of the universe ; for which reason the Apostle views him not merely as the head of the human race, of the Church, but as the Head of all creation, "the first-born of every creature" (Col. i. 15), unto whom all things are created.   For we may say of man that he is the centre of creation, the point in which the spiritual and the sensuous world meet, nobler than the angels ; the same things must be true in the highest sense of the second Adam, in whom the heavenly and the earthly, the invisible and the visible, the forces of the entire universe, angels, principalities, and powers, are summed up and combined.

In this sense we maintain that even if sin had not entered our world, Christ would still have come. Not until an insight has been gained into this, the metaphysical and cosmical significance of the Mediator, shall we find the proper foundation on which to build our doctrine of the Redeemer.

§ 132.

The doctrine that the eternal Logos became man has been supposed to involve an inner contradiction, because " He by whom the universe was made, and who sustains all things, cannot become His own creature ;" but this is to assume the existence of an irreconcilable contradiction between the idea of *creation* on the one hand, and the idea of *incarnation*, on the other hand. Revelation, however, knows nothing of such a conflict between creation and incarnation ; for it represents Christ as at one and the same time the completion of human nature, and the Incarnation of God Himself. When we say God creates, we undoubtedly imply, that brings forth something other than Himself ; but we equally imply that He Himself acquires an existence in the objects He creates, that He takes up His dwelling in them, that He constitutes them His organ and temple. Now, if even the natural universe can be considered as a temple of God ; it must be true, in a far higher sense, of the world of men, for not merely humanity as a whole, but every individual soul, is destined to become a temple of God. And if we thus meet with the idea of the incarnation of God everywhere around us in the human creature ; surely where God's creation of man reached its climax, there also must God's incarnation in man reach its climax ; and the creation of the second Adam, of the first-born of every creature, of the Man who is destined to be the Mediator between God and man must be identical with the incarnation of God : in other words, the *creative* activity of God must at this point undoubtedly be one with the activity of His *self-revelation*. One may indeed say with a certain amount of truth—the new Adam is a creature of the Logos ; but if we refuse to go further, if we abide by the plain sense of the proposition, it will become untrue. The truth of the matter is, that at this particular point creation has no independence apart from the Incarnation, but is originally involved and absorbed in it; the truth is that the second Adam does not possess a created altereity of being* *outside* the uncreated fulness, as is the case with individuals at the periphery, who strive to attain to the fulness of eternity, and yearn for a Mediator who shall aid them in their efforts; but in this central individual the fulness of the Godhead was originally and indissolubly inclosed in created nature as in a frame, and this *indissoluble relation between the uncreated image of God,* was the fundamental, all-determining feature of the personality of Christ.

It has also been considered self-contradictory, that the eternal Logos should become man, "because the eternal and omnipresent One could not be *born* in the midst of time." We, too, are far from imposing the task of conceiving that the eternal Logos ceased with the Incarnation to exist in His general revelation in the world; or that the Logos as a self-conscious, personal being was shut up in the womb, was born as a child, grew in knowledge and so forth: for such circumstances are incompatible with the very idea of birth. Birth in time is necessarily connected with the notion of a progress from unconsciousness to consciousness, of possibility to actuality, of a grain of seed and germ to ripe organization; and any view of the birth of the God-man inconsistent with these conditions must be characterized as docetical. Accordingly when we say that the divine Logos consented to be born, we mean that He planted Himself as a possibility, as a holy seed in the womb of humanity in order that He might be able to rise forth in the midst of the human race as a mediating and redeeming *human* revelation; we mean that the fulness of the divine nature individualized itself under the form of the life of a single man, in such a manner that the entire sum of holy powers was *involved* therein. The Scripture also gives us a hint, that the Son of God was in the womb, not as a self-conscious divine Ego, but as an unripe unborn child, in the words of the angel to Mary, "The holy thing which shall be born of thee shall be called the Son of God," (τὸ γεννώμενον ἅγιον, Luke i. 35). But the holy thing which was born of Mary, whilst advancing in years and becoming more and more conscious of itself as a human person, became also in the

* Anderssein.

same measure conscious of its deity ; it felt itself to be a divine-human personality, because the fulness of the deity was the ground of its life as a man ; it felt itself to be, not merely a participator in the divine Logos, but also the *divine-human* continuation of that eternal life of the deity which was from the beginning.   Although, therefore, Christ says, " I and the Father are one " (John x. 30), He never says, " I and the Logos are one."   For He is the human self-revelation of the divine Logos ; for which reason also He styles Himself directly the light and life of the world (John viii. 12) ; and the one who proceeded forth from the Father, who descended from the heavenly glory, in order to carry out the counsel of love.

§ 133.

We follow, therefore, the Apostle Paul, who represented to himself the Incarnation of God as a self-emptying ($\varkappa \acute{\epsilon} \nu \omega \sigma \iota \varsigma$) of the divine Logos, manifesting itself primarily as a self-abasement.   " Although He was in the form of God, He thought it not robbery to be equal with God ; but emptied Himself, and took upon Himself the form of a servant," (Phil. ii. 6, 7.)   Whatever explanation be adopted of the disputed words " He thought it not robbery," the thought of the apostle must be clearly allowed to be—that although the eternal Logos existed in divine form ($\acute{\epsilon} \nu \ \mu o \rho \varphi \tilde{\eta} \ \Theta \epsilon o \tilde{\nu}$), He humbled Himself when He resolved to exist in the form of a man.   He was not minded to live merely in pure divine glory, in metaphysical majesty ; but emptied His fulness into the mean form of a servant, to the end that He might become the Head, the Reconciler, and the Redeemer in the kingdom of love.   This self-humiliation, however, must be at the same time regarded as His self-perfection ; for through His revelation in the flesh He first became, in the full sense of the term, " Lord, to the glory of God the Father."   The idea of the deity of the Son is the *idea* of the revealer of God, of the Mediator between God and the creature ; but He is in the deepest sense the mediating God, not for the first creation, but for the second ; not for the kingdom of nature, but for the kingdom of grace and love ; and He only becomes the ruler in the kingdom of love on the ground of His having appropriated human nature as His own.   It was necessary that the mediating God should exist and live as a creature; that He should be found in fashion as a man and act as a man; that He should acquire a living and practical experience of the various phases of human existence, in order that He might be able fully to sympathize with our needs and weaknesses. In that He thus lived as a man, and, as " the Son of man," possessed His deity solely under the conditions imposed by a human individuality, in the limited forms of a human consciousness; we may undoubtedly say of Him that He lived in humiliation and poverty, because He had renounced that majestic glory by which, as the omnipresent Logos, He irradiates the entire creation. On the other hand, however, because His humiliation is the only way in which He can fully reveal the depths of the divine love, and because precisely by His poverty He makes all rich (2 Cor. viii. 9); we may also say that He first came into the full possession of His own divine glory when He became the Son of man; for love is never in full possession till it can fully communicate; and then only does it display its omnipotence when it overcomes all hearts, and " takes the strong for spoil." (Isaiah liii. 12.)

§ 134.

The relationship between the revelation of the Logos in Christ and the eternal revelation of Him may therefore be described as follows :—in the general revelation of the Logos, the Son of God is presupposed by every creature as being the one *through* whom all things are created; whereas, in His revelation in Christ, He is the goal of every creature, or the One into whom all things are created, and in whom all things shall be summed up and gathered together as in their head. In His revelation as Logos, the Son proceeded forth from the Father as God (ἐν μορφῇ Θεοῦ); in His revelation in Christ, on the contrary, He returns back to the Father as God-man. This His return is richer than His outgoing, for He comes back with an entire kingdom of children of God (" Behold, I and the children thou hast given me," Hebrews ii. 13.) Without the revelation in Christ, the leading of the world back to God would have been a leading back merely in idea, and not in fact; and created individuals would seek in vain the way and the door by which to enter in to the fellowship of redemption and perfection with the Father. Still there

are not two Sons of God, but one Son; Christ did not
add a new second Son to the Trinity; the entire movement takes place within the circle of the Trinity itself. At
the same time, it must be allowed that the Son of God leads
in the economy of the Father a twofold existence; that He
lives a double life in His world-creating and in His world-
completing activity. As the pure *Logos of Deity,* He works
through the kingdom of nature by His all-pervading presence,
creates the presuppositions and conditions of the revelation of
His all-completing love. As the *Christ,* He works through
the kingdom of Grace, of Redemption, and Perfection, and
points back to His pre-existence (John viii. 58; xvii. 5.)

§ 135.

He is very God; but in the revelation in Christ the very
Godhead is never separated from the very manhood; the
divine and human natures were never separated from each
other, and never neutralized each other.* We are to see in
Christ, not the naked God, but *the fulness of deity framed in
the ring of humanity;* not the attributes of the divine
nature in their unbounded infinitude, but the divine attributes
embodied in the attributes of human nature (*communicatio
idiomatum*). Instead of the omnipresence we have that
blessed presence, concerning which the God-man testifies, "He
that seeth me seeth the Father" (John xiv. 9):† in the place
of omniscience comes the divinely human wisdom which reveals
to babes the mysteries of the kingdom of heaven; in the place of
the world-creating omnipotence enters the world-vanquishing,
and world-completing power, the infinite power and fulness
of love and holiness in virtue of which the God-man was able
to testify "all power is given to me in heaven and on earth"
(Matt. xxviii. 18). For all heavenly and earthly powers, all
the forces of nature and history find in Him their centre of
freedom, and serve the kingdom of which He is the Head. If
any one be disposed to say, the Son is more truly God in
His general mundane-revelation, than in His revelation in
Christ; let him remember that the idea of the deity of the
Son is in reality one with the idea of the *mediatorial* God or

---

* According to the formula of the Council of Chalcedon, they are united
thus: ἀσυγχύτως, ἀτρέπτως, ἀ διαιρέτως, ἀχωρίστως.

† See also Matt. xxviii. 18.

of God as the Revealer of God. But in no form is the Son more truly and fully the mediator and revealer of God, than in the form of the Son of man.

Observations.—When Christ designates Himself the Son of man, He undoubtedly describes His human mode of existence, as in one respect *other* than and *inferior* to, that which was originally His; for which reason He generally employs this designation in speaking of His sufferings. And yet, on the other hand, He characterizes His human mode of existence as the fulfilment of His eternal destination, as the perfection of His glory. When He speaks of the glory which He had with the Father ere the world was, He refers not alone to the pure divine glory, but to the divine-human glory on which He was to enter through His resurrection and ascension, and which He possessed eternally in the divine idea. For it was eternally involved in the idea of the Son that He should become incarnate, that He should become the Head of the kingdom of love. When He says, "before Abraham was, *I am,*" He speaks not merely of the pure glory of the Logos, but of the glory of Christ; further, not merely of the glory of Christ in the eternal idea, but of the glory which He possessed in the midst of the unbelieving Jews of His own day. As the one, into whom, as the ultimate goal of creation, all things were made, He is the presupposition for Abraham, the presupposition for every period of history. For Him, who is the personal eternity in the midst of the ages, nay more, in the midst of the entire creation, the sensuous difference between past and future, has but a vanishing significance; for all the ages of the world, all the æons revolve around Him as around the all-determining centre to which each owes its peculiar character and force.

§ 136.

Eutychianism or Monophysitism teaches the divinity of Christ in such a manner as to do away with the idea of the true Adam. It transfers to the incarnate Logos all the predicates which must be applied to the eternal world-Logos; and thus necessarily gives rise to a confused representation of Christ. The monophysite type of doctrine takes pleasure in such formulæ as, "God is crucified! God is dead! One of the

Trinity has suffered hunger and thirst!" This one-sidedness has manifested itself in various forms in the Church. The custom that prevails among Catholics of calling Christ " the dear God ;" and Zinzendorf's designation of the *Lamb* as the Creator, the Sustainer, and Ruler of the world ; rest on an Eutychian confusion of the twofold revelation of the Logos. Although the Church condemned the monophysite error in the most distinct terms, the current orthodoxy still contains monophysitic elements, which manifest themselves particularly in the doctrine of the union of the divine and human *attributes*. This doctrine, namely, supposes that the divine attributes were communicated to the human nature, in the unlimited infinitude, with which they embrace the entire creation ; a supposition which is irreconcilably opposed to the idea of the human development of Christ, as is particularly evident when viewed in connection with Omniscience, Omnipresence, and Omnipotence. It has been maintained, for example, that Christ, when a child in the manger, according to His divine nature, ruled the world with divine omniscience in a hidden manner ($\varkappa\alpha\tau\grave{\alpha}$ $\varkappa\varrho\acute{\upsilon}\psi\iota\nu$), although according to His human nature, He grew in knowledge and wisdom. It has been maintained that Christ, during His death-struggle on the cross, omnipotently and omnipresently ruled heaven and earth : —two things which it is impossible to conceive united. Such representations destroy the unity of His person, and force us to the supposition of two different series of consciousness in Christ, which can never blend and unite. We get as it were a Christ with two heads ; an image which produces the impression, not merely of the superhuman, but of the monstrous, and which is incapable of producing any *moral* effect. What this theory lacks is the rightly understood conception of $\varkappa\acute{\epsilon}\nu\omega\sigma\iota\varsigma$, of the divine self-limitation. If the Incarnation and the idea of the mediatorship of Christ are to be realities, it must also be a reality that God felt the limitations of human nature as His own limitations, that He experienced the states of human nature as His own states. We must conceive, therefore, of the deity as wrapped up or clothed in the humanity of Christ ; of the external infinitude of the divine attributes as converted into an inner infinitude, in order that it might find room within the limits of human nature. In the measure in which the human nature grew and developed, in that measure did the divine nature also grow in it; in the measure in which, whilst thus advancing in development, He became conscious of His *historical* significance, in the same measure did the *recollection* of His pre-existence and of His going out from the Father rise more clearly in His mind.

§ 137.

He did not possess His deity outside of His humanity, but His true humanity was grounded in His true divinity. It is the idea of human nature not to be independent, but to be an organ, a temple for the divine nature. To the extent to which human nature is filled by the divine, to that extent does it attain its true idea; and we may say with perfect truth of every human individual, that he is a true man only in proportion as a divine word becomes incarnate in him. The capacity of an individual man to realize and manifest true humanity, must therefore be measured by his capacity for receiving the divine, by his capacity for becoming the organ of God. And that individual alone will be the perfect revelation of humanity, or the true Adam, who is able to embrace in Himself the entire fulness of deity. In describing Christ as the ideal of humanity, we do not mean that He embodies all the relative perfections and partial excellences which are to be found in the human race; but that He is the central man, in whose perfection all partial excellences and therewith every sort of partial bondage to nature are done away. This again signifies that His humanity was destined, not merely to express the divine in one special relation or in broken rays, but to be the perfect brightness and image of the divine nature; so that it was not merely *a* divine word which became flesh in Him, but *the Word* which is God himself. We must accordingly regard His personality as the free moral evolution not of single powers, but of the fulness of the powers of the deity, or of the divine glory (δόξα); as the human revelation of the undivided mystery of the divine essence. Not that the human nature of Christ had the capability of rising by its own power to this union with the divine; for such a notion would be decidedly heathenish. The divine nature must be conceived as taking the initiative in the union; and the entire conception of

Christ first acquires steadiness and fixity when we recognize
with the Scriptures that it is God himself, the eternal Logos,
who has here made Himself man.

Observations.——Both moral and æsthetic Rationalism represent
Christ as the ideal of humanity, but refuse to acknowledge
Him as the incarnate God.   Dogmatic theologians of this
class are like the painters whose heads of Christ express
merely the so-called " purely human element," that is, the
human element without the divine; in other words, a
κένωσις in the worst sense.   No mystery is reflected in the
features; no divine depths shine forth out of the looks of
these representations.   Such heads offer either the expression of a dry sobriety and seriousness, or of an exag-
gerated sentimentalism.   Those of the former class
answer to moral rationalism; those of the latter to
æsthetic rationalism.   The picture, on the contrary,
contained in the gospels, shows us " the brightness
of deity in the face of our Lord Jesus Christ."   The
appearance of every genuine hero in religion and
morality, produces not merely a moral impression, but
also the impression of lofty, natural, intellectual qualities;
——it impresses with a sense of the nearness of deity, of
the presence of the divine nature in the human.   If this
holds good of every such case, it holds good unquestionably
and absolutely of Christ, whose entire human appearance
makes a superhuman impression, and therefore at once
inspires confidence and fear, love and awe.   Without the
mysterious divine ground-work of the nature of Christ,
His moral qualities would be powerless; His compassionate love would not be a power of God unto salvation
for man; He would not be able by His holiness to kindle
a fire on earth, capable of purging and judging the world.
His very humility and obedience depend for their effect
on His majesty; for humility first reveals itself in its
entire inward, quiet greatness, when He to whom it is
given to have life in Himself refuses to be anything of
Himself, and receives everything from the Father alone.
If, therefore, we would recognize Christ as the second
Adam, we must conceive Him at the same time as the
incarnate God.   Christ must stand before us, to quote

the words of one of our writers,* "as the immediate manifestation of the divine sanctity on earth; the highest love, the profoundest humility of heart, the greatest submission to the will of God, must be conceived as blended in one with a fear and awe inspiring expression of righteousness whose foundations nothing can shake, and with the mystical expression of a power which is able to employ all forces in its service.

A distinctive position among the representations of Christ set forth in recent times belongs to that contained in the theological system of Schleiermacher. Taking for his starting-point the antagonism between sin and redemption, Schleiermacher views the Saviour as the second Adam, as the perfected creation of human nature, and recognizes His consciousness or sentiment of God as the expression of the actual presence of the deity in Him; he deems Him to be typical for all times and generations, the living head of a new community, which constantly draws from His fulness. But the defects of this Christology may be reduced to two points—to the divine aspect and to the mundane aspect of the existence of Christ. In relation to the divine aspect, we miss the idea of the *pre-existence* of the Son; and with it also that of the revelation of the condescending love of the eternal Logos. It is merely the impersonal divinity that acquires personal existence in Christ. In relation to the mundane aspect of the existence of Christ, He has merely religious and ethical, but not a cosmical significance; it is true, He is the perfected creation of human nature, but not as the sum and close of *all creation*. Accordingly, those passages of Scripture which declare that principalities and powers and forces are subject to Him, must be content with a merely moral explanation. Schleiermacher's picture of Christ has become, through the vigorous truth and vigorous life which it unquestionably embodied, a source of blessing to many who by it were led nearer to the fountain of faith. Not, however, until we recognize the incarnation of God in Christ as the free self-revelation of the creative Word from the beginning; not until we see

* Sibbern: Om Poesie og Konst I. p. 351.

in Him, who is the Head of His Church, at the same time the Head of the whole of creation, have we the Christ who is fitted to be the object of the absolute appropriation of faith. Not till then do we return to the consciousness of Christ, in which the apostles lived, in which Christian antiquity lived.

§ 138.

In opposition to Eutychianism, Nestorianism sought to keep firm hold on the *ethical* significance of the God-man. But the adherents of this view, by representing Christ merely as the free *organ,* or as a *temple* of the deity, reduce the relation between the divine and human in Christ from that of a veritable incarnation, to a mere union or alliance between the man and the Logos, to an inhabitation of the latter in the former. By attributing to the human individuality of Christ a certain independence prior to and apart from the union with the Logos, they constituted Him as a mere creature, and as far as His human individuality was concerned, could never conceive Him to be anything more than a sort of genius, or a *specially-selected instrument.* They failed to see that the creation of the humanity of Christ by God was absolutely one with God's incarnation in Christ, and apart from this incarnation has no independent significance. This might be expressed in another way by saying that Nestorianism rests satisfied with what the Scriptures term the first creation. It views Christ merely as *a* man, not as *the* man, as the second Adam, the first-born of all creation, who is the fulness of the creation. That creature, however, which is the fulness of the creation, and thus also the fulness of the incarnation of God, is not merely an organ or a temple of the deity, but temple and God at one and the same time. Genius (the genius of the poet or of the wise man) has its vocation; prophets have their mission; but the only-begotten Son *came* down from heaven,[*] *went* out from the Father.[†] It is true He also frequently speaks of His *being sent;*[‡] and thus puts Himself on the same level with the holy men and prophets of the past; but the reason of this lies in the circumstance of His being God in the form of a servant, and that He was meant

---

[*] John iii. 13, ὁ ἐκ τοῦ οὐραμοῦ καταβάς.

[†] John xvi. 27, ἐγὼ παρὰ τοῦ θεοῦ ἐξῆλθον.   [‡] John x. 36; xvii. 3, ὃν ἀπέστειλας.

to earn for Himself the glory which originally belonged to Him by a free moral development, or a free *obedience* to the divine law (Phil. ii. 9.) From this point of view alone is it possible to explain the opposed elements in His consciousness. Speaking in agreement with the eternal relation of His essential nature to the Father, He says, " No man hath ascended up to heaven, but He that came down from heaven, even the Son of Man which is in heaven ; " whilst as the One who was to be made perfect in time by obedience and suffering, it was necessary that the hour should come when He would have to say, " My soul is exceeding sorrowful, even unto death." (Matt. xxvi. 38.) As to His eternal and essential relation to the Father, He says, " I and the Father are one " (John x. 30) ; whilst as the One who in time was not so far perfected as to enter into His glory, He says not only " The Father is greater than I," but even " Why callest thou me good ? there is none good but One, that is, God." (John xiv. 28 ; Mark x. 18.)

THE DIVINE-HUMAN DEVELOPMENT.
§ 139.

The union of the divine and human natures must, on the one hand, be conceived as gradually effected by a continued development ; and, on the other hand, be assumed to have been an accomplished fact from the very first moment of conception and birth. As the prior condition of the divine-human development of Christ, the conception formed of His birth must be such as to ward off both the error of the Gnostics and that of the Ebionites ; in other words, the birth of Christ must be conceived both as a miracle and as a true human birth. The second Adam, who sets forth the type of a new humanity, and is the starting-point of a new human creation cannot be supposed to have come into existence according to the old Adamitic type. According to that type arise only beings who bear but in a restricted sense the image of God ; all who are thus born after Adam's type are concluded under sin : and yet, nevertheless, the birth of Christ must have been a truly human birth. It would not do for Him to belong to the race merely as a stranger, " without father, and without mother, and without generation," (Heb. vii. 3) ; He must at the same time be born as a Son of David. This requirement, that the new Adam be born in the midst of the race, without the sinful race having any sort of self-determining and independent part in His birth ; that He should be conceived and born of a woman without being linked by the fact of His conception into the connex of sinful human nature—is met by the Creed of the Gospel, and of the Church, which says, " *conceived by the Holy Ghost, born of the Virgin Mary.*" He is born not of the will of a man, nor of the will of the flesh ; but the holy will of the Creator, took the place of the will of man and of the will of the flesh,— that is, the creating Spirit, who was in the beginning, fulfilled the function of the plastic principle. He was born of the Virgin Mary, the chosen woman in the chosen people. It was the task of Israel to provide, not as has often been said, Christ Himself, but the mother of the Lord ; to develope the susceptibility for Christ to a point when it might be able to manifest itself as the profoundest unity of nature and spirit—an unity which found expression in the pure virgin. In her the pious aspirations of Israel and of mankind, their faith in the promises are centred ; she is the purest point in history and in nature, and she, therefore, becomes the appointed medium for the new creation. And while we must confess that this virgin birth is enveloped in a veil impenetrable to physical reasonings, yet we affirm it to be the only one which fully satisfies the demands of religion and theology. This article of our Creed, " conceived of the Holy Ghost, born of the Virgin Mary," is the only sure defence against both the Ebionite and the Docetic view of the entrance of the God-man into connexion with humanity.

Observations.—The virgin birth has continually been looked upon as a *mythus*, the usually adopted description of the birth of genius. For genius has an earthly mother, but as to its spiritual source it is without father, without genealogy. According to this view, the birth of Christ is regarded as a miracle in history, but not a miracle in nature ; it is ranked as one of a class of historical miracles occurring at creative epochs in history. But upon this supposition the essential idea of the Incarnation, of the second Adam, is destroyed. It may with truth be said that the birth of genius is a birth of the Spirit, a birth not of the spirit of nature, of a nation, of the world, but of the Divine creative Spirit. But he reveals Himself in genius as the Spirit of *power* and *energy* only, not as the Spirit of *holiness*. Genius is only a *cosmical* spirit, and even in religious genius as such, what is holy is restrained by cosmical hindrances, and grows out of the impure soil of natural disposition. Genius needs redemption for itself, it must be regenerated by the Spirit of holiness, for it discovers in itself a discrepancy between the natural and the holy. The idea of the Incarnation, on the contrary, implies natural holiness, *i.e.*, the union of holiness and nature. We are, therefore, unavoidably led to an Ebionite Christology, we deny the idea of Redemption and of the New Creation, if we take the birth of Christ to be no more than an interruption of the *historical* laws of human development, and not an interruption of its *natural* laws. The recognition of this interruption of the course of natural law leads us back to the evangelistic account of the miraculous conception of the Lord. Schleiermacher endeavoured to evade the virgin birth, and to harmonize the naturalistic view of Christ's birth with the supernatural account by the following expedient :——He supposes that all the natural conditions necessary to an ordinary human birth must have been present in the case of Christ's birth, but that to these there was added an absolutely creative act, which did away with the traducian sinful influence. Such an explanation has no sanction in Holy Scripture ; it increases the difficulty instead of obviating it. The miraculous is enhanced by this contradiction—the man is looked upon as co-operative in the process, yet not really co-operative. The generative influence upon the man's part which, in the order of nature transmits his individual life, and propagates the Adamic nature, must, according to Schleiermacher's hypothesis, be at the same time obviated or altered by a divine act ; and thus the co-operation of the man in the Incarnation is presented in a singularly Docetic light.

The statements of Scripture concerning the supernatural birth of Christ are only indirectly confirmed by the declarations of Christ Himself, and by the preaching of

His apostles. It was natural that the Lord, who in the power of the Spirit proved himself to be the Son of God, who had proceeded forth from the Father, and had come down from heaven, should not refer to the fact of His virgin-birth : such a reference by way of proof would not only have been useless, it would have been inconsistent with the mind of the Spirit and of freedom. And as to the apostles, it was natural that they—having in their preaching to labour by means of the full power of the revelation of their Lord, and to present the doctrine of His person in connection with the doctrine of His work —should give prominence to this particular fact of the gospel history indirectly rather than directly. In the history, on the other hand, the account is given in the early chapters of Matthew and of Luke. It has repeatedly been said that these chapters, like the birth which they describe, are of a mysterious origin ; that the narratives they contain do not possess the same historical worth and character as the accounts of our Lord's public life. This, however, is certain, that the doctrinal principle involved in these narrations, the principle in which both traditions coincide is precisely that which the Church recognizes in her apostolic symbol, " *Conceived of the Holy Ghost, born of the Virgin Mary.*" The criticism which refuses to recognize this either falls inevitably into Docetism or Ebionitism ; or if it tries to evade these, as we have above seen, it must have recourse to arbitrary and fantastic hypotheses as to the miraculousness of Christ's birth.

§ 140.

Care must be taken in considering the development of our Lord's complex nature, that the human part of it shall in no point contradict the divine, and that the divine shall in no point belie the human. We define this development negatively when we say that Christ was wholly *without sin ;* (" Which of you convinceth me of sin ?" John viii. 46 ; " In all points tempted like as we are, yet without sin," Heb. iv. 16), *sinless,* whether sin be viewed as a state of mind or as an outward act. Positively, we express the truth by saying that Christ's life on earth, while it had a normal develop-

ment, revealed also that *ideal perfection* which qualified Him
alone to become the Mediator between God and the world,
and which made His life throughout the *historical* realization
of the divinely human ideal, according to His own words,
" Take my yoke upon you and learn of me, for I am meek
and lowly in heart, and ye shall find rest unto your souls,"
(Matt ix. 29) ; " I have given you an example, that ye should
do as I have done to you" (John xiii. 15) ; and to the words
of St Peter, " Because Christ also suffered for us, leaving us
an example that ye should follow His steps." Thus, whereas
in the sinful life of man the worldly prevails over the spiritual, and the consciousness of God is restrained and crushed
by the consciousness of the world and self; in the Second
Adam this relationship is reversed. Christ's earthly existence
is completely determined by His relation to His Father. In
proportion as His self-consciousness grows He becomes conscious of His relationship to the Father ; and in proportion
as His consciousness of the world increased in clearness, He
arrived at a perception of His native, essential, and holy relationship to the world as its Redeemer.

§ 141.

As every human life is developed by contact with the
world ; as we all, from the first dawn of consciousness, in-
hale, in a spiritual sense, the air of this world, and as the
mode of thought which the moral atmosphere of each age
forms contains a mixture of the true and the false, the pure
and impure—so that error steals upon us and seizes us from
the first moment of our existence—it follows that the Second
Adam could not have escaped its contamination had He not
possessed the safeguard of His own holy nature ; in virtue of
which He repelled the impure and sinful as alien to His very
being from childhood upwards, and received and appropriated
only what would serve as an element for His normal development. His destined office, His mission as Redeemer,
wherein all others would be recipients, and He alone the dis-
penser, required that His own susceptibility to this world's
influences should be perfectly controlled by the inner independence and uniqueness of His individuality, whether this
be viewed as taking the form of clear self-consciousness, or,
as in His childhood, of holy instinct and spontaneous im-

pulse. His mind was moulded by impressions and thoughts coming from without, only in proportion as He himself selected these, and at the same time even transformed them in conformity with His own holy nature. Although the history of His childhood has not come down to us, one glimpse of it has been preserved which serves to indicate, and even to give us a clear conception of what it was : I refer to the picture of the Boy of twelve years old in the Temple (Luke ii. 41–52). This narrative not only shows us how the consciousness of Christ's own peculiar relations to the Father shone forth in Him like the rays of dawn—"Wist ye not that I must be about my Father's business?"—ἐν τοῖς τοῦ πατρός μου δεῖ εἶναί με ;—but representing Him as it does surrounded by the Teachers of His people, not only hearing them, but awakening their astonishment by His questions and answers. We see in it the first manifestation both of His divine origin and of His productive power upon outward circumstances ;—*discendo docuit.* This power in relation to circumstances kept pace in its development with the growth of His self-consciousness. What is true of every genius, that he makes traditional forms of thought the material and element of his own creative power and activity, holds good of Christ ; with this difference, that whereas in man this power is limited by that law of sin which obliges even the greatest genius to pay tribute to the errors of his age, in Him it was not thus limited. The importance of this fact is obvious, when we remember that Christ was born, not among heathens, but among the chosen people, whose traditional ideas and prophetic images were moulded beforehand expressly for Him, and expected Him as the One who alone could breathe into them their true spirit and fulness. The development, therefore, of His essential perfection and inherent holiness was favoured by the consciousness of sin and of the law of holiness fully presented to Him in the thoughts, wants, and aspirations of His countrymen, and also by the fact of His childhood having unfolded itself in the purest and holiest circumstances possible in the midst of general sinfulness. The human forms that surrounded Him in childhood presented to us in the Christmas gospels—the holy family, the calm and silent ones of the country who now waited for the consolation of Israel, may be

looked upon as a sort of inner circle of elect ones among the
elect people.   The childhood of the Second Adam is spent as
if in a paradise in the midst of the sinful history.

Observations.——Inasmuch as temperament in man forms not
only a strengthening foundation, but also a limiting barrier to his development, the sinlessness of the Second
Adam required that He should not thus be fettered by
any sinful peculiarity of disposition, and His essential
perfection was characterised by the fact, that no one-
sidedness of temperament could be specified as unduly
prevailing in Him.   We discover in the new Adam the
hopeful, unanxious state of mind which leaves each day
as it comes to look after its own cares (Matt. vi. 24),
which is as unconcerned as the lilies of the field and the
birds of the air ; and side by side with this, the oppressive and painful and sorrowful heart, from whose lowest
depths the lamentation arises, in a far keener sense than
that of the ancient prophet, " Is there any sorrow like
unto my sorrow ?" (Lamentations i.)   In Him we behold
alike a calmness which the world cannot disturb, that
peace which the world cannot give nor take away
(John xvi. 32), and a deeply-stirring, intense zeal and
fervour of soul (John ii. 17) ; yet neither of these
contrasted feelings are perverted by any excess or partiality.   While, however, this perfection is inherent in
Him, it is strengthened and matured by His progressive
freedom of development.   Thus, Heb. v. 8, 9, we read,
" Though he were a Son, yet learned he obedience by the
things which he suffered : And being made perfect, he became the author of eternal salvation unto all them that
obey him."   As there can be no human life without some
impress of nationality, Christ cannot have been wholly
without this, and yet withal His sinlessness required that
He should not be subject to that partiality which is inherent more or less in all nationality.   Hence the Jewish
nationality appears in Christ not as something absolute,
but only as the medium or dress through which the eternally typical in Him manifests itself ; and this it does
because the typical is the true interpreter of Israel's nationality, whereby its individual peculiarities are done

away, and it furnishes the materials for that revelation which is intended for all people ; and indeed the true Messianic hopes of Israel exceeded the bounds of this distinctive nationality. This nationality in Christ was not a principle, but only an instrument of action, and the carnally-minded Jews therefore, who prided themselves upon it, and considered it something inherently excellent, charged Christ with being unpatriotic. "They answered him, We be Abraham's seed, and were never in bondage to any man : how sayest thou, Ye shall be made free ?" (John viii. 33.) But it is precisely because patriotism in Him expands into humanity, His eternal ideal, that He can be all things to all men, whether Jews or Gentiles, and that the new Adam finds an access among "Greeks," and "the philosopher Christ" is at home among the barbarians of the North.

As, moreover, *physical nature* in man is not only an instrument for mental development, but in some respects a restraint and fettering barrier, the question of our Lord's physique is connected with that of his sinlessness and ideal perfection. We must ever remember that though without sin, He yet lived, not in an incorruptible body, for this He did not possess until his Resurrection from the dead, but in a body like our own, subject to the same wants, susceptible of the same pains and griefs, and mortal. "God sending His own Son in the likeness of sinful flesh," εν ὁμοιώματι σαρκὸς ἁμαρτίας—"and for sin, condemned sin in the flesh," (Rom. viii. 3). " Forasmuch then as the children are partakers of flesh and blood, He also Himself, likewise took part of the same,—καὶ αὐτὸς παραπλησίως μετέσχεν τῶν αὐτῶν,—that through death," &c., (Heb. ii. 14). Accordingly—though upon this point no particulars have come down to us—we cannot but think that His bodily form must have been a temple meet for, and corresponding with, his spiritual nature. The Church, indeed, in harmony with "the sufferings of this present time" (Rom. viii. 18), has sometimes represented the Lord in a bodily form afflicted and oppressed, yea even marred, according to Isaiah liii. 2, "He hath no form nor comeliness, and when we shall see him, there is no beauty that we should desire him ;" but it is clearly inconsistent with the idea of Christ's perfect manhood to attribute to Him deformity or weakness. As deformity excluded a man from the priesthood in Israel, it must have been still more incompatible with the office of the Messiah. If again the opinion be advocated that the body of our Lord was not only endowed with general health, rendering it meet to be the instrument of his soul, but was gifted over and above this with an ideal beauty, according to the Psalmist's words, " Thou art fairest among the children of men " (Psalm xlv. 2), this may be understood as literally true ; but we must guard against the notion, which through the indirect influence of heathenism has gained ground in the Greek Church, that Christ's physical beauty was something that shone forth from Him—possessing in itself a distinct significance ; for in this case we reach the low standpoint of artificial religion, in which the inward expands into the outward, and beauty of bodily form shines forth as in a Jupiter or Apollo in distinct self-importance. The ideal beauty, which we may attribute to our Lord in the days of His flesh, is the beauty of holiness which shines through the servant's form, the union of majesty inspiring reverence, and of redeeming love, visible only to the eye of faith. Whenever pure Christian art has endeavoured to paint a likeness of the Lord, it has done so with the consciousness that the beauty to which expression is to be given, is not that which is to be seen, but far rather that which is pre-supposed, and which can be explained only by the living WORD.

§ 142.

Christ's growth was from His birth a holy growth,—" He increased in wisdom and stature, and in favour with God and man " (Luke ii. 52,)—and as His human nature advanced, so also did His divine nature. Had His life been only a spiritual development, it would have been nothing more than a religious glorification of the Grecian idea of the blessed gods. That it might reveal the ideal perfection by which alone He could become the Mediator, it must not only have been an ever-advancing growth, but also a progressive warfare and conquest on the side of Freedom, according to the ideal of the

Servant of Jehovah in the Old Testament (Isaiah xlii. 1-4).
He must have been "in all points tempted (πεπειρασμένον)
like as we are, yet without sin" (Heb. iv. 15.) As temptation is the inseparable law of the life of man, it was necessary that the first Adam should be tempted; and it was
equally necessary in the case of the second Adam. It behoved
Him to be tempted not by this or that kind of evil merely,
but by evil in and for itself, by the evil principle, the
devil; for as Satan already triumphed over the princes of
this world, he only could have had to do with the Mediator
between the Father and the world. It is only natural that
this testing should take place with special force at that
point in His life when He had arrived at maturity, and that
by means of it with clear self-consciousness, and with deliberate act of will, He should elect for Himself to undertake
the office of Messiah. He must now have chosen the Messiahship according to its true ideal, because He now rejected a
false Messiahship (Matt. iv. 1-11.) And after the first
temptation, when the devil departed from Him for a season,
having by progressive development realized His ideal, He was
still exposed to demoniacal attacks upon Him, and to all those
temptations, oppressions, and sorrows which His struggle with
the world involved. As the eternal Son, and in relation to
His divinity, this was His life-task, by free endeavour to maintain and manifest His unity with the Father, and the reality
of His incarnation, steadfastly and uninterruptedly to establish
the certainty of the truth that He came forth from the Father
(ἐγώ εἰμι),* through all His bitter conflicts with the powers of
the world, and notwithstanding the hour of darkness and the
powers of darkness. As the Son of Man, and in relation to
His humanity, the aim and work of His life depended upon
this, that notwithstanding His appointed warfare against the
sin of the world, by which He incurred the world's hatred,
He should establish an indissoluble fellowship of love between
Himself and the race, hindered and circumscribed though this
love would be by the growing hostility of the world against
Him. The object and labour of Christ's life was thus an
absolutely perfect one, none higher can be conceived as to
purport or to range than to become, as He did, the Mediator

* Luke xxii. 70, "Art thou then the Son of God? Ye say that I am."

between God and the world, the founder and builder-up of
the kingdom of God. The conflict which He accomplished
was the one all-important and all-deciding conflict, than which
no greater is conceivable. It was a struggle not only between
His individual will and the whole outward necessity which
universal history seemingly witnessed to, but still more
between that individuality and the cosmical principle itself,
the principles of this world, the kingdom of Satan and its
chief. This warfare is not merely apparent, it is real; for
though the fulness of the Godhead did essentially dwell in
Him, neither His own knowledge of the relationship between
Himself, as the only-begotten, and the Father, nor His love
to humanity, could have attained this highest standard of
inward perfection, had not the development of His personality
been accomplished by progressive, continual, and ever-renewed
obedience. This is what Scripture calls His τελείωσις.* But
in proportion as His life advanced, the world's hostility increased, and the contrariety between outward circumstances
and facts, and His inward steadfastness. As far as outward
appearances were concerned, everything seemed to go against
Him, and in the issue He seemed a king without a kingdom,
His disciples scattered every man to his own, and Himself
left forsaken and alone. But herein lay the evidence of His
sinlessness and original perfection; He triumphed in defeat,
He conquered through suffering, before Pontius Pilate He
witnessed a good confession, and laid down His life upon the
cross as the foundation of an everlasting reconciliation.

§ 143.

The fact that the Second Adam experienced all temptations—enticements to sin, threats and tortures of body and
mind—is to be explained upon the ground, not of His moral
freedom only, nor of the progressiveness of His nature, but of
both these combined. The propositions, *potuit non peccare,*
"it was possible for Him not to sin," and *non potuit peccare,*
"it was impossible for Him to sin," so far from being distinct
or contrasted, may be said to include and to presuppose each
other. The first, which means that sinlessness was only a
possibility for Christ, implies that He experienced temptation

---

* Hebrews v. 9, "Being made perfect (τελειωθείς), He became the author of
eternal salvation unto all them that obey Him."

as an actual power; for while it came upon Him from without, it must, if it were not a mere pretence, have excited some corresponding feeling within Him; through which alone He could have been really tempted. And as the contrast between the cosmical and the sacred—the natural and the spiritual—was necessary in the Second Adam in order to a twofold influence upon the will;—as the Second Adam cannot be viewed as Monotheletic, which would be in fact to consider Him Monophysite, but Duotheletic,—the same principle must have been active in Him which made the fall of the first Adam possible. The possibility of evil existed in the Second Adam; but this possibility never became active, was never realized; it served only as the dark and obscure background to show forth His perfect holiness. This was guaranteed, not by the force of virtue or innocence, which the very idea of temptation makes uncertain and doubtful, pending the trial, nor again by the force of the Divine nature as distinct from the human, or the human as distinct from the Divine, but in virtue of the indissoluble union of the divine and human natures in Him; that *bond* which might indeed be strained and shaken to the greatest apparent tension and contrast of the two natures, but which never could be broken. This is expressed in the second proposition *non potuit peccare*, " it was impossible for Him to sin." Though the temptation itself and the conflict against it were not apparent merely but real and sternly earnest, the result could never have been doubtful; for the bond between the Divine and the human natures, which may be severed in the creature, was indissoluble in Him who is the Mediator between the Father and all His creatures. This bond may be broken only when the connection of the divine with the human is merely relative and representative; never when it is essential and archetypal, as in Him, in whom the counsels of the Father were comprehended before the foundation of the world.

Observations.—The doctrine of the sinlessness of Christ has been handled by its opponents in a twofold way. Kant, in accordance with his views of the unconditional commands of the law, held that it must be possible for a man every moment of his life to fulfil its requirements, because the denial of this possibility would interfere with

the validity and obligation of the law.   But, says Kant,
it can be proved concerning no one that he is without
sin, for we cannot search the heart ; we can only judge
the outward act, the moral character of which depends
upon hidden motives and springs of action which we cannot
see ; hence the representation of sinlessness can have no
value save as a practical ideal to stimulate our endeavours.
Such language bears the impress of a habit of thought
widely estranged from Christianity.   If Christ be looked
upon merely as a man, a single and ordinary individual
of the race, His sinlessness must certainly appear very
problematical.   But the case is wholly changed when we
infer His sinlessness from the idea of Him as the Mediator, the Second Adam, the incarnate God, who was " justified in the Spirit," ἐδικαιώθη ἐν πνεύματι, 1 Tim. iii. 16, in
and through the new Creation of which He is the Head.
From this stand-point only—which realizes the new creation—can the necessity and the reality of Christ's sinlessness be asserted.

While the rationalism of the critical school allows at
least the possibility of sinlessness, that of the speculative
school distinctly denies even this, on the ground that sin
is inseparable from our idea of the finite.   On this point
this new philosophy reaches no farther than that of the
heathen Epictetus, who proposed to himself the question,
" Is it possible to be faultless ?" and answered, " No, it is
impossible : this only is possible, to endeavour to be
faultless."   When Heathenism, which as heathenism may
be worthy of respect, takes upon itself to enter the domain
of Christian theology, it is pleased to express itself thus :
—There was in Christ a *minimum* of sin, and a
maximum of holiness.   But in this *maximum*, as well as
in this *minimum*, that ideal is denied which admits of
no superlative, but is a definite and simple positive.   The
assertion that goodness and holiness have no existence in
the world except as they may be included between the
extremes of a wholly undefined *minimum* of sin, and an
equally undefined *maximum* of holiness ;—from which it
further follows that truth can have no other reality than
what may be included between a *minimum* of folly and

a *maximum* of wisdom—this assertion is of course in harmony with the spirit of this world (ὁ κόσμος οὗτος) which consists in this impure mingling of folly and wisdom, falsehood and truth, vice and virtue, hatred and love ; but it is (strictly speaking) a diabolical assertion.* To calumniate holiness is the very essence of the Devil's nature, and it is accordingly his to lower it into something merely relative, so that he may thus claim an equally relative position for himself and his kingdom. If there be in Christ a *minimum* of sinfulness, if He ever for one moment gave way to evil, or failed to do battle against it, He cannot be the God-man, He cannot be the Saviour. We must in such a case apply to Him the words of the Apostle, "he who is guilty in one point is guilty of all ;" had He sinned in one moment, He must have sinned in several, because that first moment could not have been without its consequences ; and with the first imperceptible *minimum* of sin, the sinful principle itself must have entered, which is ever active. As we cannot conceive of sin existing without the imputation of guilt, as no justification can ever be made of sin, but at the very best only excuse or palliation ; He himself must have needed forgiveness as well as we, and must in penitence have known this. But whereas He never did this ; whereas we never hear from His lips confession of sin and sorrow on account of any contradiction between what He was, and what He should have been—a confession, a sorrow, which we hear from all the noblest and best of men—whereas instead of this we hear Him promise the Spirit who should convince the world of sin, of righteousness, and of judgment (because they believed not on Him, and because the Prince of this world is judged), (John xvi. 8–10), it is impossible for us to attribute to Him a so-called *maximum* of holiness ; He must either have been more blinded than most men, or (what is still more heinous) He must have given Himself out to be something wholly different from what He was.

To the faithful He proved Himself in word and deed, in life, sufferings, and death, to be the perfectly Holy One ; but

---

* See Daub's Judas Iscariot, 2nd part, 222-4.

to the unbelieving, who refused to submit to the power of His holiness, no convincing proof, it must be granted, could be given.   The main part of this proof consists in that *experience* which each must for himself attain, when, being born again, he enters into the kingdom of Christ; by it alone is he practically assured that the source from which that redeeming and sanctifying power springs could never itself have been tainted by sin.

THE CONDITIONS OF THE LIFE OF THE INCARNATE SON.

§ 144.

During the temporal life of the Divine Son on earth, His manifestation could not, strictly speaking, have been in harmony with his eternal existence.   In every moment of his life, indeed, He was what, according to the counsels of the Father, He should have been; this present world, this present time (ὁ κοσμος οὗτος and ὁ αἰών οὗτος), had no power over him; but His manifestation in time required, that so long as His earthly historical life lasted, there should be a contrast between the partial and the completed work, between the partial, relative, and restrained manifestation of His glory and its perfect fulness.   In the holy life of the God-man, viewing it as a manifestation, there is an ἐκ μέρους, in contrast with a τέλειον.   He was not yet glorified; and He who asked, "Which of you convinceth me of sin?" also said, "Why callest thou Me good? none is good save one, that is God."   He was without sin, but not yet "good" in the last and highest sense, in the sense of fulness and glorification; for though He was in reality one with the Father, His outward life was subject to the limitations of history, to the change and conflict of time, and so far must have been wanting in infinite perfection.   The doctrine of the church, therefore, rightly distinguishes between His state of humiliation and exaltation (*status exinanitionis* and *exaltationis*);* the one referring to Christ's life on earth under the limitations of time and of history, the other to His resurrection life, His Ascension to the right hand of God the Father, and His presence in the everlasting kingdom, the ful-

---

* Phil. ii. 8, 9, "Being found in fashion as a man He humbled Himself, and became obedient unto death, even the death of the cross.   Wherefore God also hath highly exalted Him."

ness of bliss, where He lives the unseen Head of the Church and fills all in all with His spirit. This carries us onwards to His *second Advent* at the end of days, when the revelation of Him shall perfectly correspond with His infinite being, and when we, as the Apostle says, "shall see Him as HE IS" (1 John iii. 2).

§ 145.

This contrast between His humiliation and exaltation is traceable within the limits of Christ's earthly life, which was throughout developed in alternate lowliness and majesty. Had His life been throughout a manifestation of power merely, He would have been only an earthly Messiah, such as the carnally-minded Jews desired, a Messiah treating faith and the soul's salvation as things superfluous and needless, and His glory would not have been the glory of the God-man, for it would have evaded that pledge of reality and humanity, the cross. Had his life, on the other hand, been one of humiliation only, without any signs and wonders, a struggling will through which the Divine glory never shone forth, it could never have been a revelation of the eternal Son. The contrast or non-conformity of humiliation and exaltation in His life consisted in the fact, that the conditions of majesty and lowliness were blended in Him, and the glory of the Only Begotten was hidden as well as revealed, being seen as much in κρύψις as in φανέρωσις. He who was transfigured on the holy Mount, appears in ordinary human form in the streets of Jerusalem, and must endure "the contradiction of sinners" (Heb. xii. 3) who believe not upon Him, because He gives them no sign from heaven. He who performs miracles of healing, who raises Lazarus from the grave, must in Gethsemane agonize in prayer, and upon the Cross hear the mocking taunt, "If He be the Son of God, let Him now come down from the cross, that we may see and believe." These, the conditions of His humiliation, involving the lowliest obedience, the deepest humility, patience, and meekness, limit the conditions of His majesty and glory. The king of holiness could not, like an earthly conqueror, flaunt his glory before men as a spectacle or a spoil. In Him every manifestation of it must have been limited by the most perfect obedience, and the law must in its highest sense have been applicable even to Him, " Whoso

T

exalteth himself shall be abased." From this alternate action of the conditions which limited the earthly life of the incarnate Son, it followed that during it He could give no absolutely convincing proof of the reality of his nature as the God-man ; this truth in Him could only be discerned with the eye of faith. These conditions of humiliation, by which His divinity was veiled and hidden, are expressed in the title " Son of Man," which He so often uses of Himself with special emphasis, and sometimes in a tone of holy sadness. While He knows that His manifestation as the Son of Man is the highest revelation of His love, He also knows that from this it would be that mistake concerning Him and offence would arise. Accordingly, we find that many of Christ's contemporaries, who could only have been assured of the truth of His Messiahship by inward experience of His grace, felt and advanced the same doubts and objections, that have since been often urged by many who say they could readily have believed, if only they had been eye-witnesses. But while carnally-minded eye-witnesses were fancying that signs and wonders would enable them to believe in Him, His divinity faded from their sight, and the opposite part of the life of the God-man——the conditions of His humiliation——became more prominent, and confirmed their questionings and doubts. " Is not this," said they, " the carpenter, the Son of Mary, the brother of James and Joses, and of Judas and Simon ? and are not his sisters here with us ? And they were offended at him." (Mark vi. 3).

Observations.——The alternation of humiliation and glory here referred to is the expression of a general law, holding good of every revelation of truth in time, of every manifestation of divine Providence. What is temporal cannot be conceived of without a seeming incongruity between the ideal and experience; not that a harmonizing of these is impossible, or as if there were between them an irreconcilable contrariety, but because it involves the thought that the contrast between the idea and experience should be dissipated in time, and by the conflict of mind and will fulfilling itself in time. Yet a point must be reached in the progress of time when time and eternity shall meet, and experience shall find its consummation and transfiguration in eternal truth ;—otherwise its development in time would exhibit the continual struggle of truth, not its advancing triumph ; and that sure resting-place in truth would be wanting, in virtue of which truth, though in the midst of what is temporal, anticipates the end of time. Inasmuch, however, as this eternal revelation is a revelation made in time, it can only be momentary and evanescent, and it must be held fast in faith ; for experience will still demand a multiplicity of signs to be adduced as evidences to the objector. Thus, though the advent of Christ is the clearest proof of the providence of God, yea the bright and shining fact in which it culminates, it is nevertheless subject to this universal law. Nay, more ; we may even say that Christ is the full exponent of this law, because in Him, in most outward and clear embodiment, we see the law of temporality,—the contrast, I mean, between what is revealed and what is hidden in the counsels of the Father with the righteous, all that can strengthen and confirm, all that can give offence. Further, to require that Christ should, during His manifestation in time, give demonstrative evidence of His truth, would be to set up the unreasonable demand that He should reveal Himself now in the same manner as He will when He comes in the end of days, when the temporal shall be separated in heaven and in hell, and when all uncertainty shall be taken away ; it would be to require that He should not be "a sign spoken against," that He should not be " for the fall and rising again of many;"—there being no room upon such a supposition either for faith or for un-belief.

And what is true of our Lord is also true regarding His gospel and His Church. The history of the Christian Church necessarily presents a continual alternation between κρύψις and φανέρωσις, between circumstances of humiliation and of glory. Manifold as have been the signs and wonders which the Church has furnished in the history of the world, many as have been the times when the sun of Christianity has shone high in the firmament of history, there must nevertheless occur in its annals partial, yea, total eclipses of that sun, serving as grounds of objection for unbelievers, and demanding and developing " the patience and faith of the saints" (Rev. xiii. 10).

§ 146.

The believing view recognizes the same Christ in humiliation and exaltation ; recognizes that the human nature in Him never so prevailed as to contradict the Divine, nor the Divine so as ever to contradict the human ;—it perceives that at no moment of his life did this distinction in His nature ever become a schism. He exhibits the finiteness of human nature so far as it can be presented in Him, for " He was in all points tempted like as we are, yet without sin." Without sin ; for sin is an actual apostacy of the human nature from the divine; but His finite development—His growth from childhood upwards—involves only a contrast, and a yielding tension or expansiveness, without which the nature of that development must have broken the bond of unity. That the bond of union between the two natures never was broken, that it continued though unseen in the circumstances of the lowest humiliation, is manifest from the fact that He came forth out of every temptation triumphant and glorious. Even upon the cross, when He cried, " My God, my God, why hast thou forsaken me ?" even then it was unbroken. This word does indeed denote the utmost limit to which the tension between the natures can be stretched ; it is the cry of suffering, of agonizing human nature itself giving way, and giving itself up. Not only does it indicate anguish because of the contradiction between outward fact and the inner consciousness of rectitude ; not only does it express the sense of the terrible weight of bodily suffering, which seemed almost about to triumph over the eternal ; an agony through which the holy and pious of all times have had to pass, the thought that they had surrendered the eternal ideal, that their heart of hearts had deceived them ;—it indicates a deeper agony still, an inward idea of abandonment by God, which the holy and righteous also know, and which they have described as that state when a person is without the consolation of God.*

Not only in the saint's outward circumstances, but in his inward spiritual state and disposition, there is an alternation

* Compare the beautiful chapter in *De Imitatione Christi*, by Thomas à Kempis, entitled *De carentia omnis solatii*.

of κρύψις and φανέρωσις, of light and darkness, emptiness and
fulness. Those blissful seasons when his soul is satisfied with
divine consolations, with heavenly peace and joy; so that he
readily and joyfully endures all tribulation, because the Spirit
affords him more abundant recompense,—these seasons must
alternate with hours of darkness and desolation, when God
seems estranged because consolation and joy are gone, hours
withal which are designed, through TESTING, PATIENCE, and
DELAY, to accomplish in him a higher perfection and glorification. For, as Thomas à Kempis says, "it is not difficult to
despise human consolation when one possesses a higher—that
of God. Hard it is, very hard, to do without the divine as
well as the human, and out of love to God willingly to endure
exile of heart, as one banished from the land of consolation.
What glory is it to be joyous and zealous when favour compasses you round? All rejoice in such seasons of consolation
and pleasant hope; and what marvel is it that he feels no
burden who is sustained by the Almighty arms, and led by
the omniscient Guide? Real progress in the spiritual life is
made not only when grace fills thee with consolation, but
equally when grace seems to forsake thee, and thou bearest it
patiently, in humility and self-abasement, while thy earnestness in prayer cools not, and thy desires after righteousness
do not wane." Now, as it certainly behoved Christ to be in
all points tempted like as we are, yet without sin, He must,
in His inner life, have experienced these alternate states of
darkness and of brightness, of emptiness and of fulness.
Though He never was alone, because the Father was with
Him ever; although in Him dwelt the fulness of the Godhead bodily, yet He not only experienced those states, in
which divine fulness broke through its earthly limitations,
and the Only Begotten rested blissfully upon the bosom of the
Father; He experienced those also when the fulness of His
Godhead withdrew itself into the hidden depths of His being,
lying low and unperceived at the foundation, while in holy
activity He was called to fight the battle of patient endurance,
to sustain a great fight of afflictions. These conditions of
inward emptiness and desertion of soul multiplied and pressed
upon Him chiefly in the hour of His last sufferings and death;
and these were the feelings which found their expression in those

words of the ancient Psalm, " My God, my God, why hast thou forsaken me ?" by which He shewed us what He was suffering upon the cross. At the moment when those words escaped His lips, the fulness of the Godhead was in its deepest concealment; it lay still in the depths of His suffering nature. At that moment there was an eclipse of it within Him like that of the sun which took place in nature. But there was no variableness nor shadow of change in His perfect sinlessness and holiness. That cry which now we hear is not the cry of impatience, nor of doubt abandoning itself to despair; it is the cry of the patient sufferer, who knows that this word of Scripture must be fulfilled in Him, that the counsel of the Father must be accomplished, that all the sufferings of the righteous, not excepting this very sorrow, this very darkness of soul, must now be blended together in the cup which He is to drink to its very dregs. But as He gives expression to the agony He was enduring in a word of holy Scripture, He also shews His knowledge that He is still within the economy of the Divine purposes and love in that other word, " It is finished !"

§ 147.

As Christ's human nature never contradicts His divinity, so also His divine nature never belies His humanity. The manifestation of the divine nature in the human reveals to us the principle that human nature is the central point in creation, being that nature in which heaven and earth, God and the creature, meet. Christ's miracles are tokens that the Son of Man is Lord of Nature, and proofs of the union of free-will with nature. Hence His power over nature is by no means arbitrary or unlimited ; it finds its bounds in the law of holiness, and its exercise is controlled by His obedience to His Father's will. Resurrection from the dead is not a contradiction of human nature ; it is its glorification—the solution of the mystery of life and death. At His ascension, Christ does not lay aside His humanity, but, raised up to the right hand of the Father, where all power and wisdom are given to Him, He abides the heavenly Adam (1 Cor. xv. 42, 47), in whose likeness the Church shall grow ; and He shall come again as " the Son of Man," to judge both the quick and the dead. (Luke xxi. 27.) All shall thus be judged by the

Son of Man, by their own ideal, their eternal exemplar and antitype.

THE MEDIATORIAL WORK OF CHRIST.

§ 148.

Christ came as the world-perfecting and world-saving Mediator, in order to institute a new relationship with God, a new covenant; in order to establish not only a new consciousness of God, but a new life for man in God, whereby the abnormal development of human nature might be stayed, and a new development introduced, by the progressive destruction of sin. His office as Mediator may be viewed under the threefold division of PROPHET, PRIEST, and KING. As the Prophet under the old covenant appeared as a witness in behalf of truth, as the High Priest presented the offering for the sins of the people, as Israel's King guarded and protected the people of God, these mediatorial offices were to be united in the Messiah, and in Him were to find their perfection and spiritual glory. He is the Mediator of the new Covenant in virtue of His Testimony, in virtue of His Atonement, and in virtue of the establishment of a kingdom whose everlasting King, whose Lord and Head He is.

THE PROPHETIC OFFICE OF CHRIST.

§ 149.

Revelation is vouchsafed to men by means of the WORD, and Christ therefore was to appear among men as a Prophet. A prophet is more than a teacher of God's Word. A teacher of God's Word does no more than unfold, explain, and witness to, what a given revelation contains. The Prophet, on the contrary, brings us something *new*, his appearance always denotes a new turning point; and the prophetic word is itself an historical act in an evil age, a powerful, saving, and reconciling word, spoken in order to purify and reform the times. The Prophet stands in the midst of the swelling stream of the people's life and history, and proclaims the advancing fulfilment of God's eternal counsels. He stands between the past and the future, and while he shews how the types of the past are fulfilled in the present, he announces in the present visions of the future.

§ 150.

While the elder Prophets indicate only points of development in the preparatory Dispensation, Christ announces a new Dispensation, of which He is the head. His appearance as Prophet marks an absolute turning point in the times, for in the fulness of time He declares the fulness of all prophecy. We may indeed say that the prophetic work of Christ is the *end* of all prophecy, that after Him no new prophecy can be looked for, but that every following announcement is only the unfolding and explaining of His.

§ 151.

He appears among the people and preaches the Law and the Gospel. As the prophets of old had ever to give new life to the spiritual meaning and intent of the law in opposition to the carnal apprehensions of priests and people, and to lead them back from a literal observance of its outward requirements, to the fulfilment of its spiritual demands; so in like manner does Christ proclaim the law in its spirit and intent, in contrast with the righteousness of the Scribes and Pharisees; he interprets the Mosaic law, not in order to destroy it, but in order to fulfil it. And as the ancient prophets added to the law the promises of God's grace, so Christ announced Himself to be not only the fulfiller of the law, but the accomplisher of the promise likewise. For herein lies the difference between Christ and the ancient prophets; the main characteristic and distinctive feature of Christ's testimony is His *self-assertion,* His witness concerning *Himself* as the Mediator between God and the world. He testifies of Himself as the fulness of all grace; "Come unto ME, all ye that labour, and are heavy laden, and I will give you rest," (Matt. xi. 28). He testifies of Himself as the fulness of the law. "Who among you convinceth me of sin?" In most striking contrast with this world, He testifies of the *kingdom of heaven,* which is not of this world, and proclaims faith in His Person as the indispensable condition for participation in His kingdom and its blessedness. In comparison with this, every other aim possesses only a temporary importance, and must unhesitatingly be sacrificed should the kingdom of God require it. He therefore compares this heavenly kingdom to a pearl of great price, in order to obtain which the merchantman sells all that he has, (Matt. xii. 45–46). For what shall it profit a man if he gain the whole world and bring ruin upon his soul ? Accordingly, He declares that whosoever loveth father or mother more than Him, is not worthy of Him ; that whoso putteth his hand to the plough and looketh back, is not fit for the kingdom of God ; while to one who would become His disciple, but wished first to go and bury his father, he declares, "Let the dead bury their dead ; but go thou and preach the kingdom of God," (Luke ix. 59–62).

§ 152.

As the prophets of the old dispensation uttered visions of the future, so also did Christ. In his announcements regarding the future, however, His self-annunciation is the main and central feature, for He prophesies concerning Himself that He shall come a second time to judge both the quick and the dead. His apocalyptic discourses (Matt. xxiv., Mark xiii., Luke xvii., xxi.), may be called the unfolded and full blown flower of prophecy ; and the new world,—the times of restitution of all things, the new creation—is in its main features revealed. From this high point of prophetic vision He explains the meaning of the times and the intent of history. In his prophetic view he sees neither a continual revolution nor an unending advance ; the development of his kingdom has a definite goal, when this present world shall be dissolved, and there shall be a new heavens and a new earth ; and his design was, that His Church on earth should ever live in the perception and experience of this contrast between this world and that which is to come, between this side the final goal and that which lies beyond. The notion, however, so congenial to the natural mind, of an harmonious and progressive growth of the kingdom of God on earth, is foreign to His prophetic view. For while the kingdom of God is described as growing and spreading secretly and calmly through the world, and like leaven leavening the whole lump, yet the world appears to Christ not merely as the *natural* world, gradually improving and advancing towards perfection, but as a world which lieth in wickedness, and which entertains against the gospel an hostile, yea, even a satanic opposition. It is the

fundamental principle of the present dispensation that a conflict is being now carried on between two opposite principles,
between the kingdom of the world and the kingdom of holiness, between the Prince of this world and Christ ;—a conflict in which all must bear a part, for he who is not with
Christ is against Him (Matt. xii. 30),—a conflict in which all
powers, all spirits in the universe, are involved. The advance
of this conflict is indicated by the opposition and contrast
between the contending forces becoming more and more marked
and manifest. And so far from confirming the philosophic
dream of a final and everlasting peace, brought about by a
progressive civilization and enlightenment of humanity upon
earth, Christ rather sanctions the Norseman's myth of Ragnarok,* that in the last days there shall be upon earth a corruption, a conflict and a misery such as there never had been
before since the beginning of the world. Perfection and
glory are to ensue only upon the bitterest conflict.

Observations.—The conflict of life presented itself to our Lord
as a conflict between the kingdom of heaven and *this*
world, and for this very reason He foretells nothing concerning the advance of mankind in civilization and culture.
The contrast which is presented in Christ's declarations
and prophesies is not that subsisting between the thinking and the unthinking, about which culture is concerned,
but that between the spirit of the world and the Holy
Spirit. That current philanthropy which makes history
merely the progressive march of culture, an advancing
triumph of mind and reason over nature, over matter and
substance, over the unthinking and unreasoning, does
not really differ essentially from nor rise above Hellenism,
because it takes no cognizance of the all-important contrast and conflict between the spirit of the world and the
Holy Spirit of God ; it has no conception that a profound
worldly knowledge and a most refined culture may be
enlisted in the service of a principle hostile to the kingdom of God—such as is involved in a false teaching
which is by no means identical with a mere want of intelligence. The power of culture and of civilization is
intermediate, and derives its importance only from the

* See § 120.

relation in which it stands to these two great principles, striving for the ascendancy in history, about which the real life of men consciously or unconsciously is concerned.

§ 153.

Although Christ's knowledge, when on earth, could not be called omniscience, although it was limited, it was nevertheless perfect. He confessed indeed that the Son knew not that day and hour which the Father had kept in His own power (Mark xiii. 32), but He also declared that heaven and earth might pass away, but that His words should not pass away (Matt. xxiv. 35). This distinction between the unlimited and the limited in Christ's knowledge is explained only upon the principle of a *central* fundamental and typical knowledge. His knowledge possessed an inward rather than an outward infinitude; it was infinite in depth though not in range. As the perfection of His Person was not the mere sum total of all relative perfections, so His knowledge was not the mere sum total of all relative truths, but the eternal and fundamental truth. As He is the centre of all creation, for it was the Father's good pleasure that in Him all fulness should dwell, His personal consciousness necessarily involved clear perception and knowledge of God, of man, and of the world. As personally and in virtue of His essential being, He knew the mysteries of the kingdom of God, He also knew the secrets of the human heart; and considering the mysterious relation in which He stood to every human soul, every one who came within the range of His personal influence—whether a Nicodemus or a Samaritan woman, a Nathanael or a Judas—was necessarily known and seen through by Him. " He knew all, and needed not that any should testify of man; for He knew what was in man," (John ii. 24, 25). And as He knew what is in the human heart, He must also have known what is in the world. With the piercing and unerring eye of His wisdom, He searched out and knew the powers of heaven, of earth, and of hell; He saw through those spiritual powers by which things temporal and human life in its development are influenced—powers which do not perish in time, but era after era rise up anew with redoubled effort, appear and re-appear through the long range of historic periods, until the last great judgment day. Christ's prophecy is therefore the key for the ultimate and conclusive solution of all church history, of the history of the world, and even of nature itself.

Observations.—As He is Himself the Word of God incarnate, the word which He speaks is a divine word uttered in a way suited to the comprehensions of men. He speaks in similitudes and parables, and thereby divine truth in His lips is intensely human, plain to the consciences of the simple as well as of the wise. "I thank thee, O Father, Lord of heaven and earth, because thou hast hid these things from the wise and prudent, and hast revealed them unto babes," (Matt. xi. 25). This is the true idea of ACCOMMODATION (συγκατάβασις) a coming down, an adaptation to the narrowness of human understanding. The rationalistic idea of accommodation which supposes that Christ intended to convey two truths—the one hidden and the other obvious,—contradicts the inherent principle of revelation. "If," says Luther, "He had possessed a better gospel, He would have given it to us." It was, however, necessary to the principle of the *economy*, that His gospel should contain some things which He could not tell His disciples, because they could not bear them then, (John xvi. 12), and that in His discourses generally there should words occur, the depths of whose meaning no one has ever yet fully fathomed.

§ 154.

He speaks as one having authority and not as the Scribes, (Mark i. 22). This holds good of every true prophet, but above all and in a special sense of the only begotten Son. The words of Christ derive their authority, not from Inspiration, like those of the prophets, but from the Incarnation. Inspiration implies a fundamental distinction between God and man. The prophet feels that he is himself, in common with all, a sinner in the midst of a sinful world, and he needs to be raised up by the power of God's Spirit to a higher range of view ; he has originally unclean lips, and must be purified in order that the seraph may touch his lips with the live coal from off the altar (Isaiah vi.) Christ, on the contrary, speaks as one who is essentially in the Father, and the Father in Him, and accordingly He declares "No man knoweth the Father but the Son only, and he to whomsoever the Son will reveal Him" (Matt. xi. 27), and in contrast with the prophets it is written concerning Him, " No man hath seen God at any time ; the only-begotten Son, which is in the bosom of the Father, he hath declared him," (John i. 18). His authority is, therefore, higher than all the prophets : " Verily, verily, *I* say unto you !"   But while he speaks with this unlimited authority he does not demand the obedience and submission of the slave, but rather that of freedom, that of the inner man.   " Blessed are they who do hunger and thirst after righteousness, for they shall be filled."   " If any man will do the will of God, he shall know of the doctrine, whether it be of God, or whether I speak of myself," (Matt. v. 6 ; John vii. 17).

§ 155.

He is a prophet mighty, not in words only but in deeds (Luke xxiv. 19).   While the power of working miracles was a gift conferred upon the prophets of the old dispensation, in Christ's person it was inherent, the spontaneous outgo of His earthly life.   His words and His miracles are but different sides of the same truth, the manifestation of the fundamental miracle of the Incarnation.   " Go and shew John again those things which ye do hear and see : the blind receive their sight, and the lame walk, the lepers are cleansed, and the deaf hear, the dead are raised up, *and the poor have the Gospel preached to them*," (Matt. xi. 4, 5).   His word, His doctrine, is itself a miraculous act, named in this list as one of the restorations of the order of nature ; and each of His acts is an embodied word, a sign of the wonderful origin and power of the gospel. The carnal desire after signs and wonders as the ground of faith is condemned by Him, (John iv. 48), because they who misunderstood his words, misunderstood also his miracles, and at length were offended at his humiliation.   Hence He does not refer merely to the evidence of miracles (John v. 36), but to the witness of the Spirit in the heart of man, and to the signs of the times, which throughout the history were confirming prophecy.   The power of His word upon the heart ever depends upon the influence and impress of His Person, and the acceptance or rejection of His word cannot be separated from the acceptance or rejection of Himself.

THE HIGH-PRIESTHOOD OF CHRIST.

§ 156.

The office of prophet leads on to that of high-priest, a title which gives expression to the idea of propitiation. All priesthood, all sacrifices, in the religions which preceded Christianity, rest on and spring from this idea as their foundation and main root. But as Christ is the end and fulness of prophecy, all priesthood and sacrifice find their consummation and fulfilment in Him, who is Himself the true High-priest and the true Sacrifice. No created being—to say nothing of a *sinful* creature—no creature but the Son only can be the reconciling Mediator between God and sinners, and the setter-up of *the new covenant.**

§ 157.

The necessity for propitiation arises out of the separation produced by sin between God and man. As this separation certainly concerns God as well as man, the necessity for propitiation is not only a human, but a divine necessity. We must not suppose that by means of propitiation some change is produced in the Divine Being (viewing His Being as a metaphysical abstraction); for it is from the Divine Being that the Atonement springs. The plan of redemption, the decree for propitiation, was itself devised and determined in the depths of HIS everlasting love, who is without variableness or shadow of turning (Eph. i. 5 ; 1 Peter i. 20.) Neither should it be said that the Atonement produced a change in the essential relations of God to the world ; for through the presence of the eternal Logos God still continued in actual connexion with the world, though fallen ; and the world, notwithstanding its fall, is still *His* world. But nevertheless it is right for us to say not only that it is man who needs to be reconciled, but that God himself must become a reconciled God.† The living action of God's love in His world has been hindered and stayed by sin ; and consequently it hovers round the divine holiness and rectitude as a demand which has not

---

* See the Epistle to the Hebrews, *passim.*

† Conf. Augustana, Art. iii. Ut reconciliaret nobis *Patrem,* Art. xx. Quod propter Christum habeant *placatum* Deum.

been fulfilled in the world of unrighteousness ;—a requirement which finds its expression in this—that the divine love, which *must* be manifested actively, must yet remain in abeyance ; that God must retain the revelation of His love in the depth of possibility instead of allowing it to flow forth freely.

Observations.—The idea of atonement may accordingly be defined as the solution of a certain antithesis in the very life of God as revealed to man, or of the apparent opposition between God's love and God's righteousness. Though these attributes are essentially one, yet sin has produced a tension or apparent variance between these two points in the divine mind. Though God eternally loves the world, His actual relation to it is not a relation of love, but of holiness and justice, a relation of opposition, because the unity of His attributes is hindered and restrained. There exists also a contradiction between the actual and essential relations of God to mankind ; a contradiction which can only be removed by the destruction of the interposing principle of sin. The expression, the *wrath of God*, simply embodies this truth, that the relations of God's love to the world are unsatisfied, unfulfilled. The expression is not merely anthropopathic, it is an appropriate description of the divine pathos necessarily involved in the conception of a revelation of love restrained, hindered, and stayed through unrighteousness. For this wrath is holy love itself, feeling itself so far hindered because they have turned away from its blessed influence whom it would have received into its fellowship. This restrained manifestation of love, which in one aspect of it may be designated wrath, in another aspect is called *grief,* or *distress*, in the Holy Spirit of love ; and wrath is thus turned into compassion. It is only when the wrath of God is allowed that any mention can be made of His compassion. That heathen antiquity had no idea of God's love is attributable to the fact that it had no living conviction of the world's being under God's wrath. Plato and Aristotle rise only to the bare representation of God as a jealous God ; and men who in our day speak of dispassionate love rise no higher than they. The Old Testament, on the contrary, speaks of the wrath of God who is "a consuming fire," in the Psalms and in the Prophets, almost on every page; but it speaks also of the tender mercy and grace of the Lord, and of His love as like a mother's!

It is not a living, but a dead notion of the unchangeableness of God, which asserts that it was man only, and not God, who needed to be reconciled. For God's unchangeableness cannot be an empty, meaningless notion; it must be conformable with the fact of a living activity in Him by which He holds free intercourse with His creatures. This fact it must not exclude. And while God's attributes are all in their essence and foundation one, yet if this oneness be not empty and meaningless, those attributes must be viewed as different forces in the living activity of God; and their living manifestation in the moral government of the world must be conditioned and limited by the free relations of moral beings. Now, righteousness expresses a relation of contrast between God and man; and if the reality of sin be allowed, it is evident that this relation of contrast is of such a nature as to hinder and destroy the relation of unity. But God, in virtue of the very unchangeableness of His nature, must require that this relation of unity be maintained. A mere proclamation of the forgiveness of sin, without the actual removal of sin, would be only an apparent, a seeming reconciliation, and sooner must He leave the world to sink in ruin than violate the eternal laws of His holiness and rectitude. *Holy* love, which possesses the right of unconditional demand upon the human heart, must notify itself to the conscience as a creditor who cannot be refused, who continues to knock till his demands are satisfied. The debt *must* be paid; but as man has no resource, no means of meeting it, eternal love itself must devise an expedient. Thus the scheme of reconciliation divinely planned, so far from violating God's unchangeableness, is in reality the result of it.

The fundamental principle of the Church's teaching, upon the doctrine of atonement, is that it must have been a reconciliation accomplished not only on earth but in heaven, not only in the hearts of men, but in the heart of God.   This principle was scientifically developed in the middle ages by Anselm of Canterbury in his work *Cur deus homo,* and it is equally the fundamental idea of the Reformation doctrine.   In opposition to this,—the objective doctrine of atonement,—according to which Christ has averted wrath, and has reconciled heaven and earth,—Abelard had already propounded the doctrine of a subjective and merely psychological reconciliation ; a doctrine revived at the time of the Reformation in Socinianism, and in the present day in Rationalism.   According to this doctrine, God cannot be reconciled and needs no atonement, for He is eternal love without variableness or change.   Mankind only needed to be reconciled, because they could not believe in God's love.   Addicted to sin, they were ruled by the spirit of fear.   A sign was therefore necessary as a manifest token and pledge of God's grace, and this pledge we have in Christ.   He has come not to avert wrath—an unworthy notion—but to drive out fear.   His life of love, His affecting self-sacrifice, awakens trust and confidence in men's hearts, and leads them back to the Father.   The reconciliation is thus accomplished in man, not in God, who is pure unchangeable love, too high, too sublime to require a sacrifice or atonement.

But though we also teach that the essence of God is unchangeable love, we at the same time maintain that the active life of God's love in the world must needs have been interrupted by sin, and that a love, whose holy and righteous claims could not thus be injured and wounded would not be true love.   The notion of God's greatness, which considers Him too high to require an atonement, differs nothing from the notion that He is too high to be grieved by sin, that as the atonement does not affect Him, so neither does sin affect Him.   We, on the contrary, believe that sin is against God, that it does concern Him, that it disturbs His divine relations towards us, and therefore we cannot rest satisfied with that seeming reconciliation which is effected on earth but not in heaven. He has only a superficial perception of sin who can rest satisfied with it.

However much of pious energy we may grant to an

U

Abelard, and to other Pelagian natures, experience teaches
that those spirits who have felt the sting of sinfulness
and the weight of human guilt, amid the struggles of an
alarmed conscience, who have felt sin to be, not merely a
disturbed relationship to an impersonal law, but a violation of their religious relations to the living God,—St.
Paul, for example, and Augustine, and Anselm, and Luther,
and Pascal, and Hamann,—have been able to find consolation simply and alone by faith in a reconciled God ;
only then, when in faith they laid hold upon the gospel,
that the wrath of God was taken away, did love within
them drive out fear.

§ 158.

The contradiction between God and the world, and the
restraint put upon God's living revelation of His love through
sin, might have been removed had it been in the power of
the human race to offer a perfect sacrifice ; could they collectively have sacrificed—not this thing or that of the things
of this world, as in the religions of antiquity—but the inter-
rupting principle itself; could they have withdrawn from and
mortified the sinful self within, and have returned again to
God in unconditional obedience.   But the human race could
not make such a sacrifice, could not bring such an offering.
Human freedom could never produce true goodness, save in
fellowship with God, and from that divine grace to which it
owed its origin.   But in this sin really consists, that
fellowship is broken, human freedom is a freedom without
grace, man's best work is only a work of the law, and springs
not from the fountain of holy love, not from love's creative
inspiration.   Hence all the ancient sacrifices were insufficient,
and could never purify the conscience (Heb. ix.).   Unconditional surrender of the heart was impossible, because freedom
was alienated from its divine source, and could not surrender
itself.   To bring in a perfect sacrifice, two requirements must
be complied with, which our sinful race were unable perfectly
to accomplish ; namely, man must *himself*, by an act of the
purest free will, retrace and retract his sinful life, and begin a
new development in love, in obedience, and in rectitude ; and
withal this act of human freedom must at the same time be
the act of the purest grace, God's own act in sinful history.

These requirements are nowhere met but in the gospel : " God was in Christ reconciling the world unto himself."

§ 159.

Divine love, that knew from eternity the possibility of the Fall, found also from eternity the way of Redemption. In free grace and love the Father gives up the Son to humiliation, obedience, and suffering ; and by His willing obedience the Son, as the second Adam, satisfies the demands of holy and righteous love, offers up the sacrifice which our sinful race should have offered, but could not, drank to its dregs the cup of suffering for sin, which must needs be emptied, that the growth of sin might be retraced and destroyed, and that a new life might begin. This work of Christ's is really God's work of love and grace towards the race ; it is as really in the highest sense the act of humanity ; for it is God in human nature, who satisfies the demands of righteousness. On earth and among men the wall of partition between God and man is taken away ; amid our sinful race is the pure and sacred centre found, in which the disturbed relations of God towards us are again restored to harmony, and from which divine love can again stream forth abundantly upon the world. As God beholds the whole race represented in the new Adam, it follows that as One is righteous so are all righteous, as One died for all, all died ; and " as in the first Adam all die, so in the second Adam shall all be made alive " (2 Cor. v. 14 ; 1 Cor. xv. 22).

§ 160.

The second Adam also takes the place of humanity ; and His sacrificial work must be looked upon as the actual work of humanity itself (*satisfactio vicaria*). But our innermost consciousness demands that the righteousness and obedience rendered, should not only be *without* us in another, but should also become personally our own. Now this demand is satisfied by the fact that Christ is our *Redeemer* as well as our *Reconciler :* our Saviour who removes sin by giving a new life to the race, by establishing a living fellowship between Himself and mankind. All merely external and unspiritual confidence in the Atonement arises from a desire to take Christ as Reconciler without taking Him as Redeemer and Sanctifier. The gospel, " God was in Christ reconciling the world unto himself," must not be separated from the following call, "Be ye reconciled to God!" that is, "appropriate to yourselves the reconciliation accomplished in Christ, by the healing and purifying, the life-giving and sanctifying power which emanates from Christ!" As Christ is appropriated to ourselves by FAITH, He is a Redeemer not only *for* man but *in* man ; and with faith,—which is a new principle of action, and includes the giving up of the heart to Christ—a new fountain of life is opened, the beginning of salvation in man. To say that God in Christ beholds the reconciliation of the world is the same as to say that He anticipates the redemption and salvation of the whole world in the perfection of Christ and the perfection of His sacrifice,—the actual destruction of sin in man. But redemption as the foundation of faith in man's heart, while a work of grace, is at the same time *conditioned* by man's will, which can resist grace ; and the gospel of reconciliation, while it embraces the whole world, proves to be for the fall of many, and for the rising again of many, a savour of death to them who will be lost, and a savour of life to them who allow themselves to be saved ;— a truth which is unfolded and developed in the doctrine of predestination.

§ 161.

When the evangelical doctrine treats of the Atonement under the two-fold heads of the active and passive obedience of Christ, *obedientia activa et passiva,* it must be remembered that this contrast is simply relative. We cannot conceive of any part of Christ's *active* life in which there was not suffering also, as the result of the world's sin : the story of His sufferings does not begin in Gethsemane ; His whole life of obedience is a tale of sorrow. At the same time we cannot conceive of any suffering in Christ which was not also an active act, which was not in its truest sense a holy act of His free will ; for His whole life of obedience is the history of a struggling and conquering will. Remembering, therefore, that the distinction is only relative, we say that Christ is our righteousness in as much as He in active life fulfilled the law (*obedientia activa*), and by His sufferings and death offered Himself up for our transgressions (*obedientia passiva*).

§ 162.

He is our *Righteousness* before God, in as much as He overcame the world by His sinless and ideal perfection, and fulfilled the law in the midst of all temptations (Matt. iii. 15 ; v. 17 ; Heb. x. 7), and thus has realized the ideal of human nature. He fulfilled the law not as a single casual individual in the course of generations, but as the head of the race, under whom all must be included. Again, by the realization of His own ideal in His own Person, He has realized not merely the ideal of a single man, but that of human nature and human life. He has also fulfilled the law in *our stead*, and can say to His disciples, that in the world they should have tribulation, but in Him they should have peace, because He had overcome the world (John xvi. 33). The righteousness of the whole Body is included in Him as the Head, and as the Father beholds the race in Him, He beholds the race as one in whom He is well pleased. When it is objected that the imputation of the righteousness of another is akin to unrighteousness, this rests upon a conception of mankind as an outward aggregation of individuals, and the mystery of organism and the union of the body with the Head is ignored. This atomic view contradicts the idea of one spiritual body, one common consciousness, and one historic inspiration. It consequently forbids the spiritual appropriation of an external perfection ; and disallows that feeling of virtue in which a nation not only sees in her heroes examples for imitation, but appropriates their deeds as her own, as of national right and citizenship hers. This deep feeling of inseparable unity in multiplicity pervades all religious bodies, and finds in Christianity its highest and holiest realization.

§ 163.

As Christ is become our atoning Righteousness before God, He is also made unto us *Redemption* (1 Cor. i. 30), in order to our freedom from sin. As He reveals in His life an embodiment of the law, He awakens in man the knowledge of sin, and the desire after a perfect and holy life. To those who receive Him He gives power to become the sons of God (John i. 12). This liberating gift depends, not only on the force of His Word, but upon the direct influence of His Person; for He Himself becomes an *animating* and inspiring principle in all whom the Father gives Him. Even Plato had already said that we are allured to virtue, not by teaching, not by our own nature, but by the influence of the gods, and that intercourse with a divinely-minded man, nay, even nearness to him, gives us power for good, just as one becomes courageous when by the side of a courageous warrior. This is the mystery which the apostle Paul gives expression to when he says, "I live no longer myself, but Christ liveth in me" Ζῶ δὲ οὐκέτι ἐγώ ζῇ δὲ ἐν ἐμοὶ Χριστός (Gal. ii. 20). But all whom Christ receives into the fellowship of His life, He appoints to the fellowship of His sufferings and death. For by the death of the Lord comes the perfect knowledge of sin, and death is perfectly expiated thereby alone. As the law must be perfectly fulfilled, so also must the *guilt* be perfectly blotted out.

§ 164.

The Lord's death is the perfect revelation of the sin of the world. It is not merely relative goodness that suffers: still less is it one party laid low by an opposite sect; He who now suffers the death of a malefactor is the incarnate Righteousness itself raised high above all parties. This death must therefore be described as the consummation of the world's unrighteousness. It is not merely an isolated act; all the sin previously developed in human history reaches, in this act, its highest culmination. To so deep a depth had history now sunk, that those very powers in Judaism and heathenism whose province it was to embody and maintain righteousness upon earth, those spiritual and secular powers unite to crucify the personal Righteousness itself. It is not only Caiaphas and Pilate who bring the Redeemer to the cross; spiritual principalities and powers are engaged in the work; on the one hand unbelieving Judaism, the spirit of Pharisaism, idolizing itself in the letter of the law; and on the other hand, spirit-denying heathenism recognizing itself in the Cæsar of Rome as a god on earth. Had Caiaphas, and Pilate, and Judas never lived, those powers would nevertheless have brought Christ to the cross. The death of the Lord Jesus is therefore the perfect manifestation of the world's sin and guilt. But this very death, which seems to consummate the condemnation and perdition of the race, in reality atones for the sin of mankind; Golgotha's cross, which seems to be set up for all history as a sign of the curse, is the symbol of salvation, the true 'tree of freedom' for all history. This is the deepest mystery of love displayed in the Atonement.

§ 165.

The solution of this strange anomaly can be found only in the mysterious relation subsisting between Christ and the human race. Mankind are represented not only in those who stood beneath the cross, but in Him also who hung upon it. It is the old Adam that we see beneath the cross, he is the new Adam who hangs upon it. The second Adam has no share in the sin of the race; but his self-consciousness must not be separated from the consciousness of union with the sinful race itself. The suffering and death which he endured of the race—which was inflicted by the race, He Himself transformed into a suffering and death *for* the race; in the boundless sympathy of His love He felt the guilt of His brethren as if His own; as our High Priest He was able to bear the guilt of the race upon His heart. By His incarnation Christ is so intimately united with our sinful race, that He can say (as Luther expresses it), "I am this sinner, that is, his guilt and punishment belong to me;" and the sinner can say by faith, "I am Christ, that is, his death and his righteousness belong to me!" From this point of view it becomes clear that "He was made sin for us, who knew no sin," that "He was wounded for our transgressions, and bruised for our iniquities," that "the chastisement of our peace was upon Him, and with His stripes we are healed" (2 Cor. v. 21; 1 Peter ii. 24; Isaiah liii. 5).

§ 166.

The atoning sacrifice, which the race of man cannot offer, is free surrender to, and voluntary undertaking of, that suffering by which the power of sin is slain. That suffering must now be described as consisting of the consciousness of guilt, the conviction of sin, and *repentance*. Repentance is the life- and death-struggle of the soul, in which the sinner slays not only particular sinful habits, but all his previous sinful life. Now, though Christ, as sinless, had nothing to repent of, yet holy sorrow, on account of human sin, was the secret and soul of all His sufferings.   His was the pain of a pure and true nature, on account of the sinful development which reaches its culmination in the sufferings of the second Adam.   The knowledge of sin, on the part of mankind, expresses itself in the dying Redeemer.   In the very centre of history, pure and perfect pain, on account of sin, is endured,—that spiritual pain, by means of which the past is remitted—the development of sin retracted and removed.*   On the cross the new Adam offered up Himself—the principle of self—that cosmical principle, from which the kingdoms of this world derived all their false glory—a principle which stirred even in Him, though it never became actual sin.   And as the second Adam has been Himself perfected by destroying the possibility of sin, the human race in Him has died unto sin—for, if One died, all died.

§ 167.

The atoning power of Christ's death consists not in His physical sufferings as such, not in His blood and His wounds merely, as such, but in the infinite offering of His love.   But this perfect offering of His love would not have been accomplished had He merely died in a spiritual sense, and not bodily, for the race.   The perfect sacrifice to atone for sin consists not only in the perception of sin, and sorrow on account of it, but in the voluntary endurance of *its penalty*,— of the suffering which is the consequence of it.   Now, all the consequences of sin, all human misery is summed up and consummated in death, which is *the wages of sin*.   Christ being the spotless One, has no sin of His own for which to suffer, yet He suffered what sinners deserve to suffer,—He submitted to death, to death which has in it the sting of sin.   When we say that the Lord died the death of a malefactor upon the cross, we express the truth that He died that death which is the wages of sin.   But the sting in His death is the sin of the world, which He bore upon His heart, as our High Priest, the judgments of God which were laid upon His soul.   By thus voluntarily enduring the punishment, voluntarily giving His entire personality up to death, He nailed our sentence to

---

* Romans iii. 25, εἰς ἔνδειξιν τῆς δικαιοσύνης αὐτοῦ, διὰ τὴν πάρεσιν τῶν προγεγονότων ἁμαρτημάτων.

His cross. The penalty being endured, justice is satisfied, and a perfect sacrifice is offered for "the remission of sins." Thus, as this act of sacrifice is the act of the new Adam, it is really the act of human nature, of human freedom ; but it can be the act of human freedom only, because it is the act in history of God's merciful grace, because the suffering Adam is none other than the suffering God—God himself in the lowest humiliation of humanity,—the dying God-man.

For the faithful, death has now lost its sting : by Him, in whom they possess a reconciled God, they are delivered from the fear of death (Hebrews ii. 15),—of that death whose sting is sin and the righteous judgment of God.

§ 168.

In the suffering and dying Redeemer, the human race conquers death, because it becomes dead to sin. But the race becoming dead to sin in the new Adam, implies that it dies not only to the will of the flesh, but to its worldly ideals likewise. Now, the natural heart will not of itself die to all that in a spiritual sense makes the world *this world,*—to all that fancied perfection which the race has ever sought for in some kingdom of worldly ideals. The spirit of man sought to realize that perfection in the earthly ideal Messiah of Judaism, —in a kingdom of temporal prosperity, which hope decked out in the garish colours of the imagination. He sought it again in the æsthetic ideal-world of Greece,—in a kingdom of sensuous beauty in the dream-world of art. He sought it once more in the political ideal-world of Rome,—in a kingdom of action, full of earthly greatness, honour, and luxury. But it must be confessed that according to the law of necessity these ideals must come to naught in the general oblivion and death of this world's history : this was the inevitable fate of the old world ; its glory faded away like the leaves of the forest. But one place there is in history where the power of fate was broken—because humanity there, by a sacred act of will, offered up its worldly ideals, freely surrendered the glory of this world, for that kingdom which is not of this world ;—and that place is Golgotha's Cross. There, be it remembered, was accomplished a sacred act of self-sacrificing will, because it was the act of divine self-sacrificing grace.

By this perfect union of the Divine with the human, the death of Christ was the sacred focus for the revelation of Providence in history ; whereas Judaism was in bondage to the yoke of the law, and Heathenism to the yoke of blind fate.

§ 169.

When the Redeemer cried "It is finished !" as He hung upon the cross, the veil of the temple was rent in twain from the top to the bottom ; because thenceforward the entire service of sacrifice pertaining to the old dispensation was abolished. That perfect, that satisfying sacrifice was offered up as an odour of a sweet smell, well pleasing to God. The odour of this offering ascended from the sacred heart of humanity ; and when that heart broke, to live again for evermore, this world and the prince of this world were overcome. The death of the Lord was alike atoning and redeeming in its efficacy. The crucified Redeemer is the principle and foundation of expiation and conversion for the world. His sacrifice is the central truth, the main theme of apostolic preaching. "I am determined not to know anything, save Jesus Christ, and him crucified !" Through the forgiveness of sin, we are made partakers of everlasting life. Accordingly, the Article of "the forgiveness of sins," and of "justification by faith," is justly esteemed by all evangelic churches the central and fundamental doctrine of Christianity. The new obedience, and the imitation of Christ in the fellowship of His sufferings, these alike grow forth from that one centre : for it is only when we die with the Lord that we can live with Him. But fellowship with Christ's sufferings possesses this characteristic, all human suffering is spiritually glorified thereby ; yea, death itself, after the pattern of the Lord's, becomes a free, a world-overcoming death. And the more the Faithful are drawn into fellowship with Christ's sufferings, the more do even *their* sufferings in turn become vicarious for the world, as is clearly witnessed by the history of the Christian martyrs and the Christian heroes.

Observations.—The intercession of Christ as our Advocate with the Father is usually included in His office as High Priest. But as we have throughout described His propitiatory offering as one which He continually presents to the Father, this subject finds its appropriate place in the doctrine of His kingly office, or of His continual working in His Church.

THE KINGLY OFFICE OF CHRIST.
§ 170.

Our Lord reached the goal of ethical perfection in His humiliation. " He was made perfect through sufferings." But as in death He was perfected in an *ethical* sense, His Person and His Work were to be manifested after death in the fulness of their *cosmical* import. In the days of His flesh, the unity of His ethical and cosmical power appeared only partially and fragmentarily, through the limitations of time ; it appeared only in alternations between concealment and revelation. But by the voluntary act of self-sacrifice accomplished in His death, He brought human nature into perfect harmony with the divine ; He died to what was in part, that the perfect might come, and that He might reveal Himself as the Lord of Glory, to whom the Father had given the kingdom and the power. Exalted above the limitations of time and space, He reveals Himself now eternally as the Head of the KINGDOM OF GRACE ; a kingdom which is not only the centre and goal of all human history, but which embraces within its range the world of spirits also : that kingdom of grace which is to take up into itself and to glorify the entire kingdom of nature, and thus become in the end one universal KINGDOM OF GLORY (*regnum gloriæ*). This grand conception of Christ's exaltation is unfolded in the three articles of Christian dogma, the Descent into the realm of death (Hades), the Resurrection, and the Session on the right hand of God the Father. The entire series of Old Testament prophecies regarding a triumphing Messiah is fulfilled in this exaltation of Christ ; prophecies which constitute an antithesis to those describing a suffering Messiah, and which usually represent the Messiah under the type of a theocratic KING who is the head of the people of God.

Observations.—During His humiliation Christ was still a king, and exercised at times His kingly prerogative. He chose Apostles ; instituted the ministerial office, and the sacraments; and gave the Apostles the power of loosing and binding. But He did not assume His royal rule with power until after His death.

§ 171.

It was a fundamental article of apostolic tradition,* and the general belief of the Christian Church, that while His Body lay in the grave, our Lord descended in spirit into the kingdom of the dead, and preached to the spirits who there were kept in prison. Great as is the darkness in which this doctrine is involved, it nevertheless expresses the idea of the universal and cosmical efficacy of Christ's work; the idea of the efficacy of the work of atonement for the generations of men who lived before Christ's advent, for all who had died without the knowledge of salvation, and for all who had died in faith of the promise. Those spirits of men who still stood in a mystical union with the organism of humanity, as members of the great family of man, were made partakers of that Restitution which had now been realized in the centre of the organism. By his descent into Hades, Christ revealed Himself as the redeemer of all souls. The descent into the realm of the dead gave expression to the truth, that the distinctions Here and There—the limits of place—are of no significance regarding Christ, and do not concern His kingdom; and on this ground it is that we include this Article in the doctrine of Christ's exaltation. No powers of nature, no limits of space or of time can hinder Christ from finding His way to souls. His kingdom has extended even into the region of the dead, and still includes that region; and the distinctions of living and dead, of earlier and later generations of men, of times of ignorance and times of knowledge, possess but a transient significance. All fatalism regarding different individuals and races of men is thus obviated and destroyed. Each spirit determines its own destiny, because all temporal and circumstantial differences are finally absorbed and nullified in the one great distinction,—that namely which finds its

* 1 Peter iii. 19, "By which also he went and preached unto the spirits in prison."—Eph. iv. 9, "Now that he ascended what is it but that he also descended first into the lower parts of the earth."—Phil. ii. 10, "That at the name of Jesus every knee should bow, of things in heaven, and things in earth, and things under the earth."

efficacy in Christ,—the grand distinguishing principle of
FREEDOM, between the believer and the unbeliever, between
those who accept and those who reject salvation.

Observations.—We have included the descent into Hades in
the doctrine of Christ's exaltation. Yet viewing it in
another aspect, it may certainly be taken as part of His
humiliation. We must take it as belonging to His
humiliation when we look upon Christ as now fully sub-
mitting himself to the law of death, undergoing the common fate of man, by descending into the valley of the
shadow of death ; because the spirit is then separated
from its corporeity, and lives in an uncompleted being,
waiting for its re-union with the body. So far therefore
as Christ's humiliation and exaltation are viewed as successive states, the descent into hades may be described as
the connecting link, and is at once the lowest step of His
humiliation and the beginning of His exaltation.

Had this doctrine of the descent into the realm of the
dead been recognized as possessing the same significance
for all times which it had for Christian antiquity, those
fatalistic conjectures in which modern orthodoxy has indulged regarding the final blessedness of the heathen
might have been avoided. Lutheran orthodoxy, afraid of
recognizing an intermediate state lest it should seem to
sanction the Catholic purgatory, would only assert the
distinction between eternal life and eternal fire. The
explanation it gives of the dogma is simply, that Christ
descended into the realm of the lost, and triumphed over
the devil. But we only suppose that this triumph over the
devil was something real and definite, when we believe,
with the early Church, that Christ took from the devil his
prey, and led captivity captive (Eph. iv. 8) ; that He
delivered the generations who had died before His advent,
the generations of heathen, from that dominion of Satan
and of fiendish powers, under which we must believe they
had hitherto been. Great confusion has arisen from the
expression " the Descent into *Hell*," because the word
hell, which in the older languages denoted the realm of
the dead generally, soon came to mean the abode of the
damned. The original meaning is necessarily maintained

here, but it has been time after time supplanted by the later and narrower meaning, in both the Lutheran and the Reformed Churches. The Reformed Church deprives this dogma of any distinctive meaning, understanding it as wholly figurative. It explains it thus:——Christ upon the cross endured the pains of hell, and so far it may be said of Him that He descended into hell. The confessions of both churches must therefore on this point be tested and corrected according to the testimony of Scripture and the witness of the early Church.

§ 172.

On the third day the Lord rose from the dead in order to a revelation thenceforward of the kingdom of glory (*regnum gloriae*). In the resurrection is anticipated the perfecting of the world. That regeneration, including renewal and glorification, which mankind and all creation look forward to as the consummation of the world's development, in which spirit and body, nature and history, are perfectly reconciled,——human nature being glorified into a temple for the Holy Ghost, and material nature being brought into the glorious liberty of the children of God,——that regeneration which necessarily involves and demands the belief, that the contradiction between the physical and the ethical, between the kingdom of nature and that of grace shall not continue as if eternal and indissoluble ——is revealed ideally in the resurrection of the Lord. The resurrection of the Lord is not the mere *sign* of that regeneration, it is itself the actual *beginning* of it. It is the sacred point where death has been overcome in God's creation; and from this point the spiritual as well as the bodily resurrection of the entire human race from the dead proceeds. Now, for the first time, as a risen Saviour can Christ become the real Lord and Head of His Church. Now that the perfecting of the world is in His person ideally accomplished, He becomes the actual Perfecter of the world, and can replenish this present world with the energies of the future.

Observations.——There is also a close connection between the resurrection of the Lord, and the perfecting of the church. That blissful future, that idea of victory, which hovers before the Church's hope, is already reached in the risen Redeemer. Easter is therefore the chief of the Christian festivals, and Sunday, as the day of our Lord's resurrection, is universally a festival day for Christians. The Church dates her existence from that historical fact in which she beholds the pledge of her blessed future, and which has ever been before her eyes as the goal of her development and her conflict. In this fact, more than any where else, she recognises the deep and close connexion which subsists between prophecy on one hand, and history on the other. Prophecies regarding the future of the kingdom of God must be viewed in the light of the historical fact of the resurrection, and this historical fact must in turn be looked at in the light of prophecy. Apart from the resurrection of the Lord, the prophetic view of the world which forms the hope and expectation of the Church, would, have no foundation in actual fact. "If Christ be not risen," as the Apostle says (1 Cor. xv. 14), "then is our preaching vain, and your faith is also vain." Eternal life would then be no more than an hereafter. Apart from prophecy, the resurrection would be a bare fact without meaning, an isolated wonder answering to and connected with no new order of things. Prophecy and history, promise and fulfilment are blended together in the Church's joy on account of the resurrection ; her Easter rejoicing is a joy not merely on account of this or that single fact, but a joy in Christ and the kingdom of Christ as that which is all in all.

The denial of the miracle of the resurrection is not, therefore, the bare denial of a single historical fact, it is a denial of the entire prophetic aspect of the world which Christianity presents ; which finds in the resurrection its beginning in fact. A view of the world which makes the present order of things perpetual, and which considers the eternal to be only a continual present, naturally allows no room for the resurrection of Christ, which is an interruption of the order of this world by the higher order of creation still future ; and which is a witness to the reality of a future life ; yea, it is even that future life itself in the actual present ; the beginning of "the last things," concerning which the Apostles witness that we who live after the resurrection of the Lord live "in these last times" (1

Peter i. 20), and that it now remains for the risen Saviour again to manifest Himself to judge both the quick and the dead. This, the Christian view of the world, overthrows the mythical interpretation of the resurrection advocated now-a-days, and the biblical criticism resting thereupon. As Hegel omitted this Christian escatology, it was natural that those who followed in the steps of his philosophy should go on to deny the resurrection as something which had no foundation in fact. And when Schleiermacher, though reverence for apostolic testimony prevented his denying the fact of the resurrection, yet could attribute to it no doctrinal significance, nor draw any inference from it ; this in like manner arose from the well-known uncertainty and indistinctness of his teaching in relation to future and final realities. Among modern religious philosophers Steffens may be named as having asserted the prophetic significance of the resurrection in connection with a noble view of nature.

Criticism has taken great exception to the want of harmony in particulars, which marks the accounts of the resurrection given by the Evangelists ; and the inference is drawn from this, that those accounts lack an historical basis. But we challenge any impartial critic, assuming for the sake of argument that the resurrection did take place, to ask himself whether it was not to be expected that the great and unequalled impression which that event must have made upon the first witnesses of it, would not naturally have incapacitated them from treating all the minute circumstances connected with it microscopically, and would not involve a want of exact harmony in their accounts of it ? while the main assertion of the fact of the manifestation of the risen Saviour, must have been the same on the part of them all. In other words, whether, upon the supposition that the resurrection did take place, we must not expect to find the accounts of it, generally speaking, just as we do find them ? If, on the contrary, we suppose that the resurrection did not really take place, we are brought face to face with the psychological impossibility, that the disciples, who upon the death of the Lord had sunk low in despondency and were in a despairing state, should suddenly be able to inspirit themselves by means of a self-invented vision, which appeared equally to them all, nobody knows how; and criticism must submit to the difficulty of explaining how the disciples were transported into that visionary state (for deception is inconceivable in this case), in which they saw this imaginary resurrection.

There is, however, a greater difficulty and contradiction than that between the several evangelists when compared together; a difficulty which is not divided among them severally, but which occurs equally in each. It is this:—All the four gospel accounts of the resurrection seem to introduce two contrasted representations concerning the nature of the resurrection-body of the Lord. The risen One seems now to live a natural human life, in a body such as He had before His death. He has flesh and bones, He eats and drinks: again, on the contrary, He seems to have a body of a spiritual transcendental kind, which is independent of the limitations of time and space; He enters through closed doors, He stands suddenly in the midst of the disciples, and as suddenly becomes invisible to them. This contradiction, which occurs in the appearances of the risen Saviour during the forty days, may be explained upon the supposition, that during this interval His body was in a state of transition and of change, upon the boundary of both worlds, and possessed the impress or character both of this world and the next. Not until the moment of the ascension can we suppose that His body was fully glorified and freed from all earthly limitations and wants, like the spiritual body (σῶμα πνευμαιχόν) of which Paul speaks (1 Cor. xv. 44).

§ 173.

The ascension of the Lord forms the close of the resurrection and the perfecting expression and act of the exaltation. We cannot conceive of heaven as any distinct place—some sphere, some distant world, or the like—some distinct "where," according to the ideas of our present sensible perceptions; because heaven is everywhere that God is. Yet we must persuade ourselves of some more definite place in heaven where the cosmical, the created life, is perfectly realized; where God himself is all in all; where the fragmentary, the imperfect, inseparable from existence in time, is lifted up into the fulness of eternity. Christ is received up into heaven, and this involves the glorious truth that He is received up into a sphere in which His life and being are in perfect harmony with His nature. Even concerning His earthly existence He could say that He was in heaven (John iii. 13); yet He also declared that He must leave the world and go unto the Father (John xvi. 28), for He still was subject to the limitations of time and of development. His heavenly life, now that He is ascended, is the expression of His perfect union with the Father;—"I am in the Father, and the Father in Me;"—and it is equally the expression of His perfect Being in redeemed humanity;—"I am in them and the Father in Me" (John xvii. 12). During His earthly life He could compare Himself to the Vine, and believers to the branches; yet He also said, "I, if I be lifted up from the earth, will draw all men unto me!" (John xii. 32). When He was lifted up above the limits of time and space, then for the first time was He able perfectly to unfold and display His organic relations to the children of men, by the all-attractive power of His Spirit and His Word.

§ 174.

Holy Scripture describes Christ's heavenly glory as His "sitting on the right hand of the Father" (Mark xvi. 19). The *right hand of the Father* (ἐκ δεξιῶν τοῦ Θεοῦ) means the power of the Father, and conveys the same idea as that expressed by the words, "All power is given unto Me in heaven and on earth." This kingly power of Christ is not exactly the same as His divine power, which was revealed in the first creation, and belonged to the Son as the λόγος. The *power of Christ,* manifested upon His exaltation, is not a creative, but a perfecting power, penetrating all ranges of creation, spiritual and natural, and perfecting the works of His omnipotence in the first creation. This kingly power of Christ is not revealed in its full strength and widest range, whereby all at last shall be subdued unto Him, until after His exaltation.

§ 175.

The session of Christ at the right hand of the Father must

not be taken as a state of inactive rest. The declaration, " My Father worketh hitherto, and I work," still holds true of Christ after His exaltation. The session of Christ must be viewed as compatible with, and inseparable from, that eternal activity by which He reveals His kingly power. A twofold activity must be recognized here ; an activity in relation to the Father, and an activity in relation to the world. The one is expressed by the representation of Him as our Advocate, making intercession for us to the Father (*intercessio Christi*) (Rom. viii. 34 ; 1 John ii. 1 ; Heb. ix. 24). The other is expressed by the term His *second advent,* which includes His continual and progressive coming to establish His kingdom in the world, and His coming to the faithful for their salvation, and to the world for judgment. When we say that He *sits* at the right hand of the Father, that He *intercedes* for us with the Father, that He *comes* again into the world, we express only different aspects of His exaltation.

§ 176.

Christ's intercession for us with the Father denotes that, as Mediator and Reconciler, He continually represents before Him the human family as a race well-pleasing to the Father, such as may be the object of His love. But this movement, *ad intra,* is conditioned by a corresponding action *ad extra,* for Christ continually comes to the human family, and penetrates it with His holy energy, with His personal and progressive workings. As the redemption of the human race is not a mere process of nature, but is conditioned on the part of the race by the power of freedom and conscience ; so also the spiritual coming of Christ, now set forth, is conditioned by an historical *economy,* according to which mankind are brought progressively under His influence, and are made susceptible of His active power. As it is He who comes in the Spirit, He comes alike in His *Word* and in His *Sacraments ;* and by this progressive advent, He obtains an ever-strengthening hold upon humanity, an ever-deepening root ; and can continually confirm before the Father the efficacy of His redemptive work. As His organic relations to humanity are thus subject to a beginning and a growth, we must recognize a rising and an increase also in His heavenly glory. It may be said even of Him who has gone up heavenward that He grows and advances, not indeed in wisdom, but "in favour with God and man;" in blessedness and fulness of life;—a growth which shall reach its consummation, its ἀκμή, when His Church, which is His spiritual Body, shall have arrived at maturity and perfection; when all things shall be gathered together under Him as under the Head. " Till we all come in the unity of the faith, and of the knowledge of the Son of God unto a perfect man, unto the measure of the stature of the fulness of Christ" (Eph. iv. 13.)

Observations.—Though Christ has continued to be the personal Head of the human race ever since His departure from earth, He refrains from all personal and visible appearances. The influence of such appearances upon earth has been either impersonal and merely ideal, so that the personality has been obscured by the thing bestowed; or so far as their activity has been personal, it possessed only a narrow and transitory reality for a single point in the organism of humanity, and passed away into the visionary realm of mere memory. He who has gone up to heaven, on the contrary, is not merely an historical Person, but is above all history, and continues to penetrate and to fill all history with His presence : all regeneration and salvation proceeds from His personal working; and there can be no workings of the Holy Ghost in the Church which are not in reality the workings of Christ. The sensuous understanding takes exception to this doctrine, on the ground that the material limitations of sense must necessarily form a barrier between Christ, who is in heaven, and ourselves, who are on earth. It therefore considers that our relation to Christ is only one of historical recollection, and it refuses to recognize any other kind of influences from Christ which can be called His working, since He appeared upon earth; it disallows that there is any immediate and direct connection of Christ with us now. But a believing perception of the person of Christ necessarily discerns how this material sphere of time and space, in which human nature lives,—this sphere which, in the very conception of it, possesses only a temporary importance, and is limited thereby,—must come to an end, and be transformed, so as to exclude the possibility of that higher and heavenly sphere into which it must be absorbed, being impenetrable,—unpenetrated by Him who is the centre not only of humanity, but of the whole creation. This organic and abiding connection between the Church and her unseen Head is the fundamental mystery upon which the Church reposes, and all minor and individual mysteries rest upon this. This lies at the foundation of the mystery of edification in the congregation of the Church—"I am with you always," and "Where two or three are gathered together in my name, there am I in the midst of them." Upon this foundation the mystery of the Sacraments rests, and, in a word, all Christian mysticism—all that individual experience of a personal fellowship with a heavenly Redeemer (*unio mystica*) described by the Apostle John, with all the intensity of fervent Christian feeling.

§ 177.

The doctrine of the Session of Christ at the right hand of the Father is developed in the doctrine of His Ubiquity; the doctrine that Christ's presence penetrates all things; that He fills all in all (τοῦ τὰ πάντα ἐν πᾶσι πληρουμένου, Eph. i. 23). Christ sits at the right hand of the Father, but the right hand of the Father is every where, (*dextera dei ubique est*), because it means His all-pervading *power;* the ascended Saviour must therefore be everywhere. This is the profound conception of the Lutheran theology; but in the exposition of it, it has overlooked the fact that the omnipotence of Christ is not a world-creating, but a world-perfecting, a world-redeeming power. It makes the kingly power of Christ immediately one with that of the Father, instead of viewing it as the consummation of almighty power; the point from which the powers of redemption and regeneration stream forth into the first, the old creation, which is the presupposed sphere of Christ's kingdom. It thus confounds (as they should not be confounded) the presence of Christ and the presence of the λόγος, a confusion which intimately affects the entire doctrine of the union of divine and human attributes in Christ. (*Communicatio idiomatum*). All that is predicated of the eternal λόγος is predicated of Christ who has ascended up to heaven; the creation of the world, the sus-

taining of the world, and the government of the world, are
attributed to Him.   He who has ascended up not only penetrates with His regenerating and redeeming power the
kingdom of nature, but is everywhere; wherever God's
omnipotence is, there also is Christ, not only in His divine but
in His human nature;—not only in power and in action,
but in immediate personal and bodily presence, though super-
naturally and incomprehensibly;—He fills heaven and earth,
He is in all creation, in every leaf, in every grain of wheat.
If we hold fast and maintain the idea of Christ's presence in
heaven and on earth as thus unlimited, we cannot avoid
evaporizing and doing away with the individuality of Christ;
for even a glorified individuality, a spiritual body, cannot be
conceived of without limitations;—and we are in danger of
that error, which has so often appeared among Mystics and
Theosophists, which loses sight of a personal Christ in the
general life of the godhead; of the Christ of grace and salvation in a pantheistic Christ of nature, who fills heaven and
earth, the air and the sea, who is in every blade of grass, in
every ear of corn, in every vine branch,—so that the whole
creation becomes one great sacrament for those who know
how to see and to use it.   Nothing is more foreign to the
Lutheran faith and the fundamental principle of Lutheranism
than is such a Christ, who is only an allegorical picture in
nature of the real Christ.   Such a view bears the same relation to Lutheranism, as the empty vision bears to the reality;
yet the manner in which that school has developed the doctrine of ubiquity, is not without a false leaning to the pantheistic mode of treating the subject, a mode of thought
adopted by many poets of nature of the last generation who
gave it poetical expression; in the same way as it is found
before them in many of the writings of Lutheran mystics and
Theosophists.

§ 178.

The Reformed doctrinal system adopts a more relative, a
narrower view of Christ's presence; a presence realized by
the working of the Holy Spirit in the soul, and which is
limited to the fellowship of the faithful,—to the Church.
While the Lutheran system lays special stress upon the
cosmical power of Christ, the Reformed Church maintains

specially the eternal prevalence of His ethical and religious influences. While the Lutheran interpretation recognizes Christ throughout nature, and attaches so unlimited an importance to His cosmical influences, that it runs the risk of confounding the Christ of grace and holiness, with a pantheistic Christ of nature; the Reformed Church recognizes the Christ of grace and holiness, but limits the sphere of His energy to the kingdom of the souls of men; and hence runs the risk of losing sight of Christ's cosmical power. While Lutheranism inculcates a universal presence of Christ, which is the deepest mystery in nature, the reformed doctrine acknowledges only the moral, religious, and spiritual influences of a Christ who has gone up to heaven. The world of nature and of matter is quite impenetrable to Christ, who in His present state submits to the general laws of sense and corporeity. We have not here, therefore, any mystery of nature but only a subjective mysticism, in which the soul experiences communion with the ascended Lord. In a literal sense, He who has gone up into heaven is separated from His Church;—high above the stars He sits enthroned at the right hand of the Father,—an expression which, according to this view, denotes a distinct and actual *place* in heaven;—He cannot Himself in bodily form come down into this material sphere of time and space, but He holds fellowship with the souls of men by the secret workings of His spirit. This is a point of doctrine which specially appears in the explanation of the Sacrament maintained by the Reformed Church, in which is recognized a psychical or spiritual mystery, but no mystery or miracle of nature. By making the world, nature, and corporeity, wholly impenetrable by Christ, and separate from Him, the Reformed doctrine misses the idea of Christ as the perfecter of the world; for in this capacity He is the Redeemer and perfecter, not only of spirit and soul, but also of body and nature; and it necessarily belongs to the Christian view, not only that the realm of souls be penetrated by Christ's spirit, but that the realm of body, the material world, be penetrated by His glorified corporeity.

§ 179.

If we desire a doctrine of ubiquity which shall be free from the two contrasted extremes which I have described, we must

seek it according to the principles already developed in that
view of the kingly power of Christ which defines it, not as
direct omnipotence, but as a world-perfecting power, penetrating *in progressive* development all ranges of creation in
nature and in history. The presence of Christ in the universe must be looked upon, not so much as an actual *being*,
but rather as an essential *becoming;*—it must be treated of
as a progressive advent, a continual coming, in virtue of
which, by the growing development of His fulness, He makes
Himself the centre of the whole creation ; and the creation
itself is thus being prepared and created anew as a living,
organic, and growing *temple of Christ*. The kingdom of believing souls, the church, is the innermost circle of His pervading presence. He fills it with His power, His workings,
and His gifts, by the agency of the Holy Ghost. But in all
His gifts to His believing people, He gives *Himself*. " I
live," says the apostle, " no longer myself, but Christ liveth
in me." The presence of Christ is displayed with growing
power, not in the Church alone, but in the world also. Uninterruptedly He comes into the history of the world, not only
with the might of judgment, which spiritually discerns between
the true and the false, and the presence of which is recognized
in the *signs of the times;* but with redeeming and perfecting
power, which attracts to Himself, as the Head, all that is truly
spiritual, and penetrates it with His sanctifying energy.
Once more ; in the realm of spirits, as well as in the history
of the world, is His presence displayed with growing power ;
for time and space cannot raise any insuperable barrier to His
advance.

As therefore the separation between soul and body, matter
and spirit, is done away with in the risen Saviour, who has
passed into the heavens, the kingdom of matter and of nature,
as well as that of spirit, is open to His workings. In the
Sacraments, which are the expression of the most sacred presence of the Ascended Lord, in His Church, He makes the
kingdom of nature and of sense the instrument and means of
those secret workings by which He makes believers partakers
of the reality, not only of His spiritual, but of His glorified
corporeal nature, and nourishes and strengthens in them the
future men of the resurrection. But the perfect revelation of

this, His spiritual and corporeal presence, will not be made until the fulness of time, in the last great transformation of the world ; when the spirit-world, the world of souls, and the world of matter, shall be blended together into one great kingdom, the kingdom of glory (*regnum gloriæ.*) Thus will the whole creation be builded together into a holy temple in the Lord ; thus will its great manifoldness be illuminated by the glory of One—Christ, who filleth all in all. Yet it always holds true of Christ's presence, as of the divine omni-presence generally, that its appearance, both as to the nature of it and the manner of it, is determined by the distinctive natures and susceptibilities of the several ranges of creation.

§ 180.

We conclude by repeating the caution, that in this doctrine there must ever be kept in view the distinction between the action of the Son as Mediator, in the revelation of the λόγος, and in the revelation of the Christ ; between His world-creating and world-perfecting energy. This distinction will have force and hold good even if we suppose that the king-dom of glory has appeared to us. Even in the life of the redeemed we cannot conceive that the relation of contrast between God, the Creator, and the creature, will be entirely removed, because it is involved in the relation of union. We must also distinguish a two-fold activity in the Godhead. The one activity *proceeds forth* from God, establishes and sustains created life in a relative existence apart from God ; and this is exactly the conception of an all-creating, all-sus-taining, all-enduring λόγος-energy. The other activity *leads back* to God, and makes perfect, transforming the relation of contrast into one of union, that God may be all in all : this is exactly the conception of the Christ-energy. This twofold Mediatorial activity can never be conceived of as suspended or destroyed.

The kingly dominion of Christ expresses the idea of a future kingdom of glory, and the idea also of a heavenly kingdom upon earth, in which Christ himself is the invisible Head. Both these ideas find their further development in the doctrine of the Spirit.

THE DOCTRINE OF THE SPIRIT.

THE PROCESSION OF THE SPIRIT FROM THE FATHER AND
THE SON.

§ 181.

IN the inner life of God as revealed to man, the SPIRIT is God
returning in upon Himself,* the heavenly master-builder, who
brings the eternal possibilities of the Son to an inward reality.
(Compare *The Doctrine of the Trinity,* § 56). That distinguishing activity which belongs to the Spirit in the Trinity
of absolute existence, belongs to Him also in the Trinity of
the economy. In the beginning of the creation the Spirit of
God moved upon the face of the waters; by the Spirit of God,
the divine Logos sowed the holy seed in men's hearts, and
spoke through the prophets, before the coming of Christ,
among both Jews and Heathens. And as the Spirit of God
brooded over the waters in the beginning of the first creation, so likewise by the agency of the same Spirit upon
humanity, our sinful nature is prepared for and made capable
of the second, the new creation. In virtue of His power,
Christ could be conceived and born of a woman; and since
Christ has been manifested it is the Spirit who glorifies Him.

As in the preceding sections we have designated Christ
the Perfecter of the world, this name must also be given to
the Spirit, but in a different sense. What Christ is in unity,
the Spirit is in manifoldness. The design of the world is
ideally accomplished in Christ; but it is through the Spirit

-----

* 1 Cor. ii. 10-12, "God hath revealed them unto us by his Spirit; for the
Spirit searcheth all things, yea, the deep things of God," &c.

that the one Christ obtains a place in the manifoldness of souls, and that the kingdom of God comes in the world. Here also is the Spirit the heavenly master-builder, who moulds the fulness of the Son into a temple of glory ; who models and prepares the manifold natural idiosyncracies of men and the distinctive peculiarities of nations into an organ for the one Christ.

Observations.—In describing the Spirit as the forming and glorifying principle, we have given a definition which may be taken to apply to every spirit. We discern a revelation of the Spirit, wherever we perceive a plastic architectural power in manifest activity. As the Spirit is the moulding principle, He is not the first but the last ; and as it is true of every spirit that its dominion is conditioned by its circumstances, upon these depends what depth it fathoms, what mystery of life it solves and forms. Accordingly, the Christian doctrine of the Trinity places the Spirit in indissoluble union with the Father and the Son. It recognises the Spirit as He "who does not speak of Himself," but draws continually from the fulness of Christ. The philosophic idealism of our day has in many respects become Formalism, because it would make all, not only in religion, but in the various departments of life, to consist of Spirit ; without considering the material of life upon which the Spirit works, without having any regard to the mystery of life, which the Spirit is to make clear. Were the Spirit separated from His given conditions, He would speak only of His own, and would be bare spirit. "He shall not speak of Himself but He shall take of my fulness, and shall glorify me ;" this declaration of Christ is true of the Spirit's method in every range of life. It is universally true that the spirit must derive its origin from a *living* source ; and it is as certain that the philosophic and poetic idealism which separates itself from the springs of life can present only barren forms of truth, unreal forms of art.

§ 182.

The Spirit who proceeds from the Father and the Son, and who is Himself divine, designates Himself in Scripture as the *Holy* Spirit. He is thus distinguished from all the spirits of this world, not only because these have fallen into sin, but because, according to their original idea, they pursue altogether different aims. The spirits of this world, whether the spirits of nations or of states, spirits of art or of science, have for their object the establishment and spread of their kingdom, and individual persons serve only as means or instruments towards this end. These spirits accordingly only ask the question, How may individuals be wanted in the service of the idea," to help towards its realization ? no matter what the individual may be in his earthly sphere : they do not ask concerning the individual himself, and for his own sake. The Holy Ghost, on the contrary, aims at establishing a kingdom of redeemed and blessed persons ; His object is the salvation of souls. " I seek not yours, but you," said the Apostle Paul, (2 Cor. xii. 14) ; " I seek not your natural help and bounty, not man or woman, Jew or Greek, but you yourselves, the hidden man of the heart in you." The Spirit's aim is indeed always a kingdom, but a kingdom in which each individual soul is sought for, for its own sake ; a temple in which each stone is itself a temple (2 Cor. vi. 16). This temple, the spiritual abode of God, which consists of many, nay, of innumerable abodes of God, is the Church of Christ, the assembly and communion of the saints.

Observations.—The conception or idea of the Church brings back our thoughts to the LORD, from whom the Spirit proceeds ; to Christ as King ;—and together with Him, to those whom Christ appointed ;—to the office of Apostle, and to that of teacher. The idea of the Church, again, leads on our thoughts to individuals and souls. By the one is chiefly or mainly expressed the objective, and, by the other, the subjective aspect of the kingdom of God, in its revelation in the course of history.

§ 183.

As the Son did not reveal Himself fully until He became man in the act of His incarnation, so the Spirit does not fully manifest Himself until He comes not only as a temporary visitor, but as taking up a permanent abode, and forming an abiding union with mankind, until He becomes the Spirit working in Christ's kingdom. It is only as *the Spirit of Christ* that the Holy Ghost can enter upon an abiding union with mankind. When the ideal union of the divine nature with pure and sinless human nature, was accomplished, when the Mediator between God and the kingdom of God had come, then only could the kingdom itself advance in power, then only could that general union of the divine nature with sinful human nature be accomplished, which is the copy or fac-simile of the union of these natures in Christ. In Christ dwells the fulness of the Godhead bodily ; in Christ the union of the two natures is such that the human nature possesses no individuality apart from or before its union with the divine. But in the case of the Spirit, human souls possess a natural and earthly individuality, apart from and before their union with Him ; and they need to be transformed by the Holy Ghost, by little and little, into the image of that perfection, which belongs naturally and essentially to Christ. While, however, this union of the Spirit with sinful humanity is not precisely the same as that which took place in the Incarnation, but is an *inhabitation*, it is none the less a permanent, yea, an indissoluble union. For as the union of natures in the person of Christ can never be dissolved, but must continue through eternity, so, in virtue of the mediatorial office of Christ, the Holy Ghost dwells for ever in the kingdom of Christ ; and amid all earthly and national or party spirits which bear sway in history, He, the Holy Spirit, will ever reveal Himself as the strongest. " He who is in us is greater than he that is in the world." (1 John iv. 4.)

Observations.—In thus describing the Holy Ghost as the Holy Spirit dwelling in the Church, we do not take away His personality, but rather confirm it. It is only because He is in Himself a holy and a personal Spirit that He can be the Spirit in the community of the holy, that He can have for His object the salvation of individuals, or can become the heavenly Pastor. An impersonal and indefinite Spirit in the Church—the Spirit of the Church—could only work more or less blindly and instinctively, and for this reason could not be the Holy Ghost ; such a spirit could only have a general influence, it could not make the winning of individual souls its aim. It is the pantheistic element of Spinoza in Schleiermacher which leads him to describe the Spirit as an impersonal Spirit in the

Church, and thus unavoidably to confound the Spirit of
God with the created and sinful spirit of man.

§ 184.

As the Spirit has been sent into the world by Christ, and
evermore is and will be sent (*procedit a patre filioque*,
John xv. 26), He, the Holy Ghost, reveals Himself as the
Spirit of *Gospel history,*—the Spirit of Tradition handed down
to us pure and unfalsified. Were it conceived possible that
the Spirit could separate himself from sacred history, He
would cease to be the Spirit of Revelation, and would become
only a mythical, mystical, and apocryphal spirit. In opposition to this it must be affirmed that the Holy Ghost is far
more than the Spirit of Tradition. He is not only the Spirit
of *Recollection,* but the Spirit of *Illumination ;* He not only
puts us in remembrance of Christ (John xiv. 26) as an historical person who once lived on earth, but He ever proceeds
from Christ as from the ever-living Saviour, and glorifies Him,
as the object of the soul's contemplation, and as in the soul
itself. "He shall glorify me, for he shall take of mine, and
shew it unto you (John xvi. 14.) Thus it is that while the
Spirit represents Himself in a dependent relation to Christ,
this relation is nevertheless one of freedom and individuality,
so that He never ceases to be the free *creating* Spirit. If the
Holy Ghost were merely the Spirit of tradition, the Church
could never have sung *Veni* CREATOR *Spiritus !* But as He
is the Spirit not of Tradition only, but of enlightenment and
glory, He is the life-giving, liberating, and plastic Spirit. All
that the Spirit moulds is after the pattern of Christ ; and
speaking after the manner of men, we may say, that as the
human artificer regards in every work some eternal and ideal
pattern which is ever in his mind, and embodies this his fundamental thought in his manifold productions, so the Holy Spirit,
the great invisible Master-builder and Artificer of the temple,
has ever before Him the model and pattern of Christ, and does
nothing but what He seeth the Son doeth. But inasmuch
as the Spirit ever moulds human nature according to the one
original type, yet into ever new forms, ever new repetitions
and varieties, He reveals Himself as the Spirit of freedom, who
displays eternal truth. The principle of free development,
continually creating the new upon earth, He renews and

restores to youth and vigour the life of Christ in individual souls, and in the entire kingdom of Christ; He moulds the Christian doctrine and worship into new forms. He devises and finds out new means and plans for the spread of the kingly empire of Christ. He, the holy, ever-present principle of Providence, reveals Himself as the PARACLETE, who, on the one hand, convinces the world of sin, of righteousness, and of judgment (John xvi. 8 ;) and, on the other hand, as the Comforter not only of individual souls, but of the Church, wherein all the promises of history find their accomplishment. As the ever-present principle of renewal and of living development, He proves Himself the Spirit of *power;* and thus through Him the kingly dominion of Christ never dies away, never grows old.

It is evident from what has been said, that the relation subsisting between the operations of the Spirit and the kingly activity of Christ in His Church, may be described as one of *simultaneousness* and unison. There is no operation of the Spirit in the Christian fellowship which is not in reality a display of Christ's working; " He shall take of mine and shew it unto you ;" and conversely, there is no act of Christ's which is not carried on by the Spirit, " for no one can say that Jesus Christ is Lord, but by the Holy Ghost" (1 Cor. xii. 3.) This mutual and simultaneous working of the Lord and of the Spirit is manifested in the ESTABLISHMENT, the MAINTENANCE, and the PERFECTING of the Church.

THE ESTABLISHMENT AND MAINTENANCE OF THE CHURCH.

§ 185.

Essentially the Church was founded by Christ during His life on earth, but outwardly and actually it began with the outpouring of the Holy Spirit on the day of Pentecost ; it was established, in other words, by Inspiration. Inspiration is the entrance of the Spirit of God into the human spirit, thus forming a permanent union ; and it corresponds with the miracle of the Incarnation. It is the setting apart of the Church as the instrument whereby the world shall be made Christian and be born again; as the channel through which the redemption and fulness of life which are in Christ shall be imparted to sinful humanity. Nothing was more unlikely, no supposition is more untenable, than the notion, that the Church might have been introduced into the world merely by a series of human impulses and outward circumstances, of pious recollections and holy feelings; or, again, by a number of sporadic, vague, and instinctive movements and agitations of the divine Spirit. Upon such a supposition the Church would have been launched upon the world, wandering to and fro after a principle for its development, and driven, like a ship without helm or compass, now in this direction, now in that. At the best, by such uncertain and haphazard beginnings, a multiplicity of religious sects and Gnostic schools would have been set up; but certainly not a CHURCH, a living organization for revelation and redemption, spreading itself wide through all times and nations, and flowing throughout history with a full tide of revealed truth and grace. The Christian Church could not have been ushered into the world except by a definite act, declaring her to be " the new creature " in Christ, who was to be developed through all time, to increase and grow up into Christ who is the Head; and who possesses the all-embracing principle of her future development, in the new regenerate consciousness with which she is endowed. The first act by which the Church made known her existence and power in the world, must have been an assertion and display of that principle of development whereby a new history was set up among men; and accordingly the Church does begin with the *fulness of the Spirit*, with the full and sweeping power of holy energies, graces, and gifts. The first stage of the Church's historic development, I mean the apostolic age, was not the most imperfect, but on the contrary, the most intensively perfect. As Christ, the new Adam, is the first begotten among many brethren, not only because He is the first member of a newly developed race— first in the order of time—but also because He stands foremost as a model for all; in like manner the Apostolic Church may be said to be the first born among many sisters in relation to following states of the Church, and succeeding epochs of church history; because all the development which followed depends upon and is measured by her internal and essential wealth, by her primitive excellence and fulness.

Observations.—The development of the natural spirit and genius of the Church confirms the fact that as a new spiritual creation, it must have begun, not with a mere approximation to, but essentially with the fulness of, the Holy Spirit. We have indeed, in the early church, a model which is only relative, because the development of its natural spirit was in many ways limited and interrupted. Yet must we not allow that the period of its first inspiration, when its true genius was first manifest, and won its earliest results, must be taken as the prototype of its entire subsequent development; a development which, though advancing in a certain course of productions, must nevertheless be considered as already planned and included in its fundamental intuitions? Must it not be said that the law of normal development concerning genius is, that it remain true to its primary inspiration, that amid the later struggles of reflection, it abide by those fundamental intuitions by which the Spirit revealed Himself to it, and elected it as His instrument? Now so far as the Church may be viewed as one great and spiritual individual, its inspiration must be the same as regards its development, with that of the most highly gifted genius among men. The period of its first inspiration must be the rule for all subsequent advances. The true existence and reality of the church is manifest only in that life and activity which preserves its connection with its primary inspiration; in every activity different from this it departs from its proper genius, and derives its strength from the working of some alien spirit.

It has been ingeniously remarked, that there were authors who had not yet received their pentecost; and that we may suppose genius to exist, which has not yet received the power of actually beginning its productivity. The spirit, the invisible master builder, had not yet come upon them in his plastic power. This view serves to explain the position of the Apostles before the outpouring of the Spirit. Essentially they possessed the Spirit in the manifestation of Christ, and His election of them; but they were not yet possessed by Him actively, they were still unproductive. The *susceptibility* for inspira-

Y

tion was developed in them when the visible presence of Christ was taken from them, and they sat still and waited in retirement at Jerusalem.

INSPIRATION AND THE APOSTOLIC OFFICE.

§ 186.

Inspiration could only have its beginning with a breaking forth of the Spirit of God in the natural spirit of man. The Apostles were assembled together on the Day of Pentecost, when suddenly they were filled with the Holy Ghost, and spake with tongues (Acts ii. 3). There has been much disputation as to the meaning of this gift of tongues, but we may content ourselves with the explanation given by the Apostle Paul, who describes it as a state in which consciousness is not active, a state of ecstasy or of transport, the outward result of new spiritual impulses and strong movements in the depths of the soul; and it bore the character rather of a spiritual ecstasy of nature, than of clear and living consciousness.[*] This speaking with tongues was the outward expression of the first extraordinary penetrating and overflowing inspiration by which the Apostles felt their whole being thrilled, as if by a lightning flash. They felt themselves carried away with the overwhelming power which came upon them; and hence arose the impious explanation which refused to recognize the real import of the occurrence, and mocked them as drunken, saying, "These men are full of new wine." But when the others, who were present, heard them speak, every man in his own tongue in which he was born, we need not suppose that they spoke different languages, but that each one for himself, in his own inward individuality, felt himself addressed; that the inner man of the heart in each so felt himself spoken to in this language of ecstasy, that his soul was roused from its natural and wonted narrowness, and was in a wonderful manner revealed to itself.[†] We need not, however, suppose that the circumstance of ecstasy constituted the Inspiration. It denoted only the moment of the spiritual

---

[*] 1 Cor. xiv. 2-4. "He that speaketh in an unknown tongue speaketh not unto men, but unto God; for no man understandeth him, howbeit in the spirit he speaketh mysteries."

[†] Compare Steffens, Religions-philosophie, ii. 346.

birth, when the spirit broke the husk of naturalness, and it at once passed on into a state of clear consciousness and discretion. The distinct and historical consciousness of revelation ensued upon and rose out of the transient state of agitated nature. Natural religious powers were brought under the government of historical development; speaking with tongues passed into prophesying, and Peter came forward, spoke the word of salvation in a thoughtful sermon, explained the event as having its foundation in the economy of revelation, and as the fulfilment of the predictions of the prophets; he proclaimed that the Dispensation established by Christ was now being realized in its power, and exhorted to repentance and baptism ; and about three thousand were on that day baptized. Thus the great event terminated with the preaching of the apostolic mission, and with the first all-embracing missionary baptism. Everything was organized on an historical and ecclesiastical basis, and we may take Peter's sermon as a type of the actual consciousness of revelation which now appeared among the Apostles. The new apostolic tongue which thenceforward spoke on every hand throughout the world and explained the mysteries of the kingdom of God to the wise and to the unlettered, was to be a glowing tongue, a tongue of fire ; but it possesses this characteristic, that it speaks words which are intelligible, sound, and accurate.*

Observations.——If that first gift of tongues had not given way to prophecy, but had remained as an isolated phenomenon, the apostles would have been looked upon only as " the awakened," and extravagance and fanaticism would probably have ensued. Paul found it already necessary to warn the Church against overrating and unduly prizing this outward display of spiritual influence ; and he urges that prophesying, that is, the clear and easily to be understood word of revelation, is a far higher gift. The history of the Church most amply teaches, that in times of spiritual influences and awakening, if the religious powers are not historically organized, extravagance and error are the inevitable result.

* 2 Tim. i. 13. " Hold fast the form of sound words which thou hast heard of me."—Titus ii. 2.

§ 187.

The day of Pentecost may be viewed as a type of the whole period during which INSPIRATION continues, the period whose essential principles are presented in the apostolic history. Inspiration was not confined exclusively to the apostles. Not only men who stood near the apostles—a Stephen, for example, or a Barnabas—a Mark, or a Luke—were thus inspired; but we often find that a manifestation like that on the day of Pentecost was experienced in the case of private individuals admitted into the Church, of whom we read, " They spake with tongues and prophesied."* But as this whole period, including the birth and infancy of the Church, is spoken of as the period of inspiration, we must necessarily assume different *degrees* of inspiration, and allow that inspiration has been possessed in different degrees at different times. We must attribute the fulness of inspiration as appropriate and necessary to that inner circle of those who from the beginning had been followers of the Lord, and who were set apart by His own holy election to be the pillars and buttresses of His Church. Inasmuch as the Holy Ghost is the Spirit of sacred history, *they* must in an especial manner have been singled out as the instruments of inspiration, who had been with our Lord from the beginning, who possessed the clearest perceptions of Him, and were the possessors of the true tradition : and again, inasmuch as the Holy Ghost is the Spirit who not only brings to remembrance the things of Christ historically, but who glorifies Him, *they* must especially have been selected as the organs of inspiration whom the Lord had set apart to Himself out of the world, admitted to His confidence, and whom He had thus cleansed and sanctified.

Observations.—When the eleven apostles, after the apostacy and death of Judas Iscariot, completed their circle by the election of a new apostle, both Joseph and Matthias (Acts i. 23), who were set apart as candidates, possessed the qualification of having been with the Lord from the beginning to the end of His public life ; and the apostles

---

* Acts xix. 6. Compare also Acts viii. 17 ; x. 45.

themselves considered them as belonging to an apostolic class, to the original number of Christ's followers, from among whom the candidates for the apostleship were to be chosen.* These men seemed to hold a position similar to that of the apostles; the apostles looked upon them as being upon the same footing with themselves, so that they did not hesitate to leave it for decision to the mere casting of a lot, in order to discover (ἀνάδειξον ὅν ἐξελέξω) the actual election of the Lord. As to the apostle Paul, he certainly did not originally belong to this sacred and primary stock, but as a wild branch he was afterwards grafted upon it. His apostleship depended upon an extraordinary call. He was chosen by the Lord in that wonderful revelation which took place on the way to Damascus, to which he always refers his apostleship; and though he had not known Christ after the flesh, and was not, in the sense in which the others were, a possessor or depository of the sacred tradition, yet we must allow that he stood in such a relation to those who were pillars (Gal. i. 18; ii. 9) that he must have received of the Lord a perfect understanding of the sacred history—a knowledge of it so perfect that he could deliver to the Church historical facts of our Lord's life as something which he had received from Him (1 Cor. xi. 23).

§ 188.

As the instruments of the Holy Spirit in the establishment of the church, the apostles were in a position of the most absolute dependence upon Him: and yet they possessed the fullest freedom. "It is not ye that speak," said our Saviour to them (Matt. x. 20), "but the Spirit of your Father who speaketh in you." The Truth was in them, undarkened by error or by human imperfection. So far, however, from losing their personal characteristics and talents by becoming the Spirit's instruments, the apostles became in their own persons witnesses of the power of the Spirit in building up individual character, permanent types of Christian individuality and character; and accordingly the apostolic age may be appropriately called the age of HEROES, or

* Compare Schleiermacher: Dei Chr. Glaube ii. 364.

representative men, following upon the age when the Lord himself dwelt among men. Their relation, therefore to the Spirit must be looked upon not as one of bondage, but of *freedom* and development ; and their inspiration must be described as the progressive communication of the Spirit, going hand in hand with the progressive development of consciousness and of freedom. But the revelation of the Spirit was given to them for this purpose, *to profit withal* (πρὸς τὸ συμφέρον,) 1 Cor. xii. 7 ; and the progressive development of inspiration in the apostles was therefore conditioned by the historic relations and the historic progress of the apostolic church. The revelation of the Spirit was given to them only for their official work. As church questions arose in the course of church history, and moulded themselves into form (Acts xv. 10), questions relating to doctrine or church organization, the Spirit gave them the power of deciding ; and the decision which was thus given them from above came also from within, from the depths of their own consciousness. "It seemed good to the Holy Ghost and *to us.*" These words concerning the apostolic council at Jerusalem clearly express the freedom of self-consciousness in inspiration.

Observations.—As to our Lord's words to Peter, "Thou art Peter, and upon this rock will I build my church," we must not infer from them what the Romish Church has endeavoured to maintain. We may, however, take them as indicating the great importance and weight attaching to apostolic individuality. We may indeed say that not Peter, but the Faith, and the knowledge of the Faith, is the ROCK on which the Lord builds His Church ; but the church cannot be established by the faith or the knowledge of the faith *in abstracto ;* it cannot be built up by such impersonal instruments ; instruments only instinctively and dimly conveyed by the power of the Spirit to men's minds ;—yet this must have been more or less the case had the church been given over to a conglomerate and unorganized life. The church, as such, could not have been founded save by particular men, in whom the Holy Spirit who pervaded all attained the freest and most personal revelation. As the believing Peter, prompt to confess his Lord, stood at that moment before Him as the representative of the apostles, the Saviour designates *him* "the rock" of the faith; and thus expresses the value and importance of what was personal and distinctive in the characters of His apostles, as furthering the establishment of His church. It holds true concerning every age of the church's history, that its development cannot progress, cannot surmount the agitation to which it is liable, unless its spirit be centralized in individuals, from whom an organizing energy may go forth to the many, springing from them as from personal and life-giving fountains: individuals in whose spiritual authority the church finds its attracting and uniting centre, and who therefore may be designated pillars and buttresses of the church. It is evident in all ages of the church, as for example at the time of the Reformation, that the great ecclesiastical characters who speak and work not of themselves, but actuated by the spirit of the age in which they live, and which they embody,—are the heroes of freedom and self-determination, in whom the dependent multitude find their mainstay. What we thus find true in the case of subsequent and relative eras of the church's development must prominently hold good concerning the original era of its development, concerning its first establishment.

§ 189.

As the instruments by whom the Spirit worked in the establishment of the church, the apostles stand in the relation not only of the greatest freedom and unity with the Spirit, but of the greatest freedom and unity one with another. There are diversities of gifts, but the same Spirit; there are diverse forms of apostolic doctrine, but it is the one fundamental truth that actuates them all. It is by distributing His power in different forms and forces that the Spirit reveals His fulness and His stores of wealth. The perfect expression of the Spirit's revelation in the formation of the church is not to be found in the phase of thought or teaching of any one apostle, but in the sum total of apostolic consciousness; and this again is the only perfect embodiment of the church's consciousness regarding its fundamental relations to the Lord and to the Spirit, to the world, and to itself. As the representatives of the mother church, the apostles not only express the consciousness of the church at one particular time, they are the representatives of the Christian Church for all time.

THE ESSENTIAL ATTRIBUTES OR NOTES OF THE CHURCH.

§ 190.

The epoch of inspiration and of extraordinary gifts came to an end; but the Spirit abides permanently in the Church. Inspiration had to do with the establishment of the Church, but not with its subsequent growth. By it the true foundation was laid, the perfect principle of development was bestowed. But what has once for all been given by inspiration still needs to be confirmed, to be expanded, and to be made fruitful throughout a long historical probation. The progressive development of the Church advances in close connection with the life of the world, which is to be renovated and regenerated by the Church. And inasmuch as the Church becomes a power in the history of the world, and developes herself in a free and reciprocal action upon all other agencies in human life and history,—on various nationalities and periods, on various stages of natural enlightenment and cultivation;— she must subject herself in turn to the laws of worldly development. As the Church has travelled on from that paradisaical state which inspiration had described and secured, it cannot be denied that the due relation between the divine and the human in her constitution has been in many respects very inadequately maintained; but this arose from the fact that she had necessarily to submit to the general laws of historical development, and was beset with every form of worldly influence, limiting, from without and from within, her normal growth. But in all vicissitudes of her history, in all changes of her forms of rule and modes of work, the Church has remained essentially the same; after each season of corruption and adulteration she has been renewed again to the purity of her ideal; and thus she furnishes abundant proof that she has never been forsaken by her Founder, that the spirit of her Founder has never left her.

Observations.—We here stand at the very point where Catho-

licism and Protestantism begin to diverge. Placing ourselves in imagination at the point of time when the last
of the Apostles died, we ask the question, "Where is the
Apostolate now?" Catholicism answers—"It is in the
living successors of the Apostles to whom the true tradition is intrusted, in Bishops, Councils, and Pope, who are
to be recognised as the representatives and possessors of
continual Apostolic inspiration." The Evangelical Church,
on the other hand, replies—That the only full and valid
embodiment and expression of the Apostolate is to be
found in Holy Scripture, which is the abiding voice of the
Apostles in the Church. While Catholicism assumes a
progressive inspiration continued through all times, Protestantism traces inspiration back to, and derives it from
the Church's foundation. Historical criticism has now
sufficiently proved, that progressive inspiration, such as
the Catholic Church lays claim to, is the very opposite of
what it gives itself out to be. Ideally, the divergence between the two Churches arises from their entertaining a
widely different conception of what the historical development of the Church really is. Protestantism views the
history of the Church as a *free* development, because with
the Apostolic ideal before it, the Church ever aims at and
endeavours after the perfect union of its divine and human
elements—"Not that I have already attained, either were
already perfect, but I follow after, that I may attain it."
Catholicism looks upon Church development as a mechanical and self-progressive development of tradition, in which
the divine is rendered so prominent that the human element becomes a mere name. Protestantism, on the other
hand, makes the essence of development to consist in their
free reproduction on the part of the Church, by active
labour, and continual efforts of historic reflection, of what
has once for all been given her by inspiration. Catholicism considers development to be a quantitative prolongation of the beginning; forgetting that the various forms
lying dormant in that pregnant beginning must become
manifest in analysis, in free reciprocal relation, and even
in alternate strivings with one another.

§ 191.

The fundamental relation of the Church to her Lord and to His spirit remains firm amid all changes.   The true Church —as the Church of the Holy Ghost, and the Church of Christ —is both INVISIBLE and VISIBLE.   The article of our Creed— " *I believe in* one Christian Church " involves the truth that the Church is not only visible, but moreover that she is invisible ;—otherwise it would have sufficed to say—" *I see* one Christian Church."   The Church is invisible in so far as it is the fellowship of the Saints, a fellowship not merely of *known* but of true believers, scattered among all nations, in all ages, in all conditions and positions ; who, however separated by time and space, nevertheless constitute one spiritual mystical body.   The Church is invisible in so far as it is a kingdom of invisible powers and gracious activities which constitute its organism, and bring it to the fulness of Christ, to the fulness of Him who filleth all in all (Eph. i. 23).   The Church is invisible in so far as Christ its Head is invisible.   But the Church is *visible* in so far as its invisible essence witnesses for itself and makes itself recognisable to the world ;—in so far as its existence is conditioned by the historical revelations of Christ ;—in so far as the workings of grace are conditioned by the *means of grace* appointed by Christ,—by the Word and Sacraments,—and through these, she appears in power.   As, therefore, on the one hand, it holds good of the true Church that we cannot say of her, " Lo here ! or lo there ! " it is on the other hand equally true concerning her, that she is " the city set on an hill which cannot be hid."   Both these truths are expressed in the Augsburg Confession, where the Church is described as a fellowship of the holy in which the gospel is rightly preached, and the sacraments are duly administered— " *Congregatio sanctorum in qua evangelium recte docetur, et recte administrantur sacramenta.**

Observations.—Roman Catholic Theology objects to the notes
    here given of the true church, upon the ground that they
    are inadequate.   Supposing, it is argued, that the right
    preaching of the gospel, and the due performance of the
    sacraments, are the notes of the true church, we must

* Confessio Augustana, Art. vii.   Eph. iv. 4-6 ; Acts ii. 42 ; John xv. 3.

further define what the right preaching of the gospel is,
and what efficacy is to be attributed to those sacraments
which are the true ones. In the case of the Evangelical
Church, this difficulty is solved by the principle that
through the guidance of the Holy Spirit, apart from the
Roman chair, the church is in a position to apprehend for
itself the contents of the gospel, and the true import of
the sacraments; as also the church in the earliest times
pronounced regarding her spiritual apprehension of these
things in her symbols. In Catholicism the outward is
one and all; the Evangelical Church on the contrary
recognises that the truth consists in the reciprocal proportion between the outward notes and inward experience; between what is visible and what is invisible in
the Church; between Tradition and the Spirit. The
very idea of an historically free development necessitates
that this proportion should be variously understood in
the course of church history; and that even opposite
views should be taken of it at different times; and as
long as this development progresses, there will be, yea,
there must be, controversy regarding the question,
"Where is the true church?" unless indeed tangible
proofs can be presented. The visible notes of the church
can avail only for those who recognize and experience the
invisible also.

§ 192.

As there are not Lords many, but one Lord; as there are
not many Spirits, but one Holy Ghost; as there are not
many humanities, but one Humanity; which is to be united
with Christ the Head; so certainly there is but ONE Church
(Eph. iv. 6). But this true unity reveals itself in variety and
manifoldness. We see, even in the first and apostolic church,
how the One Spirit revealed Himself in many gifts, and how
the One Christ is represented in various aspects by the
Apostles. In its relation with the world, with various
nationalities, and at different stages of human development,
the one Church has been divided by a variety of confessions,
and by different *formulae,* or church symbols. The differences
and separations involved in these different confessions must
be viewed as arising from our sinful nature, in so far as they

maintain points of truth exclusively relative and partial, or even errors, to be absolute truth. These various confessions are in reality individual embodiments of Christianity, the germs of which lay hid as *possibilities* in the apostolic church, but which did not become active until the fulness of the times, and which, as they appear, are to be looked upon as so many progressive stages in the education of Christendom and its advance toward perfection. In so far as these differences of Creed are the result of sin, they must be looked upon as perishable fragments, which must be cast away ; but so far as they have their foundation in the necessary varieties of human life, they will be established and purified, and they should be viewed as gifts of grace, and types of apostolic doctrine. These various confessions must be looked upon as various chambers, various dwellings in the house of the one Lord. "In my Father's house are many mansions," (John xiv. 2). To distinguish what is erroneous and sinful in these confessions, from what has its foundation only in the actual varieties of human life, is among the most difficult tasks of ecclesiastical history ; and constitutes the main difficulty in all questions of church union.

§ 193.

The one Church is at the same time the UNIVERSAL Church ; universality or catholicity is the outward and historical expression of its unity. The unity of the Church must thus become manifest in historical activity. If there were not a common, universal bond of ecclesiastical union, historically uniting the various particular churches, the unity of the Church would be merely an ideal thing, a mere invisibility. The ecclesiastical universality, which stands high above all individual differences, whether confessional or national, is the APOSTOLIC. The only really Catholic Church is therefore the Apostolic, because it is founded upon Apostolic tradition, and preserves the connection with the Apostolic mother Church as that tradition advances from generation to generation,— holding fast the primitive and apostolic doctrine as of continual value and universal authority. The authentic statement of this apostolic tradition is furnished in the New Testament; and hence it follows that the really Catholic Church must also be the Church which is conformable to Scripture.

But the present Church has its connection with the apostolic
community in virtue also of that fundamental confession, the
apostolic symbol, in which the early church expresses the
doctrine received from the Apostles, and hands it down as a pattern and type to the present day.   This apostolic confession
of faith was afterwards more accurately defined and developed,
—in opposition to individual and heretical notions,—in the
Nicene and Athanasian creeds.   Throughout church history
these œcumenical symbols have ever been esteemed the fundamental types of all church confessions ; not only on account
of their traditional authority, but on account of their Scripturalness and eternal verity ; and all the various confessions
are tested as forms of the Catholic Church by their recognition of these œcumenical fundamental creeds ; which exist
anterior to and independently of the separations of Greek
Catholic and Roman Catholic, of the Lutheran Church and
the Reformed.

Observations.—This recognition and adoption of the œcumenical fundamentals, in the various confessions of Christian Churches distinguishes them from the sects.   Sects
hold only what is individual and partial, as contrasted
with what is universal and œcumenical.   They profess,
indeed, to connect themselves with apostolic doctrine, but
they have lost the thread of historical development, by
which alone they could thus be really in union therewith.   The confessions, while embodying the various
powers of Christianity, contain—each and all of them—
the common sum total of apostolic doctrine ; whereas the
sects give expression to fragments only (*disjecta membra*),
broken off from the whole.   The sects possess the Christian religion in a sporadic or fragmentary manner.
Having lost connection with historical organization,
they have sunk into merely natural developments, indistinct and fermenting, turbulent, and garish.

Even supposing that the so-called Neo-Catholicism had
its foundation in a deeper religious consciousness than
manifestly it has, it could still be looked upon only as a
sect, because it has divorced itself from primitive Catholicism, and even rejects the Apostle's creed—*symbolum
Apostolicum.*   This Neo-Catholicism is a separation and

Dissent not only from Rome, but from the universal Church.

§ 194.

The Church, one and universal, is also HOLY. True unity and universality have their basis in what is holy, and apart from holiness all is partial and perishable. The holy church stands out distinctly from the world : it does not take its rise from a merely natural development, like the kingdoms of the world, nor from the self-development of the spirit of man. God, the Holy Ghost, is the author and principle of its growth, and its aim is not merely the culture of the human race, but the redemption and sanctification of every man. But inasmuch as the church necessarily has the world within its pale as well as without—the divine spirit being united in her with sinful humanity—her development is not absolutely but only relatively perfect. The church is absolutely faultless as regards her *principle* and her *beginning ;* absolutely faultless also as to her *final aim ;* but in the interval between these extremes, in her historical and free development, her relative fallibility lies. The historical development of the church is not, as Catholicism asserts, normal ; it is subject, like a ship upon the billows, to the undulations of the times ; and there are seasons when she fulfils her mission as " *the steward of the mysteries of God,*" only in a most imperfect way. *Ecclesia potest deficere.* But the Holy Ghost, who abides within her, is her invisible preserver and Reformer, withstanding the encroachments of worldliness ; and though particular churches may lose their spiritual life in the world, the church herself can never become secularized. Notwithstanding corruptions, notwithstanding relative pauses and backslidings, the church holds on her course, and cannot miss her final goal. *Ecclesia non potest deficere.*

§ 195.

The ideal holiness of the Church affects alike the whole community and each individual member, and its healthy development depends upon the reciprocal influences of both these upon each other. The growth of the individual Christian towards Christ-like perfection is conditioned by the degree of perfection attained by the entire fellowship ; and on the other hand, the perfection of the fellowship is influenced

by the state of each individual member;—being advanced by
those in whom the ideal of a free personal vitality is realized,
in whom the idea of a universal priesthood of Christians
(1 Peter ii. 9), has become a truth, and whose piety and
spirituality leaven the entire lump. This mutual relation
between the community as a whole, and the individuals com-
posing it, is traceable in church history, not only as a normal
reciprocity, but even as a counteracting and opposing force,
appearing in a new form time after time, from the first century down to the present day. The Church endeavours after
the attainment of its ideal holiness by a progressive solution
of this contract; by a continual conquest of the extremes
which occur when one side of the relation (whether the individual or the body) is maintained and insisted upon at the
expense of the other. All one-sided Catholicism, all partial
orthodoxy, arises from the circumstance that the Church is
resting satisfied with a holiness that exists only in the community—in the institutions, the doctrines, the representations
of the Church—while it is indifferent to the state of its
individual members, whose piety is considered as a mere
opus operatum. All one-sided Protestantism, Pietism, and
Sectarianism, arises from the fact that holiness is made to
consist in individual character alone, and that these individuals imagine that they can dispense with the Church which
is their mother, or even turn round upon her in fanatical
opposition. In both cases it is only worldliness, only fleshly-
minded selfishness which has supplanted holiness. The
principle of the Reformation promotes the conquest of both
extremes, for its interests are in behalf of the true objective
reality of the church; in behalf of its authority and mater-
nity, quite as much as in behalf of the freedom of each individual Christian man.

§ 196.

For as much as the Church has the world without as well
as within her pale, she is the holy church MILITANT. Whereas
the Roman Catholic Church carries on its contest, chiefly with
the outward world, and is content to rid itself by external
means of the hostile elements which she finds within her, (by
excommunication for example, and the burning of heretics);
the Evangelical Church strives, on the other hand, by spiritual

means to solve the inward contradictions which exist in relation both to doctrine and to practice, to realize her holy ideal, and to obtain the victory over her spiritual foes by the power of the *Spirit* and the *Word.* The true Church, seeing that we have to wage war, "not against flesh and blood, but against principalities, against powers, against spiritual wickedness" (Eph. vi. 12), acknowledges her own sinfulness and her infinite distance from the ideal. "Not as though I had already attained, either were already perfect" (Phil. iii. 12). The true Church is ever putting forth new endeavours to reform and purify herself according to the reforming patterns. We can trace this criticizing and reforming movement in the Church's history from the first century downwards; it never dies; even in the darkness of the middle ages, there have not been wanting witnesses of evangelical truth (*testes veritatis*) who have criticized the corruptions of the Church;—a line of witnesses which cannot fail, because the Holy Ghost has never wholly forsaken His Church. Even in the darkest days the word spoken to the despairing prophet Elijah has been true, "Yet have I left me seven thousand in Israel, who have not bowed the knee before Baal" (1 Kings xix. 18.) A reforming activity appears within the Church in every age; but the chief era of reformation, the greatest reforming *catastrophe,* took place in the sixteenth century; and this is pre-eminently styled *the Reformation.*

§ 197.

The Church militant is also the Church TRIUMPHANT; the gates of hell shall not prevail against her. The Church's victory is not only a final one at the end of time; it is a progressive victory in every age. After the pattern of her Lord, she is herself developed, not only by a progressive course of sufferings, but also in an ever-advancing course of *joyous resurrection.* "Destroy this temple," said our Lord, "and in three days will I raise it up!" This saying holds good in reference to the Church, as well as to our Lord. Herein consists the triumph of the Church in history;—in virtue of the indwelling spirit, she continually renews herself; after every interval of corruption and dissolution, when she lay in ruins, when faith seemed to be vanquished by the world, she has risen anew, like life from the dead. That vision of the prophet Ezekiel—wherein he saw the valley of dry bones, and, behold, they were very dry, and the Spirit of the Lord came from the four winds, and breathed upon the slain, and they lived again, and the breath came into them ;—that vision is a parable of the spiritual resurrection of the Church, repeated in her history from age to age. This fact that the Church has never wholly died out, but ever rises anew from the dead, is a pledge, a certain surety, of her future glory.

§ 198.

The Church's aim, or her appropriation of the grace of God in Christ, is accomplished by the operations of grace and by the means of grace. By the *operations of grace* are to be understood the activities of the Holy Spirit in human nature, in order to redeem it from sin, and to build it up into a new creature in Christ Jesus. But as the Holy Ghost is the Spirit of Christ, His workings are in reality the works of Christ, so that the workings of His grace are carried on through the agency of those *means of grace* which Christ has instituted, through His Word and His Sacraments. The indissoluble connection between the means of grace and the workings of grace, depends not only on the fact that the Holy Spirit proceeds historically from Christ, and testifies of Him, but also upon the truth that He ever proceeds from Christ as the invisible Head of the new creation, which has been begun by Him. Every explanation of the workings of grace, which denies their living connection with the means of grace, leads to a false subjectivity ; to Mysticism, Quakerism, and the like : every theory of the means of grace, which separates them from a life-giving connection with the workings of grace, leads to a false objectivity ; to a literalness of faith, *opus operatum ;* such as is in various ways manifest in Catholicism. The true doctrine of the Church rests upon the organic reciprocity of both the means and the operations of grace ; and these, though distinguished here for the sake of argument, are in life and activity indissolubly connected.

THE OPERATIONS OF GRACE.

§ 199.

The relations in which human nature was at first created

z

require that it shall attain the perfection of its destiny only by means of divine grace, and the sanctifying operations of the Spirit of God. The innate and fundamental principle of human nature is *its* NEED *of God*. Human nature is not created as a nature perfect within itself, but to be the vessel, the instrument of revelation; or a temple for another—a higher nature than itself—for the divine nature. But human nature thus created became sinful by the fall, and needs not only perfecting, but redeeming grace. Nature and grace mutually presuppose one another. Nature seeks after grace like the plant that bends towards the light; for the instinctive longing after the kingdom of God is inextinguishable in sinful humanity; and this leads man on by sense of need, pain, and aspiration towards the fulness of grace. And grace in like manner inclines towards nature, in order to satisfy its need, and to pour its fulness into nature.

FREEDOM AND GRACE.

200.

Although the contrast between nature and grace is done away by Christianity, it still presents itself as the deepest anomaly of human existence; an anomaly which requires practically to be solved in every human life, and which therefore presents itself in manifold forms to human thought. In its original and essential form it is the anomaly between freedom and grace; for freedom is the purest expression of human nature, the distinctive feature of humanity. There is the idea of human freedom as a perfect self-determination, and there is also the idea of freedom as determined by grace in every point of its activity. Round these two principles, concerning these two determinations, the great dogmatic strife between Pelagianism and Augustinianism rages; —a strife which has repeated itself in various forms and modifications in every age, because it has to do with the deepest questionings of the human heart.

§ 201.

PELAGIANISM insists exclusively upon the principles of freedom and self-determination, or the power of choice, in man. From this point of view grace is made to signify, partly the innate powers and gifts of nature, and partly the historical ordainments of Providence for the nurture of humanity; among which Christianity, in virtue of its pure teaching and the example of its Founder, may be reckoned as the chief:—*gratia juvans.* Sin, moreover, is not a violation of nature, but a mere infirmity, which may be healed by the healing powers of nature, and may be conquered by the individual exertions of freedom. The idea of creative grace (*gratia creans*), of a communication of new redeeming power, of a communication of the Divine nature as necessary conditions of the holy and free development of mankind, involves, according to Pelagianism, a degradation of human nature, whose essence is self-development. Upon the principles of Pelagianism, humanity finds its goal within the limits of nature, *i.e.*, of its original creation; free will possesses within itself, and in the natural gifts of its creation, all necessary sources and means of self-perfection and self-appointment. Man can and must attain his destiny by his own power, by pious effort and progressive culture; and there was no need that any such miracle as regeneration should interrupt the sure and advancing progress of human development.

§ 202.

The misapprehension of grace on the part of Pelagianism arises from a misconception of the true nature of humanity and of freedom. It must be allowed that man is free, only in proportion as he governs himself according to the laws of his own being. But Pelagianism forgets, or does not adequately realize the fact, that the essence of man's being is God's likeness, that he was created in God's image, and that accordingly human liberty governs itself according to its true nature, when it governs itself according to the all-determining will of God, which has its authority as recognized in the very depths of freedom. And when Pelagianism itself lays down the principle that human freedom must fulfil the will of God, how is this possible, unless it be made to partake of the divine essence; unless the human spirit be brought into an actual and living fellowship with the Divine? Pelagianism, however, not only mistakes the essence of humanity and freedom as resembling the Divine, it misinterprets also the outward reality of freedom, for it takes this to be a *res inte-*

gra with freedom. In the Pelagian consciousness there is no experience of the serious contrariety between the flesh and the spirit, between the practical reality of human liberty and its abstract essence, between the subjective and the absolute will. It fails to recognize the deep-seated consciousness which convinces us that we possess the glorious gift of liberty only in essence or idea, while our actual liberty, as far as it goes, is wholly inadequate for true self-government according to the sacred ideal of its essence. "I delight in the law of God after the inward man. But I see another law in my members, warring against the law of my mind, and bringing me into captivity to the law of sin which is in my members" (Rom. vii. 22, 23). When the conscience is thoroughly pierced with this experience of the incapacity of the will to fulfil that ideal of holiness, which rises from its depths as an unalterable demand, and which is presented to us in the holy nature of Christ, the man renounces his own virtue and his own merits, and turns to the redeeming God ; he discovers his need of a grace which will not only be a means of advancing human virtue, a medium of strength for the healthy, but medicine for the sick, a power which reforms human nature from its foundation, and enables him to live a life whose inward springs are wholly new (Ps. li.; John viii. 36 ; Phil. ii. 13).

§ 203.

In contrast with Pelagianism, AUGUSTINIANISM dwells upon the remembrance of man's having been originally created in the image of God, and upon the stern experience of the all-prevailing power of sin ; and whereas Pelagianism insists upon the notion of self-development, Augustinianism is engrossed in the thought of God's grace in creation—*gratia creans*—which it imagines to be a holy activity to renew the human soul, and to form it anew for the kingdom of God. It is, accordingly, only as the instrument of grace, as the organ of Christ, that man is really free. Even a deeper Pelagianism must perceive how it is only when man is thus the instrument of something higher than himself, that he is truly free. Fichte says, "One must pass his life upon some idea, and that life only which is moulded by the idea is truly a life of freedom." Augustine says, "It is only a life in God which is truly a life of freedom ; then only is man free, when he gives himself up, not only to the thought and idea of God, but to God himself, as his creating and moulding strength ; that God may be the all-working and all-moving power within him. *Da quod jubes, et jube quod vis !*" By this view Augustine did not violate the freedom of humanity, but confirmed it. For grace is not anything hostile to human liberty, but is one and the same in spirit with its real essence; the object and aim of grace differs nothing from the object and aim of true liberty. In that essential freedom which is after the image of God, the point of union for nature and grace lies ; in the essential depths of freedom, grace exists *as* nature. It must, however, be allowed that Augustinianism, both in its great founder and in many of his followers, has been developed in a way which contradicts the idea of human liberty. Augustinianism has insisted so much upon the one factor, that the other has been forgotten. It has so insisted upon the idea of grace, and of spiritual development, that liberty has become a mere shadow and name. While it rightly views human nature as "a vessel" for grace, —the material out of which Christ the moulder of humanity forms it into a new creature after His own image,—it has far too often overlooked the fact that this vessel is itself a " person," that this material is itself " I." This is especially manifest in the assertion that grace is irresistible, *gratia est irresistabilis ;* and nature and grace have too often been so opposed to each other, that no point of union and harmony could be found, and the relation of grace to nature was made merely external and mechanical. The operations of grace have thus been looked upon merely as the operations of supernatural power, without at the same time recognizing them as the carnal aspirations and deepest stirrings of human nature. Such representations, moreover, as they were not without reason styled barbarous, gave to Pelagianism a relative right and worth, because it vindicated despised humanity and liberty ; although it failed to perceive the deeper religious kernel which lay hid in imperfect theological forms.

Observations.—The prevailing notions of the cultivated world of our day are Pelagian, though in a very different way. How greatly does the Pelagianism of ordinary Rationalism differ from that which has been developed by a Kant

or a Fichte, a Schiller, and a Göthe? This Pelagianism
owes its power in virtue of its opposition to a dead orthodoxy in which the Christian doctrines of sin and grace
appear only as an external tradition, possessing no living
root in consciousness. The free spirit of man turned away
from the heap of Christian tradition, and endeavoured to
renew its youth after the grand patterns of the ancient
world. Down to the time of the Reformation the human
and natural thus wandered away from a lifeless scholasticism, and tried to regenerate man according to the ideal of
humanity held by the heathen world. The idea of an
harmonising self-development of human nature prevailed
among the leaders and teachers of that age. But this
humanitarianism failed to realise and explain the fundamental conviction of sin, and the perception of the ideal of
holiness, which consciousness had lost in its manifold endeavours after this world's ideal. Yet the elder Pelagianism was not wholly without a germ of truth for the kingdom of God; for in proportion as it was thorough, it led
to a deeper self-knowledge, even to the knowledge of the
law and the prophets in man's own heart, and thus on to
the refutation of itself.

§ 204.

According to the pattern of the individual development of
Christ as the God-man, the new creation which Christianity
introduced must be viewed as a blending of an holy natural
development, with an holy development of freedom. The individual man *is made* the subject of an higher fulness of life,
—which as a sacred *natura naturans*, works itself out, grows
and takes form in him;* and, at the same time, he *makes*
himself the instrument, labours and strives after his own salvation (Phil. ii. 12). But this union of freedom and grace
would not be a truly spiritual union were it not developed by
the fundamental distinction between the two; by an inward
crisis and a reciprocal strife between both factors. This is
especially evident in that most important era of human life,
conversion. Therein we see how grace differs from mere
power; how it does not work irresistibly and by force, but
has regard to human freedom, gives it a power of choice, of

* John iii. 6; Phil. i. 6; 2 Cor. iii. 5. See *Sibbern's Pathol.* 65, 334.

deciding, an alternative of *either—or, Gratia trahit, non cogit.* It is immanent grace, in the yielding heart of man, which constrains free will to surrender itself to the grace which seeks an entrance, which enables it to open to its influence, like the flower which opens to the sunbeam ; yet it is the internal power of the natural will which bears witness that the natural will is not a mere name but a reality, and that it can close the heart against the operations of grace, and shut itself up in a self-chosen darkness. " To-day, if ye will hear his voice, harden not your hearts " (Heb. iii. 15).

Observations.—It was a serious misconception on the part of the old Pelagianism, that looked upon the freedom of choice as the whole of freedom, and that made the essence of liberty to consist in the power of deciding otherwise at any moment of time regarding any act. But it was no less a misconception on the part of Augustinianism which denied the reality of freedom of choice *in toto,* instead of realising it as the necessary point of transition from grace to actual liberty. This was the truth recognised in that form of semi-Pelagianism called *synergismus* which found advocates within the pale of the Lutheran Church in Melanchthon and Strigelius. The error of Synergism consisted in its attributing to the subjective will an active part in the work of conversion, whereas grace is the source of all productiveness. For when man surrenders himself —allows himself to be drawn by grace, this power of surrender is not native to the natural will as such, but is involved in that essential liberty, that innate grace, which finds its expression in the natural will. In this sense the Lutheran orthodoxy is right in maintaining that the human will, *i.e.,* the native natural will, possesses the power to *withstand* or resist grace, but not the power of surrendering itself to grace. For when man gives himself up to gracious influences he does this in virtue of that inward glimpse of God which is inseparable from the divinely modelled essence of freedom, and which must, strictly speaking, be designated grace in nature. If, on the contrary, he resists grace, this is an act of the natural will as such, the merely human will, which, in the act of resistance, separates itself at once from its own divinely modelled essence.

§ 205.

The inward reciprocity between nature and grace that has
now been described, is not confined to the beginning of the
work of conversion, but continues throughout the whole
Christian life. The combination of freedom and grace as
blended in one is chiefly observable in the first act of conversion and regeneration. But not till the life of the man has
become wholly a life in God, can the actual unity of grace
and freedom be fully manifest ; a condition which Scripture
describes as the glorious liberty of the children of God, and
which receives its full glory in future blessedness. The progress of the new creation in man, or, as we call it, the development of Christian character, presents a continual blending of
liberty and grace, in which grace not only seeks the attainment of liberty, but freedom also endeavours after grace, and
works hand in hand with grace. There are seasons in the
Christian life when the sense of a spontaneous growth in
holiness is strong ; when there is felt a still calm increase in
the Lord ; an imperceptible yet real advance in wisdom and
in grace ; but seasons such as these are interspersed with
other and critical times, in which there is a struggle on the
part of freedom, where freedom (through the influence of
grace) endeavours with toil and effort to obtain more grace,
wrestles with God in prayer, waits patiently for the Lord,
and strives to preserve the oil in the lamp. It is only in the
most blissful moments of the Christian life, moments which
are, in fact, anticipations of future perfection, that the harmonious unity of grace and freedom is revealed, when the
man is divinely ruled as well as self-ruled, at once *governed*
and *self-governing* ; when the act of God in the man is the
act of the man himself in God ; and when a blessed rest in
the Lord is one and the same with toil and service for the
Lord. The twofold and variegated view of the Christian life
which is here referred to, is the result of what is temporal,
and pertains to the scaffolding of the building, which shall be
taken down when it is complete. We have seen now that
even in Christ himself there was this alternation ; states and
circumstances in which the human element was prominent,
while the divine was comparatively hidden ; and states and
circumstances again, in which the Divine gloriously broke

through the limitations of the human. As this changeful alternation is inseparable from our present life in the midst of what is seen and temporal, it is very clearly expressed and dwelt upon in Holy Scripture. The Bible now encourages the believer to a holy freedom from anxiety, because the kingdom of God is "a seed which grows in the man while he sleeps, he knoweth not how" (Mark iv. 27); and again, it exhorts; "Strive with earnestness!" "Seek that ye may find, so ask that ye may receive, so knock that it may be opened unto you" (Luke xiii. 24 ; xi. 9). Now it declares that "it is not of him that willeth, nor of him that runneth, but of God who sheweth mercy" (Rom. ix. 16); and again it exhorts, "Watch and pray that ye enter not into temptation!" "Work out your own salvation with fear and trembling!" "Draw nigh to God, and he will draw nigh to you" (Matt. xxvi. 41 ; Phil. ii. 12 ; Jas. iv. 8).

Observations.—While these two aspects of the Christian life are both of them essentially manifest in every Christian, yet there are varieties of Christian character arising from the fact, that one of them may become, throughout the life of some, the most prominent and prevailing. Thus there are characters, of which the Apostle John may be taken as the type, that specially bear the impress of a calm growth in the Lord ; the course of whose life resembles a peacefully-flowing stream. In them grace expresses itself in a beauty of soul, and a natural security, which carries them through life undisturbed by violent conflicts, or by times of anxiety or suspense.* In contrast with these are ascetic characters, whose life bears the impress of internal restlessness, of a continual endeavour after freedom, and who, with untiring efforts, strive to realize the blessings of grace. Natures such as these, though the subjects of grace, can never attain to perfect peace in the full assurance of faith. Their life is spent " in fear and trembling ; " they are continually sighing for that redemption, after which all creation longs. Asceticism in the Roman Catholic Church, and Pietism among Protestants, alike furnish instances of such characters. We may here name Pascal among the distinguished cha-

* Compare, however, concerning the Apostle John, Mrk x. 37; Luke ix. 54

racters which Church history presents, as an example of
an ascetic and struggling nature. The truly Pauline
characters, on the other hand, foremost among whom we
may name Luther, present the healthy blending and due
proportion of these contrasted dispositions ;—peace of mind
in the fulness of grace, and energetic endeavour after
the realization of blessedness ;—confidence and fear, freedom from anxiety and carefulness of soul ; and in their
life we see the twofold picture of a heavenly growth and
a free endeavour after holiness.

THE ELECTION OF GRACE.

§ 206.

Although the new creation in man cannot be accomplished
without the assent of his will, its foundation is neither human
will nor human resolve. When grace begins its work in the
soul, it is not the result of man's counsels ; neither does it
depend upon human determinations that grace shall continue
to work contending with slowness of nature and hardness of
heart, until at length it conquers the opposing will, and brings
it into captivity to the love of Christ. It does not depend
upon any human choice that the new Christian life should be
kindled in certain souls, while the great mass of men are
strangers to it ;—that some should be regenerate and believing, while the majority remain under the dominion of worldliness ;—this has its foundation in the determination of Divine
Providence.

§ 207.

The appointments of Divine Providence concerning the souls
of men, when viewed in the light of eternity, must be designated PREDESTINATION. But predestination, or the eternal
pre-determination concerning all souls, can be conceived of
only as a pre-determination of all men to regeneration and
blessedness. God's grace is universal ; and from eternity it
has been concluded that all shall be gathered together under
Christ as the Head. In eternity God looks upon all human
souls according to their essential destiny—looks upon them
as possible subjects of regeneration—candidates to become
new creatures in Christ. Dualism does not appear till time

begins. When the divine counsels advance out of eternity into time, they assume the character of a development in history, and must begin to work at some single point of time and space, thence to spread in their activity throughout the whole. Predestination fulfils itself under the form of an election of grace, which chooses and prepares certain persons successively from the sinful mass, for the new life which is in Christ. All cannot be first who are received into the kingdom of God; some must be first, and others last. All cannot at the same time become equally susceptible of the operations of grace within the soul; many must certainly be called, and few chosen. But this Dualism prevails only in time; as it is excluded from the eternal counsels of God, it must be excluded from the final issue of the world's development. The two conceptions, therefore, of predestination and the election of grace must be kept distinct from one another. Predestination is an eternal act; the election of grace is temporal and historical. Predestination looks upon all souls as subjects of God's grace; the election of grace distinguishes between souls, and divides them as the chosen and the disregarded. Grace must submit to the conditions of time and the relations of creation, which assign to every generation, to every individual, a certain "fulness of time:" it must submit to the limitations of human freedom; for grace cannot accomplish its work in humanity without the will of man, but only by an actual *dialectic* or reasoning process of the will.

§ 208.

The true doctrine of predestination depends upon the right distinguishing between the temporal and the eternal, the divine and the human, in the revelations of universal grace; and all one-sidedness of view regarding it arises from some disturbance in the due relations of these to one another. This is the case especially with Calvin's theory. CALVIN confounded predestination with the election of grace. The separation which is only temporal he made eternal, because he laid its foundations in the eternal counsel of God. God, according to him, made from eternity a twofold election, because He has fore-appointed certain persons to faith and to blessedness, and certain others to unbelief and everlasting damnation. Here Calvin disturbs and violates the relations between what is temporal and what is eternal. This awful election, he further maintained, to be purely unconditional, and thus he mistook the true relations between the divine and the human. The divine does not concern itself with the voluntary act of man in conversion, it fulfils itself simply as a development of nature. We have not before us here an election on the part of man, it is God who has chosen once for all time. From Calvin's point of view, man has *no history*, so far at least as history includes the idea of a temporal and free life, in which, what is as yet undecided, will be decided. All *is* decided already; existence, life, destiny,—every individual man, with his distinctive lineaments of character, and outward circumstances,—already have been present before the eye of the omniscient God, with a necessity as fixed and certain as the paths in which the planets move. And though Christ offers His grace to all, in His work and by the means of grace, and calls all to repentance and conversion, the doctrine of predestination shows that this is merely apparent; for in reality Christ is come into the world to fulfil an eternal election,—for the fall and rising again of many,—for the rising again of those who were created for the resurrection, for the fall of them who were created for destruction.

§ 209.

Calvin's doctrine has been further developed and remodelled by Schleiermacher. Schleiermacher does away with the confusion of Predestination and Election, and distinguishes between what is temporal and what is eternal in the revelation of grace. Eternal predestination, in his view, determines the final blessedness of all in Christ; but election is the temporal form in which this gracious will of God fulfils itself. Though Schleiermacher thus obviates Calvin's fatalism, by allowing that universal grace will release the now fettered freedom of all men, yet he has avoided fatalism only in theory, not actually; because he maintains Calvin's idea of God's unconditional counsel, and leaves no room for human choice in the matter of eternal blessedness. The relation between the divine and the human is still somewhat confused. For the final accomplishment of human blessedness is, according to this view also, exclusively a development of nature. From Christ, the holy centre of humanity, the prevailing beams of

grace shine forth, working in men's hearts, effectually renewing their natures and building up their characters, and in
successive generations penetrating that humanity which, apart
from Christ, is only an unorganized mass, in which the light
of true personality has not yet been kindled.　Just as the
tree must wait till the gardener comes to transplant it to a
better soil and a more genial aspect, so must every human
being tarry until his hour comes, when the heavenly husband-
man shall transplant him out of the kingdom of nature into
the kingdom of grace, and shall draw forth into life the
slumbering germ of his personality.　Whatever sanction this
mode of treating the subject may derive from the fundamental
representations given in revelation, Schleiermacher, as well as
Augustine and Calvin, has taken a one-sided view of the
truth that man is "a vessel" for grace.　The freely choosing
self-determining *ego*, according to this view, has no part whatever in the realization of its own blessedness.　By a process
of nature merely, every one is born again when his appointed
time arrives ; and, as Calvin foretells a kingdom of the saved
and a kingdom of the lost, as the issue of this world's development, upon the very same principle of necessity does
Schleiermacher predict a universal restoration.

Observations.—As Schleiermacher's speculative fatalism [De-
terminismus] excludes freedom of choice, he cannot entertain the idea of the *history* of the kingdom of God, but
can speak only of the *evolution* of that kingdom.　In his
doctrine of sin, as well as of grace, he persuades himself
only of the essential union subsisting between freedom and
necessity, forgetting that this union is effected by that
power of choice in man whereby good as well as evil is
developed in him to complete personality.　As the Christ
of Schleiermacher was overcome by no temptation, but
unfolded His holy nature harmoniously and consistently,
He is looked upon as the type of all the subjects of grace.
This view of grace is not perfectly ethical ; a one-sided
æsthetic sentiment pervades it.　The Christian life, according to it, is in fact only a still, calm growth in the
Lord, and the ideal of personality is in fact merely the
ideal of "the beautiful soul," and "the higher nature."
We bow down before grace, which works as a higher

genius in the man, but we lose the strengthening perception of the free warfare sustained by the man himself. In
like manner man, in his state of sinfulness, is made the
subject of merely æsthetic treatment. For as that power
of choice is wanting, whereby alone sin can become a
personal act in the man, the sinner can only be the subject
of *compassion*, and holy *wrath* against his sin cannot
justly be manifested. The consciousness, moreover, of his
sin can only be accompanied by a holy sorrow; conscience
can only experience a sense of spiritual need, an anxiety
for the salvation of the soul; self-contrition and self-
condemnation cannot justly be experienced. Those emotions do indeed form part of the Christian's consciousness;
but this consciousness feels itself violated if other additional and corresponding emotions are excluded, if the
spiritual ordainments of nature be not blended with the
self-determinations of freedom.

§ 210.

The true basis of the doctrine of election is given in the
LUTHERAN teaching regarding *universal grace* and *conditional
decrees*. The eternal decree of God determines the blessedness
of all who are in Christ (John iii. 16; 1 Tim. ii. 4); for
Christ is Himself the true Book of Life in which they all are
written; but that decree is not unconditional in such a sense
that human action in time should be only the dependent reflection of it. As the eternal decree, when it passes into time,
assumes the form of election of grace, it submits to a corresponding connection with the will of man, and conditions
itself as a *calling*. The election of divine grace enters upon
a new relation with the power of choice in man, and thus
begins an actual *history*. The *calling*, indeed, as well as the
election, proceeds after the manner of a holy and yet natural
development; the sower sows the heavenly seed, which grows
even while the man sleeps; the potter forms whatever he
wills out of the clay;* but this natural development is conditioned in its progress by the will of man (Matt. xi. 28
Mark xvi. 16; Luke xiv. 17; John v. 40; Matt. xxiii. 37.

* Matt. xiii. 3-9; Mark iv. 26-28; Rom. ix. 21. Compare *Confessio Augustana*
Art. v.; "Spiritus sanctus—fidem efficit, *ubi et quando* visum est Deo, in iis, qu
audiunt evangelium."

for man may refuse the call and resist the attracting grace. Grace may indeed overcome the opposition of man, but it does this in a manner consonant with human freedom, by leading on the resisting will through a course of purifying experiences till it reaches the turning-point at which it humbly gives God the glory, and elects to find its freedom in God—surrendering itself by a moral, not a physical necessity, to the all-prevailing power of love (Acts ix. 5, 6.) Thus the kingdom of God in man becomes more than an *evolution*, it becomes an actual *history;* a history both as regards the race collectively and each individual soul; thus, too, both the requirements of the Christian consciousness—the sense of dependence and the consciousness of freedom—are met and fully satisfied.

Observations.—An unfortunate turn is taken by the Lutheran theory, arising perhaps rather from an imperfect view of it than from any inherent religious principle which it lays down. It is that God bestows His grace upon men *ex prævisa fide,* and that He also rejects men *ex prævisa incredulitate.* This formula involves a return to Calvinism. Freedom of choice is transformed into a mere shadow, for whatever is the subject of eternal foreknowledge, must have its foundation in an eternal law of necessity. The relation in which the free choice of man stands to the divine election of grace, cannot be the object of God's *fore*-knowledge, though it is certainly the object of His *joint*-knowledge.

§ 211.

If we now consider the progress of the election of grace as it is carried on in history, in order to understand the dealings of God with men, we find our knowledge limited in this part of the subject also, because the election of grace does not accomplish its work wholly in this present life, but carries it on beyond the grave. This is distinctly involved in the dogma of the Descent of Christ into the region of the dead. Our present state of existence affords only a partial and imperfect revelation of God's universal grace; and regarding no other point of Christian doctrine does it hold more true that our knowledge is but fragmentary. This earthly life presents to us only the first act of the divine drama which universal grace began in the creation; and the problematical, the entangled threads of which indicate a great catastrophe, to be realized only in a future world.   It is not the province of learning, in our present state of being, to fathom all the depths of the teleology of grace,—much is hidden from us and must continue so to be ;—our endeavour must be to discover only the general type presented in the historical course of the election of grace, that type which reveals this election as a work of divine wisdom.

§ 212.

As the kingdom of God embraces the human race as a whole, and the individuals also who compose it, the teleology of election must be looked at in this twofold light.   In the ideal, and in the *perfected* reality of facts, the race and the individual cannot be viewed separately, but not only must we distinguish between them when we come to treat of them, they are already distinguished in the progress of election in time.   The fact that the entire mass of mankind, that all nations, shall be christianized, by no means involves the notion that grace will be shared personally by every individual.   Experience itself witnesses that this is by no means the case.   The election of nations is only one step in the history of election, the conditional basis for the subsequent election of particular persons.   Election, therefore, in its historical progress, presents itself to us as an election of nations, and an election of individuals ;—as *vocatio gentium* and *vocatio singulorum.*

§ 213.

The supernatural bestowment of that new life which Christianity brings depends upon the susceptibility of human nature ; and the new creation can be revealed in power only where the first creation has prepared the way.   Election is never realized save by the combined workings of supernatural and of natural powers—the powers of the first and of the second creation.   This is revealed as the law of divine wisdom in the calling both of nations and of individuals.   The ELECTION OF NATIONS, for example, depends partly upon their position in the world's history, and partly upon their natural gifts, which specially have singled them out and fitted them to become the recipients and instruments of the spirit of Christianity.   "No man can come to the Son unless the

Father draw him" (John vi. 44). This passage denotes the obvious connection between the kingdoms of nature and of grace. If, in the teleology of the first creation, the Father had not qualified the nations for the kingdom of God, the Holy Ghost would strive in vain, and grace would fail to accomplish its work—in virtue of the necessary conditions of nature—labouring in vain upon a resisting material. Upon this principle it is that we read in the book of the Acts, how the Holy Ghost forbade the apostles to preach the gospel in certain places, because in them a receptive soil was wanting.* In like manner, no nation can, in the fulness of time, be chosen, unless it possess not only the preparations of grace, but the inward conditions of nature also, viz., receptivity, and a sense of need.† Nations are chosen in the manner described by our Lord in His parable of the Labourers in the Vineyard;—some are called at the third hour, some at the sixth or at the ninth hour, and some at the last, the eleventh hour. (Matt. xx. 1-16.)

Observations.—Augustinian theologians have often maintained that the operations of Christianity are never fettered by natural restrictions, but that grace can accomplish its object "*what, when,* and *where*" it will. They think that by this doctrine they extol the power of grace. But this is not only contradicted by the universal experience of church history, it is in itself false; it magnifies the second creation at the expense of the first, which on such a principle is violated; it glorifies the Son at the sacrifice of the Father's glory.

§ 214.

The division of nations into those which are *chosen,* and those who may be described as set aside, or at least *postponed,* must be viewed as the work of divine wisdom, having respect to the condition of the creature; and not beginning the new creation, until the first creation is so advanced in its teleolo-

---

* Acts xvi. 6, 7 : "Now when they had gone throughout Phrygia and the region of Galatia, and were forbidden of the Holy Ghost to preach the word in Asia, after they were come to Mysia, they assayed to go into Bithynia : but the Spirit suffered them not."

† Acts xvi. 9 : "And a vision appeared to Paul in the night; there stood a man of Macedonia, and prayed him, saying, Come over into Macedonia and help us."

2 A

gical development, as to present the spiritual conditions of nature (among which we may reckon the conditions upon which culture depends) necessary for the new. This was the method followed by divine wisdom towards mankind collectively ; for Christ did not come into the world until the first creation, and the active preparations for redemption were so far developed, that the soil was ready, and a receptivity secured ; and this typical instance is repeated in the experience of every nation. It is true of many peoples, and especially of those children of nature who spend their lives apart from any connection with historical culture, that, viewed only in the light of nature, they are spiritually in an unripe, an embryo state; so that it may be said of them that they needed first to be brought into the kingdom of nature, in order that the kingdom of grace might come to them. For, to name only one point, who does not perceive that the language of a nation must be developed to a certain degree of spirituality, in order that the ideas and truths of the gospel may be expressed in it ? We must ever keep in view the fact that there must not only be a development of the new creation, but that the first creation also, which includes a moral as well as a physical order of things, must also advance ; and that it would be of little use to any nation for the gospel to be preached to it, or for the Son to draw it to the Father, until it has itself so far progressed that the Father also can draw it to the Son.

§ 215.

The distinction between nations that are chosen and those who are left or postponed must vanish in the development of history. For it may be said of the chosen nations that they have been favoured before others, in order to the benefit of others ; following, as they must, the rule of the economy, and becoming a leaven for the unregenerate mass ; missionaries to bring to them Christianity as well as culture. But the conversion of a nation does not depend only upon Christian missions and the advance of culture ; it is contingent also upon that hidden development which silently progresses in the innermost spirit of the nation, and which precedes the mysterious moment when the Father draws it to the Son. We need not, however, take account of the exact time *when* any particular people were called, nor of the many

problems which suggest themselves, provided we fix our
thoughts upon the distinction between what is temporal and
the eternal destiny of nations as imaged in the divine mind.
Though the reality of history in time presents to our view
whole nations who for centuries have lived a merely animal
and sensual life, over whom no spirit hovers,—nations that
for centuries remain in a state of spiritual petrifaction, without a single trace of living progress ;—we nevertheless cherish
and hold fast the faith, that the time will come when the
word of the Lord shall be accomplished, and when baptism
and Christianity shall be brought to all nations.　And as for
those generations which have been born and have died without partaking of the blessings of the Gospel and of the Spirit ;
—as for those generations whom we may compare to the
great multitude of children dying immediately after birth ;
without experiencing any spiritual development ;—we can
only find rest in the thought, that this earthly existence is
but a fragment, which cannot be seen by us in its completeness, save in a future state.　To assume, in accordance with
the Pantheistic doctrine of predestination, that all these generations are only of transitory import ;—to assume that a
multitude of human germs of life fall to the ground, just as
yearly in nature myriads of seeds are scattered abroad, of
which only the smallest number grow and come to perfection ;
—this is forbidden us by the principle of the divinely ideal
existence in man, and of the eternal difference between him
and nature.　Even were we to allow that certain nations are
only dying and vanishing points of transition in the history
of mankind, we dare not apply this assumption to the individuals that compose them ; for experience teaches that there
never has been a nation whose individual members were
entirely void of a moral sense,—of conscience,—that inextinguishable witness to their destiny as candidates for
eternity.

§ 216.

Although the distinction between nations as the chosen,
and the " left " or postponed, shall finally disappear, there is a
distinction which is not transitory, a distinction becoming progressively more and more marked among those nations which
have been chosen, and which arises from the deep connection

between nature and grace.   Natural peculiarities of national life shall indeed be made pure and perfect by the supernatural influences of Christianity ; yet they cannot be wholly obliterated.   As the realm of nature contains within its range original and essential varieties of noble and ignoble, higher and lower natures, it may be inferred that while all nations are chosen, there must necessarily be among them vessels unto honour, and vessels unto dishonour, for the uses of grace ; and among all nations which have played a part in church history experience has testified to the fact, that as was the nation so were the Christians who belonged to it.   All Christianized nations bear the image and superscription of Christ, yet great variety is found to exist in the material on which the image of Christ is impressed.   " In a great house," says the Apostle, " there are not only vessels of gold and of silver, but also of wood and of earth" (2 Tim. ii. 20).   Though Christian nations are all members of one spiritual body, of which Christ is head, and must not be severed from the body, because no one member can dispense with the others ; yet in virtue of this inextinguishable variation of natures some members must possess a central and important office, while others must occupy a lower and subordinate place.   The election of grace fulfils itself within the range of the chosen nations, and in this sense it coincides with predestination, which determines from eternity concerning the nations conformably with the economy of the whole.   It is a pure supposition to think that this could involve unrighteousness on the part of God.   Righteousness is developed by means of wisdom ; yet it is also wisdom's law, that in a kingdom composed of individuals, all points must not have the same centralization ; there must exist a manifold variety of individualities from the lowest and comparatively imperfect forms, up to the highest and most perfect.   Wisdom embraces distributive justice, which fulfils in every case the *suum cuique*, gives to each his own, imparts to every member just so much fulness of life as conformably to its nature it can receive, wisdom is also inseparable from love, which gives to all the one thing needful—salvation.   If some natures possess a deeper susceptibility, and a greater power of spiritual activity in God's kingdom, there can be no injustice in this towards those who do not possess the same degree of susceptibility or strength of productive energy, who yet find perfect satisfaction for their inmost wants, and for the highest powers of their own being.

Observations.—The truth here presented is not far removed from the possibility of error ; the error, I mean, into which a nation falls, when, in the consciousness of its natural election and its special susceptibility for Christianity, it acts haughtily, as if it were the head of all civilization and Christian development, instead of being simply a member of the great body ; and when it over-estimates special gifts of grace above the ordinary gifts, the national above the universal church. The possibility also is at hand of erroneously judging of the power of Christianity from a national point of view ; whereas nationality owes its real value to Christianity, which alone possesses intrinsic worth. Amid the prevailing idolatry of nationality, so common now-a-days,* this possibility of error has in many ways been realized. But neither the possibility nor the fact of the error, can hinder our recognizing the truth, that there are original and natural diversities in the relations of nations to Christianity, which Christianity neither can nor will extinguish ; and that Christianity can obtain neither entrance nor progress among a people—except by its supernatural powers working consentaneously and hand in hand with the natural susceptibility and flexibleness of the people ;—features which are by no means alike in all. Yet the truth is by no means violated or destroyed, " that God has included all under sin that he might have mercy upon all " (Romans xi. 32).

§ 217.

The election of nations is not the final end of grace. Its final end is the election of INDIVIDUALS ; for grace can reveal itself as effectual for the formation of character in a kingdom of individuals alone. But the election of particular persons is in no way connected with that of nations. The children of Israel who are a permanent type of an elect nation, were emphatically *the* elect people, yet there was only a small remnant of elect individuals among them (a holy election) who repre-

* Compare Rudelbach : *Christendom og. Nationalitat.*

sented the true and spiritual Israel.   So do we find it in every Christian nation.   All, perhaps, have been baptized and incorporated into Christ's kingdom and outwardly united to Him, and yet in every period there is to be found but a small remnant of really awakened and regenerate persons in whom Christianity dwells as a subjective and personal life.   Thousands within the pale of Christendom spend their whole lives without being brought into any personal relation with Christ; remaining, in an undefined, external, and general way, under the influence of Christianity.   It is not enough to explain this exclusively on the ground of their personal responsibility and guilt: awakening is not contingent upon the resolve of any man; neither does it depend upon his own individual purpose that grace shall continue to seek a man, notwithstanding his indifference and opposition, until he finds that it is in vain "to kick against the pricks" (Acts ix. 5), and yields himself to the power of love.   Experience teaches that this special grace is not vouchsafed to all alike; and the word is continually verified, "a man can receive nothing except it be given him from heaven" (John iii. 27).   We are thus led to the conclusion that grace interests itself in an especial manner about some, whom it will make its personal subjects and instruments, while it interests itself about others only in a general way, in so far only as it is solicitous for the entire kingdom, within which they are included, as parts of the great whole, without possessing any individual importance.   Within the pale of the Church, also, it is true, that many are called, but few chosen.

§ 218.

The apparent severity involved in the conception, that God incorporates so many within his kingdom without giving them an actual and personal participation of its blessings, can be explained only upon the principle of successive steps in the revelation of grace.   Just as in the doctrine of divine Providence we distinguish between a manifestation of Providence to the race as a whole, and a manifestation thereof in the lives of individuals, we find that this distinction repeats itself in the sphere of grace: here also we must distinguish between general and special grace (*gratia generalis et specialis*). Those who are simultaneously admitted to the church, and incorporated into the kingdom, cannot all of them be simultaneously raised to an equal standard of personal character; here too we find that some lead the way, while others remain behind. Those who are not brought into personal connection with Christ, are subjects of the general influences of grace only;—though, undoubtedly, individualizing and personal grace exists as a latent power and possibility in those general gracious influences. Grace meets them in the first act of its manifestation, and includes them in its election of the nation or of the mother church to which they belong, without manumitting them to a distinct and personal life. The new life implanted in them by baptism, lies dormant, and as if in an embryo state; the time for their awakening, or in other words, the testing point of their free development,—is not yet come. General grace must accordingly be described as *preparatory,* *prevenient,* a term which is employed in reference to its action beyond the pale of the church, but which is likewise applicable to some of its workings within the church. Being preparatory, it endeavours to go beyond a merely general working, it seeks to *individualize* its influence, and to become *special* grace. The range of preparative operations of grace includes manifold diversities: and between those on the one hand who, though incorporated in the church, are quite abandoned by grace, and seem to be spiritually dead, and those, on the other hand, who have been awakened, and are really regenerate, there lie manifold religious changes and differences of character, which can be exhausted in no list, but may be seen in real life in innumerable forms.

§ 219.

If we now consider the election of those who are actually awakened and born again, and brought into personal union with Christ, we shall find that in their case the preparative and combined working of nature and of grace—the factors of the first and of the second creation—attains its final aim. It is impossible to tell *when* this "fulness of time" arrives in the case of any individual man; it depends upon the mysteries alike of the old and of the new creation. Again and again does it occur, that the first,—those who seemed to be nearest to the kingdom of God,—become the last; while grace breaks forth where it was least expected; so that we are constrained to exclaim, "How unsearchable are his judgments, and his paths past finding out!" (Rom. xi. 33.) It is beyond the power of any human understanding to calculate or foresee what individuals are elected as the subjects of God's special grace; for there is no outward sign marking those who are thus singled out. No natural morality on the part of the individual secures his election, for we see many who are distinguished for the righteousness of the law, and for moral endeavours, passed by, while publicans and harlots enter before them into the kingdom of God (Matt. xxi. 31). And though we must allow that the self-determination of the man himself is a *condition* of the progress of the new creation in him, this certainly cannot be called the *cause* of it. The choice again is not regulated by the natural gifts of this world possessed by individuals, for many the most highly gifted with genius, worldly wisdom, and skill, many a Coryphæus of the intellectual world (ἄρχοντες τοῦ κόσμου τούτου) are passed by; while those who belong to the classes of so-called ordinary men enter into the kingdom of God. If we ask holy Scripture for a mark whereby to distinguish the elect, it replies—"Base things of this world, and things which are despised hath God chosen" (1 Cor. i. 27). But Scripture affords no criterion whereby to pronounce who are the despised of the world; and experience overturns every outward criterion that human calculation sets up. Not only the low, but the high and mighty, not only the simple, but the wise and understanding also, are chosen, and the despised of the world are found thus scattered among all. That which is despised of the world and chosen of God, we can only suppose to be a living susceptibility of nature for grace,—that poverty of spirit, that hungering and thirsting after righteousness, which our Lord in His Sermon on the Mount pronounced blessed;—that infinite craving for redemption which cannot find satisfaction in the springs of this world, and which in its very essence must be "that which is despised of this world," despised and disesteemed by a world that fancies it has enough within itself and in its own resources. But there is no outward token to indicate the living presence of this fruitful susceptibility; it is a secret of the heart: the awakening and regeneration following upon it are themselves the only

sure evidences of its presence. All we can say is, that whenever that need of redemption and of regenerating grace, which
is inseparable from the sense of sin, is felt, the "fulness of
time" begins in the experience of that person : or, in other
words, the "fulness of time" appears whenever the Son
draws the individual to the Father, and the Father draws him
to the Son ;—when those words are fulfilled in the individual's own life, " No man cometh unto the Father, but by
me" (John xiv. 6), and " no man can come unto me, except
the Father which hath sent me draw him " (John vi. 44).

§ 220.

It must also remain an inscrutable mystery to human enquiry, why just *these* individuals should be chosen, while others
are passed by. As grace is certainly general, and real freedom
possessed by all, it follows with equal certainty that there exists
a general susceptibility in all. But the mystery of election lies
in this, that, while this susceptibility in the case of many remains in a hidden and slumbering state, or manifests itself
in a barren, or at best a sporadic form, in the case of others
it is awakened as a *fruitful* susceptibility. This awakening
is produced partly by the powerful impulse of grace, which,
like the lightning flash, cleaves the hard natural heart, or
lures forth the spiritual germ as with a gentle warmth ;
partly by the special leadings of the soul's life, by which the
will is nurtured and moulded for the kingdom of God ; and
partly again by the soul's innate religious dispositions, its
natural instincts ; in virtue of which the striving after God's
kingdom and righteousness is developed in some more rapidly,
more easily, and with greater energy than in others. It is
on this account that the apostle Paul does not date his calling from the lightning flash which arrested him on his way
to Damascus, but declares that he was set apart for the kingdom of God from his mother's womb—ὁ ἀφορίσας με ἐκ κοιλίας
μητρός μου (Gal. i. 15). The apostle had the mystery of the
election of grace in view when he said, " It is not of him that
willeth, nor of him that runneth, but of God that showeth
mercy"—as the Scripture saith, " I will have mercy on whom
I will have mercy" (Rom. ix. 18) ; and with this mystery of
creation before his eyes, he silences every complaint regarding those left or *postponed* with the words, " Shall the thing

formed say to him that formed it, Why hast thou made me thus?" (Rom. ix. 20.)

§ 221.

Though election is an inscrutable mystery, it must not be forgotten that we may recognize in this mystery a manifestation of the divine wisdom. If we can rise to the contemplation of the teleologic world-plan—of God's final design in the creation of the world—we shall find it to be a necessary law of wisdom, that by means of nature and of grace, alike in the first and in the second creation, it behoves God to ordain, that there shall always be just so many individuals in the communion of saints, as are needed to represent the activity of His kingdom upon earth, and to be the chosen instruments for the spread of that kingdom, the salt of the earth for those around. Election is inseparable from the idea of activity for the spread of God's kingdom, of effort for the salvation of others. Every one who is really regenerate, feels an irresistible impulse to communicate the new life, which he possesses, to those around. Those who are elect must so minister to those who are left behind, that they in turn may be awakened to participate in the same new life. The elect are lights in the world which give light, centres of life which impart life. The eternal pattern according to which this law of election works, is illustrated for us in the gospel history of the Apostles and first disciples, who were chosen before the mass of the people that had been indistinctly yet really impressed by Christ's life, in order that by their election good might be done to that multitude. That just *these* individuals and not others, were made the instruments of good, arose out of the arrangement of the economy as a whole ; or because the hidden threads of nature and of grace were so intertwined at these particular points, that new personalities, new characters, could here be formed, such as could not be formed at any other points, in the then present era of the development of the work of creation.

Observations.—" God always seeks out the most useful nation for his government."* We may compare with this a declaration of Luther's in a sermon upon the conversion of Paul. " Because Paul did the work (the persecution of

---

* Richard Rothe ; Theol. Ethik. 2, 259.

the Christians) so earnestly, our Lord Jesus had him in
His thoughts, and said thus to Himself—"This man may
become good, for what he does, he does in earnest. This
earnestness which he now employs in a bad work, I will
sanctify with my Spirit; I will employ him in a good
cause, and will set him against the Jews." "In the same
manner," adds Luther, "our Lord and God makes use of
me at this day against the Pope and his whole party."

§ 222.

Divine providence reveals itself most distinctly and specially to the elect, (*providentia specialissima*). They possess
the pledge of their election in their faith, in the witness of
the Spirit with their spirits, that they are the children of God.
By faith they perceive that the kingdoms of this world serve
only as means and elements for the kingdom of God; that all
must work together for good to them who love God, and that
no creature, present or future, neither height nor depth, is
able to separate them from the love of God, which is in Christ
Jesus our Lord.* But the fact that the chosen in Christ
Jesus know that they are the subjects of God's special and
personal grace, cannot engender any human pride. In the
parable of the labourers in the vineyard, the Lord teaches us
that they who were called at the eleventh hour, received the
same reward of grace as they who were called at the third
hour. In other words :—the elect are before those left behind as regards time only, not in virtue of the eternal appointment which is the same for all. And he who is chosen must
act with humility towards his brethren who are left, because
he cannot tell when their time may come, and when they, like
Himself, shall be moulded by the Lord into better qualified
labourers. The warning is given to all the elect, by prayer
and labour, to make their calling and election sure (2 Peter
i. 10).

§ 223.

Electing grace therefore accomplishes its end by a temporal
distinction between the chosen and the left. But there is yet
another and more clearly defined distinction in the history of
the election of grace, the contrast, I mean, between the chosen

---

* Rom. viii. 28-39—A passage which, above all others, must be looked at
from a consolatory and *paracletic* point of view.

and the *cast away*—the *obdurate*—who place themselves in positive hostility against the kingdom of God. The Apostle Paul speaks not only of vessels of dishonour, but of " vessels of *wrath* " also, " fitted to destruction," whom God endures with great long-suffering, in order to shew His wrath, and make his power known (Rom. ix. 22). The apostle views this contrast also as having its foundation in divine appointment, for it was God, he argues, who rejected Pharaoh—yea, regarding the twin brothers Jacob and Esau, when they were still in their mother's womb, he employs those words of the Lord, " Jacob have I loved, but Esau have I hated !" (Rom. ix. 13).   How can we recognize in this contrast a revelation of divine wisdom ?

We must not look upon obduracy in the same light as election ; for while election is the final end of God's ways towards men, obduracy is only a means employed by Him in the historical world-plan.   It belongs to the economy of nature and of history that in this world of sinful men there should be individuals and multitudes who are centres and embodiments of general corruption, and who prepare the way for the kingdom of evil.   God tolerates these vessels of wrath in His economy, *i.e.*, He allows sin to pursue its necessary course, that it may become manifest and ripe for the revelation of His righteousness.   It is the law of history that all that is hidden —all that passes in secret in the heart of hearts, in the depths of the spirit, must be made manifest and brought to light.   A teleologic and reciprocal relation may be traced, therefore, between the vessels of mercy and the vessels of wrath.   By the instrumentality of the vessels of mercy—by the glorious revelation of the kingdom of God in the elect—the hostility of those who are the representatives of corruption, according to their economic position in the kingdom of sin, is aroused and accelerated ; and by their increasing exasperation against the ideal of holiness, they reveal their hidden corruption, and so grow ripe for judgment.   Thus we see how the first appearance of Christianity in the world, bearing the living witness that man is justified by faith alone, aroused the greatest opposition in the preponderating mass of the Jewish people, accelerated the full manifestation of the false spirit of Pharisaism, and made it ripe for judgment : and this opposition on the part of the obdurate, reacted in turn upon the faithful, who appropriated the gospel in greater simplicity of heart, and with stronger conviction;—with an intense earnestness which prompted them to large undertakings, so that, when scattered abroad among the heathen, they went everywhere preaching the Word ; and thus the obduracy of the former, the vessels of wrath, became the historical cause of the salvation of the latter, the vessels of mercy.* Instances answering to this have occurred in all ages. The more lively and vigorous the proclamation of the Faith in the world, the more has it become a sign every where spoken against ; and thus the world has been roused to shew its hostility against the truth, while the truth in turn, in virtue of this opposition, has increased in power. And in that portion of the human race which is given up to the spirit of the world, and abides under the influence of the chiefs of this world, there have never been wanting those who may be described as vessels of wrath, because they are centralizations of the enmity of the world against the ideal of Christian holiness. Yet we cannot venture to pronounce with confidence concerning the final destiny even of these ; for the germ of God's kingdom may lie dormant beneath obduracy, and God is able to transform vessels of wrath into vessels of mercy. Thus the apostle Paul declares that the branches of Israel which were broken off shall in the end be graffed again into their own original noble and chosen stock. And even Paul himself, during a considerable period of his life,—while he was the Saul who persecuted Christ with vehement hatred,—even he had been a vessel of wrath whom God transformed into a vessel of mercy. It is a significant fact that this apostle is distinctively the great asserter and maintainer of the doctrine of election.

§ 224.

To sum up our progressive development of this subject, we see that mankind are divided into various groups in the great economy of universal grace (*gratia universalis*). We have, first, the narrower circle of the elect, who stand in a personal connection with the Lord, in which God's design in the creation of the world has already been commenced, and is

* See Romans x. and xi.

progressing towards its accomplishment. We have, secondly, the circle of those within or without the Church, who are under the influence of prevenient grace. Thirdly, we have those who are left behind or overlooked, who have not yet been recognized by the Holy Ghost, and who still continue to be a large multitude. And lastly, we have the vessels of wrath burning with hatred against the light of holiness, and offering energetic resistance against the kingdom of God. Electing grace must be looked upon as moving through all these different circles of existence,—perfecting the elect—strengthening the weak—giving life to the dead—conquering the hostile—until the fulness of redeemed humanity is gathered together in Christ (πλήρωμα). It thus appears that the last catastrophe must issue in a general restoration, with the bringing back of all free beings to God. Yet here the great question suggests itself, whether, in virtue of the power of free self-determination in man, some individuals may not carry their opposition to grace so far as at last to cease to be in any degree the subjects of gracious influences, because they have carried on their resistance beyond the last boundary of development in time. When the development of mankind is brought to a close, the kingdom of God completed, the building of the temple perfected, the conditions necessary for the conversion of the individual seem no longer to exist;—conversion being conceivable only in a kingdom of freedom still developing itself. The question, moreover, is suggested, whether some may not continue their resistance so long, that repentance is now *too late*. If this be so, the conception of the *fulness* of humanity does not denote the complete numerical sum total of human souls, but the total which expresses the realized idea of humanity ; and those individuals who remain behind, through determined and voluntary obduracy, might be likened to dry and withered branches upon the tree of humanity—chaff which is good for nothing but to be burned,—dregs which must be separated from the purified and glorified Church. The doctrine of Predestination here leads on to eschatological questions. We therefore discontinue our enquiries here, in order to resume them when treating of Eschatology.

THE PLAN OF SALVATION.

§ 225.

The various powers of development, by which the election of grace is accomplished in each individual, are summed up and included in what we call the plan of salvation. The development of the new life in the soul, from its first unseen beginnings, onwards to its perfected state in bliss, embraces a multitude of human circumstances, and holy influences of the Spirit; and presents an inexhaustible mine of study, in the departments of Ethics and Moral Psychology. Nevertheless, the whole may be grouped together under the two great heads REGENERATION and SANCTIFICATION; and in the development of these two main doctrines, the dogmatic principles pertaining to the subject will be presented.

§ 226.

REGENERATION is for the individual man, what the coming of Christ is for the human race: it is the absolute turning point, where the earlier development of character is broken off and terminated, and a new and holy development of life begins; a turning point which has been heralded by a series of external and internal workings of preparatory grace. Regeneration may be described as the breaking out of grace in the man; or, with equal propriety, as the breaking out of freedom in the man; for regeneration denotes precisely that these two factors have henceforward found their living point of union, and that a *new personality* is established, a copy of the divine and human personality of Christ, "If any man be in Christ," says the Apostle, "he is a new creature: old things are passed away; behold, all things are become new."*

Regeneration is not indeed a metamorphosis, a transubstantiation of human nature; the *ego* in man, his personal identity, is the same in essence after regeneration as it was before; but by regeneration the essential principle of the *ego* is realized, and it becomes the free instrument of divine grace. Those, moreover, who have been born again, do not cease to be subject to the influences of worldliness and sin; but the principle of worldliness, the sinful habit of life, is broken off;

* 2 Cor. v. 17.   See also John iii. 5; James i. 18.

and a new and holy habit of life is formed within the soul. In the consciousness of the regenerate man, Christ has become the sacred centre, round which his whole life moves ; and though the flesh has not wholly ceased to be a power within him, the Spirit is the ruling and determining principle of his life ; though this world has still some share in him, yet his inmost will, turning away from it, strives after the ideal of Christlike holiness.

Observations.——Regeneration must not be confounded with AWAKENING, though there is a striking similarity between them, and they are often blended together in real life. Awakening precedes regeneration, but it does not constitute it. Awakening is certainly a work of grace, affecting the entire personality of the man, raising his consciousness to a higher religious state,—a state to which he could not raise himself by his own natural powers merely ; and in which he is brought out of the wonted sphere of his psychological life. Grace kindles a new light in his soul *(illuminatio);* the kingdom of God rises within the man; and he looks upon the world and upon himself in a new light : it impresses the will with a grievous sense of sin and corruption *(contritio)*, and a life of fellowship with Christ appears to be the highest good. But although regeneration is certainly initiated thus ; awakening is a state which precedes regeneration ;—it is the spirit seeking its home, in answer to the effectual call of grace ; but it is not yet the permanent indwelling *(inhabitatio)* of grace within the soul. The awakened man is as yet only roused by grace, he is not actually endowed with grace ; he is still only one of the *called,* not of the *chosen.* There is still wanting the deciding resolve on his own part. Awakening, as such, is only a state of religious distress, a pathos, in which the man is involuntarily influenced ; it must be viewed as analogous to those congenial circumstances in a person's life, which must not be identified with his own free discretion and action. Grace cannot advance towards its goal except through a voluntary act of surrender on the part of the man himself ; by means of this it becomes creative and renewing grace, which as an incorruptible seed (1 Peter i. 23) sinks into the will, takes root in the heart, and thus forms the abiding principle of a new development of character. It is only when this principle of a new development after the image of Christ has taken root, that regeneration is begun ; and there is, accordingly, no surer sign of regeneration than the progress of this development of Christian character throughout the life. But it is obvious that when grace becomes the source of a new development in a man, he must be placed in a new position in relation to that Kingdom which is the organism of the Spirit, to the historic economy of revelation, to the means of grace, and to the rules of Church organisation. We thus perceive the close connection which subsists between regeneration and the sacrament of Baptism. Objectively, regeneration has been already begun in baptism; for by baptism the individual is united to Christ, incorporated into His kingdom, prepared for a new personality : but subjectively, regeneration actively begins when the man enters upon a personal and living relationship to the historical order of God's kingdom, as a member of the body of which Christ is the Head ; and thus derives his spiritual life, not only from individual · religious impulses and experiences, but out of the fulness of the whole.

From what has now been said, it is evident that the time of awakening is the critical and jeopardous point in the progress of man's conversion. For here he is placed in that critical and testing position in which he may resist grace. He may be unwilling to surrender himself self-denyingly to the obedience of truth, although he was willing for a season to rejoice in its light (John v. 35) ; or by indolence he may let slip and lose the acceptable time of grace ; or by self-will he may arrest the awakening in its progress, instead of letting it lead him on to regeneration. Here it is that extravagant enthusiasm or fanaticism begins ; for all such extravagance arises from men's viewing awakening as a prize in itself, eagerly to be seized upon, instead of letting it lead them, in patient and calm submission, on to conversion, and to their appropriate place in the kingdom of God. Hence, too, religious extravagance or fanaticism is usually associated with that religious pride, clad in which the man imposes upon himself, and which he passes off before others as a sort of armour of security for the elect. He thus confounds the light kindled by God with his own whims ; he hates order and discipline, and a lawless, easy-going geniality is the natural counterpart of his temper of mind. The religious systems of enthusiasts, which present such a strange mixture of depth and of confusion, have their foundation in thus impurely confounding the higher light of awakening with the notions of the natural heart. Indications of a naturally genial disposition are often observable in these characters. But as enthusiasts prevent alike the germs of nature and of grace from coming to perfection, according to the laws of historical development,—by conscientious resolve and obedient self-surrender,—the only fruits of such excitement are spiritual abortions, untimely births, caricatures of holiness, such as history affords abundant examples of.

The danger in awakening is forcibly described by Suso * when he says, that many men who have begun to soar high above time and space arrive at a point which may be compared to a deep sea in which many are drowned. For when these men began to look into eternity, they discovered that they had been blind and poor and without God. But now they think that they will be full of God, and grasp at this far too hastily and in an unseemly way. Their patience is like fermenting must ; it is with them as with bees in gathering honey ;—when they first fly out of the hive, they fly about waveringly and unmeaningly, and know neither out nor in ; some go astray and lose themselves, but others are brought back again into the hive.

§ 227.

Regeneration, being the setting up of a new personality in sinful man, includes CONVERSION. The conversion of man is a work of creative grace, breaking the fetters by which his personality had been held bound under the dominion of this world. But it is equally conditioned by human liberty ; man may delay and hinder his conversion (Luke xiii. 3, 6-9) ;

* Heinrich Suso, born 1300, died 1365, was one of the Mystics, a disciple of Eckart, and a contemporary of Tauler. *Tr.*

and it is in this that the power and danger of liberty appear.
But real conversion advances when free will, having surrendered itself to awakening grace, now throws off foreign
dominion, in the strength of creative grace which has found
place within the man, and breaks forth in all its earlier and
normal and living development. It accomplishes this by
means of REPENTANCE (2 Cor. vii. 10). Repentance is not
only grief on account of this or that particular act, it is a fundamental grief, a deep-seated sorrow, on account of the discrepancy and division between the outward acts of the will
and that ideal which is presented to the conscience in the
new Adam, the typical man. Man cannot experience this
repentance by his own spontaneous power, but only through
the holy influences of Christ, which shine into the soul like
enlightening and kindling rays. Genuine and fruitful repentance includes a new *tendency of the Will*, and is thus
associated with FAITH, the personal act of union with Christ,
a trustful self-surrender to Him as the Saviour of the world,
and as the author of a new development of life in harmony
with His own image.

Observations.——No man can be a partaker of salvation without
conversion; and the demand for it, the necessity of it, is
so universal that we must extend it even to those who
have been received into the Church by Infant Baptism.
For though such persons have been incorporated into the
kingdom of grace, and are subjects of the constraining
influences of grace, yet salvation cannot be attained by
them individually, without a *personal* awakening, and
conversion following thereupon. There must occur an
era in the life of the individual, when sin in all its awful
import rises before him, and when a personal surrender
to Christ is made, and a union with Christ is really
brought about. There must be a time when the individual consciously discerns between light and darkness, and
with fixed resolve obeys the apostolic exhortation "to put
off the old man," to stay his sinful habits, and to "put on
the new man." Even they who from childhood upwards
have preserved the innocence of the Christian life,——who
have been steadfast in the faith into which they were
baptized,——are not wholly free from the struggle of free-

dom involved in conversion, although they may experience it in a way different from others. Even in them sinful peculiarities of disposition and habit still possess an opposing power ; and as their life is full of unconscious states, and circumstances unforeseen, the abnormal influences of nature in many ways assert their power over them. When, however, the individual reaches that point in his life at which a free development of character must begin, this development can become a Christian development only by a turning-point in consciousness, whereby a separation is made between the old man and the new. It is certainly the natural law that this should take place at the time when the individual begins to awake to self-consciousness, and to the recognition of the principle of natural development in human life, and must arrive at some decision regarding life's problems ; but it may also take place at a later period, in the experience even of those who have been baptized.

Having thus established the position that awakening and conversion must be experienced by all who shall be saved, it is withal necessary to add, that psychologically the way and manner in which these changes are experienced vary greatly in different persons. That methodistic view, according to which conversion is not real unless it be the result of a so-called struggle of penitence,—in which the man, in anguish, terror, and compunction, feels himself as if sunk in the abyss of ruin, and then at last is raised by grace to joy and peace in believing ;—is based upon mistake and ignorance concerning the great diversities of individual life and character always conditioning the operations of grace. We by no means deny that there are cases of conversion in which great struggles of soul and agitations have been felt, arising from the strength and clearness of the consciousness of sin in the individual. No one indeed can be converted without a living and personal consciousness of general depravity, but certainly the sense of sin in different persons who are converted cannot be equally strong, neither is its sting in the pricks of conscience equally piercing, nor can be. The keenness of the consciousness of sin depends upon temperament, and upon the general complexion of natural

character. Luther, for example, during the period of his
conversion, often wrote to Staupitz, "Oh, my sins, my
sins !" and yet in the Confessional he could name no actual
sins in particular which he had to confess ; so that it was
clearly a sense of the general depravity of his nature which
filled his soul with this deep sorrow and pain. Now, this
feeling must certainly be present in every case of conversion ; but the greatness and intensity of it varies according
to the original and natural disposition of the man. Again,
as the strength of the sense of sin is conditioned by the
psychological possibilities of the individual, it is also influenced to a great extent by diversities in the previous life.
The woman who was a sinner, and who anointed Jesus,
experienced the stings of conscience on account of sin, in a
manner very different from the pure maiden, the Mary who
sat at the feet of Jesus, and heard His word concerning
the " one thing needful ;" though they both had essentially
the same need of redemption. The erroneousness of the
methodistic rule is equally clear from the manifoldness and
variety of the narratives of conversion, which Scripture
presents to us, partly in the Gospels, and partly in the
Epistles. To name but one instance :——How different is
the conversion of Paul, which was attended with a very
deep agitation of soul——trembling and astonishment——
from that of a Nathanael or a John, in whom the change
from the old to the new man was imperceptible, and without any sudden revolution of soul. And yet in them,
equally with Paul, the most thorough transformation of
personal character and life took place ; so that we cannot
unconditionally give the preference to either mode of conversion as superior to the other. The main point in conversion is its thoroughness ; I mean the reality of the change
in the relations between the holy and the worldly principle ;
and this can be realized, according to the peculiarities of
different individuals, quite as well by the still and hidden
movement of the inner man, as by violent agitations.

The idea is equally erroneous that a man must necessarily be able to date his conversion from some particular
moment of time. Narratives of conversion are not wanting, telling us the exact point in the person's life at which

the soul was struck by the lightning flash of grace. But conversion cannot always be traced back to such moments. If, for example, we consider that which happened to Paul on his way to Damascus, not only is it clear from the history of the Apostle, that he had psychologically been prepared for this moment beforehand ;—for this is evident from the divine voice which said to him, " It is hard for thee to kick against the pricks " (Acts ix. 5), implying that there had been something in his conscience which in secret witnessed against him, and told him that he was in the wrong way ;—but it is also plain, that his conversion was not wholly completed at that moment ; because in calm thoughtfulness he had to reflect upon what had happened to him, and with clear deliberate consciousness to surrender himself, in obedience to the Lord who had called him. Accordingly we find that he retired for a season in order to silent reflection, that he received comfort from a disciple, and submitted to the rite of baptism. Thus even his conversion was accomplished by a series of different states of mind. We cite this example as a witness, not, as some take it, that conversion takes place at a definite moment, so that the day and hour can be given —about which there is always much self-delusion—but, on the contrary, to shew that it occupies a section of the man's life, forming an epoch in his history, of longer or shorter duration in different individuals. But as there can be only one period in a man's life which can be called the period of conversion, there may be many different times of awakening, which prepare the way for the deciding turning point.

§ 228.

FAITH in Christ as the Saviour of the world is faith in Him as the Restorer of the normal relation between God and man, or faith in the justification of man through Him. The JUSTIFICATION of the sinner before God means that the decree of God for the redemption of the world, which has been fulfilled in Christ, is appropriated by electing grace to the individual, as the *forgiveness of sins*, and *adoption* into the family of God (Rom. iii. 28 ; v. 1 ; viii. 15 ; Heb. x. 22).

This takes place *essentially* in every one who by baptism is received into the kingdom of redemption; but *actually* and in fact is it accomplished only by an act of human freedom, an act of the deepest self-consciousness in man, appropriating the redeeming love of the Son of God by the power of awakening and life-giving grace. This act is faith, and the justification of man is, therefore, justification by faith.

§ 229.

JUSTIFYING FAITH, as the teachers of the Evangelical Church have specially insisted, is not only an assent of the understanding, but *trust ;* a confidence of the heart, a trustful appropriation of the article of the forgiveness of sins, a heartfelt *certitude* that the Son of God died not only for all, but for *me* (Gal. ii. 20), the individual ;—a faith which, as it is the personal act of the man who ventures to appropriate the redemption provided for the world, is, strictly speaking, the gift of the Spirit of God, the heart of man being in itself too weak for this infinite trust. This believing appropriation of the *crucified* Saviour brings with it actual fellowship of life with the *risen* Saviour in His Church : a fellowship in which the believer possesses the righteousness of Christ, not only outwardly, but inwardly, as a creative principle for a new development of life. Christ dwells in the heart of the man by faith, yea, faith is itself the living bond, the secret point of union between Christ and the individual soul (*unio mystica*) (Gal. ii. 20).

Justification contains a positive and a negative power, which are respectively conditional upon each other. A man cannot be a partaker of the new life unless he have a good conscience, purified from the sense of guilt and of God's displeasure,* and in like manner the forgiveness of sins and the cleansing of the conscience cannot exist without a real and living fellowship with Christ, His fulness and righteousness being the animating principle of individual life.†

---

* Heb. x. 22 : "Let us draw near with a true heart, in full assurance of faith, having our hearts sprinkled from an evil conscience, and our bodies washed with pure water."

† Col. ii. 13 : "And you, being dead in your sins and the uncircumcision of your flesh, he hath quickened together with him, having forgiven you all trespasses."

§ 230.

Justification is not contingent upon the fact of the transformation of the sinner, as to his immediate actions, into a holy and righteous man ; it has its foundation in this,—that God now outwardly *declares* the man righteous, without anything new being implanted within the man himself. It consists in this, that the individual is through Christ placed in the true fundamental relation to God, and therefore can be looked upon by God as just. Thus, as Christ is objectively the pure and holy centre of the human race, in whom the Father determines beforehand the future blessedness of mankind, faith is the holy centre within the individual, in which the Father determines beforehand *his* future blessedness in particular (Rom. viii. 1). For faith is like the grain of mustard-seed, a small, insignificant, but fructifying seed corn, which contains within it the fulness of a whole future. In His gracious contemplation God beholds in the seed corn the future fruit of blessedness ; in the pure will, the realized ideal of freedom

§ 231.

The evangelical principle that faith alone justifies (*sola fides justificat*) rests upon the presupposition that Christ alone justifies. It is only in virtue of the righteousness of Christ, in virtue of the new fundamental relationship with Christ, that man can be reconciled to his God ; and by faith alone, as the profoundest act of susceptibility and subjectiveness on the part of the inner man of the heart, can Christ be appropriated ; by faith alone can man obtain blessedness in its indissoluble completeness. When he resorts to works and to his own pious endeavours, he enters upon the realm of the outward and the manifold, where all is fragmentary and partial. Pelagianism, which would justify men by works, can never even for a moment bring to man the complete certitude of his reconciliation with God. For as the purest pious endeavour is at best but an imperfect approach to the goal, as it alternates between pious progress and retrogression, between a more and a less, the certitude of redemption, which must be built thereupon, is subject to the same imperfection. But no conscience can find rest in a self-persuasion of forgiveness which is only an approach to certitude, and which wavers to and fro between a limited "more" or "less." The Roman Catholic Church teaches, according to her semi-Pelagian theory, that

man is justified not by faith alone, but by works *also*. She
thus weakens the sinner's assurance of his redemption, makes
man's salvation contingent upon his own imperfect endeavours, and affords no true resting-place for the troubled
conscience, convinced of the insufficiency of all human works.
The Evangelical Church teaches that *Christ alone, received by
faith* is the Righteousness of man ; and thus she leads man
back from what is imperfect and multifarious to ONE who is
Himself perfection ; she brings him back from his wanderings
in the desert to the pure Fountain where freedom springs
from grace, to the holy Centre where God looks upon man
not in the light of the temporal and finite, but in the light of
Christ's eternity and perfection. In characterizing this doctrine as dangerous, the Romish Church forgets what the
Evangelical Church further teaches, namely, that justifying
faith cannot possibly exist in the soul in a dead or merely
stationary condition, but that, like the living fruit-bearing
seed-corn, it contains within itself a mighty germinating
power which must necessarily beget a holy development of
life.

Observations.—The doctrine of justification by faith alone is
rightly looked upon as the corner stone of the creed of
the Evangelical Church, because in it the Reformers laid
hold upon that which makes Christian faith a saving faith,
upon the distinctive feature of the Christian's relation to
God. This doctrine made its appearance as a *reforming*
doctrine in the full sense of the word, in the sixteenth
century, not only because it led men back to the true
source of doctrine, the Word of God, but because it also
led them back to the inmost and living source of religious
consciousness, which in the Romish Church had been for
the most part hidden beneath the rubbish of tradition
and human teaching. Pelagian objections against this
doctrine spring from a conscience which has never really
experienced the sense of sin,—which has not experienced
the struggle in which alone man learns to feel the absolute majesty of the law, that holy ideal far above him ,
by which alone in the consciousness of his unworthiness
and guilt, man feels himself surrounded by the terrors of
eternity : a conflict which may vary *outwardly* accord-

ing to the varieties of human character, but whose inward reality none can be ignorant of who personally participates in the blessings of salvation. As to the Romish Church, she has weakened the high solemnity of this doctrine by her semi-Pelagian theory ; and this theory, she must confess, has been practically objected to in the stern realities of life and death, by many of her very members, who, in the inmost experience of their souls, have borne witness for the evangelical doctrine. It has been said with truth regarding the evangelical doctrine, that although it is rejected by the Romish Church, it nevertheless lives within her pale as a hidden esoteric tradition, and is practically embraced by thousands in place of the outward tradition, which in theory is maintained. Not only have the great teachers of the Middle Age, an Anselm and a Bernard, not only have the host of witnesses who are called the forerunners of the Reformation, given their testimony for this doctrine, but the history of the pastorate, the cure of souls, within the Romish Church, abundantly proves that the evangelical doctrine alone can give real comfort to troubled and helpless consciences. Thus it brought peace to Luther, when, as a monk, and experiencing great struggles of conscience, he was referred to Romans iii. by an old Augustinian brother, in proof that a man is justified by faith without the deeds of the law. The evangelical truth is also implied in the old custom of the Romish Church, clearly symbolical, of holding a crucifix before the dying. For what else could this custom mean, except that the man now in the solemn hour of death, must rely, not upon his own merits, not upon the merits of the saints, but solely upon the crucified Christ, as the only Mediator ?

This crucifix it was that Pius VII., the noblest and most severely tried Pope of modern church history, pressed to his breast in his dying moments, while with strong words he refused the name " most holy Father," which some one addressed to him. " What!" he exclaimed, " *most holy Father !* I am a poor sinner."*

---

* H. Thiersch, Vorlesungen über Katholicismus u. Protestantismus II. 129.

§ 232.

In conversion and justification, regeneration or the establishment of a new personality has really taken place; and from this source SANCTIFICATION proceeds, sanctification or the development of the new character, by which the entire natural individuality is builded together into a personal and living Temple of the Holy Ghost (2 Cor. vi. 16 ; Rom. viii. 5-10). As Christianity is both a redemption and a new creation, as regeneration includes the forgiveness of sins and a new germ of life, sanctification also must give expression to both these truths. The development of Christian character must be carried on by a continual dying unto sin, and a continual rising again to newness of life (Rom. vi. 4), a progressive realization of personal perfection, which solves a given problem in the kingdom of God by pious fruitfulness. Both processes are inseparable from the true conception of the imitation of Christ. If the negative process be exclusively maintained, it presents merely that ascetic pietistic holiness, which aims only to purify the life from sin, without building up anything new. It keeps in view the death of the Lord, but not His resurrection ; it makes the gospel, a gospel only of suffering ; and life, nothing but a continual dying in the school of the cross, a continual penitential conflict. If, on the contrary, the positive process be exclusively maintained, there follows a false geniality in Christian piety, a mixture of the Christian ideal with that of the ancients, which considers the laying down of the cross and neglect of repeated penitence quite compatible with pious fruitfulness and personal perfection. Both processes must be combined in order to true Christian development, and no work deserves the name of Christian which is not on the one hand a purifying and testing work, whose aim is to banish the power of sin, and on the other hand, a holy and creative work, which accomplishes a new thing upon earth.

§ 233.

No character can be conceived of without talent, without some original and natural gift, which receives a moral quality from the will ; indeed the very idea of character involves a union of talent and will. This is illustrated in the development of Christian character. The innate and natural capacities of the individual are sanctified by grace; the gifts of nature become gifts of grace—χαρίσματα. The Charisma, therefore, is in part a gift of nature *purified* by grace;—for it is only by grace that talent can be freed from the one-sidedness and egotism originally bound up in it, and can unfold its innate power;—and in part it is a gift of nature, *elevated* by grace, the natural gift being penetrated by the holy influences of God's kingdom, as by a fructifying blessing. As, therefore, the essence of the charisma lies in regeneration, sanctification may more accurately be described as the progressive development of the charisma, a development realized partly in the growth and partly in the work of freedom. " Neglect not," says Paul to Timothy, " the gift that is in thee, which was given thee; . . . . meditate upon these things, give thyself wholly to them that thy profiting may appear to all. Take heed unto thyself and unto the doctrine; continue in them: for in doing this thou shalt both save thyself and them that hear thee" (1 Tim. iv. 14-16).

§ 234.

As the kingdom of God embraces a kingdom of regenerate persons, it is also a kingdom of CHARISMATA (1 Cor. xii.) There are diversities of gifts, but one Spirit. As there are many members in the natural body, and a distinction must be made between the more honourable and the less honourable members, so also is it in the spiritual body, the kingdom of God. But all the several special gifts of grace find their bond of union in those *general* gifts of grace, which are common to all, and in all times; namely, *faith, hope, and charity;* of which again charity is the chief, because it lives beyond time, and never fails (1 Cor. xiii.). The individual can develop his charisma only by the reciprocal action of love, blending it with the various other charismata which all belong to the one great kingdom. He cannot accomplish his sanctification by leading an egotistic, morbid, and isolated life; but only by blending his own life with that of the community. Just as Christ must truly live in the individual, so must the Church of Christ, with its sufferings and its triumphs, carry on an actual life in Him likewise. The ideal of Christian perfection which is before the true christian in all his efforts, is involved in the ideal of the Church. The apostle describes it, when he says, " Till we all come in the unity of the faith and of the knowledge of the Son of God, unto a perfect man, unto the measure of the stature of the fulness of Christ" (Eph. iv. 13), a state wherein the Church, in the fulness of her developed gifts, will represent the pure and spotless image of Christ's perfection ; and accordingly the apostle, in that passage, represents the church as if a single individual, as " one perfect man."

Observations.—If we keep in view the distinctions which exist among the regenerate, we are led back again to a general contrast which we have already considered in the first creation. As we saw in considering the contrast between Creatianism and Traducianism, that in the economy of the first creation there are some individuals who prevailingly embody creative force of character, and others who prevailingly illustrate preserving grace ; we find this repeated in the economy of the new creation. For while all regenerate persons are new creatures in Christ, while each of them is a new personal centre of life ; we can here also discern a relative difference between such individuals as are points of beginning to new developments of the kingdom of God, and who may in a special sense be called chosen instruments ;—individuals who become fructifying springs of life for the neighbourhood around, in larger or smaller spheres, and who may accordingly be called the creative points for the kingdom ; —and persons who only repeat and reproduce the established order of God's kingdom, the religious and moral tradition handed down by the whole fellowship, though certainly in a living and personal way. The difference is only relative; for every regenerate man possesses in reality both powers. But the relative difference becomes apparent in action, although it is again done away in the unity of love, and in the fact that every one born again possesses the whole Christ by justifying faith.

§ 235.

As the regenerate, who are also the subjects of sanctification, do not move towards the goal of perfection in undisturbed progress, but with continual warfare against their old sinful nature, which does not cease to oppose the principle of holiness ; and as the possibility of another fall and declension in sanctification is presented : the question occurs whether there can be an absolute FALL FROM GRACE ; so that the work of the new creation in the individual would be wholly undone. We deny this ; and we must, on this point, give our approval to the theologians of the Reformed Church in opposition to those of the Lutheran. The most grievous falls may indeed take place in the life of the regenerate man ; he may suffer many shipwrecks through the temptations of the world, as regards the Faith as well as the life ; only we maintain that the injury cannot be absolutely fatal. For the essential idea of regeneration is, that grace is implanted as an incorruptible seed in the will, and has formed in the individual a new principle of heart, of will, and of character ; a principle which cannot be rooted out, but which strives continually against sin, and leads to sorrow and repentance on account of it. From this point of view only, can we understand the Apostle's declaration, that " he who is born of God, cannot commit sin because his seed remaineth in him, and he cannot sin, because he is born of God " (1 John iii. 9). In cases where experience seems to witness that the regenerate have wholly fallen from grace, we must say, either that the fall has not really taken place ; *i.e.*, no absolute and final apostacy ; —as, for instance, in the case of many who have fallen by denying Christ when suffering persecution, or affected with bodily torture ;—or, that regeneration had not really taken place, but was only an awakening, about which, not only ourselves, but others, are liable to the greatest delusions. Very much which has the appearance of regeneration is wanting in its power. A pietism, which rests securely in Christian feeling and delights in Christian phrases, is not necessarily regeneration, but may very probably be " *without root.*" An orthodoxy, enthusiastic for the creed and for a system which is exclusively saving, is not necessarily actuated by saving faith ; thorns and briers may be within it, and a stony ground. A merely apparent regeneration, such as this, may easily degenerate and come to nought. But when we assert that the truly regenerate cannot finally fall from grace, we by no means imply that they are exempt from the sternest conflicts. For as no one can tell by experience when he actually entered upon a state of grace, trust in God's grace must ever be linked with watchfulness and circumspection ; and in this respect the Lutheran view will ever retain its practical worth. The dark possibility of being cast away must have a subjective validity and power in the consciousness, even of the regenerate man, who experiences the hidden power of sin in the prevailing conflict of life; and who, under the sense of his own weakness, cannot but tremble for and mistrust himself. Thus we see that even the Apostle Paul once expressed a fear lest having preached to others, he himself should be a castaway ; (1 Cor. ix. 27) ; a fear which, doubtless, was subjectively most real ; although we cannot allow the objective possibility, that Paul could fall from grace ; for the Apostle himself elsewhere (Romans viii. 38, 39) gives expression to the most perfect confidence in the unchangeable grace and election of God. " I am persuaded," he says, " that neither death, nor life, nor angels, nor principalities, nor powers, nor things present, nor things to come, nor height, nor depth, nor any other creature, shall be able to separate us from the love of God, which is in Christ Jesus our Lord."

Observations.——Our Lord warns us against a merely apparent regeneration, not only in the parable of the sower, but also in the parable of the wise and foolish virgins (Matt. xxv. 1-13.) The foolish virgins had certainly some faith, some hope, some love ; they were delighted with the new light which burned in the lamps of the spirit ; but they had neglected to take oil. They wanted that which should provide the new flame of life with its proper nourishment ; they lacked the true foundation of mind and will ; they were awakened, but not born again. The wise virgins, on the contrary, though they fell asleep like the foolish virgins, and were thus equally chargeable with a fall, yet when they were awakened by the sudden coming of the Lord, they still had oil wherewith to trim their lamps, *i.e.*, their fall was only partial ; they were able to restore themselves, in virtue of the foundation of Christian character which was in them. They were really regenerate.——(Heb. vi. 4, we may understand as referring to the awakened only ; Matt. xii. 32, concerning the sin against the Holy Ghost, we may understand as referring to a state of perfect impenitence, in which the man offers a malevolent resistance (*resistentia malitiosa*, as distinct from *resistentia naturalis*) to awakening and attracting grace in his own heart.

THE MEANS OF GRACE.

§ 236.

If the Church were only a kingdom of invisible operations of grace, it would be strictly and exclusively a mystical and internal kingdom. But, as in the fulness of time, Christ appeared as Grace and Truth, historically revealed, so, in virtue of His eternal dominion as King, He is continually present in His Church, by means of His historical institutions. It is by the institutions of Christ that the Church becomes visible or historical; by these, moreover, the connection is organically maintained between the Church and her glorified Saviour, so that the workings of the Spirit in the fellowship may be experienced as the workings of Christ. By means of these institutions, Christ continually abides as the principle of the Church's *doctrine* and *worship:* he keeps her in the true and saving doctrine by the divine Word, which He has entrusted to her; He keeps her in the true worship by the holy ordinances and acts which He has appointed.

THE WORD OF GOD AND THE HOLY SCRIPTURES.

§ 237.

What is to be preached? What is to be taught? How shall the divine service of Christ be harmonized with that which was from the beginning? These questions bring us back to the Holy Scriptures of the New Testament, as the authentic and perfect witness of what the first and original Christianity was, of the Christianity which was first preached, and which must abide through all the changes of time. The Church, indeed, was first established by an oral revelation of the word, by a word of man regarding the Law and the Gospel, which is essentially and in fact the Word of God. But certain as it is that the Lord has not seen fit to give a continuous inspiration to His Church, a self-continuing and living apostleship, such as the Romish Church imagines, it is equally certain that the oral tradition of Christianity was subject in the course of time to all the uncertainty—the possibility of falsification—which is inseparable from the spoken word. Oral tradition would, in process of time, only too easily have ceased to be the *true* tradition of Christianity, had not the holy and apostolic Scriptures been given to the Church, whereby to decide between true and false tradition, and to govern the living, self-propagating, and self-developing Christian consciousness. The oral word is in its nature transitory and vanishing, so also is the swiftly-flowing river of time in which it is uttered; and it may be torn from its connection with another spoken word, which modifies, if it does not extinguish, the impression of the first word. But Scripture bids the swiftly-flowing stream of time stand still, and gives to the flying word an abiding unchangeable presence. Accordingly, no historical revelation can dispense with some holy Scripture. We find also that Christ did not place any reliance upon the oral tradition of the Jews; He often described it as a human planting, which should be rooted up; while, on the contrary, we hear Him say continually, "It is written;" we hear Him ask, "How readest thou?" And the first and Apostolic Church, though without the New Testament Scriptures, which had not yet been formed, referred, like our Lord, to the Old Testament Scriptures, in order to establish the due connexion between their free and spoken word, and the *historical* economy of Revelation. Thus it may with truth be said, there never has been a time in the course of Church history during which a perfect *interregnum* has found place,—an interval during which no divine and written authority was recognized. And would we discern between the true and the false in the vast multitude and variety of ecclesiastical traditions, would we arrive at a full certainty regarding what is taught us orally in relation to Christianity, we must, as Luke told Theophilus, resort to the Scriptures, ἵνα ἐπιγνῷς περὶ ὧν κατηχήθης λόγων τὴν ἀσφαλειαν (Luke i. 4.) Even supposing that the Scriptures were not needed for the founding of the Church, they are clearly necessary for its maintenance; and they must be looked upon as the work of the same divine providential activity, which revealed itself in the formation of the Church. Although, moreover, they cannot be considered the direct ap-

pointment of the Lord ;—for as we have nothing written by
the Lord, neither have we any word from Him on record,
commanding His disciples to write ;—we must nevertheless
regard the Scriptures as indirectly the work of the Lord's
wisdom ; the fruit and fulfilment of that promise of the Spirit
which Christ gave His followers.

§ 238.

The true idea of the Inspiration of Holy Scripture was
given in our exposition of the inspiration of the apostles ; for
the apostles possessed no other inspiration when they wrote
than that which was upon them in every official act. It must,
however, be confessed that betwixt the spoken word and
writing in a systematic manner there subsists this relation—
writing compresses the copiousness of the oral word into a
permanent form, and is the expression or embodiment, now
fixed and settled, and purified by careful consideration, of the
inspired thoughts ; so that we have in Holy Scripture the
ripened fruit of inspiration. As, therefore, we have already
recognized the perfect imprint of the Spirit of inspiration in
the combined consciousness of the apostles, we recognize the
same in Holy Scripture. Its perfect and canonical authority
does not depend upon any one writing, but upon the whole
collection of writings, which supplement one another, and must
therefore be taken together ; and in this dogma regarding
Scripture is involved the truth, that we have in the New
Testament, not merely fragments of the apostolic age which
have by chance been preserved to us, but an harmonious
whole, complete within itself, wherein no principle of apostolic
consciousness is wanting ; a reflection or copy of the perfect
and undivided fulness of the Apostolic spirit.

§ 239.

The apostolic consciousness embodies and represents the
central consciousness of truth, the fundamental truth concerning *the things which pertain to the kingdom of God.* " Ye received the word of God which ye heard of us," says the
Apostle, " not as the word of men, but as it is in truth, the
word of God." * In relation to those things, therefore, the
apostolic consciousness is raised above all the limitations and

* 1 Thes. ii. 13. See also John xiv. 16 ; xv. 26 ; 2 Peter i. 19 ; 2 Tim. iii. 15.

imperfections pertaining to what is temporal. But in relation to all that is not an inextinguishable article of fundamental truth, it is liable to the uncertainty attaching to the temporal and finite; and this finiteness and relativity must leave its impress upon the apostolic writings.* If unlimitedness were claimed for inspiration it would not be the representative *beginning* of a free development, it would be identical with the final display or review of all things in God, which can only be conceived of as the *end* of that development. We must, accordingly, maintain not only the union of the divine and human in Scripture, but at the same time the distinction between these two. The old proposition, *the Scripture is the Word of God*, expresses the union; the more modern dictum, *the Scriptures contain the Word of God*, expresses the distinction. The first proposition is clearly preferable to the second, which is vague and indistinct, and may be applied to many writings. The first, however, is untrue, if it be taken so to affirm the union, as to exclude all distinction of the divine and human elements in the Bible. From this point of view that theory of inspiration has arisen which looks upon the sacred writers as merely dependent instruments, which extends inspiration to every tittle and every point even in the Old Testament, and wholly ignores anything of transient and casual import, which is to be found, nevertheless, in every book. The opposite proposition, which does not venture to assert that scripture *is* the word of God, but that it only *contains* the Word of God, considers only the distinction between the divine and human elements, and overlooks the all-pervading, obvious, and typical union of these in scripture, the sacred, all-pervading, apparent, and fundamental truth, which in unsullied clearness enwraps and even subdues the temporal and human narrowness. Supposing that the evangelists contradict one another in historical and chronological details of the life of Jesus, which do not affect the substance of the revelation, this does not obscure a single lineament of that portrait of Christ, which they have painted in colours given them by the Holy Ghost. Were the historical discrepancies of such a kind as to occasion, in one point or another, a distorted apprehension of Christ's

* 1 Cor. vii. 6 : τοῦτο δὲ λέγω κατα συγγνώμην, οὐ κατ᾽ ἐπιταγήν.

person, or in the least to disturb the fundamental view of the facts on which the revelation is based, in this case only would their inspiration be invalidated. Though the words of Christ may not always be repeated (by John, for example) with literal exactness, this does not invalidate the fact that the reproduction is canonical, provided that they are repeated in the Spirit, of whom the Lord himself said, " He will bring all things to your remembrance whatsoever I have spoken unto you," and " He shall *glorify* me, for He shall receive of Mine and show it unto you " (John xiv. 26 ; xvi. 14).   Inspiration does not depend upon the exact and formal *recollection*, but upon the true *remembrance ;*—not upon the merely literal retention, but upon the fair reproduction, of Christ's discourses. A just reproduction is the main thing required, and when the Apostles bring forward new ordainments in relation to doctrine and the conduct of the Church, even in these cases their own productivity is only a continuous reproduction and glorifying of Christ.

Observations.—In the employment of the proposition, "the Scripture is the Word of God," we must also distinguish between the Word of God as it holds good for *all* times, and as it applies only to *one* particular time ; a distinction the importance of which especially appears, when we consider the circumstances of the apostolic Church.   The apostolic Church is the representative centre of union from which all subsequent stages of Church development are to spring ; yet it is itself, at the same time, only one, the first of these very stages.   Whatever apostolic regulations therefore arose merely out of the exigencies of the times, —as, for example, the community of goods, the combining of the *Agapae* with the Lord's Supper, the decisions of the apostolic college conditioning the admission of the Gentiles,—these are only of temporary obligation.   We must throughout the New Testament distinguish between what is transitory and what is abiding, between τὸ καταργούμενον and τὸ μένον (2 Cor. iii. 11).   Were we to extend the representative character of the New Testament as a pattern for our guidance, to every thing it contains, and to maintain, as many sects do, the permanent obligation of every direction in the early Church, we should fall into the same error with respect to the successors of the apostles, as if, like many monastic orders, we were to imitate the followers of Christ as literally our patterns, and to copy their habits and their dress in the outward relations of life. Meanwhile, however, we must repeat, that although many regulations were only of temporary obligation, the general practice (πρᾶξις) of the Church,—the spirit of love, the wisdom, and the discipline, manifest in those regulations,—is exemplary for her permanent guidance. Since even those regulations were prompted and illuminated by the thoughts of eternal wisdom, they contain a word of God which speaks to us also. *Est enim* PERPETUA *voluntas evangelii consideranda in decreto.*[*]

§ 240.

The older theology expressed the representative character and import of Holy Scripture, by saying, that it contains all things necessary to be known in order to salvation; and this proposition is certainly true, though it does not express the whole truth. By giving prominence to *salvation* as solely and exclusively the reference and design of Scripture, we confine our thoughts too much to the individual, and give too much occasion for the error, which has often manifested itself in the Protestant Church, of making the necessity of Scripture a necessity for the individual alone. But some individuals cannot perhaps even read, and yet may be saved by hearing and keeping the word of God; and moreover, Scripture contains much more than the individual must know in order to salvation. The necessity of Scripture is not *principally* for the individual, but for the Church; and its full import and design is stated rather in the assertion, that it contains all truth necessary for the preservation of the Church, and for its progressive development towards its final consummation. This again is to say, that by means of Holy Scripture, under the continual guidance of the Holy Spirit, the Church not only may be kept in purity of doctrine and true worship, but that in the whole course of her development there can be no new practice or law established, be it in relation to doctrine or to life, which she cannot abolish by means of the eternal principles of truth and

* Confessio Augustana, pars. ii., Art. vii., De Potestate Ecclesiastica, 33.

life laid down in holy Scripture : moreover, that on the one hand, all critical and cleansing activity in the church, and on the other hand, all building up, edifying and strengthening activity (taking this expression in its widest sense), must find its governing type for all times in the Holy Scriptures. Maintaining as we do that the Holy Ghost guides the church into all the truth by means of Scripture, we attribute to Scripture perfect sufficiency and clearness (*sufficientia et perspicuitas*) ; in so far, that is, as the Church is given through Scripture the revelation of the Spirit concerning what is advisible or useful for *any particular time,* while Scripture itself must be looked upon as for *all times,*—much that it contains not being perfectly accomplished until the latter days. Experience, moreover, teaches that whenever a true reform has been accomplished in the church, the word, *It was not so in the beginning,* has been spoken with telling power against a lifeless ecclesiasticism, because it has been spoken in the strength of Holy Scripture. This holds good not only of the great Reformation of the sixteenth century, but of the many successive protests which have been made both in the Middle Ages and in modern times. For as the church has, in every age, triumphed over that false *gnosis,* which resolves Christianity into merely human reason, by the Word of Scripture, this same word has been a safeguard against a barren orthodoxy, which has built up ecclesiasticism at the expense of Christianity ; and it has continually led back to an illumination inseparable from edification, because the apostolic illumination is in its essence an enlightenment which leads on to salvation.

§ 241.

As holy Scripture is the canon for *the Church* only, it is manifest that a necessary reciprocity must continually subsist between it and ecclesiastical tradition. By the transmission of the Church, Scripture has been handed down to us, and the Church it was that collected the books of the canon, as they are in living use at the present day. We cannot indeed look upon our traditional canon as a work of inspiration, yet we cannot but recognize the fact that the ancient church had a special call to this work ; and that this collection of books, —which has obtained unanimous recognition in the most contrasted quarters in the Church, and thus has received *œcumenical* ratification,—has been determined under the guidance of the Spirit who was to lead the Church, according to her Lord's promise, into all truth, and who must above all have guided her to discern the genuine works of the Spirit, and to distinguish them from the mass of apocryphal writings. To deny that the early Church performed this task, is to deny that the Scriptures given by God have the power to claim for themselves admission and recognition in the Church. The fact, however, that the early church did solve the question regarding canonicity, by no means excludes the possibility that this or that writing which has been received into the canon of tradition, may be only of doubtful genuineness ; for the early church itself has in a manner recognized this by her idea of the ἀντιλεγόμενα : neither does it exclude the possibility that those canonical writings which must be looked upon as authentic in a doctrinal point of view, *i.e.*, as the work of the Spirit of tradition, may have proceeded from another apostolic author than him whose name they bear. Accordingly we must say, and this is the Protestant antithesis to the Catholic view—that the canon must be capable of correction by that growing perception of what is canonical, whose improvement in the Church must never be regarded as having ceased. In the strength of this it was that Luther expressed his condemnatory judgment regarding the epistle of James and the Apocalypse. And though his judgment was certainly one-sided, yet he thus illustrates a principle which the church must never surrender,—namely, that having received the Scriptures only by tradition, we must again demand that tradition shall establish its proof by the internal structure and actual contents of the writings transmitted, rather than by a new revision of old witnesses or independent investigation.

Observations.—Even if the books of the New Testament were anonymous, they would internally witness to their antiquity or *primitiveness* by comparison with other works which Christian literature has preserved ; and this is strikingly manifest, if we compare them with the writings which we assign to the following period, those of the Apostolic Fathers. We certainly find tokens of a deep

Christian life in the works of the Apostolic Fathers, yet the remarkable lack of new thought, and the constant repetition of words from the Apostolic Scriptures, alike witness that, in a spiritual sense, an ebb has ensued upon a mighty flood, or that the Church is no longer under the influence of extraordinary powers of inspiration, but that now, though by no means forsaken of the Spirit, she is subject to the prosaic law of natural development. And even where we recognize a lofty flight of the spirit, as in the Ignatian Epistles, the inspiration repeatedly is merely a religious enthusiasm, a subjective romance, showing itself in an almost revelling desire for martyrdom, moving and even infectious; so that many who read an Ignatian epistle for the first time, feel themselves doubtless more excited and stirred than by a Pauline one; but this very feature proves that it is not really inspired; for the Spirit who founded the Church does not tolerate the extolling of one isolated tendency in the soul, and cannot bear such subjective partiality of view, be it ever so strong, ever so apparently admirable. The consciousness of the man really inspired, is absolutely ruled by the pure and objective power of the truth, and notwithstanding the greatest depth of internal feeling and of soul, notwithstanding the most overwhelming fulness of the stream of thought, its language ever bears the impress of the rest of eternity, of omniscient wisdom and thoughtfulness, which, side by side with warmth and fulness of life, is to be found *only* in the writers of the New Testament.

We readily allow that there may be reason for distinguishing in the New Testament itself between protocanonical and deutero-canonical portions. It is the work of biblical criticism to cultivate the mind to appreciate the canonical Scriptures in their peculiar features as distinct from other contemporary and subsequent writings; a faculty which is comprehended according to its true import in that "proving of the spirits" of which the Apostle speaks (1 John iv. 1). We see this critical faculty in its purest state in the early Church who collected the writings of the New Testament into the canon; while it has been reserved for the modern Church, by a continual examination of particulars, to educate the delicacy of this sense. As for a newer kind of criticism, which fancies that all must be begun anew, and that the canon must now first be discovered, it may perhaps be distinguished for learning and acuteness, but cannot claim the appellation "theological," because no theological criticism could begin with an entire mistrust of œcumenical tradition, but, on the contrary, must proceed upon the pre-supposition that the fundamental question has been solved. And now that the latest criticism of our day has taken upon itself to argue, that in fact we are not in possession of any canonical Scriptures whatever, and that the church itself is labouring under a perfect delusion as to its own origin ; such criticism may certainly give a new impulse to theological criticism, in order to the surer establishing of the truth, but it can possess only a transient and vanishing importance, and must be ranked in one and the same category with the old gnostic attacks upon the Scriptures.

§ 242.

The correspondent relation between Scripture and tradition will further appear if we examine the question as to the interpretation and meaning of Scripture. "Understandest thou what thou readest ?" This question will always call forth the answer on the part of the individual : "How can I, except some man should guide me ?" (Acts viii. 30, 31). Were we to say that it is the Church's province to explain the Scriptures, by the same Spirit that produced them, we certainly could not, like the Roman Catholic Church, insist upon an inspired collection of churches, or an infallible apostolical chair of doctrine, to which we should go for the true interpretation. But it by no means follows that the interpretation of Scripture is to be left to a merely subjective discretion, or a *judicium privatum.* For there lives within the Church a general historical and fundamental consciousness, a consciousness, not merely invisible and undefined, but which already expressed itself in the primitive age of Church history in œcumenical confessions, of which the Apostle's creed stands first in order. The Church knows itself to be in organic connection with this œcumenical tradition, which stands on higher ground than the *judicium privatum* of the individual, and far above the individual limitedness of any one man's confession. But though she thus makes use of the *guidance* of tradition in order to the understanding of Scripture, this by no means violates her principle, that tradition must in turn be tested, purified, and more perfectly developed by Holy Scripture. It is true even of the Apostles' Creed that being a work, in its present form, clearly post-apostolic, it cannot possess the same critical authority as Holy Scripture. And it is only because this symbol proves itself to have been in each of its parts the purely biblical symbol of the first three centuries, springing from the same source as Scripture, that it approves itself to us as a *symbolum irreformabile.* (Compare what has already been said in the Introduction.)

Scripture and Tradition stand in indissoluble and reciprocal relation to each other, and "what God hath joined together let no man put asunder." We behold the severing of Tradition from Scripture in the Roman Catholic Church of the Middle Ages, and arising therefrom the uncritical confusion of what is sacred and profane, of the Word of God with the propositions of men, of revelation and mythology—a tradition running to seed, which, with its proud ramifications, soon overspread the whole life, and formed a religious labyrinth out of which the Reformers succeeded in finding their way, only by the help of Holy Scripture and the old œcumenical tradition. If, on the other hand, Scripture be separated from tradition, there ensues that merely spontaneous subjective use of Scripture, which we see variously in the Protestant Church, that *judicium privatum,* which considers not only that the symbols of the Church are beset with relative imperfection, but that now, apart from all pre-suppositions, it must again be made the subject of enquiry what Christianity is.

§ 243.

Regarding the question, lastly, how Christ, as the Head of the Church, maintains and guides His Church by means of Holy Scripture, we may say that He keeps her in the true tradition by the Spirit, through whom He dwells continually within her; and He carries on her normal development by means of Holy Scripture. But as the Church can be guided

only by the instrumentality of living men, a teachership has
been instituted by our Lord, whose distinctive duty is personally to witness to the faith of the community, and to expound
Scripture according to the gifts of the Spirit possessed by them.
And in extraordinary times, when a fermenting influence pervades men's hearts, and when problems of reformation suggest
themselves, the Lord, in an extraordinary manner, raises up
chosen instruments, men gifted with a prophetic spirit, by
whom the faith and the progress of the Church are re-estab-
lished ; and who, in virtue of the new treasures of wisdom and
knowledge which the Lord reveals to them out of His holy
Word, are ably qualified to lead the Church on to a new progressive stage of her history, to a *progress* which in the
deepest sense of the term is ever a *retrogression*, a return to
the original and first truth ; by which means the spiritual bond
between the Church and the apostles is made more genuine
and sure. In the sense thus explained, we say, that the Lord
continues His prophetic office in the Church by means of Holy
Scripture.

THE ORDAINMENTS OF THE LORD.

§ 244.

As the Lord strengthens His Church by means of saving
doctrine, He also maintains her by true worship ; for doctrine
and worship are as inseparable from each other as truth and
life. In a general sense, the whole Christian life may be
called a service of God, a worship ; but as the kingdom of God
was not only to be a secret thing in this world ; as it consists
not merely in hidden and internal piety, not only as leaven
penetrating human life, but is also to make itself known in
its own independent reality, the service of God must be embodied in a range of sacred observances, in which the Church
can unite, apart from the labour and strife of worldly life, in
order to realize the true purpose of the kingdom of God, in
spirit and in truth, and free from admixture with the aims and
business of this world. The distinctive mark of true worship
is, that not only human will, but divine grace also fulfils the
object of the service, namely, union with the Lord, and union
of the faithful with each other in the fellowship of the Lord ;
or, again, true worship is not only a relation in which man

puts himself with God, but equally a relation wherein God puts Himself towards man.   It is, moreover, the fundamental mystery of Christian worship that Christ, as the eternal Lord and King of His Church, is not absent from the congregation, but truly present (Matt. xviii. 29), and puts His invisible activity into the holy ordinances appointed by Him, "for the perfecting of the saints, for the edifying of the body" (Eph. iv. 12.)   The holy observances, which present themselves not only as acts of the fellowship, but as acts of Christ living within the Church, and which remain as the permanent fundamentals of worship, are the preaching of God's Word, prayer in the name of Jesus, and the Sacraments.   "They continued steadfastly in the apostles' doctrine and fellowship, and in breaking of bread, and in prayers" (Acts ii. 42.)   This picture of the first community of believers in Jerusalem is applicable essentially to every Christian community.   However manifold the forms which Christian worship has assumed in the course of time, they may all be traced back to the fundamental elements here named.   Liturgical formularies are only the permanent expression of what should be the subjects of preaching and of prayer.   Praise is connected with prayer in the name of Jesus, and is the form by which the whole community prays aloud.   And all pictorial art, all symbolism in worship, is connected with the idea of the Sacraments, with the idea of embodying what is holy in outward form.

THE PREACHING OF GOD'S WORD.

§ 245.

"Faith cometh by hearing, and hearing by the Word of God" (Rom. x. 17.)   Christian preaching, as the living witnessing for Christ, as the living proclamation of the Law and the Gospel to awaken and to strengthen faith, to build up the fellowship of the Lord, is not merely a spontaneous work of a private individual, not merely an arrangement made by the Church ; it rests upon the command of Christ himself.   The command of Christ for preaching—" Go ye into all the world, and preach the gospel to every creature" (Mark xvi. 15)— relates, in the first instance, to missionary work ; but the newly converted ever need new instruction and edification ;—

" if ye continue in my word (ἐαν ὑμεῖς μείνητε ἐν τῷ λόγῳ τῷ ἐμῷ) then are ye my disciples indeed, and ye shall know the truth, and the truth shall make you free " (John viii. 31) ;—and herein is clearly implied the appointment of preaching as a permanent and constituent part of Christian worship, just as we hear from the apostle that the Lord has ordained " Pastors and Teachers " in His Church, " for the perfecting of the saints, for the edifying of the body of Christ " (Eph. iv. 11, 12.) It is not that there are merely speakers and hearers who edify one another by the preaching of the Word ; it is the Lord himself who builds up His Church by this means of grace. As the heaven-ascended Saviour, He is present with His Word in the power of the Spirit, He gives to the preaching its due authority and its proper unction, invisibly He works together with His preachers. " They went forth, and preached every-where, the Lord *working with them* " (Mark xvi. 20.) Chris-tian preaching, therefore, is not merely a word of man *about* Christ, it is Christ himself who in it gives His presence for the world and for believers, continually coming anew by His Spirit, of whom He said, " He shall bring all things to your remembrance, whatsoever I have said unto you, and He shall glorify me " (John xiv. 26 ; xvi. 14.) This is the mystery of Christian preaching, which distinguishes it from all other speaking which may be carried on about an historical person, that in proportion as it is preached in the name of Christ, the word exerts essentially the same influences in order to awaken and strengthen faith in the *Person* of Christ, as if He moved about here below in bodily form,—with really the same in-fluence, in order to awaken and to strengthen faith unto salvation, which is given us in Him. All this is clear if we remember that the Church does not possess merely an absent, but a really present Christ, who proves His living power in His Word. If Christian preaching were only a continual reminding us about the Lord, notwithstanding all endeavour put forth in order to refresh our memory of Him, this remem-brance would no less certainly fade away according to the universal law of history ; His image could in no way exercise a life-giving power ; and we who have never known the Lord after the flesh would be far behind the first Christians who saw and heard Him. Now, on the other hand, we affirm, that when the Word of Christ and the remembrance of the Church livingly unite, it is not merely the spirit of the preacher who puts the spirit of the Church in remembrance of the history of the Lord ; it is that the Lord himself is among them by His Holy Spirit, so that they experience the power and efficacy of history (*effectum historiæ*) as a present power and influence in the heart.

It is evident, from what has now been said, that the preaching of God's word in a legitimate manner must be a preaching by means of Holy Scripture ; not only that Scripture must be the touchstone of all thoughts and feelings expressed in the assembly of the faithful, but that the effectual and original power of the address must be derived from Scripture ; so that it is this which is opened out and explained, and its force which is brought to bear upon the given circumstances and relations of the congregation. When some one in these days affirmed that the task of the preacher is to declare the consciousness of the fellowship, to be " the mouthpiece of the congregation," he certainly stated an important truth ; but he also uttered a serious error if he intended to make this the only or the highest object. For the consciousness of the Church, as it may be found at this time or at that, is in many respects very undefined and variable, composed both of spiritual and worldly elements. A church consciousness which does not seek by means of preaching to submit itself to the testing of God's word, and by its fulness to be edified, will very soon find itself reduced to an indistinct, powerless spiritualism, which knows no difference between the sayings of men and the saving doctrine of Christ. And the preacher who makes himself only " the mouth of the congregation," and who does not prepare himself, if need be alone,—fortifying himself with holy Scripture and the œcumenical testimony—to speak against the erring consciousness of the congregation, infected as it is with the spirit of the day, will soon become the servant of the church in such a sense, that he can no longer be the Lord's servant. The preacher therefore is rightly called " the minister of the word ;" and it is also in harmony with the Word of God, that the church shall test and prove that which they hear, according to the pattern of the apostolic church. " Let the prophets," says St

Paul, " speak two or three, and let the others judge :"—*καὶ οἱ ἄλλοι διακρινέτωσαν* (1 Cor. xiv. 29).

PRAYER IN THE NAME OF JESUS.

§ 246.

Devotion is the first step in raising up the soul to God, a relation of intercourse, of contemplation, a union with God, in edifying thought. But worship is an act ; and the exercise of contemplation must lead on to a practical surrender of the will, in the offering of the heart. This, as a definite act of worship, takes place in prayer. Prayer therefore demands a deeper and more weighty inwardness than devotion, and many may be devotional who are not yet really prayerful. For in devotion man's relation to God is for the most part only an edifying reflection ; a relation in which God is certainly present, and in which the soul certainly feels God's nearness, but in which withal, God is present, so to speak, in the third person only ; in prayer, on the other hand, God is immediately present in the second person, as a personal *Thou*, corresponding to the human *I*. In devotion, the man's relation to God is of a general kind, as the God of creation and of the whole church ; in prayer that general relation is narrowed into one purely individual and direct between the man and God. In prayer, I hold communion with the God of all creation and of the church universal, as *my* God, the God of the individual man. This immediate relation between God and the soul, when the soul breathes forth its longings for the light of God's countenance, and calls upon Him, and when God himself gives His Holy Spirit to the suppliant, this union, *unio mystica*, is the essence of all true prayer. But the distinctive feature of Christian prayer is, that it is *prayer in the name of Jesus.* " Whatsoever ye shall ask the Father *in my name*, He will give it you. Hitherto ye have asked nothing *in my name*, ask, and ye shall receive, that your joy may be full" (John xvi. 23, 24). Prayer in the name of Jesus is not only prayer about the concerns of Jesus and of His kingdom ; not only prayer for the things of Christ, but prayer which we offer relying upon the word of Jesus, and trusting His promises ; praying, in the full power and warrant which He has given to His Church, for a fulness of power from Him, who is the eternal Mediator between God and man ; the heavenly Priest, who has provided an everlasting atonement, who ever makes intercession for us before the Father, by whom we, being justified through Him, have access to the Father. As no other prayer under heaven possesses so pure and holy an import as does prayer in the name of Jesus, so no other prayer under heaven possesses the confidence which springs from the right of a child, the spirit of adoption which Christ has given us.* In the time of doubt, of need, and of conflict, the Church prays,—the individual prays,—in the strength of Him who is our Advocate with the Father ; and in proportion as the prayer offered is really prayer in His name, it will be heard ; for in like proportion it is Jesus who prays the prayer through us.

Observations.—The model prayer, which is to be offered by the Church in all ages, in the name of Jesus, is that which has been given us by the Lord, namely, the *Pater noster*. It is a model prayer, because it embodies the deepest need of the Church, and of the individual likewise ; neither in the history of the Church, nor in the life of the individual, can any want arise, which may not find here its true expression and its satisfaction. For the Lord's prayer embraces in its range the *Teleology* of the kingdom of God, as well for the Church as for the individual, and contains 'all that we have to ask.' The first petition, that the name of God be hallowed, His kingdom come, His will be done, expresses the final and eternal aim, towards which all life tends, the holy ideal which shall not be reached until the perfecting of all things, when God shall be all in all, but which may be attained in this present time, not only by the labour, and endeavour, and conflict of the Church, but by prayer also for these highest blessings ; because the suppliant, by offering up and surrendering his heart, anticipates in this earthly and temporal life, that rest of God, that giving up of man's will to God's, which is to be fully revealed in future blessedness. The remaining petitions, for daily

---

* Rom. viii. 15, "Ye have received the spirit of adoption, whereby we cry, Abba, Father."

bread, for forgiveness of sins, for delivering from temptation and from evil, indicate *the way* to the eternal end ; human life in time ; earthly wants and spiritual need ; conflict and experience. As the petition for daily bread is included among those for spiritual blessings, the kingdom of nature is represented in its true relation to the kingdom of grace. The Church prays for temporal blessings only in connection and harmony with those other petitions, " thy kingdom come, thy will be done." Not as though we would imply that prayer for the external is only a deception, that everything outward would be the same, if we were not to pray for it. It would be a still greater deception to assume, that while God, under the influence of prayer, can accomplish changes in the inward and spiritual state of man, yet that He cannot, upon the same condition, bring about corresponding changes in the outward course of human life. As we cannot wholly see through the divine world-plan, the prayer for the thing thus conditioned must be determined by the unconditioned. We must look upon all that pertains to day and hour, to outward ways and means, in the advance of God's kingdom, from this point of view. And in this sense we say that the *unio mystica* of self-surrender and of love is the essential feature of prayer, so that the suppliant, though he may not also obtain this or that particular thing, always receives God himself.

The Sacraments.

§ 247.

Worship, as an holy act, finds its highest expression in the Sacraments, for in action there is a living union of the internal and the external, the invisible and the visible, the spiritual and the corporeal. The Sacraments, as acts of the Church, are chiefly to be viewed as acts of profession (*notae professionis*), visible, sensible acts, by participating in which, each person indeed confesses his Lord and the Church. But they are at the same time mysterious acts, acts of the glorified Christ, by which our relation to God as our reconciled Father is strengthened and renewed, and the secret fellowship of life

between the Lord of the Church and those who are united to
Him is established and confirmed. Sacraments and prayer
are certainly akin to each other; but their relationship implies a still greater difference. Sacraments and prayer have
this in common, that the relation of the Christian to God in
them is not merely one of thought and contemplation, but
immediate and practical; not the general relation between
the Lord and His Church, but a special one between the
Lord and each particular member. But the difference consists not only in the fact that the sacramental act is visible,
an embodiment of the invisible, whereas prayer is internal and
invisible; not only in the fact that grace now comes to the
help of man's weakness, vouchsafing him, in the Sacrament, a
visible sign, a tangible pledge, of its presence, giving him an
outward tendency, a visible word (*verbum visibile*) of its will
towards him, to awaken and strengthen his weak faith, so
that the feeble and outward man may not be weary nor
despair through pure spirituality and inwardness; the difference does not consist in this alone, though this certainly is
one characteristic of the Sacraments, on account of which they
have always exercised a powerful *educational* influence upon
Church life. The essential difference consists in this: the
sacred tokens of the new covenant contain also an actual
communication of the being and life of the risen Christ, who
is the Redeemer and Perfecter, not only of man's spiritual but
of man's *corporeal* nature. In prayer there is only a *unio
mystica*, a real, yet only spiritual, psychological union; but in
the Sacraments the deepest mystery rests in the truth that in
them Christ communicates Himself not only spiritually but
in His glorified corporeity. The final goal of God's kingdom
is not only that history but that nature also shall be redeemed
and glorified. " Corporeity is the final aim of God's way."
This, which is the final aim of development, which can only
be realised in the perfection of all things, is anticipated in the
Sacraments. All the intuitions of Christendom are reflected in
the Sacraments, and differences of creed have arisen chiefly in
reference to them.

§ 248.

Christ instituted only two Sacraments, Baptism and the
Lord's Supper. The nature of the case shows that there

should be only these two, Baptism as the Sacrament of Regeneration, the Lord's Supper as the Sacrament of confirmation and renewal. The New Covenant must once for all be *established* in man, and must from time to time be *renewed*. The individual must once for all be incorporated into the fellowship of Christ, and that incorporation must ever be growing more close and perfect. Baptism, therefore, cannot be repeated ; but the Lord's Supper must frequently be celebrated from time to time ; because the Christian life, weakened by the world and sin, requires to be strengthened and renewed from the great sources of atonement and new creation.

Observations.—The doctrine of the Roman Catholic Church, which counts Confirmation, Penance, Orders, Marriage, and Extreme Unction, as Sacraments, as well as Baptism and the Lord's Supper, can be defended only by taking the word Sacrament in a much wider sense, in a sense in which the word was often used in the early Church. With the exception of Extreme Unction, which is rendered superfluous, according to the evangelical view, as the last *viaticum* given to the dying, by the holy communion ; we in the Evangelical Church recognize Confirmation and Penance, Orders and Marriage as holy acts which, when undertaken and performed in faith with prayer and invocation, bring a divine blessing with them, and may deservedly be called "means of grace." All we say is, that they differ essentially from Baptism and the Lord's Supper ; not only because they cannot be traced back as these can to the distinct command of Christ himself, and cannot therefore be looked upon in the same manner as institutions of Christ ; but also because they are in their own essential nature different from them. They bear the relation to Baptism and the Lord's Supper of the derived to the original ; as subservient accessories to the central point ; and they possess neither the independent nor the all-embracing import that Baptism and the Lord's Supper possess. Confirmation springs out of Baptism, and Absolution receives its true significance from the holy communion. Marriage and Orders concern only particular relations of life and offices ; while in Baptism and the Lord's Supper there is neither male nor female, neither laic nor priest, but the new man in Christ Jesus. There is, moreover, this essential difference : Baptism and the Lord's Supper, which correspond respectively to the regeneration and sanctification of the new man, according to Christ's own appointment, are absolutely necessary for the existence of the Church, and are fundamental pre-suppositions or conditions of the Church's development, her union with the Lord depending upon them ; whereas those other five are only products of this development. With these convictions the Evangelical Church, though from the beginning she has through Melanchthon asserted ordination and penance to be of the nature of Sacraments,—an application of the term which may certainly be maintained by the usage of the early Church, without in any way necessarily sanctioning the Romish view,—has nevertheless by degrees given up this wide application of the word, and has confined its use exclusively to Baptism and the Lord's Supper, in order to avoid all erroneous confusion. The other relative ordinances are not, however, to be disregarded as merely empty ceremonies. They occupy a middle place between the unmeaning and outward form on one hand, and the pure sacraments of Baptism and the Lord's Supper on the other.

§ 249.

When the Catholic Church teaches that the sacraments work *ex opere operato*, we can agree therewith so far as to say that it is the faith neither of the priest nor of the Church which constitutes the sacrament, but the word and appointment of the Lord. We must also allow that the saving efficacy of the sacrament is not conditional upon living faith ; but we must protest against the doctrine that the lack of this cannot put any bar (*obicem non ponere*) to its power. The true idea of worship involves the union between the divine and human, between grace and freedom ; and as the sacraments imply the most perfect communication of divine grace, partaking of them implies the highest act of free will on the part of man. If it be said that the sacrament establishes and strengthens faith, because the beams of divine grace are collected in it as in a single focus ; it must also be said that in no act of worship is there greater need for man to concentrate his faith; for all the power of faith which the human soul can exercise in worship, in hearing the word, in the hour of devotion and of prayer, should be present in combined fulness in partaking of the sacrament.

§ 250.

While the Lutheran and the Reformed doctrine is one and the same concerning the number of the sacraments and the necessity for faith as the condition of their saving efficacy, these Churches differ in their estimate of the mystery of the sacraments; and the Lutheran Church alone has retained the fulness of that mystery. Zwingli did away with the mystery altogether; for he looked upon the sacraments partly as mere acts of confession, and partly as commemorative signs. Calvin takes higher ground; for he looks upon them not only as memorials, but as *pledges* of present grace (*symbola non absentium sed præsentium, pignora gratiæ*), visible pledges of invisible union with Christ. He recognizes a mystery in the sacrament, because he assumes that, as pledges of grace, they are accompanied with an invisible gift of grace. Lutheranism also considers the sacraments to be pledges of grace,[*] and this coincidence of doctrine has always been insisted upon by the Philippists in this Church,—the school of Melanchthon—as the point of union between Luther and Calvin. But the distinction comes into view in the consideration of each sacrament, because Calvin does not consider that the union with Christ in the sacrament is more than a spiritual union; he will not allow that it is spiritually corporeal. We cannot maintain the full reality and distinctiveness of the sacrament, unless with Luther we recognize therein not only a spiritual mystery, but a mystery of nature likewise. If, with Calvin and the Philippists, we suppose that there is only a spiritual union, *unio mystica*, in the sacrament, its distinctive feature will be only its educational import. The *unio mystica* subsists in prayer also, and the only remaining peculiarity of the sacrament is the visible

---

[*] *Confessio Augustana*, Part i., Art. xiii. "Signa et testimonia voluntatis Dei erga nos, ad excitandam et confirmandam fidem, in his, qui utuntur, proposita." Similarly *Apol. Confess.* "Ritus qui habent mandatum Dei, et quibus addita est promissio gratiæ."

pledge which comes to the help of human weakness. If the sacrament have only a psychological or educational import, he who is strong in faith may dispense with it, because he can obtain by prayer what the sacrament gives. It may indeed be asked with truth, who is so strong in faith as to be able to dispense with the external support, the visible pledges, with which the Lord himself has met our weakness? What sort of faith is that which thinks it can with impunity dispense with any distinct appointment of the Lord? Where is there a man to be found who presumes that he is so intimately united with the Lord and the invisible Church, as to be able to do without the visible bond of union by which the Lord draws all to Himself, even as it unites all to one another as parts of one body? Indeed, if we assign to this educational aspect its weight and import in this its fullest measure, we must recognize it as that which we must have *chiefly* before us. We therefore maintain that the last definite and perfect import of the sacrament is to be sought, in the indissoluble union of the holy spiritual, and of the holy natural mystery.

Having offered these preliminary observations, let us proceed to the consideration of each sacrament by itself.

§ 251.

BAPTISM, as a human ceremony, is an act of confession, by which a person is admitted into Christ's Church; but as a divine ceremony, it is the act by which Christ, our invisible High Priest and King, establishes His Church within the individual, and consecrates him in a true relation to God; in that relation to the triune God by which Christian worship is distinguished from Judaism and Heathenism (Matt. xxviii. 18–20 : Mark xvi. 16). Baptism, as the sacrament of institution to the true relation to God, may be more exactly described as the establishment of the new covenant. The religious import of a covenant is not altogether that of an agreement which man makes with God, but that of an agreement of saving grace which God makes with man; because God chooses him, singles him out of the mass of sinfulness, makes him partaker of His promises, and brings him within the range of the Spirit's influences, and those of revelation. The Old Covenant was established by an act of election; for the

Lord separated Abraham to the true worship, made His covenant with him and with his seed, and instituted circumcision
as the sign of the covenant.   In like manner the New Covenant was established by an act of election ; for the new
Adam set His disciples apart from the race of mankind, and
established in them the new relationship to God.   "Ye have
not chosen me, but I have chosen you" (John xv. 16).   But
baptism is for all successive generations what the personal
choice of Christ was for the apostles—our ancestors in faith
—an act of election, whereby salvation begins to become historically active for the individual baptized.   And as there is
a *sacred history* provided for the race as a preparation for a
new development of life, so baptism is a *holy fact* for each
particular human life, making its whole future fruitful and
saving.

§ 252.

What Circumcision was for the children of Israel, Baptism
is, though in a far higher sense, for Christians (Col. ii. 11, 12),
a pledge that the God of the community is the God of the
individual, that the Redeemer of the Church will be the Redeemer of each member.   The object of baptism is to spread
the spirit of hope in God's election of grace throughout life, to
be a sign from heaven upon which believers may base the
certainty of their election ; a certainty which cannot be retained by merely inward convictions in the midst of life's
changes, but which must be associated with a visible *sign*,
like the rainbow, to which they can look back in the midst
of the storms of life in every time of external or inward need ;
a bow of hope in the clouds appearing as the rainbow did in
the days of Noah.   And as baptism spreads the hope of God's
gracious election over the whole life, it also spreads the all-
embracing obligation connected therewith (1 Peter iii. 21), to
keep the covenant which is in Christ, and to abide in the
fellowship of the Father, the Son, and the Holy Ghost.   For
the decree of God's counsels is not finally concluded in baptism, it needs to be developed by a free effort upon man's part ;
and in this view baptism may be described as an initiation
or consecration to the free battle of human life, to be carried
on in the strength of the promises, and under the protection
of grace.

Observations.—Though we take our stand upon the point of agreement between Luther and Calvin,—the institution of Baptism as a pledge of grace,—yet even here there appears a decided difference between the two views, arising from differences relating to the doctrine of Predestination. According to Calvin's doctrine, there is no real connection between predestination and baptism. The twofold election has been settled from eternity ; and baptism, therefore, can be of no avail to those who have not been elected in the hidden decrees of God. Lutheran predestination, on the other hand, obtains its true expression in baptism. For baptism, according to Luther, is the revelation of the consoling decree that " God will have all men to be saved, and to come to the knowledge of the truth." We do not need in agony to inquire after a hidden decree, according to which we are either elected or rejected ; for every one may read in his baptism his election to blessedness. Luther, by making God's decree something not only being accomplished, but coming into existence, in history and time, preserved intact the interests of human liberty ; and according to him, baptism was the starting-point of the Christian life, embracing all the fundamental relations with which that life is concerned on earth. Baptism affords the consoling assurance of the election of grace to the most troubled and struggling human will, promises the presence of the Lord, and the goal of victory ; but to that security which gives itself up to a false repose, baptism declares the sternest demand, " work out your own salvation with fear and trembling," because the divine decrees are not unconditional, but *conditional.* To the fallen and the penitent baptism proves to be a sacrament of repentance ; for truly to repent, says Luther, leads a man back to his baptism, from which he had fallen. We may be unfaithful ; but God nevertheless remains ever true, and He will receive the repenting sinner with outstretched arms.

§ 253.

Having described Baptism as a pledge, the question occurs, whether it simply guarantees a future regeneration, or under the image and pledge of regeneration, at the same time confers it. Our answer to this enquiry depends upon the sense in which we use the term regeneration, whether we take it in a merely moral and psychological sense, or in a more comprehensive application, not only as the groundwork of a new consciousness, but of a new life, not only of a new faith, but of a new man, who is more than the self-conscious man. As we maintain this, the deepest meaning of the term, we say that baptism is not merely the pledge, not merely the promise and declaration of God's grace, but the bath of regeneration (Titus iii. 5), which involves not indeed personal, but substantial and essential regeneration. Baptism is, in fact, the beginning of the Christian life, and it must accordingly be, to use the apostle's word, the true *bath of regeneration*, λουτρόν παλιγγενεσίας, for the final aim of the development must be included in every true beginning. But the aim of the new creation in Christianity is the new man, which shall not be perfectly manifested until the new heaven and the new earth are completed, when the body as well as the spirit will celebrate its resurrection, and spirit and glorified nature shall be dissolved or blended together (2 Peter iii. 10.) The new creation of Christianity, which embraces the whole man, body, soul, and spirit, must begin as some definite point when the spirit and nature first unite, a point which contains in germinal fulness what seems to be separate during man's development in time. This hidden point of life is the mystery of baptism. It cannot certainly be authenticated by any experience; but the believer who sees in baptism the complete *beginning* of that work which the Lord will finish " in that day," recognizes therein also not only the historical anticipation and pre-supposition of his personal life of faith, the connecting link between this life and the whole economy of revelation, not only a pledge, rich in promise, of the grace of God, but the beginning of a new relation of being between himself and the Lord, *i.e.*, creative grace itself. Again, the believer, recognizing in baptism the living beginning of the Lord's new creating work, acknowledges in it also an objective mystery which concerns that part of his being which does not come within the range of consciousness, feels that hidden part of his being appropriated by the blessed rule which is still hid with Christ in God, and believes himself to be united to Christ not only psychologically, but organically,—incorporated with

Him not merely figuratively, but actually,—engrafted into Him who is not only the Redeemer of the soul, but who will also change the body of our humiliation that it may be like the body of His glory" (Phil. iii. 21.)

If it be asked whether baptism, which, as a Church ordinance, is contingent upon circumstance and the discretion of man, is the only means whereby the Lord can establish the new creation in the soul, and whether the Lord can confer without baptism that which He confers in the ordinance, we reply that the Lord certainly cannot be bound to confine His saving power to the Sacrament; but the Church is bound by the appointment of her Lord. We therefore maintain the ancient canon, *necessitas sacramentorum non est absoluta sed ordinata.*

Observations.—The view which we have here given of the mystery of Baptism, which we characterize not as by any means the only tenable one, but as the latest and fullest, is looked upon as strange in the present day, and must wait a while before it finds acceptance with the many, as long as the psychological and educational view of the Sacrament is without difficulty received where Christian faith is present. But Christian reflection, when it searches deeply into the connection between the doctrine of the Sacraments and that of the consummation of all things in the last great day, must return again to the old Christian view, which Irenæus, for example, clearly perceived, as it is presented in the essential teaching of Lutheranism, and as it forms the necessary counterpart of the Lutheran doctrine of the Lord's Supper. If we assign to baptism a merely psychological or spiritual import, we make a beginning for the Christian life, which is wholly separate from its true unity, and which is tainted with that distinction and divorce of the corporeal from the spiritual which reflection only can make. Upon this theory the new creation which Christianity accomplishes has only a psychological reference, and the doctrine of eschatology corresponding thereto, must be only that of a purely spiritual kingdom, apart from nature and corporeity. If, on the other hand, the glorification of nature and corporeity be maintained as the final aim of all earthly development, while baptism is, at the same time, looked upon as an ordinance wholly without any mystery of nature connected with it, we arrive at the most unscientific doctrine, that the kingdom of Christ will end with something which was wholly unprovided for in its foundation, and which there is no clue to nor preparation for in the present economy.

§ 254.

Regeneration is by no means concluded with baptism, but the foundation of it is therein laid, and it is not therefore baptism alone which saves, but baptism and faith : " He that believeth and is baptized shall be saved" (Mark xvi. 16). Regeneration is completed only when the grace of baptism appears in power as *personal* regeneration. Just as the Church in its beginning was established partly by an act of Christ, who laid its foundation and gave it a beginning *essentially* in His apostles ; and partly by an act of the Holy Spirit, who established the Church *actually* on the Day of Pentecost,—glorifying Christ in and through His apostles ;— so, in the case of the individual, regeneration depends partly upon the act of Christ in baptism, laying the foundation of His Church and kingdom in the soul, in virtue of which regeneration becomes a germinal possibility ; and partly upon the actual communication of the Holy Ghost. We may therefore say, that the person baptized is not actually regenerate until his pentecost is fully come, until the Spirit establishes within him the new consciousness, and makes the grace of baptism manifest. These two acts, which are but two sides of one and the same gracious work—the objective and the subjective, the essential and the personal aspects of the beginning of the new life—*may* take place simultaneously in the baptism of such as are of riper years. But in the case of baptism in the less distinct and milder form of it, in the baptism of children, the two are separated from one another as to time, and here what is *conditional* in the grace of baptism is clearly seen, for personal regeneration cannot be accomplished without a free effort upon the part of the person himself.

Observations.—When the Baptist maintains that regeneration takes place before baptism, and appeals to the fact that the baptism of adults presupposes *faith*, he confounds awakening with regeneration. An awakening, a preparatory faith, must always precede baptism in the case of an adult. But that faith which is the starting point of a *continuous* life of faith, of the growth of Christian character, presupposes that grace of baptism which puts the individual in organic connection with all other means of grace, and with the workings of the Spirit in the community. And even were we to take baptism as the conclusion only of awakening and converting grace, it must still be said that the *organic* relation of life between the Lord and the individual begins only with baptism ; then only is regeneration in its full sense established, then only can the Holy Ghost make the electing grace of Christ apparent in a continuous life of faith ; so that we continually recur to Luther's words, "Therefore, I will not base baptism upon my faith, but my faith again shall base and build itself upon baptism."*

§ 255.

Baptism, being a consecration to the true service of God, and the sacrament of God's electing grace, involves the idea of *Infant baptism*. At the outset indeed it necessarily appears as the baptism of adults, for Christianity was established and diffused by missionary effort, and must have first appealed to adults and those of riper years ; but when mother churches were founded, in which a Christian community or family life was established, baptism was extended to children likewise. By so doing the Church—so far from departing from or violating the original institution, really brought out into view the true import of baptism, and made the rite correspond with the perfect idea it involves. Baptism in the true conception of it is infant baptism, for this very reason ; because in it is secured the foundation not only of a new consciousness but of a new man ; not a new personality, but the preparation for and real possibility of this.†

Observations.—The fact which experience attests, that many baptized persons are never regenerate nor believers, is no argument against the reality of baptismal grace. It only shows that baptism does not work by magic, that baptis-

---

* *Walch*, x. 2582.

† Compare the author's work, *Die christliche Taufe mit Rücksicht auf die baptistische Frage.*

mal grace is not unconditional, but appears in power and
activity only upon certain conditions. For the rest, this
fact must be explained as arising, partly from the personal
guilt of the individual, who has neglected to stir up the
grace given him in baptism ; and partly from the imperfect administration of the sacrament on the Church's part.
The Church has often baptized persons regarding whom,
humanly speaking, she must have foreseen that the conditions necessary for the development of the gift of grace
would be wanting, or for whom she has neglected to provide the appropriate means of enlightenment and awakening (as, for instance, those whom she has left to irrespon-
sible instruction in preparation for confirmation). Lastly,
the fact must in part be explained upon the principle of
the economic wisdom of the election of grace, which does
not confer personal regeneration at the same time upon
all who are baptized, but allows some, even within the
Church, to continue longer than others at the stage of
prevenient grace. (Compare the previous section on "the
election of individuals.")

§ 256.

Let us now turn from the consideration of the *nature* of
Baptism to the question regarding the administration of the
Sacrament by the Church. If we enquire what persons the
Church, as the steward of the mysteries of God, is warranted
and bound to admit to Baptism, it is manifest that Baptism
can be administered in conformity with its design, only when
there is a reasonable prospect of its being the beginning of a
Christian discipleship, and of the remaining stages of Christian growth having opportunity to appear in power. In
proportion as the Church exercises this discernment in the
administration of baptism, she on her part must endeavour
that among her members baptism shall be found united with
faith ; this indeed must be regarded as the main object of the
Church's activity, because as to what remains she leaves the
illimitable workings of grace, which she must reckon among
τὰ οὐκ ἐφ' ἡμῖν, to the Lord and to the Spirit. Compulsory
baptism is, therefore, objectionable, for when positive opposition is offered to Christianity, baptism cannot become the
foundation of a Christian life. There is only the prospect of

the foundation being profaned, and therefore it should not be laid; for the Lord himself has forbidden us to give what is holy unto the dogs, and to cast pearls before swine (Matt. vii. 6), an admonition which clearly concerns the Christian mysteries. But on the other hand, the Church must avoid the narrowness of the Baptist view, which will have absolute certainty that baptism and faith actually co-exist. The Church, did she embrace this doctrine, would have first to give up infant baptism, and thereupon, in order to arrive at that certainty, she would be obliged to postpone baptism indefinitely,—indeed for ever in this world. Against all such narrowness, the parable of the sower tells; for he unremittingly sowed his seed though some of it was lost, and "some fell by the way side" (Matt. xiii. 4), words which have their bearing also upon the baptismal gifts of grace. That false scrupulosity in the administration of baptism which is afraid of wasting it upon the unworthy, involves the necessity of depriving many of it who would be fruitful. We must not therefore, do more than set up the general rule, in the application of which there must always be certain limitations, that the church grants baptism to adults when there is a corresponding readiness on their part to receive it; but she baptizes children wherever mother churches are established, and Christian influence can lead the children on to faith; leaving it to the Lord and to the Spirit to decide *when and where* the baptism shall be rightly and personally appropriated by the subject of it.

Observations.— The question as to the propriety of *private baptism* is closely connected with the position that baptism is necessary to salvation. The practice of private baptism *may* presuppose an erroneous view of baptism, namely that baptism itself, without anything else, saves, and that children who die without baptism are irretrievably lost. As to the first notion, it must be maintained that baptism saves only so far as faith accompanies it. And, as to the second, it must, with equal firmness, be asserted, that though the Church is bound by the command of her Lord, and knows no other beginning of salvation than baptism, yet the Lord himself is not so bound to the visible ordinance as not to be able to bestow the essence of baptism without it. We therefore still hold to the old canon,

"*non privatio, sed contemtus sacramenti damnat.*" It is only when these principles are pre-supposed that the Church ventures to practice private baptism, and then it is the expression of a conscientious faith, which feels itself bound by the ordainments of the Lord, and finds rest in the belief that he who has a claim to the benefit of baptism, being made partaker of it, is incorporated with *that* Lord in whom the whole fellowship here below and in heaven above are united.

§ 257.

If we now enquire *how* the Church is to administer baptism, and when baptism is valid, the main point is of course that it be performed conformably with Christ's ordainment. If a baptism be administered according to the words of Christ's institution of it, " in the name of the Father, the Son, and the Holy Ghost," it is valid. It is not essential whether it be administered by immersion or by sprinkling, for it is not the quantity of the visible element, but its kind or quality which is necessary in the sacrament. But as the word and appointment of the Lord cannot be without the witnessing Church, the original Church symbol of baptism must be added, together with the renunciation, as a definite expression of the faith into which the person is baptized. This ecclesiastical confession must be regarded as intelligibly included in every baptism, and wherever the Church is properly organized, it will be expressly repeated. In modern times and in several places this confession of faith has been omitted or altered, and this betrays a misinterpretation of the words of the Sacrament, " in the name of the Father, the Son, and the Holy Ghost;" for the *symbolum apostolicum* is the Church's explanation of these words of our Lord.

§ 258.

The ordinance of confirmation is connected with Infant Baptism as its ratification. Confirmation is not an ordinance of the Lord's, but must be regarded as a work of the Spirit in the Church. If the practice of confirmation in the Evangelical Church corresponded perfectly with its theory, it would be an outward declaration that the personal life of faith was now beginning to manifest itself in power, and that a Pentecost was dawning upon the youth. For as this ordinance is upon the

Church's part a consecration to a personal life of faith, and an act of admission to the rights and responsibilities of years of understanding, the youth himself must witness the good confession before many witnesses, and thus avow himself as a member of the Church founded by the apostles. The work, therefore, of instruction for confirmation, as well as of Christian training generally, must be, so far as lies in human power, so to teach as to give confirmation a really *awakening* import, that it may serve to awaken in youth holy promises and resolutions, but, above all, holy joy on account of the grace of baptism, on account of the richness of the promises which are given to them in the new covenant.

§ 259.

While Baptism is the sacrament of children, THE LORD'S SUPPER is the sacrament of such as are of riper years. Baptism is the setting-up of the new covenant; the Lord's Supper is its renewal. By baptism man is incorporated into the new kingdom, and the possibility of, the necessary requirements for, the new personality are given therein : by means of the Lord's Supper this new personality is brought to perfection. Differences of creed gather round the Lord's Supper especially, as round a central point, because it is the sacrament of those of full age, and it has, therefore, specially to do with the reciprocal relations between divine grace and the free will of man.

§ 260.

The Lord's Supper, as a church ordinance, must be looked upon as an act of confession, appointed by the Lord to refresh our remembrance of Him. As the Passover in Israel was to be a means of renewing the recollection of the covenant of the Lord with Israel, and as an act of thanksgiving for the deliverance from Egyptian bondage, the Lord's Supper is in like manner a commemoration and a giving of thanks—a *Eucharist*—on account of the propitiation and redemption provided in Christ ; a sacred feast in which the partakers "show forth the Lord's death." In partaking of the bread, they must think with gratitude of Him, whose body was broken in death ; in partaking of the cup they must think of Him whose blood was shed for the remission of sins ; they must recognize themselves as permanent sharers in the new covenant, desiring to grow and increase in the fellowship of their Lord. But the

Lord's Supper is not only an act of confession on the part of the Church, it also involves a present act of Christ himself. He who said, " This do in remembrance of Me," also declared, " Lo ! I am with you always." It is His will that His Church think of Him, not as the absent but as the present Lord, not as the dead Christ, but as risen from the dead, as the Redeemer living in their midst. With the recognition of this truth, the recognition of the mystery begins. In the Lord's Supper the believer must not only look back to the death of the Lord and His crucifixion, he must also look up to the *risen* Redeemer, now *ascended* up into heaven, who fills His Church with the fulness of His power, and allows those words to be realized in their full import in the sacrament, when it is performed in harmony with His command.

§ 261.

If it be understood that the mystery of the Lord's Supper consists in this : that it is not only a human act of commemoration and thanksgiving, but an act of the heaven-ascended Redeemer,—a living bond between heaven and earth, —it will also be recognized as the holy *pledge* of the renewal of the Covenant. As often as thou eatest this bread, and drinkest this cup, the Lord renews the covenant of grace with thee which was established in thy baptism, assures thee anew of the forgiveness of thy sins, vouchsafes to thee anew the comfort of His atonement ! Graciously true as all this is, it does not constitute the mystery of the sacrament. The Lord has associated with His Supper not only the promise of forgiveness of sins, and a display and explanation of grace, but under the sacred pledges of grace He gives to His own people a new *aliment* of life. " This *is* my body," " This *is* my blood" (Matt. xxvi. 26-28 ; Mark xiv. 22-24 ; Luke xxii. 19, 20 ; 1 Cor. xi. 24, 25). However variously these words may be explained, they clearly indicate an actual participation of Life with the Lord. " Except ye eat the flesh of the Son of man, and drink His blood, ye have no life in you," John vi. 53 : Unless ye so appropriate Me, that not only my word and my promise, but I Myself, my whole undivided personality, become the aliment of your life, you have not life. Though these words are not spoken in immediate connection with the Lord's Supper, it is nevertheless plain, that they must find their full and complete realization in this ordinance. If, however, there is this union with Jesus in an especial manner in the Lord's Supper; if, again, this special union is, by the express words of the Lord, associated with and conditional upon the partaking of bread and wine, the question arises, In what way is this union to be explained? how is it to be defined? How are we to understand this relation between the heavenly aliment, between the invisible gift of grace and the visible gifts of nature, represented in the bread and wine? It is upon this point that creeds and confessions disagree. Some consider this controversy useless and unpractical, because these things cannot be the subject of human comprehension. But our business here is not to comprehend what in its nature is and must be above our comprehension, but to arrive at a true conception of what the mystery is. Our province is not to endeavour to solve the mystery by means of human sophistry. The Christian confessions, with the exception of the Zwinglian, unanimously teach, that in the Lord's Supper we have to bow before a most sacred mystery. The question is, What is that mystery before which we have to bow?

§ 262.

The common view is that of the real presence (*praesentia realis*) and real communication of the Lord himself. The Roman Catholic Church takes this to be so immediate, as to annihilate all that is symbolical and natural in the ordinance; according to her, the visible signs are changed into the body and blood of the Lord; the substance of the bread and wine is literally transformed into the substance of the body and blood of Christ; and earthly bread and wine only *seem* to be present to the senses. Against this doctrine of Transubstantiation,—which volatilizes the natural elements into mere appearances, and detracts from the kingdom of nature in order to magnify the kingdom of grace,—the whole Evangelical Church protests, and gives to the visible signs their due place in their natural and independent state. "Bread is bread, and wine is wine," and these are only *symbols* of the body and blood of Christ. In this sense, as the rejection and denial of Transubstantiation, the entire Evangelical Church adopts Zwingli's exclamation, "*Dies bedeutet!*"—"This is what it means." Zwingli's intelligent view obtains in this historical connection greater weight than one would otherwise feel disposed to accord to it. Zwingli himself indeed was content to abide for the most part by this protest merely; Luther, on the other hand, maintained the real presence of the Lord,* but a presence which is veiled or hidden beneath the outward and natural signs, and which communicates its heavenly gifts of grace in, with, and beneath these. Calvin endeavoured to take a middle course between Zwingli and Luther, but his theory of the real presence presents only the one-sidedness of opposition to the doctrine of Transubstantiation.

§ 263.

Calvin's doctrine is biassed by opposition to the extreme doctrine of transubstantiation, inasmuch as it somewhat unfairly *separates* what, according to Catholicism, is one and indissoluble. Calvin's doctrine rests upon a dualism, distinguishing between the kingdom of grace and that of nature, between heaven and earth, Spirit and body. The glorified Saviour cannot be present upon earth, for upon the laws of corporeity and individuality He must be in a definite place in heaven. In the celebration of the Lord's Supper upon earth, therefore, there is nothing more than the distribution and partaking of bread and wine; but when these are partaken of in faith, something occurs simultaneously in heaven, for the believing soul is as if transported into heaven, by the mystical working of the Spirit, and in a supernatural manner is united to the Saviour, and made partaker of His glorified body, as the true aliment of the Spirit (*cibus mentis*). The Lord's Supper, according to the Calvinistic view, thus divides itself into two parts, or consists of two acts, one in heaven, the other on earth; one in spirit, the other in body. It is only the faithful who take part in the heavenly act; the unbelieving may go through the outward celebration—partaking of the bread and wine, and nothing more; and could we imagine a communion in which all the guests were unbelievers, there would be no real sacrament, but only the outward semblance of one. Whereas, according to the view taken by the Catholic Church, the heavenly part is present as

---

* Compare *Confessio Augustana*, Art. x., where, however, the Lutheran dogma was not as yet fully developed; " quod corpus et sanguis Christi *vere* adsint et *distribuantur* vescentibus in Coena Domini."

an immediate object, appearing with the entire impress of the external reality,—according to the Calvinistic view the presence of Christ is purely spiritual, a presence only in the devotion and in the inwardness of the believing heart.

§ 264.

The Lutheran doctrine is opposed not only to the doctrine of transubstantiation, but to the Calvinistic separation of heaven and earth likewise. Christ is not in a literal manner separate from His believing people, so as that they must go to heaven in order to find Him. Christ is on the right hand of God; but the right hand of God is everywhere. *Dextera Dei ubique est.* And therefore He is present wholly and entirely (*totus et integer*) in His Supper, wherein He in an especial manner *wills* to be. There are not in the ordinance two acts, one heavenly and one earthly, distinct from each other, but the heavenly is comprehended in the earthly and visible act, and is organically united therewith, thus constituting one sacramental act. The heavenly substance is communicated in, with, and under the earthly substances. And as the sacramental communion is not a partaking of the corporeal nature of Christ apart from His spiritual nature, no more is it a mere partaking of the spiritual nature of Christ apart from His corporeity. It is one and undivided, a spiritual and corporeal communion.

§ 265.

If we would get at the idea which lies at the foundation of the Lutheran doctrine regarding the Lord's Supper, we must bear in mind that it is an idea independent of those scholastic forms, in which the old theology endeavoured to develop it, and especially independent of that doctrine regarding Christ's unlimited ubiquity, the one-sidedness of which we have referred to in our Christology. It is, in fact, the idea of Christ as the head of that *new* creation whose final end is the redemption and perfecting of human nature as a whole, as undivided body and soul. As Christ is not a Spirit only, but the *incarnate* λόγος; as man, created in God's image, is, in the true conception of him, the centre in which spirit and nature unite; as the resurrection of the body is the last eschatological event which Christianity presents; the Lord's Supper is an act of union with Christ, as the *principle* of that holy marriage of spirit and nature which is the final end of the creation. The Lutheran view of the Lord's Supper is thus, in the truest sense of the expression, *prophetically Christian, i.e.,* it recognizes in the Eucharist the actual anticipation of that union with the Saviour, the perfection of which will be reached in the consummation of all things. It sees, accordingly, in the Lord's Supper, not only, like Calvin, an aliment for the soul (*cibus mentis*) but an aliment for the whole new-man, for the future man of the Resurrection, who is germinating and growing in secret, and who shall be manifested in glory, in exact likeness with the glorified humanity of his Lord. Holy Scripture itself thus associates the doctrine concerning the last things with the Lord's Supper, not only in the words of the apostle Paul, "Ye do shew forth the Lord's death till *He come*" (1 Cor. xi. 26); but in the words also of our Lord himself, "I will not drink henceforth of this fruit of the vine, until that day when I drink it new with you in my Father's kingdom" (Matt. xxvi. 29; Mark xiv. 25; Luke xxii. 16, 18.) However these words may be interpreted as regards particulars, they plainly give us to understand that the Lord's Supper is an actual prophecy, type, and anticipation of the union with the Saviour, which will take place in the realm of bliss; and not only of union with the Lord, but of the inward fellowship of love by which believers shall be united to one another in that blessed kingdom. For in the Lord's Supper believers are all united together into one body, because, as the apostle says, they are partakers of one bread. (1 Cor. x. 17.)

§ 266.

We therefore recognize, with Luther, the indissoluble union of a holy mystery of Spirit, and of a holy mystery of nature in the Lord's Supper. We believe that the whole and undivided Christ gives Himself as the aliment of the new man in the Lord's Supper. And as we seek a literal interpretation of the words, " Take, eat, this *is* my body, this *is* my blood," there here presents itself a pattern or model from the kingdom of nature, the first creation. In bread and wine, viewed merely as natural means of nourishment, it is not the natural materials as such which do in reality strengthen and nourish, but the invisible *power* which lies hid therein, the creating power which we also call the *blessing*. For the blessing implies the fact that the creative principle is present secretly, even in the gifts of nature. Heathenism itself said that Ceres and Bacchus were present in bread and wine, and that mankind partook even of Ceres and Bacchus in the forms of bread and wine, *i.e.*, that the real eating and drinking was not a mere eating and drinking of the outward material, but a being made partaker of the creative principle itself, as that which truly strengthens and stimulates. But in revealed religion we know that the Son, the divine λόγος, is the creative principle in the whole kingdom of nature, that the secret power of life, in all the gifts of nature, is the power of the Son of God, who fills all things. The creative λόγος it is who gives us bread and wine, and even in the kingdom of nature we, as it were, hear Him say, "Take, eat, this is I, this is my being, my creative and sustaining power of life, which you are made to partake of through bread and wine, and which is in these elements, truly nourishing, strengthening, and life-giving!" "I would never desire to drink thereof," said Master Eckart, "if there were not something of God within it." Yet all this is only a shadow and type of the holy relation upon which our Lord enters in the holy communion. For in the Lord's Supper the point in question is not merely the λόγος presence, but the presence of Christ, of Christ's body and blood. It is not the λόγος who creates and sustains nature whom we seek in the holy Supper, for we may find him in all bread and wine; we seek the risen Saviour, the Head of the new creation, who deigns herein to make us partakers of the mystery of His atoning and all-perfecting love; a mystery that embraces not only the realm of souls, but of corporeity likewise, of *that* corporeity which is destined to be made glorious as the temple of Christ. Bread and wine, the noblest gifts of nature, are, in the sacrament, put in an inner relation to the kingdom of grace, they become the means, the bearers, the channels for the invisible communication of Christ, for that heavenly aliment by which the faithful are prepared for the future kingdom of glory. It is no more common bread and wine; it is the blessed bread, the blessed cup (τὸ ποτήριον πῆς εὐλογίας) (1 Cor. x. 16); and it is not only the blessing of the first creation, it is the blessing of salvation, of the new creation; it is the power of Christ's resurrection that is in the bread which we eat, and in the cup of which we drink. It is the communion of the body and blood of Christ; for in the blessed bread is *His* power who has called Himself the "corn of wheat" (John xii. 24), and like the corn of wheat He implants Himself in human nature, in order to germinate and to grow, to take form and to bear fruit; in the cup of blessing is *His* power, who has called Himself "the Vine" (John xv. 1), and whose undying life will glow through our natural life, that we may grow up together with Him. The act here in question is not a literal eating of Christ, according to the notion of the Jews at Capernaum (John vi. 52, 59), but it is one whereby we are made partakers of Christ, as the *principle* of the entire new creation of man, and of the future humanity of the resurrection which shall be revealed in that day. Here we have to do not with a presence of Christ literally defined according to the category of place, but with a presence in which the higher heavenly sphere invisibly penetrates the lower and the earthly, a presence in power, in working, in gift; for in His gifts He gives Himself. "Take, eat, drink, this is I, in this I give you what is the inmost power of life in myself! If ye eat not my flesh nor drink my blood, ye have not life in you!"

§ 267.

It follows, from what has now been unfolded, that the Calvinistic notion, that Christ is present only for the faithful, must be rejected. For the word and command of God, not the faith or devotion of man, make the sacrament; and as the seed-corn is the same, whether it fall into good or into bad ground, so is it with the sacrament. Accordingly, it is emphatically said, "Let a man examine himself, and so let him eat of that bread, and drink of that cup. For he that eateth and drinketh unworthily eateth and drinketh damnation to himself, not discerning the Lord's body" (1 Cor. xi. 28, 29.) Unbelievers, also, who partake of the sacrament, come into actual relation with the All-holy; and though we cannot say of them that they *eat* the sacrament, *i.e.*, make it their food, yet we must say that they receive it. It is not through want of knowledge; it is not through weakness of faith, that man eats condemnation to himself. It is the very consolation of the *objective* sacrament that the blessing is given to him who is weak in faith, and who has need of strengthening; herein

is just the comfort, that the Lord descends to us, comes to the
help of our weakness; whereas the *subjective* doctrine of the
sacrament makes all to depend upon the perfection of our
faith; and upon the frame of mind in which we are at the
moment we partake of it; and it must therefore lead to an
anxious effort, a straining of every nerve, by means of which
the man endeavours to soar upwards to heaven. It is not
weakness of faith, nor deficiency in doctrinal insight, which
causes a person to eat condemnation to himself. It is the
unhallowed sense, which fails to discern the Lord's body, to
discern between the holy and the profane, and which draws
nigh to the table of the Lord without preparation or self-
examination.

§ 268.

As we oppose the Calvinistic principle that the presence of
Christ is conditional upon faith, we equally reject the Romish
representation that the consecrated bread and the consecrated
wine are the body and blood of Christ *apart from the partaking
thereof*. For the presence of Christ in the Eucharist extends
only so far as the words of institution extend; but the words
of institution are inseparable from the *distribution* and the
receiving of the bread and wine. The Lord has instituted His
Supper as one undivided act, and to separate one single element from the ordinance for a holy use, is arbitrary and
without promise. We therefore reject the adoration of the
host in the Romish Church, a rite which depends upon the
doctrine of transubstantiation and the notion connected therewith of the sacrifice of the mass.*

§ 269.

If now we review the Romish, Calvinistic, and Lutheran doctrines of the Lord's Supper together, we shall find in them
different types of Christian ideas of life, represented in a con-
densed form. The doctrine of transubstantiation expresses a
false relation of unity of the kingdom of nature and of grace,
because the former is interwoven with the latter. But
this relation of transformation runs throughout the whole
Catholic theory. Catholicism endeavours, in a direct and

---

* Compare the detailed dissertation upon the Sacrifice of the Mass in *H. N
Clausens: Kirchenverfassung, Lehre, und Ritus des Katholicismus und Protestantismus.*

immediate way, to transform the world into the kingdom of
God, to metamorphize all worldly substances, state, art, and
science, into religious substances, and so bring about and
establish an earthly kingdom of Christ. If we view Catholicism in its relation to Eschatology, we may fairly say that
she endeavours artificially to anticipate the second coming of
Christ, by making a display of the glory of Christ in a visible
manner in this world. And she bears the impress of
heathenism, because she regards the outward and visible,
more than the invisible, in every department of her ritual.

The Calvinistic doctrine regarding the Lord's Supper rests
upon an overt principle of Dualism between the kingdom of
grace and that of nature; a dualism so thorough that the
Lord's Supper is literally divided into two distinct acts, the
one in heaven, the other on earth. But this Dualism between
heaven and earth, nature and grace, is a type answering to
the whole of Calvinism. Its stern ascetic method of thought
raises an insuperable barrier between the kingdom of God and
the world; and whereas Catholicism endeavours magically to
embody and shadow forth a visible spirit-world, Puritanical
spiritualism excludes all outward emblems, all art, from its
worship, and over-prizes the word at the expense of Church
ordinances. This form of piety presents no true relation
between the natural and the spiritual; the natural is only
the instrument, the vehicle, the starting point for the soul,
that she may rise up to an imageless devotion, bare and
abstract, and the highest blossom and bloom of such religiousness is a subjective mysticism. Looking at Calvinism in its
relation to Eschatology, we must say that it bears a Jewish
impress. For although it expects the resurrection of the
body and a new heaven and a new earth, it sees nothing in
the present corresponding to this, it has no point of union or
association with this consummation, but in the present
Dualism reigns on every hand. The Lutheran doctrine regarding the Lord's Supper rests neither upon a Dualism
between nature and grace, nor upon a transformation of the
one into the other, but upon an inner *marriage* of the
heavenly and the earthly substance. But this inner marriage
of the supernatural and the natural, of the heavenly and
earthly, is the fundamental feature of Lutheranism, and is

reflected in its whole worship; in all its services, in its poetry, in its customary world-life. In relation to Eschatology, its type of doctrine may be characterized as, in the deepest sense of the expression, *prophetically Christian,* and, so far as the anticipations of Christianity regarding the future have been truly described as *romantic,* in contrast with the ancient, the heathen, and Jewish views of human life, this epithet is pre-eminently appropriate to Lutheranism. The romantic in Catholicism is bound up in the earthly and the present, consciousness looks upon the visible and not upon the invisible, and indulges in a false reliance in this present world, and in the glory of the visible Church. In the Reformed Church, on the contrary, there is a merely subjective Romanticism, a mere mysticism, which views Christ as above, and far away in heaven, and the kingdom of glory as if at an almost infinite distance off. The soul can unite itself with its Redeemer only by soaring upwards on the wings of mystical aspiration. Now the Lutheran faith rests in an objective mystery, surrounding it on every hand, the mystery of the new creation, which already penetrates this present world with the powers of the future world ; in its faith Christ is everywhere at hand. But it differs from Catholicism in this,—and herein consists the inwardness of Lutheranism, its subjective side—it maintains that this mystery is veiled, that its presence is not immediate, but is ever " in, with, and under " the natural and visible, just as is the case in the Lord's Supper according to the Lutheran view. Faith beholds in the kingdom of nature visible types and resemblances of that invisible glory which shall be fully revealed in the day of our Lord Jesus Christ. Thus art and poetry have their true import assigned them,—not as the objects of deification and adoration, as in the Romish Church, but as possessing a temporal and intermediate position, as pictorial anticipations of future glory, wherein spirit and glorified corporeity shall be blended together in one.

§ 270.

If we now turn from the consideration of the nature of the Lord's Supper to the question of its due ecclesiastical administration, the main point is, that it be celebrated in exact accordance with the appointment of the Lord. The conse-

cration must necessarily be accomplished by the very words
of our Lord in the institution of the ordinance. The quantity and outward form of the sensible elements are non-essen-
tial, but it is necessary that bread and wine (or where bread
and wine are not to be had, what in the order of nature
takes their place) be actually distributed and eaten. If it
next be asked, to *whom* is the Church, as the steward of
divine mysteries, justified and bound to give the Lord's Supper, it is first of all evident that she must give it to the baptized only. And as the Lord's Supper is the sacrament for
those who are of full age, the communion of children must be
taken exception to, and only confirmed Christians must be
admitted to it. Again, as the Lord's Supper is the sacrament
of liberty and personality, it should not be given to those
who have lost the use of consciousness, the insane, or the
sick and dying who are in an unconscious state. Once again,
as this is the most sacred ordinance of Christian worship, the
unworthy—*i.e.*, those whose life and conduct gives offence to
the fellowship, and is a *scandal* thereto—must be debarred
from partaking of it. "*Sancta sanctis*" was a symbol of the
early Church. But the carrying out of this rule is possible
only where Church discipline is practised according to the apostolic model (1 Cor. v. 5). It is a question which theology cannot
answer in the present state of things, but which can only be
solved in practice, how far a resort is possible to that Christian discipline, the decline of which has occasioned so many
bitter and well founded complaints—a point which is closely
connected with the general question of Church government.

§ 271.

CONFESSION stands in intimate relation to the Lord's Supper as a preparation for the worthy partaking of it. Private
confession is not in the Lutheran Church as it is in Roman
Catholicism, a legally commanded enumeration of all particular sins which have been committed during a certain time ;
it is a voluntary expression of the personal consciousness of
sin. Absolution in the name of the Father and of the Son
and of the Holy Ghost, derived from the full power of binding and loosing which the Church has inherited from the
apostles, is not unconditional, but depends on the same condition on which the gospel itself adjudges the forgiveness of

sins, namely, change of heart and faith. If reform is to take place here, it must be effected either by endeavouring to revive private confession, or, as has been proposed, by doing away with the union between confession and the Lord's Supper, omitting, that is, the solemn absolution, because what it presupposes (personal confession of sin) has fallen into disuse, and retaining only the words of preparation, with the exhortation to self-examination, a testifying of the comfortable promises of the gospel, and a wish for a blessing upon the communicants.* It must certainly be granted, that the primitive church did not make confession and absolution necessary preparations for the Lord's Supper, but that the self-examination enjoined by Paul was considered sufficient. The last named method of reform is of course appropriate to a time when, on various grounds, it may count upon the warmest sympathies and the best opportunities of realization, whereas the revival of private confession at present seems to be practicable only where the Lutheran Church exists in small and separate fellowships far apart from each other.

Observations.—It cannot easily be denied that confession meets a deep need of human nature. There is a great psychological truth in the saying of Pascal, that a man often attains for the first time a true sense of sin, and a true stayedness in his good purpose, when he confesses his sins to his fellow man, as well as to God. Catholicism has often been commended because by confession it affords an opportunity of depositing the confession of his sins in the breast of another man, where it remains kept under the seal of the most sacred secresy, and whence the consolation of the forgiveness of sins is given him in the very name of the Lord. But this need is met and satisfied far more fully by the private confession of Lutheranism than by that of Catholicism. For the true need is after all only the desire to be able to tell his personal sense of sin, to confess what really weighs upon his heart. This is just the idea of private confession, whereas in the Catholic Church the individual becomes legitimately subject to be questioned and examined by priests regarding the whole

* *H. N. Causen:* Udwikling af de Christelige Hovedlärdomme, 508.

range of particular sins which have been committed within a certain time ; a questioning in which the most scan-
dalous abuses are unavoidable. Romanist confession
stands related to the Lutheran as the law to the gospel,
and whatever truly good and rich in blessing has been
accomplished by it, has been accomplished only in cases
when it has coincided in character and method with private confession. Nevertheless, the deep need of human
nature that we speak of certainly finds more satisfaction
in the Evangelical Church, where there subsists a closer
connection between the pastor and the several members
of the fellowship ; and it is a matter of regret that private confession, as an institution, meeting as it does this
want in a regular manner, has fallen into disuse ; and
that the objective point of union is wanting for the many,
who desire to unburden their souls by confessing not to
God only but to a fellow-man, and who feel their need of
comfort and of forgiveness, which any one indeed may draw
for himself from the gospel, but which in many instances
he may desire to hear spoken by a man, who speaks in
virtue of the authority of his holy office.

§ 272.

The due celebration of the sacraments and the preaching
of the Word were entrusted to the Church by our Lord himself (Matt. xxviii. 18-20 ; Luke xxii. 19), and hence the idea
of church offices necessarily arose.   "He gave some apostles ;
and some, prophets ; and some, evangelists ; and some, pastors
and teachers.   For the perfecting of the saints, for the work
of the ministry, for the edifying of the body of Christ." *
The general priesthood of Christians does not exclude a special
priesthood, which was required by the Christian community
for its due administration ; and though our Lord did not set
apart a special and direct form of consecration for those who
should be pastors and teachers, yet the ordination to the
priestly office appears even in the Apostolic Church as an
appointment of the Spirit.   In the Lutheran Church preachers
are ordained according to the apostolic method by laying on

* Eph. iv. 11 ; compare Confessio Angustana, Art. v.   "Ut hanc fidem con
sequamur, institutum est ministerium docendi evangelii et porrigendi sacramenta."

of the hands of the brethren—an emblem of the bestowment of spiritual gifts,—yet we cannot rank priestly ORDERS on the same footing with the sacraments properly so called, and we cannot suppose that extraordinary gifts are connected therewith, as they were in the apostles' time. And, withal, as little can we suppose that ordination is a mere ceremony in which nothing is conferred. For the office appointed by the Lord in its very idea seems to include a *power* and *authority* from the Lord himself, and must, to *a certain extent,* be accompanied with the promises that were in an extraordinary manner fulfilled in the case of the apostles and evangelists whom our Lord sent forth. "I will give you," said Christ, "a mouth and wisdom, which all your adversaries shall not be able to gainsay nor resist" (Luke xxi. 15.) From this authority resting in the office as coming from the Lord himself, appointing the preacher as servant, not of the Church only, but of the Lord, is developed the special priestly gift of performing the service for the building up of the fellowship, and of preaching words of warning and of comfort; a gift and an anointing that cannot be found in an orderly manner among those who lack that authority, because they possess only a subjective or merely human call. Although the Lutheran Church has not ventured to propound a dogma regarding priestly ordination, owing to a certain fear of the hierarchical principle, the faith nevertheless exists within her pale that ordination is more than a mere ceremony, as it is also the express witness of faithful ministers, that they have ever derived new strength and energy for the work of their office in their ordination. It is evident that the gift of grace, lying hid in the office, does not always appear in power, but depends for its activity upon faith and continual personal and ethical endeavour. "Till I come, give attendance to reading, to exhortation, to doctrine. Neglect not the gift that is in thee, which was given thee by prophecy, with the laying on of the hands of the presbytery" (1 Tim. iv. 13, 14.) What is true regarding the administration of the Sacrament, that it must be conditional upon the inner state of the receivers, holds good also of ordination. It must be given to him only who possesses the inner preparation and the due qualifications for the office, and on this principle Paul warns Timothy not to lay hands suddenly on any man (1 Tim. v. 22.)

Observations.—The Roman Catholic hierarchy consider themselves the true successors of the apostles, descended from them in an unbroken series by laying on of hands, branching out into various hierarchical degrees. But we deny this apostolical succession. It not only cannot be proved that the fancied chain is unbroken, but since the departure of the apostles, no one can ever produce the apostolical gifts, and the apostles did not leave behind any positive directions concerning the future guidance of the Church upon this matter, and the right accordingly devolves upon the community itself to conduct the Church in accordance with apostolic directions. If heirship or succession be spoken of, the Church is the heir. The Church it is who calls its servants, and assigns to them the office appointed by the Lord, trusting that the Lord of the community will give to those whom they elect the Spirit, according to their need. We know, indeed, that a short time after the death of the apostles episcopacy was introduced, but the relation was not hierarchical; for the life of the Church found its highest personal expression in the bishops who followed the apostles, and by whom several apostolic schools were formed; they were, in the truest sense, the servants of the Church, according to the pattern of the Good Shepherd, who laid down His life for the sheep. But indications of a tendency to pervert this relationship soon began to appear, for the bishops began to consider themselves the rightful inheritors of apostolic infallibility, the highest court of appeal, and the last resort, to whose authority every one must unconditionally submit. Every hierarchy arises out of this derangement of the due relation between special and general church officers. The special offices of the priesthood are in the Romish Church considered to form the fundamental and original stem which bears the general priesthood as branches. Hence the strongly-defined line of demarcation between *clerici* and *laici*, the priesthood considering itself to be exclusively the Church, and regarding the laity as an appendage merely. Thus the Scriptural and primitive relationship is manifestly disturbed and reversed. It is really the general priesthood of believers which gives birth to the special, and the apostles themselves must have been disciples, or *Christians*, before they could become apostles and overseers of the Christian community. And although they led the Church with the authority of inspiration, they never set themselves up in an hierarchical relation to the Church as "lords over God's heritage" (1 Peter v. 3), but considered themselves as members of the one Body, and continually laid stress upon the truth, that while there were diversities of gifts, there was but one Spirit. The Evangelical Church endeavours to maintain this relationship. And though we would not depreciate priestly ordination, we do not place it side by side with those distinct sacraments which belong to the universal priesthood of believers—Baptism and the Lord's Supper—far less rank them as above these. For this is the very secret *falsum* of a hierarchy, that it makes ordination in reality the chief sacrament; for the efficacy of all the other sacraments depends upon this, that the priest has been duly ordained. This is just the secret falsehood of a hierarchy, that the power which the Church seeks in the sacrament to obtain from the Lord, proceeds really from the priest who administers the sacrament; so that the priesthood actually becomes the constituent and sustaining principle of the Church. The Romish Church makes an exception, indeed, as to baptism, which, she allows, may, in cases of necessity, be performed by lay persons; but in the case of Absolution and the Lord's Supper, the priest alone has power to undertake their administration, and to present the offering. The Evangelical Church, on the contrary, maintains most distinctly that it is not ordination that gives the sacraments their efficacy, but the word and appointment of God alone. Even were an apostle to administer the sacrament, he cannot give any more efficacy to it than the words of institution give. We therefore must allow that both the preaching of the word and the administration of the sacraments may be carried on, in time of need, by unordained men in virtue of that general priesthood into which they were ordained in baptism,

and that, in case of need, the Church must have power
to ordain their ministers through the oldest of their lay
members if they are not in a position to obtain ministers
who have already been ordained.

What is here said of the power and authority to preach
and to administer the sacraments, namely, that it is
deputed by the congregation to the preacher, is true also
regarding the power of the keys (Matt. xvi. 19 ; xviii.
18 ; John xx. 23), as it is called, the power of binding
and loosing, of granting or refusing absolution, of admitting
to the sacraments, and of excluding from them. Orderly
Church discipline cannot be exercised as it ought by the
minister alone, but must be exercised by him in union
with the Church. Even the apostles exercised this
power, and indeed all ecclesiastical power, not with hierarchical authority as distinct from and above the Church,
but in co-operation and harmony of the Spirit of the fellowship with their spirit. " In the name of our Lord
Jesus Christ, when ye are gathered together, and my
Spirit, with the power of our Lord Jesus Christ."*

* 1 Cor. v. 4. See also Acts xv.

THE PERFECTING OF THE CHURCH.

§ 273.

As the communion of the Triune God, and as the organism of Christ, the Church *has* eternal life. But inasmuch as she is still militant, and finds herself in a world of activity which does not harmonize with her existence, this eternal life, as the full working out of her salvation and of the new creation, is still future. In hope and expectation the Church appears as free for true activity, or as the Church TRIUMPHANT. The natural foe of life is death, and its spiritual foe is sin. Fundamentally both have already been overcome. But their final destruction will not be accomplished until the resurrection and the last judgment, the issue of which will be eternal blessedness. The truth of this hope depends upon the truth and reality of that faith, in virtue of which the future is already present.

Observations.—Though Christian Eschatology is the doctrine concerning the *last* things, it nevertheless was very copiously and energetically developed in the infancy of the Church, during the first century. This arose from the teleologic tendency of Christianity. That inquiry which was ever the first proposed, naturally was concerning the last, the final end, the result to which the new gospel would lead its subjects. While other religions merely looked back upon a lost paradise, upon a golden age which had vanished and disappeared, without presenting anything future, the Christian Church begins with a grand revelation of future realities. She is redeemed in hope, and accordingly she measures and judges of the whole present activity of this world, by the standard and in the light of the future. While heathen and gnostic speculation resorts to questions regarding the constitution of things, cosmogony, and the origin of evil, Christian thought ever inquires about the end of this world and the consummation of all things, kindles her light from historical and prophetical contemplation, and thus shows her practical and ethical character. Christian Eschatology is, therefore, quite different from what is nowadays called the doctrine of immortality. What in modern times has been called the immortality of the soul, is only a meagre and faint reflection of the rich hope of Christianity. Christian hope does not merely expect immortality, which is a negative thing, but eternal life, including not only the resurrection of the soul and spirit, but the resurrection of the body. And Christianity does not merely embrace the perfection of the individual man ; the perfection of the individual is only one part of the perfection of the entire kingdom, yea, of the whole creation (Rom. viii. 18-24 ; Phil. iii. 20, 21), which is accomplished at the same time with our Lord's Second Advent, to judge both the quick and the dead. Christian hope, therefore, takes the form of an apocalyptic vision, embracing in its view Christ and His fellowship, the Church and the world, history and nature, death and Hades, resurrection and judgment, heaven and hell. Science can present the fulness of Christian hope in the generality of thought only. It is because Christian hope refers us to an activity which lies beyond the conditions of experience, because eternal life has its natural side, which within these conditions we cannot understand, our knowledge is necessarily partial and restricted. While science, therefore, can present these prophetical parts of doctrine only in general terms, it must be left to Christian art and poetry to anticipate individual views of this subject in images full of presage, those views being embodied in the canonical apocalypse, which is presented in its fulness in the Revelation of St John.

THE RESURRECTION OF THE DEAD.

§ 274.

It may be considered to be universally acknowledged in our day that no independent proof can be given of the immortality of man, but that the doctrine of immortality must be derived from the contemplation of life as a whole. In the Christian view of life immortality appears on every hand. It is implied in the doctrine of a special providence, in the doctrine of the eternal individuality of Christ, in the election of grace, in prayer, in baptism, in the Lord's Supper, all of which owe their true import to the presupposition of the destiny of the individual to eternal salvation; but the general and fundamental idea lies in the doctrine that man is created in the image of God. All questions concerning human immortality may be traced back to our idea of God. The true conception of man is, that he is the organ of revelation for the Godhead. If God be merely the impersonal spirit of the world, as Pantheism maintains,—an impersonal universality,—this impersonal spirit needs only impersonal instruments, intermediate channels for his universal life, which possess only a transitory immortality, an immortality limited to that moment only when the eternal Spirit shines through them, and like the rainbow which is formed in the clouds, only for a moment, in the presence of the sun. The Pantheistic Godhead can have no care for the personal and monadic, because it is itself impersonal. The personal God, on the contrary, cannot find a perfect form for the revelation of Himself in beings which are only impersonal mediums, but only in beings in his own image who are appointed to be permanent witnesses of his eternal power and godhead. The God of Revelation is Love, and He therefore has interest in the monadic, the minute and individual. He can find no adequate form of Revelation for Himself, save in a kingdom of individuals who are immortal, and whom He will make partakers of His own eternity and blessedness. This is the proof of immortality which Christ gives to the Sadducees when He says, "God is not the God of the dead, but of the living, for all live unto Him" (Luke xx. 38). All live unto Him, whether righteous or unrighteous, for it is their destiny, which they cannot lose, to be vessels for His revelation, that they should live to Him, and not to themselves nor to the world. Regarding the Godhead of Pantheism, it must, on the contrary, be said, that it is a God of the dead and of the mortal. For to such a God all die and vanish away !

Observations.—To teach the immortality of all men is by no means to teach the eternal blessedness of all. Immortality comes of itself; it is the metaphysical conception of man, the attribute which he cannot lose. Blessedness is, on the contrary, an attribute or destiny to be accomplished and fulfilled,—an immortality rich in its contents, divinely replenished; in other words, eternal life. Blessedness, therefore, does not come of itself; it is not merely a metaphysical, but a moral and religious destiny, obtained only by regeneration and sanctification, by progressive moral and religious endeavours. "No man is blessed *because* he is buried;" but every one must mould his own blessedness. That "particularist" doctrine of immortality, which has again found advocates in our day, arises from confounding the distinct conceptions of immortality and salvation. It assumes that those individuals alone, who have been made partakers of regeneration in this life, receive with freedom the gift of immortality, and continue their existence beyond the grave. The power of making man immortal rests in the spirit, which animates and morally perfects the individual, with the idea, elevated above the power of mortality, which makes its possessors to share its own immortality. Holy and spiritual men alone can survive the death of the body ; natural men fall a prey to death, and perish like other existences in nature. But though this view seems to be confirmed by those instances which experience exhibits of individuals wholly unspiritual, who seem in a degree to bear the mark of mortality and emptiness, and of whom it is not easy to understand what claim such a life as theirs can possibly have upon a continuance of existence beyond the grave ; it certainly arises out of a mistake regarding the essence of man's being, the innate destiny of all, to live to God, and from overlooking the universality and eternal indissolubility of conscience.

It involves likewise a fatalistic view regarding individuals who, without any guilt of their own, have been prevented from receiving the germ of immortality in this life—a fatalism which falls back upon the old Gnostic and Manichaean division of mankind into spiritual men and animal men—a distinction which is determined, not as a merely transitory, but an original and essential Dualism, destroying the unity of the race. It is wholly unavailing to call in the Scripture doctrine of everlasting death, as if it gave confirmation to this theory of annihilation; for by everlasting death Scripture does not mean absolute destruction, but misery, the conscious, self-conscious death. We therefore maintain that the unconditional destiny of all men is immortality; but we, at the same time, teach that mankind are saved only conditionally, by being born again, and made holy.

§ 275.

The positive immortality of the individual, his eternal and blessed life, begins with regeneration, and continues thenceforward beyond the grave. But as the idea of individual blessedness coincides with man's perfect manumission to that ideal of which corporeity forms an essential part, it follows that eternal life includes the resurrection of the body or the flesh. Positive immortality has its pattern and the foundation of its activity in Christ; and as Christ rose from the dead with a glorified body, the first-born among many brethren, so all who believe in Him shall rise again with a spiritual body, *i.e.*, with a body which shall perfectly answer to its true ideal as the temple of the Holy Ghost. "It is sown in corruption; it is raised in incorruption: it is sown in dishonour; it is raised in glory: it is sown in weakness; it is raised in power: it is sown a natural body; it is raised a spiritual body." "For we know that if our earthly house of this tabernacle were dissolved, we have a building of God, an house not made with hands, eternal in the heavens" (1 Cor. xv. 42-44; 2 Cor. v. 1.) When we speak of the resurrection of the body, or of the flesh, we do not mean literally these sensible materials making up our present frame, which in this life even are in a continual state of change, and are continually vanishing; we mean the eternal and ideal form (not τὸ ὑλικόν, but τὸ εἶδος, as Origen says) ; and we acknowledge, at the same time, the essential identity of that new body with the earthly tabernacle in which we dwell during this temporal life ; that it will not be another, but the same corporeal individuality which shall be raised again and glorified, according to its ideal. We have an anticipation of the liberation of humanity to its true ideal in statuary and painting—arts which would be without any true import if the dogma of the resurrection of the body had no reality, and if they could not be looked upon as a presage of a higher reality, which they shadow forth only in picture or in form. But it is evident that the deliverance of man's body, and its being raised to its true ideal, can take place only conjointly, and at the same time with the deliverance of the entire world of corporeity, of all nature from the bondage of corruption (Rom. viii. 21), and with the new heavens and the new earth in the universal transformation of the world. Scripture, therefore, assigns the resurrection of the body to the last day ; and thus the conception of an intermediate kingdom, an intermediate state for the dead, becomes necessary.

Observations.—That way of viewing the subject which makes the relation between soul and body a matter of indifference to both, or which considers the body merely the prison-house of the soul—a garment which the soul must long to lay aside in order to obtain true freedom—this spiritualism, as it is called, mistakes the idea of man as the point of union for spirit and nature, and involves the denial of the ideal involved in art, which depends upon this union. In reality it is only the mortal and transitory body which clogs the soul, not the body according to the true conception of it. A state in which the soul is separated from the body could not be an absolutely perfect state for the soul. But on the other hand, that naturalistic mode of viewing the subject which teaches that soul and body are so indissolubly united, that the one cannot survive the other, is equally untrue. This view makes the relation between soul and body an immediate relation of union between the external and the internal, between reality and ideality, form and substance, and that soul and body are only two sides of the same thing, and cannot be separated from each other. But this would be only the relation of the life of plants, the life of animals to their bodies, and the life or soul of plants and animals is only an empty inwardness of no independent existence, which is lost in its body as in its form, and must disappear when the body is destroyed. The ψυχή of man, on the contrary, is related to his body as its organ, and defines herself in relation to it in free inwardness, within which she freely acts, and from which she distinguishes herself as the inner man from the outward, yea, from which she distinguishes herself as from her tabernacle on which she is relatively dependent, yet of which she is relatively independent. Were the soul wholly dependent upon the body, upon the instruments of sense, it would be perfectly inconceivable how it could live an inner, esoteric life, turning its thoughts in upon itself ; how it could be the subject of a purely internal self-government. The more deeply we go into the matter, the more convinced we become "that the soul of man stands in most important relations to the world, both within and without."* So far from supposing that the soul is destroyed by the death of the body, Plato more profoundly inferred that the death of the corruptible body is the liberation of the soul, and its entrance upon a kingdom of ideas. He describes his philosophizing to be a progressive death, a dying daily, an inward act of freedom, which would end in a positive not a negative result, in inwardness—abstraction from the outward. And instead of arguing that, as the soul cannot be conceived to exist without a continual connection with nature and corporeity, this connection must be rendered absolutely impossible upon the death of the body ;—as if the merely material conditions of nature were the only ones conceivable ;—he held it to be wiser and more just to conclude that some other conditions of nature *must* be possible for the liberated ψυχή, now turning its thoughts in upon itself. In certain states of ecstasy and of vision, there appears for the moment a separation of the soul

* These are the words of *Sibbern* in his work upon the Relation between Soul and Body.

from the body, an existence apart from the body, in which the soul is not absolutely without the body and without nature, but lives in a manner free of the body and of nature ; and this may be described as a type or anticipation of its state after death. Thus the apostle Paul says that even in this life he anticipated the state after death, for he was caught up into paradise, and could not tell whether he was in the body or out of the body (2 Cor. xiii. 2-4). Now, although in these states the soul has not yet really escaped from its relations to its body, they clearly disprove the naturalist doctrine of the absolute dependence of the soul upon its present and material conditions, and imply or point towards a whole realm of *other* conditions.

THE INTERMEDIATE STATE IN THE REALM OF THE DEAD.

§ 276.

Neither in Holy Scripture nor in the conception of an intermediate state is there any foundation for the notion of a sleep of the soul ($\psi\upsilon\chi o\pi\alpha\nu\nu\upsilon\chi i\alpha$) from the moment of death until the last day. As no soul leaves this present existence in a fully complete and prepared state, we must suppose that there is an intermediate state, a realm of progressive development, in which souls are prepared and matured for the final judgment. Though the Romish doctrine of Purgatory is repudiated because it is mixed up with so many crude and false positions, it nevertheless contains the truth that the intermediate state must in a purely spiritual sense be a purgatory, designed for the purifying of the soul. If we inquire what hints Scripture gives regarding the nature of this kingdom, we find that the New Testament calls it HADES (Luke xvi. 23) thus reminding us of the Old Testament representation of Sheol, or the kingdom of shades. The departed are described in the New Testament as souls, or spirits (1 Peter iii. 19, 20); they are divested of corporeity, have passed away out of the whole range of full daylight activity, and are waiting for the new and perfect body with which they shall be " clothed upon." That state immediately following death must therefore be the direct contrast of the present. In contrast with the present state, it must be said that the departed find themselves in a condition of rest, a state of passivity, that they are in "the night wherein no man can work" (John ix. 4). Their kingdom is not one of works and deeds, for they no longer possess the conditions upon which works and deeds are possible. Nevertheless, they live a deep spiritual life; for the kingdom of the dead is a kingdom of subjectivity,* a kingdom of calm thought and self-fathoming, a kingdom of *remembrance* in the full sense of the word, in such a sense, I mean, that the soul now enters into its own inmost recesses, resorts to that which is the very foundation of life, the true substratum and source of all existence. Hence arises the purgatorial nature of this state. As long as man is in this present world, he is in a kingdom of externals, wherein he can escape from self-contemplation and self-knowledge by the distractions of time, the noise and tumult of the world ; but at death he enters upon a kingdom the opposite of all this. The veil which this world of sense, with its varied and incessantly moving manifoldness, spreads with soothing and softening influence over the stern reality of life, and which man finds ready to his hand to hide what he does not wish to see,—this veil is torn asunder from before him in death, and his soul finds itself in a kingdom of pure realities. The manifold voices of this worldly life, which during this earthly life sounded together with the voices of eternity, grow dumb, and the holy voice now sounds alone, no longer deadened by the tumult of the world ; and hence the realm of the dead becomes a realm of judgment. "It is appointed unto men once to die, but after this the judgment" (Heb. ix. 27). So far is the human ψυχή in this state from drinking Lethe, that it may evermore be said, "their works do follow them" (Rev. xiv. 13); those moments of life, which were hurried away and scattered in the stream of time, rise again, collected together and absolutely present to the recollection ;—a recollection which must be viewed as bearing the same relation to our temporal consciousness as

---

* Compare *Steffen's Religions Philosophie*, 2,307 : "The divine development unfolds itself within the thoughts as an evolution, which with growing distinctness announces what is the chief baptismal gift peculiar to each personality ;— it is therefore necessary that this evolution perfect itself in those who are dead a an involution ever more intense."

the true visions of poetry bear to the prose of finite life ;—a vision which must be the source either of joy or of terror, because it presents to view the real and deepest truth of consciousness, which may not only be comforting and bliss-giving, but judging and condemning truth also. As, therefore, their works thus follow departed spirits, they not only live and move in the element of bliss or woe, which they have formed and prepared for themselves in time,* but they continue to receive and work out a new state of consciousness ; because they continue spiritually to mould and govern themselves in relation to the *new* manifestations of the divine will now first presented to their view ; and in this manner still to develope themselves until the last, the final judgment.

Observations.—If it be asked *where* those who are fallen asleep find themselves after death,—nothing, certainly, is more preposterous than the idea that they are separated from us by an outward infinity,—that they find themselves in some other material world,—and so forth. By such notions we retain the departed within those limits and conditions of sense beyond which they certainly are. No barrier of sense separates them from us, for the sphere in which they find themselves differs, *toto genere*, from this material sphere of time and space. As we may figuratively say regarding the man who is asleep and dreaming, that though he is not separated outwardly and locally from the material world around him, yet that he is relatively "beyond or above the world," and "absent" or departed from it, because he is in a state of "involution," the same may be said in an absolute sense of those who have departed this life. The tendency or direction of the soul in death is not outward, but inward, a going into itself, a going back, not a going forth ;—and instead of the modern notion that the soul wings its way to the stars, which is sometimes understood literally, as if the soul were borne to another actual world, the idea is far more correct, that it draws itself back into the innermost and mystical chambers of existence which underlie the outward. The realm of the dead must be described, in relation to

* Compare the Parable of the Rich Man and Lazarus.

this world of sense, as an inward realm, or, according to
the comparison given us, as a realm *beneath* or *under*, for
this is the cosmical description which Revelation gives us
of Hades. For Christ, we are told, descended into Hades
(*descendit ad inferos*); the Hebrew descended into Sheol,
and even the heathen goes down into *Orcus.* But this
descent must not be viewed according to any theory of
sensible locality, we must fix our minds here upon the
category of *depth.* The realm of the dead in relation to
this world of sense, must be called the *deeper* region.
All here moves, not in space or time, but in essence, in
inwardness, in subjectiveness ; here is the still realm of
shades, where life lays bare its root, whereas in the upper
world it shows only the branches of the tree, its crown
and blossom.

While we thus exclude the sensible categories of place
when dealing with this question as to where the soul is
after death, we cannot in any sense exclude all idea of
space. The soul must be conceived of in a cosmical
sphere, where it not only stands in a separated relation
to itself and to God, but in a relation to the whole kingdom of which it is a part, and thus the conception of an
encircling world is suggested; and thus we cannot help
conceiving of a certain outwardness within the kingdom
of inwardness. The soul cannot be conceived of within
the realm of spirits as wholly *natureless.* For we must
necessarily suppose that some hidden development of
nature precedes and prepares the way for the future corporeity or the resurrection of the flesh ; and the apostle
Paul expressly teaches, that though we do not possess the
complete fulness and perfection of our being in the realm
of the dead,—because in death we are unclothed, and
shall not be clothed again till the second coming of the
Lord,—yet that we are not entirely naked in the intermediate state, but are clothed upon. " In this we groan,
earnestly desiring to be clothed upon, with our house
which is from heaven : if so be that being clothed we
shall not be found naked " (2 Cor. v. 2-4). We must,
therefore, entertain the idea of some sort of *clothing* of
the soul in the realm of the dead; in that cloister-like

(we speak after the manner of men), that monastic or conventual world. But although we are thus obliged to conceive, in a vague way, of some intermediate kind of corporeity in the realm of the dead, this must not exclude the fundamental idea of that realm, as one of inwardness and spirit. According to the fundamental representations of revelation, the life of man is to be lived in three cosmical spheres; first, the sphere in which we dwell in the flesh, ἐν σαρκί, our present life, whose prevailing bias is sensible and outward,—for not only is all spiritual activity conditioned by sense, but the spirit groans under the tyranny of the flesh; next, a sphere in which we live, ἐν πνεύματι, wherein spirituality and inwardness is the fundamental feature; and this is the intermediate state;—and lastly, a sphere in which we shall again live in the body, but in a glorified body, and in a glorified nature, which is perfection, the renewal and perfecting of this world to its final goal.

In modern times the idea of Hades has been separated from that doctrine of immortality which found its expression in the "Prospects of eternity" of the 18th century. This modern doctrine of immortality, which prevails in many minds, is only a poor reflection of the Christian doctrine of eternal joy, a remnant which is retained after dissolving and evaporizing the Christian doctrine; an uncertain and fluctuating notion, without any support, when it is thus torn from the system of doctrine of which it is a part, from the family of truths wherein it is at home. For that that state after death, according to the original conception of it, is not a kingdom of joy, is evident from the most ancient ideas of the human race, and the conceptions of Hebraism. Hebraism speaks of the state in Hades with a certain terror, and associates a joyous and consoling expectation with the hope only of the coming of the Messiah to earth, with which event again it links the idea of the resurrection of the dead in a new corporeity. Among the Greeks we find only the hopeless picture of a kingdom of shades, and Achilles will rather be a day-labourer upon earth than Achilles in the world beneath. It is evident that the deepest, though not always recognized, cause of this terror of death is the connection of death with sin and guilt. A morning ray of joy first broke into this kingdom of shades through Christ, through the descent of Christ into Hades. If, therefore, the prevailing idea regarding the state after death be with the many an idea of a state of joy and deliverance, which they attribute to natural religion; this has not arisen from a Socratic or Platonic view of the soul's relation to the realm of ideas; it must be explained as the reflection of the hope of resurrection which Christianity reveals. If we may more closely explain this modern doctrine of immortality, it is just this, that while its advocates reject the Christian doctrine of the connection between death and sin, while they also reject the redemption wrought by Christ, and the entire range of doctrines so closely connected regarding the way of salvation, yet they are not disposed to give up the result at which Christianity arrives, everlasting joy; a result which, when torn in this manner from its connection with the whole Christian system of mighty truths which it pre-supposes, is entirely without motive or foundation. Some, indeed, have endeavoured to give some semblance of ground and reason for the doctrine by the notion of endless perfectibility, describing the state after death as a gradual, progressive, and endless elevation of the soul's activity and enjoyment, an ascent from sphere to sphere, and so forth. Hence has arisen a doctrine of immortality which has justly been the object of philosophic attacks, and which, scientifically at least, has been robbed of all its value and credit.

§ 277.

With Christ a new morning dawned upon the realm of the dead. As death has lost its sting through Christ, the kingdom of the dead has lost its horrors for those who believe in Him. As Christ is present in *spirit*, even in the realm of death, the believer knows that death to him is not loss, but gain (Phil. i. 21.) "I have a desire," said the apostle, "to depart, and to be with Christ;" or, as he elsewhere expresses it, "to be at home with the Lord," ἐνδημῆσαι πρὸς τὸν κύριον (2 Cor. v. 8.) This expression, "to be at home with the

Lord," finds its full explanation in what has already been developed. It describes the state after death to be one in which the soul is brought back from the periphery of life to the centre—a state in which the eternal only is of any moment; and it must accordingly be for the believer a state of blissful rest in the Lord, an *unio mystica* with the Lord, and the kingdom of His love, a state of joy. The soul must here find herself at home, because she finds herself in the region whither her essential desire and will were directed when she was in the flesh, she finds herself undisturbed by the hindrances which, while we are in the flesh, continually mar our fellowship with the Lord, and exile us from Him. The state of the soul in Hades thus depends upon its relations to Christ, the centre of all souls. Before the appearance of Christ in glory, this state must be different from what it will be after that event. It must be a different state for those who have hoped for Him, and believed on Him, from what it is for them who have not believed on Him, whether these last be persons who had never known the Lord, or persons who had not decided for Him, or persons, again, who had been His avowed enemies. Various regions thus necessarily present themselves in Hades, and we must accordingly speak of a Paradise (Luke xxiii. 43), a Hell, and undetermined state. But none of these states can be considered to be fully and finally closed ; for even the blessed have still an inner history, they still need a purifying, an increase and growth in holiness and in bliss. While conversion must still be possible for the unconverted in Hades, it is also the region in which evil may imprint its whole essence, because there it must assume the impress of pure spirit. Asserting as we do that there is progress and development in the realm of the dead, we must necessarily suppose that these bear some relation to the course of development of God's kingdom in this world. For though there are two worlds, there is but one kingdom of God, one Spirit of God, and one goal of the world's development. The realm on the other side the grave cannot be completed until this earthly existence is perfected, until the Church militant has fought her fight on earth. Hence the Revelation of St. John represents the souls of those who were slain on account of their witness as weeping because their blood had not been avenged on the earth ; and they are exhorted to wait until the number of their fellow-servants should be fulfilled (Rev. vi. 9-11.) There must accordingly be some settled and corresponding relation between that realm and this, and the development of the world here must be manifest in its essential reality, to the consciousness of spirits in that other world. Spirits there must, in their inner self, government, and character, bear a relation to those moments of our development upon which they have decided some tendency of their will, and the spiritual struggle of history must be reflected in the depths of their will. When the last great catastrophe of the world shall be accomplished, when this material sphere of time and space shall be dissolved, then shall both worlds become one, united in one new heaven and earth.

Observations.—The idea that there is a reciprocal relation between the living and the dead is variously extended in Catholicism. It is expressed, for example, in prayers to the saints and in the belief in visions and manifestations of spirits from the realm beyond the grave. Swedenborg, the northern Dante, who took in earnest what the southern Dante took as poetry, adopted the same idea of a *rapport* with the spirit world, for he (in subjective conviction) paid a visit to those unseen regions, and received a visit likewise from the spirits there. The oft-repeated remark, that in all this there was much illusion and fanaticism, may always on good grounds be made ; but we must not forget that superstition and fanaticism like shadows spring from and refer back to realities, and that all conceptions and representations, however fantastical, regarding the *rapport* we are speaking of, would be impossible if such a *rapport* did not exist. We have endeavoured above to indicate in what general sense this *rapport* must be understood, in harmony with the revelations of Scripture, while we abstain from all further denial or assertion of such particular limitations, traditions, and assumptions as are not expressly contradicted by the Word of God. Every dogmatic assertion or denial would in this case be only ἐμβατεύειν ἃ οὐχ ἑώρακε (Col. ii. 18).

THE FINAL ADVENT OF THE LORD, AND THE CONSUMMATION OF ALL THINGS.

§ 278.

The end—τὸ τέλος—breaks upon prophetic view accordingly as a great, a universal catastrophe of the world, involving the transition from time into eternity. For the physical universe, prophecy announces a universal conflagration (2 Peter iii. 10); and for the moral universe, a universal judgment. But it is Christ who reveals Himself in this catastrophe, in unlimited manifestation of His kingly might, as the world-governing, the world-redeeming, the world-perfecting power. Against the supposition of such a catastrophe, the natural mind advances the old objection, "Where is the promise of His coming? For since the fathers fell asleep, all things continue as they were from the beginning of the creation" (2 Peter iii. 4). But to suppose that this material sphere of time and space is the only one possible, the only one actually existing for all eternity, would be to make the opposition between flesh and spirit eternal; —an opposition which is not only in man himself, but in all the relations of man to the material creation around. And to suppose, again, that this moral order of things, ὁ κόσμος οὗτος, with its undiscerning confusion of good and evil, truth and falsehood, that this present *time*, ὁ αἰὼν οὗτος, with its un-solved discrepancy between the ideal and the actual, with its restless alternation of progress and declension, of rise and fall, heaving like the billows of the ocean, shall flow on and on for ever through a purposeless eternity;—to suppose this would involve a denial of all Teleology, a denial of the final triumph of goodness and truth. The speculation that contents itself with eschatological representations, which it looks upon as mere pictures of the imagination, hovering before us, and stimulating our efforts, yet never being realized, reminds us only of Tantalus, the embodiment of that eternal contradiction between the ideal and the actual, the representative of all who possess only in imagination and thought, in mere speculation and æstheticism, what is truly blessed and saving only when we have it in reality and life. And that speculation which rests satisfied with the words of the poet, "This world's his-

tory is its judgment too," as an ample exposition of " the Last
Day " of Christianity, really transmutes God's righteousness
itself into a Tantalus, in continual unreality, pursuing a goal
which it never can reach.   The truth contained in the words
I have quoted, is fully recognized in and through Christianity,
but the judgment which is being accomplished in this world's
history attains its full truth and justice only in the last judgment.   Every judgment which this world's history unfolds, is
a relative judgment only, for it only partially cancels that impure mixture of truth and falsehood which is the special
characteristic of this Æon.   The judgment of history in this
world is always equivocal and doubtful; for signs are continually opposed to signs; a twofold interpretation is always possible; and it is to the last undecided whether that which
overcomes or that which is overcome is the just cause; again
and again are we admonished anew, *Respice finem!*   All
these imperfect judgments point onwards to a final judgment,
when the partial shall give place to the perfect, to an all-dis-
cerning, all-deciding, all-concluding judgment, embracing generations as well as individuals, spirits as well as human souls.
This great and final judgment can only be anticipated now in
the apocalyptic vision, because it involves the termination of
the present dispensation of things; but its coming is so certain, that even if revelation did not foretell it, the thought of
it must be postulated in order to give earnestness and reality
to any true idea of a moral Teleology of the world.

§ 279.

To spirits who are still in a state of conflict and development, it is, it must be, uncertain *when* the judgment day shall
dawn.   But though believers " know neither the day nor the
hour; " though it is not for them " to know the times and the
seasons which the Father hath put in His own power " (Mark
xiii. 32; Acts i. 7); yet they are commanded to mark the
signs of the times; and certain *prognostica* are given to them.
There are to be signs in nature; in sun, and moon, and stars.
The gospel of the kingdom is to be preached unto all nations;
and not only shall the fulness of the Gentiles be brought in,
but there is to be a great regeneration among the people of
Israel (Matt. xxiv; Romans xi).   The contrast between the
kingdom of God and the world, the opposition between Christ

and anti-Christ, will have reached its climax (2 Thes. ii.); and the fellowship of the faithful shall stand face to face with a world of sin,—a universal corruption in national life and culture,—not only with worldly and earthly powers, but with demoniacal spirits, false prophets, and false Christs.   The fundamental type of these prognostics we find in the eschatological discourses of our Lord (Matt. xxiv.; Mark xiii.; Luke xvii.; xxi.), which form the pattern and anticipation of the great apocalyptic vision in the book of Revelation, wherein, in its various parts, the last day is represented as a progressive series of world catastrophes.   But as many of these portents and signs are of such a kind as to be applicable in some way or other to almost any time, the question as to when the Day of the Lord shall come is one with the question as to the complete and final accomplishment of all these signs.

Observations.—It must be acknowledged that in the apostolic epistles there are indications of a belief on the part of the writers that the second coming of the Lord was near at hand.   "This we say unto you by the word of the Lord, that we which are alive and remain unto the coming of the Lord, shall not prevent them that are asleep.   For the Lord himself shall descend from heaven . . . and the dead in Christ shall rise first : then we which are alive and remain shall be caught up together with them."   " Let your moderation be known unto all men ; the Lord is at hand."   " Maranatha,"—" the Lord cometh."   " Little children, it is the last time : and as ye have heard that antichrist shall come, even now are there many antichrists ; whereby we know that it is the last time" (1 Thess. iv. 15-18 ; Phil. iv. 5 ; 1 Cor. xvi. 22 ; 1 John ii. 18).   If we find in these expressions indications of the limitedness of human knowledge, it must nevertheless be remembered that the truth of the fundamental representation is not hereby violated.   Though the apostles expected the Day of the Lord as near at hand, their belief was not based upon the notion that all the tokens and portents predicted had already been accomplished, but they expected only that these presages would soon take place.   Just as a young man may in spirit anticipate his life's ideal, because with the eye of hope he overlooks and overleaps the intermediate part of the finite and matter-of-fact life still before him ; so also in like manner did the Church, in its energetic beginnings upon earth. Those grand visions of the future, which seemed to follow one another in immediate sequence in the prophetic mirror, might not, and indeed could not, have been perceived by the apostles in exact accordance with the intermediate evolutions and determinations of history corresponding therewith. When we remember, too, that the contrast between light and darkness, God's kingdom and Satan's power, never appeared on earth in such clearness and strength as in those days, must we not naturally surmise that the apostles, though they did not presume to fix the day and hour, would nevertheless expect those prophecies *soon* to be fulfilled ? Granting that the Apostolic Church thus erred empirically, and were thus far mistaken, they did not err dogmatically, for the day of the Lord must ever hover in spiritual nearness before the church militant. And must we not say that the expectation that the day of the Lord is near at hand has always been entertained anew in the most energetic periods of the Church's history (as at the time of the Reformation) ? It has been entertained whenever anything new and strange has arisen in the kingdom of God, when all seemed overturned, and when it could not be decided whether the day which now was breaking would bring the last and final decision, or whether it would be only one of those greater days of the Lord occurring from time to time in the history of the world. Is it not a matter of experience, which church history in every part of it confirms, that in those times when the coming of the Lord and the last great day have been looked upon as an infinite distance off, wrapped in the darkness and obscurity of the future, Christian life also has borne an indefinite, loose, and careless aspect ? We would by no means adopt the immoral belief for which Paul blames the Thessalonians, who had given themselves up to an idle waiting for the day of the Lord ; and as little would we countenance the immoral effort arithmetically to compute the exact time when the last day shall come, by a symbolic explanation of numbers in the Apocalypse. This only we believe, that in all ages, and especially in critical times, there will be an effort on the Church's part to discern the signs of the times in the light of God's word. But whenever the signs of the times are pondered, the great Day of our Lord's coming must be present to the consciousness ; and it thus becomes the chief standard by which the times are reckoned,—their only true chronometer. And when Christ is recognized in any crisis in the world's history, and the cry, " The Lord cometh !" is repeated in lively expectation, this, in and for itself, is in perfect accordance with the church order as laid down in history. For though it is not for us to determine the day and hour, yet we must know, that in proportion as the opposition between the Church and the world resembles what it was in the apostolic age, in reference as well to the *inner power of the Christian life* as to heathen and satanic sway, in the same proportion we have a right to say, " The Lord cometh quickly !"—for the apostolic age is an abiding pattern and type for us, not only in relation to what is evil, but also in relation to what is good.

§ 280.

CHILIASM, or the belief in a thousand years' reign which is to take place on earth before the last great day, is closely connected with the doctrine of the final judgment and the consummation of all things. The apocalyptic view (Rev. xx.), which regards the development of this world's history as a conflict between Christ and the prince of this world or the Devil, foretells, that after a great conflict, a period of "a thousand years" (clearly a symbolic designation of time) will ensue, during which the devil is to be bound, and Christ is to reign with His saints on earth ; and that a first resurrection of the dead (ἀνάστασις πρώτη) is promised for this period. The promise also which we find given by our Lord in Matt. xix. 28, that the apostles shall sit upon thrones judging the twelve tribes of Israel, is also taken as bearing upon this period. So likewise are the words of our Lord's beatitude, Matt. v. 5, "Blessed are the meek, for they shall *inherit the earth.*" The devil is afterwards to be loosed again,

a great apostasy is to spread over the earth ; and then shall
be accomplished the last catastrophe, the coming of the Lord,
when history shall be closed, and the Devil for ever bound.
From these prophetic elements, which carry us back to the
Old Testament descriptions of a state of universal joy and
bliss, to be realized here on earth by the people of God,
Chiliasm has developed itself ; and the belief thus designated
has appeared again and again in various periods of church
history, now in a carnal and again in a more spiritual form ;
sometimes with the aspect of fanaticism, and sometimes associated with the purest thoughtfulness and care.

§ 281.

Though the Lutheran Church was right in her rejection of
Chiliasm, when it was urged upon her in a carnal and fanatical manner by the Anabaptists, who dreamed of a literal
presence of Christ in a sensible reign upon earth,* she has
nevertheless failed to recognise the idea which underlies
Chiliasm ; an idea of deep import, if we understand it as referring to the last form of our Lord's *spiritual* advents in history. History must at some time reach its ἀκμή, its culminating point. There must be some climax which the human
race and the church may attain to, even *within* this present
state and these earthly conditions, a period which shall present the highest blossoming and flowering of history. Christianity must necessarily and essentially be not only a suffering
and struggling power in the world, but a world-conquering,
a world-ruling power likewise. It is this idea of the universal
triumph of Christianity, as far as this can be realized *within*
the bounds of time and sense, which finds its expression in
the Millennial reign. After great struggles, after times of
terrible confusion, in which evil has revealed a terrible might,
we look forward to a period when the loftiest idea of Christianity shall be attained ; a period which shall realize the truth
hidden in the ancient Jewish notion of an *earthly Messianic
reign,* and in the more modern doctrine of the *Perfectibility*
of the human race ; a time in which the Church shall celebrate her Sabbath Eve,—the eve before the Sabbath,—because

---

* *Confessio Augustana*, Art. xvii. "Damnant et alios, qui nunc spargunt
Judaicas opiniones, quod ante resurrectionem mortuorum pii regnum mundi
occupaturi sint, ubique oppressis impiis."

the teleology of this world shall now have reached its goal. The devil shall then be bound ; *i.e.,* evil shall be—not indeed destroyed—but restrained and kept in the background. There will be no worldly power in hostility confronting Christianity, for the ideal of Christianity shall rule the actual. The states and institutions of municipal life shall then be governed by Christian principle. The ideal of Christian art and science will then display their highest perfection, and the idea of humanity will be illustrated and glorified in Christianity. A general historical resurrection will take place in the Church ; the graves of Church history will be opened, and all the past will rise again in an all-embracing, living, and spiritual re- membrance ; and under the influence of this great conscious- ness, the Church will display a universal activity, a universal development of her various gifts. Then, when the dominion of the Apostolic Church shall rise glorious in majestic Catho- licity, the true union of the various creeds and confessions shall be accomplished, and the principle of individualism shall be harmonized with that of universality. In this period also we place the engrafting of Israel, and the bringing in of the fulness of the Gentiles.

But besides this purely spiritual view, and the literal, the carnal method of interpretation, we must notice a third form of belief which recognizes the historical points here enumerated ; but at the same time maintains, that as the millennial reign is an actual prophecy of the glory of perfec- tion, nature also will exhibit prophetic indications, anticipat- ing its future glorification ; and though Christ will not be raised up in a literal and sensitive manner to His kingly dominion, yet His presence will not be merely spiritual ; visible manifestations of Christ will, during this period, be granted to the faithful, like those to the disciples after the resurrection. According to this view, the thousand years' reign would correspond with the interval of forty days be- tween the resurrection and the ascension, an interval which implies the transition from earthly existence to heavenly glory. It was an eve before the Sabbath such as this which the Apostles seemed to have hoped for, and even thought they might live to see, during which they expected that the first resurrection would take place, the resurrection and glorifica-

tion of those who had fallen asleep in Christ, and who should
then be with the Lord. We readily admit that this view,
which has much in common with that of the early Church,
must not in the present stage of our knowledge be pressed
into distinct dogmatic form. We allow that it is difficult to
distinguish the symbolical and the literal in apostolic prophecy, to decide what must be looked upon as having to do
only with time, and what must be viewed as referring to the
essential reality ; and that much in this matter must be left
to Christian presentiment to decide. But there seems to be
no difference of opinion ventured regarding the general idea
of Chiliasm, the idea, I mean, of a pre-eminent blossoming
time for the Church, before the final consummation.

Observations.—That the " thousand years " are to be understood symbolically, is evident from 2 Peter iii. 8 (where the
Apostle is speaking of the scoffers who denied the reality of
the coming of the Lord); " Be not ignorant of this one thing,
that one day is with the Lord as a thousand years, and a
thousand years as one day." These words not only shew
that time is not a limit for God, as it is for us ; they
mainly teach that God in His government of mankind
can make quite as much progress towards His ends in
in one day, as in a thousand years ; and, conversely, that
God in His wisdom can so protract human development
that the race shall advance no further in a thousand years,
than in one day.* And must we not confess that this
principle has already been realized in the advance of history ? Was not the Apostolic age, was not the Reformation, was not the Revolution, each of them " a day "
wherein as much and as great things were accomplished
as in a thousand years ? But the nearer history approaches her goal, the more rapidly does the wheel of
time revolve ; and with so much greater abruptness and
rapidity, with so much more sudden change of circumstances does the development advance ; and the man
might very much miscalculate, who thought that, as in
the present state of the world, so much remains still to be
done, the labour of centuries would still be needed, and

* *Thiersch*, Versuch zur Herstellung des historischen Standpunkts für die
Kritik der neutestamentliche Schriften, p. 107.

that the end must still be very distant.   For the Lord, if He saw fit, could accomplish all in a single day, pregnant with great events ; and without such a day it may never be brought to pass.   It would not therefore contradict the teaching of Scripture were we to suppose that the thousand years' reign will be but a short space of time, a single day, in which shall be concentrated a fulness and a brightness, that otherwise would be diffused over a course of centuries.

When Chiliasm takes the form of fanaticism, not only is a condition of things pictured by the imagination in which the triumph of Christianity in the world is carnal instead of spiritual,—a state of things in which material dainties abound, instead of the fruits of righteousness,—but a state of things is expected which shall be accomplished from without, which requires not the kingdom of God to be established within us ; and the effort is made forcibly to bring it about by a revolutionary overleaping of the conditions of historical development.   This was especially true of the Chiliasm of the Anabaptists who endeavoured to establish the thousand years' reign in the sixteenth century.   The same applies to several phenomena in profane history.   For worldly as well as religious consciousness has its Chiliasm, inasmuch as it assumes that there is a goal of perfection which the human race can reach within the present conditions of things.   Many Chiliastic enthusiasts appeared, for instance, during the French Revolution, who thought that the goal of earthly bliss would be attained all at once by establishing the dominant principle of the rights of man ; and we are mistaken in supposing that the political, the socialistic, the communistic tendencies of our own day, are in like manner pregnant with the crudest Chiliasm ?

§ 282.

As the thousand years' reign denotes only the earthly coming to perfection of the church, it must fade again and cast its blossoms.   For everything which grows up into flower, subject to earthly conditions, must have its autumn, and the season when the foliage falls.   At the end of that period, the devil, whose power had been bound, but not destroyed, shall be let loose again ; and the last great struggle shall begin, which shall be terminated only by the final coming of the Lord ; when His kingly dominion shall fully manifest its cosmical aim. The manifestation of Christ in power, coming to judge the world, will not only break forth with unmistakeable evidence and clearness in all parts of the spirit world, but nature herself will witness to that which is come to pass ; revealing in her transformation a wide range of new creative energies. And as all spirits will now have reached the final result of their lives, this coming will be absolute blessedness to the faithful, and absolute misery to the unfaithful, who have rejected the offers of divine love. To the faithful it will be absolute bliss, because it will banish the contrast between the actualities of this world and the kingdom of God, and will bring to them their final deliverance and the attainment of their ideal : to the unbelieving, who retain their enmity to the end, it will be absolute misery ; for the brightness of Christ's glory will be to them a consuming fire. "Depart from me, ye cursed, I know you not," (Matt. xxv.) These words are not only pronounced against them by the Son of Man, they echo against them from the depths of their own being, from the abused divine likeness in themselves, they echo against them from all ranges of the creation, which now unanimously bear witness for Him. There is no more peace in the glorified creation for those who are thus condemned ; they must be separated therefrom, and to any inquiry concerning their state, we have no other answer than this, "outer darkness."

§ 283.

Must this world's development then end in a Dualism ? Shall the condemnation continue for ever upon the unsaved ? or shall it finally be removed ; finally be abolished, though after the lapse of aeons ? Is this condemnation eternal? or may we venture to entertain the hope that there will be in the end a conversion even of the lost, a universal Restoration, ἀποκατάστασις (Acts iii. 21) ; a redemption of all moral beings, so that God may be, in the fullest and widest sense, "all in all ?" The Church has never ventured upon this enquiry ;* she

---

* Compare *Confessio Augustana*, Art. xvii. "Damnant Anabaptistas, qui sentiunt hominibus damnatis ac diabolis finem poenarum futurum esse."

seems to be restrained in her examination of it, not only by the declarations of Holy Writ, but also by a feeling, if not a conviction, that the Christian consciousness of *salvation* in all its fulness would lose its deepest reality, were the doctrine of eternal *condemnation* surrendered. It must, however, be allowed that the opposite doctrine of universal restoration has been espoused at various periods in the history of the church, and, moreover, that it too finds some foundation and sanction in the language of Holy Scripture: that it has not always sprung merely from levity, as has often been the case, but from a deep conviction of humanity, a conviction growing out of the very essence of Christianity. We have full warrant therefore for saying, that the more deeply Christian thought searches into this question, the more does it discover an ANTINOMY,—*i.e.*, an apparent contradiction between two laws equally divine,—which, it seems, cannot find a perfectly conclusive and satisfactory solution, in the present stage, the earthly limits, of human knowledge.

§ 284.

This antinomy meets us if we turn to Holy Scripture ; and no definite solution is given of it there. There are texts which if they be taken in their full and literal import, most distinctly refer to eternal damnation. When the Lord speaks of " everlasting fire, prepared for the Devil and his angels," when he speaks of " the worm that dieth not, and the fire which shall not be quenched ;" when he mentions sins against the Holy Ghost, which " shall never be forgiven, neither in this world, nor in that which is to come" (Mark ix. 43 ; Matt. xii. 32) ; when the Apostle John declares that there is a sin unto death, for which a man must not pray (1 John v. 16) ;—these texts, if they be taken without reservation or refinement, clearly express the idea of a condemnation in which there is no cessation, to which there is no end. But on the other hand, there are contrasted expressions of Scripture, which have an equal claim to be taken in their full sense. When the Apostle Paul says, that " the *last* enemy that shall be destroyed is death,"—therefore the other, the second death ; because otherwise there would still remain an unconquerable enemy ;—when he speaks of the time " when God shall be all in all" (1 Cor. xv. 26–28), without referring to any contrast whatever between blessed and condemned; when he states, without any reservations, that "all things shall be gathered together in Christ" (Eph. i. 10) as the Head, that "as in Adam *all* die, even so in Christ shall *all* be made alive" (1 Cor. xv. 22),—if we take these texts without limiting their full and obvious import, we shall not be far from the idea of a universal restoration; for the Apostle says expressly ALL, not some.* This apparent contradiction in the language of Scripture shews that Scripture itself does not afford us a final dogmatic solution of the question. He who seeks to establish the doctrine of (ἀποκατάστασις) universal restoration, must invalidate those texts which make mention of eternal damnation; must limit and pare them down according to this idea; and he who would establish eternal damnation as a dogma by means of Scripture, is obliged to limit and pare down those texts which speak for the ἀποκατάστασις, according to this idea: for example, when the Apostle says, "As in Adam all die, even so in Christ shall all be made alive," he must explain the second "all" as meaning "some," and he must take the first "all" in a particular and equally restricted sense. We readily grant that the Word of God cannot contradict itself, and that the antinomy here presented must really be solved in the depth of God's Word. We only maintain that this solution is nowhere expressly given; and we ask, whether we may not recognize divine wisdom in the fact that a final solution is not given us, while we are still in the stream of time and in the course of development?

§ 285.

The same antinomy, the same apparent contradiction which we find in Scripture presents itself likewise in thought. It has frequently been said that no speculation can overcome the belief in universal restoration. This seems necessarily to be established provided that thought proceeds from that point of view which is certainly the highest and most comprehensive in the range of Christianity, that of Teleology and divine love. If we reason from this principle we cannot conceive of the destiny of the world as being other than a kingdom of blessedness of which no human soul shall come short. The supposi-

* Compare Matt. xix. 26.

tion that the destiny of the world, the realization of the kingdom of God will be equally attained if some, yea many, souls
be lost, may easily be maintained from a pantheistic point of
view, which demands nothing more than the attainment of the
end in general and as a whole, and which concerns the kingdom only and not individuals ; but from a Christian stand-
point it is beset with many and great difficulties. It is very
difficult, for example, to harmonize the idea of the damnation
of particular souls with our conception of the decree of divine
love which embraces every single human soul ; it is very difficult to harmonize it with the principle of a special providence,
which repeats in every single soul the teleology of the entire
kingdom. The assertion that the destiny of the world is
attained even in the case of the damned, inasmuch as the revelation of the punitive righteousness of God, and His majesty, is made to and through them, may easily be maintained
from that point of view which limits the destiny of the world
to the establishment of a *moral* order demanding only
that the God of freedom be revealed, not *how* He is revealed ;
but this assertion is beset with great difficulty if we view it
in the light of the kingdom of God wherein all, not only as to
mankind but to God himself, depends upon this *how*,—namely,
that God shall be revealed in his creation as a God of LOVE.
A revelation of righteousness, in which love is kept in the
background, cannot be a perfect revelation of the will of God.
If there be a will supposed to exist in creation which continues
to all eternity to fight against God, a barrier is supposed which
the divine love can never overcome. The same is true of the
assertion that in the end " every knee shall bow at the name
of Jesus " (Phil. ii. 10, 11), merely because all shall be obliged
to recognize His *power*. The revelation of power is thus made
the fundamental teleologic aim, whereas, according to the doctrine of Christianity, the omnipotence of God finds its limiting
principle in His love. But the power of love attains its end
only when every knee bows willingly to its sway, because it
is *morally* irresistible. The conception of a revelation which
is one of mere power cannot easily be harmonized with the
true idea of Christ's power, which is ever the redeeming and
perfecting power of grace ; neither can it be harmonized with
the primary article of the Christian faith, " I believe in God,

the Father, Almighty;" for the *Fatherly power* is really the power of love (1 Peter iv. 19) which by a series of *attracting* influences leads on creation willingly to its goal.

§ 286.

When we thus start from the idea of God's character, and reason therefrom, we are led on to the doctrine of universal restoration ἀποκατάστασις; but the anthropological, psychological, and ethical method, *i.e.*, life and facts, conduct us, on the other hand, to the dark goal of eternal damnation. For if man can by no means be made blessed by a process of nature, must it not be possible for the will to retain its obduracy, and for ever to reject grace, and in this manner to elect its own damnation? If it be replied that this possibility of a progressive obduracy implies also a continual possibility of conversion—this is a rash inference. For our earthly life already bears witness to that awful and yet necessary law according to which evil ever assumes a more unchangeable character in the individual who chooses it. Psychological experience, indeed, equally shews that a mighty crisis may take place in the human soul whereby old habits are broken off, and the development of the person's character takes a new direction. But here the old question returns, whether there be a *terminus peremptorius* for human conversion, *i.e.*, an utmost limit beyond which true repentance and conversion are no longer possible. But we dare not venture to fix this limit arbitrarily at any point within the course of time (*e.g.*, at the end of this life); but we are unconditionally compelled to fix it at the end of time and history; and this corresponds exactly with the idea of the final advent of the Lord. While time lasts conversion must be possible, for the Christian conception of time consists in this very thing, that it is a season of testing and of grace; and so long as the sinner is in time he is the object of God's long-suffering. But when not only this or that portion of time, but time itself has run its course, then we cannot see how conversion can be longer possible, because conversion cannot be conceived of without a history of its own. The possibility of conversion does not merely depend upon the fact that the good in man is essentially there, and cannot be extinguished, for this is true of the possibility of condemnation; but it depends upon the fact that the inward and outward conditions of activity exist in order to the development of this possibility; that the sinner still finds himself in an order of things which is as yet undecided, in a state of the world wherein discipline and trial can still be spoken of. Now, the doctrine of ἀποκατάστασις must necessarily assume that time is sufficient for its realization, and that only in a relative sense, but never in an absolute sense can it be said, " It is too late !"

It was in harmony with this principle that Origen supposed that God continues to send the unconverted from one world to another, as from one school to another, until at last they are converted; and thus he arrives at an unlimited and illimitable series of worlds and of world developments. But this notion cannot be brought into harmony with the Christian view, of which the last coming of the Lord is absolutely conclusive and final, not only for a certain part of the creation, but for all creatures, so that after it no mention can be made of history and historical progress, but only of life and existence in undisturbed eternity. If we firmly maintain this, eternal damnation must depend upon the fact that the lost creature, as made in God's likeness, possesses the inextinguishable capability of good, but that this capability is absolutely cut off from all conditions of activity necessary to its development, or, to adopt the language of the gospel, that "the door is shut" (Matt. xxv. 10). For the lost there is no future; he can have no more history; he is shut up to the retrospect of a lost past, of a squandered existence. And as the innate capacity of goodness incessantly demands its satisfaction, while all the means of this satisfaction are wanting both within the man and without him, this unceasing yet unsatisfied demand of the conscience, may be described as " the worm which dieth not, and the fire that is never quenched."

Observations.—If we seek for types or examples in this present world of eternal damnation, we must look for them in those who, by sin, have been transformed into ruins of moral existence, ruins over which the Spirit grieves wit the lamentation, that here, where there is now only a ruin, there might, there should have been, a temple of God. Among poets, Shakespeare especially has portrayed such individuals, who in time are embodiments of hell. When, for instance, we see Lady Macbeth wander in sleep, washing the stains of blood from her hand, uttering those fearful groans by which conscience, pressed into the background, endeavours to ease itself;—must we not say that the idea of eternal damnation forces itself upon us as a reality? For it is no true, no fruitful repentance under which she suffers; in that grief there is only anguish and want, but no desire after good; she still maintains firmly the evil will, and the good is in her only as a capacity which cannot be separated from creatures made in God's image. But this capacity, kept back in unrighteousness and crushed, lies as a heavy burden, a huge weight upon her soul, without there being any means or hope of lightening it, or of liberation from it through a healthy repentance. And when we see her thus wandering, is it not just as she still must wander through eternity, weeping the tearless weeping of hell, of which we are reminded in the words, " Ye mountains fall on us, ye hills cover us!"

The remark already made, that the idea of God leads us to ἀποκατάστασις, and the anthropological view, on the contrary, to eternal damnation, is confirmed in the history of the Church. For it is especially among the Greek Fathers that we find the doctrine of ἀποκατάστασις, or at least a strong sympathy with it. The Fathers, who specially adopted a metaphysical view, while more profound anthropological inquiries were beyond their reach, accordingly regarded evil rather as a blemish or defect, a μὴ ὄν, than as anything positive. When, on the contrary, men like Augustine searched deep into the reality of sin, and the importance of time for man, they maintained prominently the doctrine of everlasting damnation, and of an outward limit to the possibility of conversion; and though they often fixed this barrier arbitrarily, they were ever guided by that great practical truth, that the moments of this life are of infinite importance, and that man has never *time enough,* never can reckon, as the opposite view says, upon an indefinite time, and must not, therefore, put off his conversion. As to Schleiermacher, who, like the Greek Fathers, looked upon evil as a privation, his belief in unlimited restoration, arose from his doctrine of the unlimited dependence of the creature upon the Creator ; though he called to his support an anthropological argument, namely, the Christian feeling of love. For as Christian consciousness knows that it is blessed through grace, it must find it a limitation of its own blessedness to know that there are other fellow creatures excluded therefrom.

§ 287.

Each side of the contrast, therefore, thus presented to us, finds a point of correspondence answering thereto in Christian consciousness itself. The difficulty, however, may in general terms be thus expressed :—we are unable to harmonize the idea of eternal damnation with the Teleology of Divine love. Some have endeavoured to remove this difficulty by means of the supposition that lost spirits finally cease to exist ; that they are at last worn out and overcome by their own vain and fruitless antagonism against the Creator, and by their continual torment; and that they finally sink in the depths of annihilation. By this means certainly all moral barriers to the divine love are done away with, for after the extinction of all the unsaved, a kingdom of the blessed only remains. But not only is this supposition entirely without any sanction in Scripture, it does not solve the chief and ultimate difficulty, namely, that beings endowed by their Creator with life eternal, who have been led through a life-long series of influences towards that goal, must at last be given up, abandoned by that divine Providence, by that *Fatherly* power, which is unable to accomplish its design concerning them, and has to leave them to sink in the night of annihilation. Another explanation of the difficulty has been attempted. The term " eternal " has been taken to have only a subjective reference ; that it is only in the consciousness of the lost that the punishment can be taken as never ending ; because objectively, we can speak of an eternal damnation only as meaning an inward infinity of suffering. Or again the word " eternal " is taken to mean eternal ages ($\tau o\nu$ $a\iota\tilde{\omega}\nu a$), which have to be traversed, but which come to an end at last. This explanation is directly contradicted by that passage which speaks of sins which shall be forgiven neither in this world

2 H

nor in that which is to come, οὔτε ἐν τούτῳ τῷ αἰῶνι οὔτε ἐν τῷ μέλλοντι, (Matt. xii. 32), for it requires us to add, that notwithstanding such sins shall be forgiven in some following world.   It is insisted upon that, in that text, which is perhaps the most difficult one relating to the subject, it is not said that sin shall not, at last, be entirely removed and destroyed, but only that it shall not be forgiven.   "These sins shall not be removed by means of forgiveness ;" *i.e.*, the punishment of them shall not be dispensed with.   The guilty must drink the cup of God's wrath to its very dregs.   Stern justice is to be dealt out to them ; they must undergo that consuming fire which is not mitigated by a single ray of divine grace or pity; and they shall not come out thence till they have paid the uttermost farthing (Matt. v. 26).   All punishment must be a purifying by fire, but the fire by which these sinners shall be cleansed is not a fatherly chastisement, but " the lake which burneth with fire and brimstone," (Rev. xxi. 8).   Having passed through these flames, it may be for ages, they will at last be brought to stretch out their hands after grace, and to lay hold upon forgiveness through " the long-suffering mercy of God," *   But in all this it is forgotten that the true exegesis of the passage is quite opposed to such an inter-pretation, and cannot by any means be made to indicate even the possibility of any actual conversion for these indivi-duals.   Because it is not enough for consciousness to be able to recognize the nullity and perishableness of sin, it must also discover some beginning for a new life and development in an objective world.   But it is impossible to conceive of an im-mediate passing from the lake of fire to perfect bliss.   And thus we are led back to Origen's theory of other worlds of development, conditions of discipline, and training schools, whereby this transference may be accomplished.   Thus we return again to the same point of opposition between this conception and the representations of Scripture, according to which the final advent of Christ is to be the end, not only of this present time and this one term of history, but of all time and of all history.   Upon this assumption we are com-pelled again to say, *ex inferno nulla redemptio.*†

* This interpretation was already given in the Lutheran Church by the elder Bengel.

† Compare the Book of the Revelation, in which the words occur in refer-

§ 288.

We therefore leave the antinomy as a *crux* of thought which never shall be, never must be solved by the church militant, or from her point of view. This being our position, we teach, with Lutheranism, an ἀποκατάστασις, *a parte ante, i.e.,* the universal purpose of God for the salvation of all; but as we hold that this purpose is conditioned by the free will of man and its development in time, we can teach an ἀποκατάστασις, *a parte post,* only so far as is compatible with the doctrine of the *possibility* of eternal condemnation. The theoretical difficulties which attend a closer analysis of these principles, and which we have now endeavoured to array, must rest upon the relations of man to the struggle of development and of time; and it must also be affirmed that a perfect theodicy can only be maintained on the assumed principle of blessedness. Practically, however, these difficulties are by no means insurmountable; they must necessarily be harmonised in every Christian consciousness which feels that it is still in conflict. For as the certitude that the counsels of divine love are for the salvation of all, is the foundation of that Christian love which "hopeth all things" (1 Cor. xiii. 6); so, on the other hand, belief in the possibility of eternal damnation—in the possibility of a final and eternal *It is too late !*—forms the dark background for the solemnity of life; the dark background which awakens that "fear and trembling" with which we work out our salvation; and which rouses us to make good use of the acceptable time of grace, to which God's word summons us. For if there be a final, irrevocable *Too late !* the thought of this gives a mighty force to every relative *Too late !* and imparts to the present time, yea, to the present moment, the most solemn importance.

§ 289.

The ἀποκατάστασις, " the restitution of all things" (Acts

ence to condemnation, εἰς αἰῶνας τῶν αἰώνων ; and εἰς τοὺς αἰῶνας τῶν αἰώνων ; xiv. 11 : xix. 3 ; xx. 10. The practical danger involved in limiting such expressions as these occurred to the elder Bengel himself; for he says ;—" He who has gained an insight into the ἀποκατάστασις πάντων, and proclaims it abroad, is a tell-tale and divulger of God's secrets,—*tells tales of God out of school.*"—*Suddeutsche Originalien,* 2 Heft, p. 23.

iii. 21), which Scripture expressly foretells, is described in the twenty-first chapter of the Revelation of St John :— "*And I saw a new heaven and a new earth: for the first heaven and the first earth were passed away; and there was no more sea. And I John saw the holy city, new Jerusalem, coming down from God out of heaven, prepared as a bride adorned for her husband. And I heard a great voice out of heaven, saying, Behold, the tabernacle of God is with men, and He will dwell with them, and they shall be His people, and God himself shall be with them, and be their God. And God shall wipe away all tears from their eyes; and there shall be no more death, neither sorrow, nor crying, neither shall there be any more pain: for the former things are passed away.*" This is the state which the Apostle Paul has in his mind when he says, "*Then cometh the end, when He shall have delivered up the kingdom to God, even the Father; when He shall have put down all rule and all authority and power. For He must reign, till He hath put all enemies under His feet. The last enemy that shall be destroyed is death. For He hath put all things under His feet. But when He saith, All things are put under Him, it is manifest that He is excepted which did put all things under Him. And when all things shall be subdued unto Him, then shall the Son also himself be subject unto Him that put all things under Him, that God may be all in all*" (1 Cor. xv. 24-28). The Son has now advanced the kingdom of God to that point at which the love of the Father can be perfectly realized. He has given up the kingdom to the Father, laid aside His mediatorial office, for by the perfect destruction of sin and death, no more place is found for the mediatorial work of making atonement and redemption, because all the saved are matured for the glorious liberty of the children of God. But the meaning of the apostle by no means is that the mediatorial office of Christ is in every sense terminated. For Christ abides eternally the Bridegroom, the Head of the blessed kingdom; all communications of blessing from the Father to His creatures pass through the Son, and now it is for the first time, in the full sense of the words, true that Christ is present in all creation, for He now fills all with His own fulness.

§ 290.

The state of the blessed may be described as one of perfection, which is not only without sin, and without merely transitory existence, but from which every thing which is in part is done away, (1 Cor. xiii. 10). Now it is described as *Rest* in the Lord (Heb. iv. 9 ; Rev. xiv. 13), as a Sabbath, as everlasting joy ; but at the same time this rest is represented as activity, in the joy of the Lord (Matt. xxv. 23) ; now it is described as a "seeing face to face " (1 Cor. xiii. 12) ; and again, as a fellowship of love with God, and with the angels and all the elect—in fact, the life of the blessed includes a blending of all real contrasts which seem to be separate in time, or which here are only relatively united. And this imperishable union of the true contrast of life is the glorious liberty of the children of God. The supposition that this terrestrial life, which here we live, is the only one possible to us ; that a state of perfect bliss is inconceivable, because life is made up only of repeated endeavours towards the goal ;— this supposition misjudges that in a state of bliss the goal has been reached, as well as shall ever anew be reached, that the blessed life *is* as well as shall be. So far from life being done, when this portion of it is accomplished, we should rather say that life is now only so far advanced that it may truly be said to *begin* ; all this temporal and partial work, all the commotions and agitations of history, and the long conflict of the Church on earth, prepares only for this beginning ; because herein the creation of man is only now at length fully accomplished. This beginning, being the beginning of an endless life of bliss, is the beginning of a *progressus in infinitum* ; of an advance εἰς τοὺς αἰῶνας τῶν αἰώνων. But this life of bliss is the centralization of human progress ; time is no more this historical time with its cuttings to waste, its losses, and its imperfect works ; but the fulness of eternity now streams through the course of ages, so that an entire eternity is contained in every moment of time. In that blessed kingdom there will be an endless progress, because therein in that land of perfection, there are perennial springs, uncreated possibilities of new joy, and new activity, new knowledge, and new love.

Observations.—In " that which is in part, which shall be done away," the Apostle includes a multiplicity of spiritual gifts, χαρίσματα, which are of use only in the development of the church on earth. But as we cannot conceive of any individuality among the redeemed without certain distinctive χαρίσματα, must we not suppose that there will be some analogy between the spiritual gifts with which believers have served God here, and those with which they shall serve Him hereafter? As human liberty cannot be conceived of without the possession of some particular talent, and as many talents are wholly dependent for their exercise upon the present order of things, apart from which they are entirely useless, how are we to understand the relation of the redeemed individually to the talents which constituted so essential a part of their spirituality during their earthly life? We think that we have the analogy of Scripture doctrine with us, when we say that talents must undergo some metamorphosis, that the charisma disappears only so far as it has been the outward covering for some underlying capacity which now is to be unfolded. As to the spiritual organism through which man is to work in that kingdom, we adopt the same method of reasoning as the Apostle when he says, that "it is sown in corruption; it is raised in incorruption" (1 Cor. xv. 42), and that there is a difference between the earthly and the heavenly body; though he at the same time insists that the body we shall have at the resurrection is not another but the *same* body. And we may in this connexion bear in mind the words of our Lord to those entrusted with the talents; "Thou hast been faithful over a few things, I will make thee ruler over many things," (Matt. xxv. 23)—words which not only denote an increase of activity outwardly, but a new capacity within the soul.

The talent, however, and the different kinds of talents, shall remain, as far as these are inseparable from the idea of individuality. We may, therefore, go a step further and enquire, Will the distinction of male and female continue in that kingdom? We certainly cannot doubt that it will, seeing that it has so comprehensive an influence upon the whole individuality of the spirit. Yet we know of a certainty that there is something in this distinction which having once disappeared will not be counted worthy of the resurrection from the dead. For, said our Saviour, "They that shall be accounted worthy to obtain that world, and the resurrection from the dead, neither marry, nor are given in marriage; neither can they die any more, for they are equal unto the angels."*

We are unable with any minuteness to discern what will for ever die away, and what will be raised incorruptible in our spiritual, and our corporeal nature, because here we see only as in a glass darkly; leaving particulars we must ever recur to the fundamental and precious consciousness that God will sanctify us through and through, in body, soul, and spirit (1 Thes. v. 23); and that every man shall be presented perfect in Christ Jesus.† Many questions suggest themselves, which must be left to pious expectation and presentiment to answer. Among these we may reckon that raised by the older theologians, viz.—In what state, as it regards age, shall the blessed re-enter the heavenly body? Lutheran theologians, who have entirely overlooked the doctrine of the intermediate state, have for the most part entertained the idea that each one shall rise again in the glorified state of that age in which he was laid in the grave; the aged as aged, the child as a child, the maiden as a maiden. But as we are left to presentiment here, we throw out the suggestion whether our Christian consciousness does not afford some ground for that view which was adopted in the middle ages, and put forth especially by Thomas Aquinas, viz.—That our heavenly bodies shall possess that state, as it regards age, in which our Lord rose from the dead and went up into heaven in His glorified body? For our Lord Himself must ever be the perfect ideal, both of the absolute and unchanging youth, and of the absolute maturity of eternity. "Till we all come," says the Apostle, "in the unity of the faith, and of the knowledge of the Son of God unto a perfect man, unto the measure of the stature (εἰς μέτρον ἡλικίας) of the fulness of Christ," (Eph. iv. 13).

---

* Luke xx. 34—36. Compare 1 Cor. vi. 13; xv. 50.
† Compare Col. i. 28.

§ 291.

God and blessed spirits are the exhaustless constituents of the life of bliss.   Each spirit not only reflects God, but the entire kingdom of which he is a member.   When God shall be all in all, it may be said that all are in all, in one another ; and the multiplicity of *charismata* unfolds itself, in this unlimited and undarkened reflection of love and of contemplation ; in this ever new alternation of giving and receiving, of communication and of receptivity.   The medium by which the blessed in a spiritual manner communicate with each other, and are in each other, we designate as *light* (Col. i. 12), according to the indications given in Scripture, and we take this word both in a spiritual and in a corporeal sense.   Thus we read of " the inheritance of the saints in light."   The kingdom of glory, is the kingdom of light, and accordingly the kingdom of clearness, and unlimited manifestation ; and our heavenly bodies will possess the nature of light ;—" the righteous shall shine forth as the sun, in the kingdom of my Father (Matt. xiii. 43) ; just as at the transfiguration Christ's face " did shine as the sun, and his raiment was white as the light " (Matt. xvii. 2).   But though this kingdom in which God and His creatures, spirit and body, shall have fellowship in light ; in which God shall in the fullest sense be revealed as " the Father of lights," from whom cometh every good and every perfect gift " (Jas. i. 17) ; in which one star differs from another star in glory, and yet each shines in perfect clearness : —though this kingdom is by no means inconceivable, for it is the pre-supposition of our thoughts, the subject of our inmost desire, and the desire of all creatures ; yet we can only speak of it as those who are themselves in the midst of the conflict between light and darkness, and are not yet matured.   *Unutterable* is an expression which must necessarily appear in our words upon these things.   We therefore conclude with the words of the Apostle John, " *Beloved, now are we the sons of God ; and it doth not yet appear what we shall be : but we know that when He shall appear, we shall be like Him ; for we shall see Him as He is* " (1 John iii. 2).

INDEXES.

1.—PASSAGES OF SCRIPTURE INCIDENTALLY EXPLAINED OR ILLUSTRATED.

II.—SUBJECTS MORE OR LESS FULLY CONSIDERED.

Abraham, and Moses, their relation to Israel, 233, 234.

Absolution and Confession, 443.

Accommodation, the true, 300.

Acosmism, 75, 188, 189.

Adam, the first, 148 ; Creatianism attains its full significance in, 150 ; his relation to God, 149. 152, 153.

Adam, the second, 307.

Advent of our Lord, the continuous, 323.

Advent, the final, of our Lord, 465, prognostics of, 466 ; belief of the nearness of, among the primitive Christians, 467 ; the time of, not fixed, 468 ; the chiliasm connected with, 469.

Αἰὼν οὗτος, ὁ, 185.

Angel world, apostacy in the, 198.

Angels, their characteristics, 126 ; the world of, corresponds to the world

natures in, 258, &c.; the self-emptying of, 265; relation between the
revelation of, and the eternal Logos,
266; God in, 267; why he calls himself the Son of Man, 268; the ideal
of humanity, 270; the Divine-human
development of—birth, 274; sinlessness of, 277; His sinlessness preserved Him from contamination by
contact with the world, 278; His physique, or bodily form, 281, 282; the development of, a progressive warfare,
—tempted, 282-284; the fact that He
experienced temptations, how explained, 284, &c.; the sinlessness of,
how treated by Kant and the Rationalist School, 285-287; conditions of
His earthly life, 288; the contrast
between His humiliation and exaltation traceable in His earthly life,
289; recognised by faith as the same
in His humiliation and exaltation,
292; no contradiction between His
divine and human natures, 294; His
Mediterial work—prophetic office,
295; prophecies of, 297; His knowledge, 299; His word a divine word,
300; speaks with authority, 300, 301;
mighty in deeds as well as in words,
301, 302; a High-priest, 302; His
atonement, 302, 303; offers the sacrifice which man is unable to offer,
306; His work, God's work, and
humanity's, 307; His work within
us, 307, 308; His active and passive
obedience, 308; our Righteousness
before God, 309; our Redemption,
309, 310; His death, a perfect revelation of the sin of the world, 310; the
relation subsisting between, and the
human race, the solution of the efficacy of His work, 311; nature of
His atoning Sacrifice, 311, 312; in
what the atoning power of His death
consists, 312; in His sufferings the
human race conquers death, 213;
His death rends the vail of the temple, 314; His kingly office, 315; His
descent into Hades, 316-318; His
resurrection, 318; connection between His resurrection and the perfecting of His Church, 318, 319; the
import of the denial of the resurrection of, 319; exceptions of criticism
to the want of harmony between the
accounts of the resurrection of, 320;
His ascension, 321; the heavenly
glory of, and session at the right
hand of God, 322-323; the intercession of, 322, 323; union with His
Church, 324; His ubiquity, 325;

continual coming of, 465; final advent of, 466-469.
Christian and heathen conceptions of
humanity, 138, 139.
Christianity, and the Christian Church,
15; the essence of, 17; the objective
canon of, 31; a life, 376.
Church, the Christian, 24; various
forms assumed by, when either its
material or formal principle is set
aside, 44-49; the evangelical,—two
forms of, 49; the founding of, 335;
essential attributes, or notes of, 334,
346; the early, a model, 336; built
on Peter, 342; visible and invisible,
346; Catholic and Evangelical, 346,
347; unity and manifoldness of,
347; universal and apostolic, 348,
349; confessions of, 349; holy, 350;
militant, 351; triumphant, 352; her
appropriation of the grace of God,
353; relation of, to Scripture, 405;
the perfecting of, 450-452.
Conception, the, of Christ, 275.
Condemnation, eternal, 474, &c.
Confessio Augustana. [See Augustana
confessio.]
Confession, 443, 444; meets a want of
human nature, 444.
Confessions, the Catholic and the Protestant, 25; and dogmatics, 54;
œcumenical, of the Church, 349.
Confirmation, 451.
Conflict, the, between good and evil, 187.
Conflicts, the, endured by Christ, 298.
Conscience, 6.
Consciousness, three eternal acts of
God's, 110.
Conversion, 386; its necessity, 387;
various modes of, 388; not necessary
to know the time of, 388-399.
Cosmogony, the Mosaic, 116; of the
Greeks, &c., 117; and creation, combined in the Johanean view, 119.
Cosmological argument, the, for the
existence of God, 74.
Creatianism, and traducianism, 141,
&c.; attains its full significance in
the first Adam, 150.
Creatian-moment, the, forces on us its
recognition, 144.
Creation, the ground of, 115; the aim
of, 114, 115; from nothing, how to
be understood, 116; and cosmogony,
116, 117; not recognised by the Heathen, 118; and cosmogony, in the
Johanean view, 119; the Christian
dogma of,—in time,—its deep religious and moral significance, 122;
the antithesis between, and sustainment, 126, 127.

TURNBULL AND SPEARS, PRINTERS, EDINBURGH.

T. and T. Clark's Publications.

Just published, in demy 8vo, price 12s.,

INTRODUCTION

TO

THE PAULINE EPISTLES.

BY PATON J. GLOAG, D.D.,

Author of a ' Critical and Exegetical Commentary on the Acts of the Apostles.'

' Those acquainted with the author's previous works will be prepared for something valuable in his present work ; and it will not disappoint expectation, but rather exceed it. The most recent literature of his subject is before him, and he handles it with ease and skill. . . . It will be found a trustworthy guide, and raise its author's reputation in this important branch of biblical study.'—*British and Foreign Evangelical Review.*

' A work of uncommon merit. He must be a singularly accomplished divine to whose library this book is not a welcome and valuable addition.'—*Watchman.*

' It will be found of considerable value as a handbook to St. Paul's Epistles. The dissertations display great thought as well as research. The author is fair, learned, and calm, and his book is one of worth.'—*Church Bells.*

' A capital book, full, scholarly, and clear. No difficulty is shirked, but dealt with fairly, and in an evangelical spirit. To ministers and theological students the book will be of great value.'—*Evangelical Magazine.*

' It bears the stamp of study and of calm, critical power. It is a good defence of the orthodox views, written in a style which combines dignity, strength, and clearness. It may be read with pleasure by any lover of theology, and will be a valuable addition to the book-shelf as a book of reference.'—*Glasgow Herald.*

' We honestly and heartily commend the work.'—*United Presbyterian Magazine.*

' Most fair, comprehensive, critical, and effective, disposing of modern as well as ancient difficulties in the most satisfactory way.'—*Homilist.*

' This work will commend itself to all competent judges, alike by the candour and earnestness of its spirit, the breadth of its learning, and the cogency of its reasoning.'—*Baptist Magazine.*

' We congratulate Dr. Gloag on his production of a work at once creditable to our sacred scholarship and helpful to the cause of truth. His aim is to furnish an introduction to the Pauline Epistles, each of which he takes up in the chronological order which he accepts. . . . The volume has a real and permanent value, and will take a high place in our biblical literature.'—*London Weekly Review.*

' We recommend it as the best text-book on the subject to students of theology and to clergymen—as a most reliable guide, from the orthodox standpoint, to a knowledge of the present position of the historical criticism of the Pauline Epistles.'—*Courant.*

' It everywhere bears the marks of an impartial judgment and of thorough research.'—*New York Evangelist.*

' A safe and complete guide to the *results* of modern criticism. At the same time it gives a fair idea of the processes by which those results are arrived at.'—*Literary Churchman.*